ID0207831

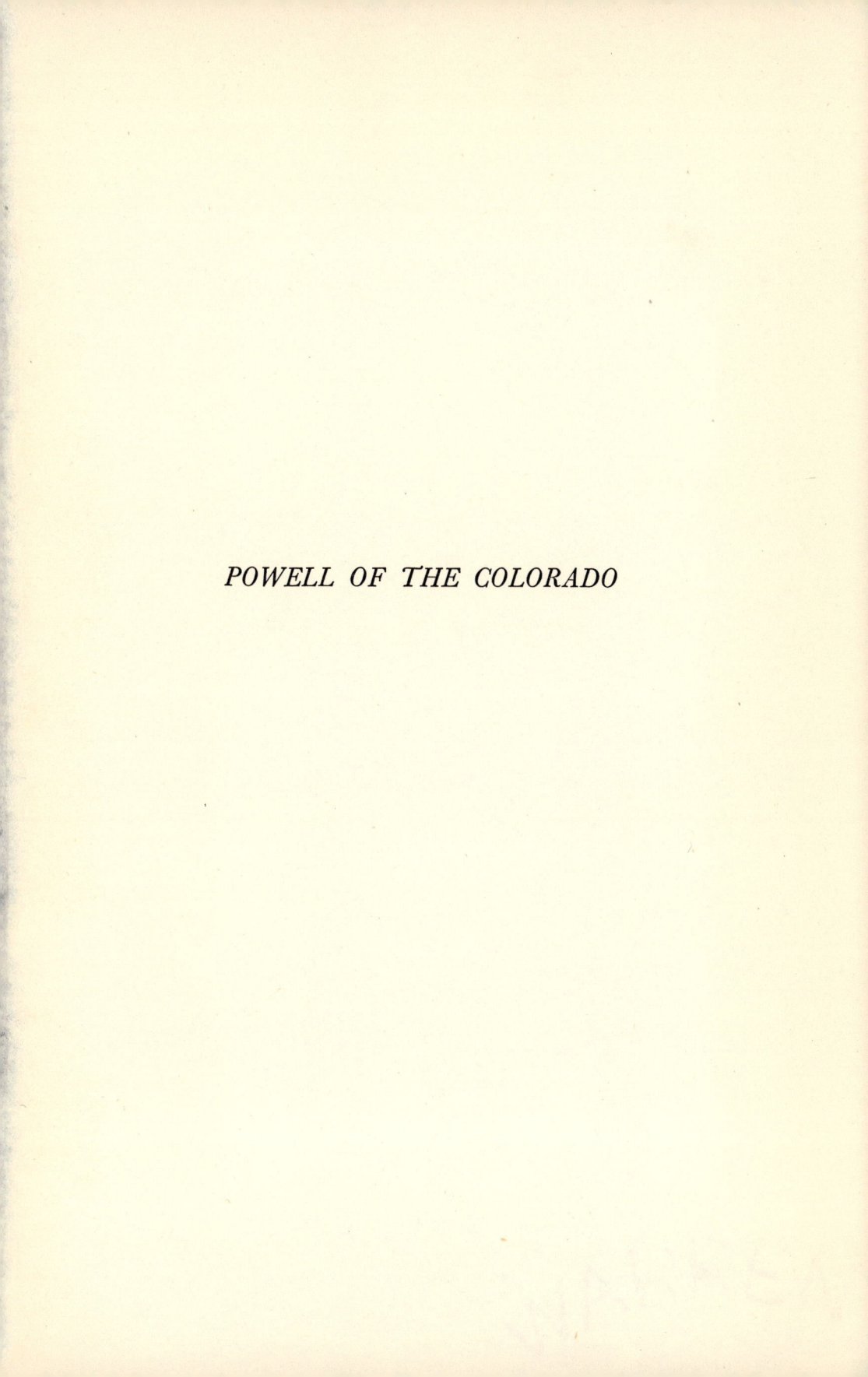

POWELL OF THE COLORADO

Powell

OF THE COLORADO

BY WILLIAM CULP DARRAH

PRINCETON

PRINCETON UNIVERSITY PRESS

1951

Printed in the United States of America
By Vail-Ballou Press, Inc., Binghamton, N.Y.

Preface

NEARLY a half century has passed since John Wesley Powell, known simply as "the Major" throughout the West, was buried in Arlington National Cemetery. It seems strange that time has so quickly dimmed his memory. It is seldom realized how one man can by his own acts set in motion movements which change the minds of great masses of people. As the struggle is won the role of the individual loses identity. The few panegyrics that appeared immediately after the Major's death distort rather than portray one of the most colorful figures on the American scene.

Overcoming a desultory education and the loss of an arm on the bloody field of Shiloh, Powell led the first expedition through the canyons of the Colorado River and explored the last unknown region in continental United States—the canyon country. The prairie had led him to the high plains, then in turn to the Rocky Mountains and the wilderness beyond. Major Powell went to Washington as a scientist, not a politician, and began one of the greatest campaigns in American politics—to force upon an unwilling government measures to reclaim the arid West and preserve the natural wealth of the country against ruthless exploitation and monopoly control by vested interests. The conservation movement, the development of a federal land policy, the elevation of science in government bureaus to a position of dignity, were in large part inspired and directed by Major Powell.

But this biography is not the story of the West, nor of conservation, nor of science in government. It is the story of a man who enjoyed everything he did with boundless energy and insatiable curiosity. The Major was surrounded by loyal associates—frontiersmen, Indians, soldiers, scientists, and statesmen. He won stanch supporters. He earned bitter enemies. In private life John Wesley Powell was simple homespun—in public life an enigma.

Looking backward, I realize this book began in my student days nearly twenty years ago when, in a superficial manner, I attempted to trace the genealogy of the philosophic views of certain American scientists who took sides on Darwinism. Out of that little group—Louis Agassiz, Asa Gray, Leo Lesquereux, Lewis Henry Morgan, Lester Ward, John Wesley Powell, and Edward Cope—one personality, Major Powell, intrigued me.

Since that beginning I have retraced many of Powell's footsteps, read his works, and read the books that he read. Gradually the man emerged from the legend and in 1940 I began assembling materials for this account.

Biography is written by the subject himself. The "author" selects that which he believes delineates the character. Nearly 6,500 items of Powelliana have come my way—photographs, letters, manuscripts, reminiscences, newspaper accounts, and published articles. It would be pure show to cite them all in this book; only the most important are included in the bibliography. Mere mass, mere weight of numbers is meaningless. Were it not for the assistance and interest of many, many friends, acquaintances, and willing correspondents, the vitality, sympathy, and color of the Major would have been elusive, if not entirely lost.

Major Powell's skillful avoidance of letter writing, except for professional correspondence, adds to the confusion which results from his versatility. During life the Major was literally all things to all people.

Four persons have steered me through the confused later years of Powell's life: Mr. Eric Parson; Miss Margaret Whittemore; Mrs. Klotho McGee Lattin; and the late Dr. Alfred C. Lane. Mr. Parson provided me with much of the material found in Chapters 23 and 25 and helped to identify and place the minor characters in Maine and Washington. Dr. Lane, in many conversations and in his manuscript, "Reminiscences," written for me, reconstructed the early days of the Geological Survey, its staff, and the issues involved. Miss Whittemore, grand-niece of the Major through his sister, Martha Powell Davis, loaned family records, letters and photographs, canvassed kin for other data, and compiled for me an enumeration of the living descendants of Reverend Joseph Powell and Mary Dean Powell. Mrs. Lattin, daughter of W J McGee, loaned many family papers, and offered more I could not use. With a candor and detachment seldom encountered, she revealed the intimate family affairs of the Powells, McGees, Newcombs, and Langleys, and of life in Washington.

Other intimate recollections came from scattered sources: Mr. Francis Dean Schnacke, a grand-nephew of Major Powell; Mae F.

(Mrs. Marshall S.) Jackson, a grand-niece; Miss Mae Clark; Dr. Fred S. Herrick; Elsie May Bell (Mrs. Gilbert) Grosvenor and Marian Bell (Mrs. David) Fairchild, daughters of Alexander Graham Bell; Mabel Powell (Mrs. Lester W.) Bradley, daughter of W. Clement Powell; Frances Dean (Mrs. Laurens D.) Whittemore, daughter of Martha Powell Davis; Reverend H. H. D. Sterrett; Reverend A. B. Parson; Mr. John Parson; Miss Emma Tibbetts; and the late Mr. W. J. Freethey.

Dr. Margaret Garfield Stanley-Brown permitted me to examine two manuscripts of recollections by her father, Joseph Stanley-Brown.

For personal recollections and source materials of Powell's professional career, I am especially indebted to the late Dr. Nelson H. Darton and to Mrs. Darton; the late Dr. Bailey Willis; the late Dr. Robert Tracy Jackson; the late Dr. Clark Wissler; the late Mr. Gifford Pinchot; Dr. John R. Swanton; Dr. F. H. Hodge; Dr. W. C. Mendenhall; Dr. George R. Wieland; Dr. William H. Hobbs; Dr. L. O. Howard; Dr. T. Wayland Vaughan; Dr. Arthur C. Spencer; and Dr. Kirk Bryan.

Descendants of associates of Major Powell have provided letters, notes, manuscripts, and photographs: Mr. Frederick S. Dellenbaugh, Jr; Miss Ethel Jones; Mrs. John K. Hillers; Mr. E. Wright Allen; Mr. L. W. Keplinger, Jr; Mr. Edward L. Morss, grand-nephew of George Bradley; Mrs. Walter A. Boyle, daughter of Lyle Durley; Mr. W. Mark Durley; Mrs. Amy McLaughlin and Mrs. Mattie S. Stetson, nieces of Andrew Hall.

Many persons have assisted in uncovering local information and suggesting leads which could be pursued further. The following have simplified and brightened the search: Mrs. Blanche H. Mace of Kanab, Utah; Mr. Quiller F. Scott and Mrs. Romaine (Benner) Jones of Jackson, Ohio; Mr. Frank C. Morrow of Wellston, Ohio; Amanda (Mrs. Asa) Messenger of Xenia, Ohio; Mr. Pearson H. Corbett of St. George, Utah; Mr. Jay Monaghan of the Illinois State Historical Library; Mr. J. W. Wentworth of Globe, Arizona; Miss Nellie Thompson of Lacon, Illinois; Mrs. Mabel Kowalsky of the Decatur Public Library; Miss Mary Davis of the Medford Public Library; Miss Anne S. Pratt of the Yale Library; Mr. James R. Joy of the New York Methodist Historical Society; Mr. Frank T. Darrow of Chicago, Illinois; and Dr. Elmo S. Watson.

Mrs. Lewis Burchard granted me access to the papers of her father, Robert Brewster Stanton. No adequate understanding of Colorado

River history can be gained without study of Mr. Stanton's collection in the manuscript division of the New York Public Library. Mr. Robert W. Hill, keeper of manuscripts, has extended many courtesies.

For information on the Civil War years—the service records of individual soldiers, muster rolls, regimental data, etc.—I am particularly indebted to: the United States Adjutant General; the Veterans Administration; the Adjutant Generals of Illinois, Ohio, Iowa, Michigan, Missouri, Minnesota, Tennessee, and Mississippi; Mr. William H. Glover and Mr. Blair Ross of Shiloh National Military Park; Mr. James R. McConaghie of Vicksburg National Military Park; Mr. F. E. Snider of Cape Girardeau Teachers College; the Illinois State Historical Library; and the Army Medical Library.

The officers and staffs of many institutions have assisted in the search. To the following I owe special thanks: the National Archives, Library of Congress, Smithsonian Institution (particularly the cheerful assistance of the Bureau of American Ethnology), New York Public Library, Boston Athenaeum, Widener Library, and Library of the Museum of Comparative Zoology of Harvard University; Illinois State Normal University, Illinois Wesleyan University, Oberlin College, Wheaton College, Illinois College, University of Illinois, Johns Hopkins University, University of Rochester, George Washington University, University of Pennsylvania, Pennsylvania State College; the public libraries of Boston, Chicago, Detroit, Denver, Salt Lake City, Cincinnati, Decatur, Aurora, Utica, Palmyra, Brooklin (Maine), Los Angeles, and Omaha; the U.S. Geological Survey and the Commission of Indian Affairs; the Geological Society of America, American Association for the Advancement of Science, National Academy of Sciences, American Philosophical Society, Cosmos Club, Chicago Historical Society, Newberry Library, Chicago Academy of Sciences, New England Genealogical and Historical Society; the Union Pacific Railroad; and the state libraries, in addition to those previously mentioned, of Arizona, Utah, Wyoming, Ohio, Wisconsin, and Kansas.

For other courtesies and assistance I express gratitude to Dr. Wallace Stegner; Mr. Otis Marston; Mr. Bruce Nelson; Dr. Herbert E. Gregory; Rev. Robert Dale Richardson; Miss Louise Bradley; Dr. R. V. Chamberlin; Dr. Walter P. Hendrickson; Mr. Murray D. Green; Mrs. Olive B. Seaman, and Mr. George W. Grant, Jr.

A special word of appreciation is due to Mrs. Margaret Sinclair Reusser, Mr. Dale Morgan, and Mrs. Elizabeth Lauchnor of the Utah State Historical Society for many favors. The Utah State Historical

Society invited me to edit the various journals and records of the 1869 Colorado River expedition and to collaborate with the editing of the journals of the second Powell expedition of 1871–1872, which have been published as Volumes fifteen, sixteen, and seventeen, of the *Utah Historical Quarterly*.

To my secretaries, Mrs. Josephine Wardrobe Norris and Mrs. Lillian Palmieri Menelly, who served also as research assistant with enthusiasm and ingenuity, I am forever grateful.

To my wife, Helen Hilsman Darrah, I make inadequate acknowledgment. For more than eight years she has serenely ignored untidy papers, listened patiently to long discussions about minutiae, and as circumstances demanded, acted in the capacity of researcher, reader, critic, and amanuensis. Last but not least, a word of appreciation is due to our daughters, Barbara and Elsie, who have for some years been asking a little impatiently, "When are you going to be finished with Mr. Powell?"

There are doubtless errors of fact perpetuated in these pages through ignorance or accident. I have invented no detail, nor deliberately used questionable material. A number of cherished legends about the Major have been sentenced to limbo. For errors of judgment and interpretation I beg lenience.

Wm. C. Darrah

Medford, Massachusetts
December 15, 1950

Contents

Illustrations

The illustrations listed below are to be found in the section following page 210. The author wishes to express his appreciation to the U.S. Geological Survey and the Bureau of American Ethnology for their courtesy in permitting the reproduction of the photographs indicated.

1. John Wesley Powell, 1859. *William Culp Darrah.*
2. Emma Dean Powell, ca. 1869. *William Culp Darrah.*
3. Major John Wesley Powell, 1865. *William Culp Darrah, courtesy of Francis Dean Schnacke.*
4. Start of the second Colorado expedition at Green River Station, Wyoming, May 1871. *William Culp Darrah.*
5. Lodore Canyon. Jones, Hillers, and Dellenbaugh in the *Emma Dean, William Culp Darrah.*
6. The Colorado River near the upper end of the Grand Canyon. *U.S. Geological Survey.*
7. Repairing boats at First Granite Gorge, Grand Canyon. *U.S. Geological Survey.*
8. Lava Falls, Grand Canyon. *U.S. Geological Survey.*
9. The Sockdologer Rapid, Grand Canyon. *U.S. Geological Survey.*
10. Glen Canyon, Utah. *U.S. Geological Survey.*
11. Marble Canyon, Arizona. *U.S. Geological Survey.*
12. Another view of Marble Canyon, Arizona. In the foreground is the *Emma Dean* showing the armchair in which Major Powell sat. *U.S. Geological Survey.*
13. Hillers, Dellenbaugh, and Johnson repairing the *Cañonita. William Culp Darrah.*
14. Major Powell and a Paiute Indian, 1873. *Bureau of American Ethnology.*
15. A family of Uinta Utes, ca. 1873. *Bureau of American Ethnology.*
16. Across the house tops at Zuni, 1879. *Bureau of American Ethnology.*
17. John Wesley Powell, 1898. *Bureau of American Ethnology.*

POWELL OF THE COLORADO

1

1830-1846 · Wilderness Bound

ON AN unexpectedly pleasant March day in 1881, John Wesley Powell, known to millions simply as the Major, quietly took the oath of office as director of the United States Geological Survey, an agency destined to play a leading part in the development of America's natural resources. "John Wesley Powell," an admirer wrote on that occasion, "is a pattern of the American self-made man, and well illustrates what may be accomplished with honest, steady adherence to a definite purpose." [1] There is more than folklore in the democratic tradition.

Powell was born of the frontier; he had explored the wilderness; he had lost an arm for Union. But the age of the frontier, the boundary between settlement and wilderness, the age of inexhaustible free lands, was past. The old frontier had ceased to exist. The uncertain beginnings of a new age were about him. The plundering of the wealth of the public lands had reached unbelievable proportions; technology and industry were fast changing the life of the nation, and the full impact of modern science would soon burst upon the world.

Powell stood upon the threshold of a new age and knew it. He had been prepared for it.

It was free land, the dream of independence and opportunity, that lured John Wesley Powell's father, Joseph Powell, to America with his wife and two children, Martha, aged two, and Mary, three months. They had come by sailing ship to New York in 1830. Finding the city scourged by epidemic fever, they booked passage by steamship to Albany. From there they proceeded by way of the Erie Canal to Utica where other families from England and Wales had settled.

Joseph Powell had been born about 1800 in the ancient town of Shrewsbury in that part of England bordering upon Wales. Joseph traced his ancestry among both Welsh and English, and showed in his

[1] Lester Ward, *Pop. Sci. Monthly*, 1881, p. 390.

manner the unconquerable Celtic love of freedom. As a young journey-man tailor he had gone to London to seek employment, and in that great city had been singled out and licensed "to exercise his gifts in the Methodist Episcopal Church so long as his doctrines, practice, and usefulness comport with the discipline of said church." In January 1828 Joseph Powell married Mary Dean, a comely young woman from Hull who was several years younger than he. Both Joseph and Mary had dedicated themselves to Methodism and now had come to America to build a home and to carry the Gospel to the border cabins. Their worldly goods included a few chests of personal belongings and domestic linens, two dozen books, and a small sum of money. Mrs. Powell's brother, Joseph Dean, and his wife had planned to come to America at the same time, but for some reason failed to meet them. They had waited vainly; the ship sailed without a word of explanation from the Deans.

Joseph Powell did not find the opportunity he sought in Utica. Tailor-ing was not satisfying; it was but a means to an end. A licensed exhorter of the Methodist Church was expected to follow his regular trade or profession, but there had been little chance for him to carry on religious work. There were six churches in the town, and all who desired to attend services had an opportunity to do so. Joseph Powell wanted to bring religion to those who were beyond its reach.

The Powell family moved on to Palmyra, New York, as another station on the road to wilderness. The town was still excited over the new sect which called themselves Mormons. The first printing of the *Book of Mormon,* of five thousand copies, had but recently been finished. A few years earlier, Joseph Smith, a young farmer, had re-ceived a vision revealing to him the existence of a record of the full-ness of Christ's Gospel, and on September 22, 1827, two gold tablets bearing cryptic characters were delivered into Smith's hands. The tablets were found, it was said, not far from Joseph Smith's home on a hill between Palmyra and Manchester. With the aid of miraculous transla-tion, the revelation was recorded in the *Book of Mormon.* Despite op-position and ridicule, the new faith was showing surprising vigor. Mis-sionaries were sent into the rural districts of New England and among the Indians living on the reservations of New York State. The "Church of the Latter Day Saints of Jesus Christ" was planning to migrate to Ohio to establish an earthly kingdom.

Could such a cult take root? Joseph Powell turned to his books, William Wilberforce's *View of Christianity,* Charles Wesley's *Sermons,* and John Fletcher's *Works,* and read from them to his wife. The battle line for the Lord was thin indeed. Powell's impatience to reach the frontier to win souls for Christ's kingdom and thwart the teachings of false prophets was fired anew.

While the Powells weighed their hopes for the future, a son, Fletcher, was born in the summer of 1832, but died in infancy. Shortly after this disappointment they took up residence in the little town of Mount Morris on the stage road southwest of Palmyra. Joseph Powell held regular meetings and visited among the neighboring communities, according to the practices of the Methodist Church. He did a little tailoring and a bit of farming, but he was restless. Fervently, Joseph hoped to place himself so that he could devote himself to the ministry. In three years he had not been able to come any closer to this calling. There was but one course open: to work his way westward and take up land. With some measure of security for his growing family, he would be free to ride circuit. On March 24, 1834, a second son was born and the parents, hoping that he would follow in the ministry, named him John Wesley Powell.[2] A few months later the family was on the move again. In 1836 William Bramwell Powell was born in Castile, New York.

Mrs. Powell raised her children after the tradition of Susanna Wesley, teaching them their letters, to read the Bible, to seek knowledge, and to build character. At the age of five, to the delight of his parents, Wes could recite the Gospels from memory, and Bram, three, could quote many verses from the Bible. With the slightest prompting both would repeat Wesley's adage:

> Do all the good you can,
> By all the means you can,
> In all the ways you can,
> In all the places you can,
> At all the times you can,
> To all the people you can,
> As long as ever you can.

Joseph would sit straight in his favorite chair and with a proud smile listen intently to these recitations of his children, but his part in their

[2] The principal source of information concerning Powell's childhood and youth is the biographical sketch written by Mrs. M. D. Lincoln ("Bessie Beech") published originally in *Open Court*, Vol. 16, 1902, pp. 705–15, and reprinted, with slight revision, in 1903 in G. K. Gilbert, ed., *John Wesley Powell: A Memorial to an American Explorer and Scholar*. The sketch was based upon interviews with Major Powell during the period 1885–1895. Scattered through Powell's letters and publications are many references to his childhood homes in Ohio and Wisconsin. Anecdotes and instances used in this book have been substantiated by collateral documentation.

education was discipline—obedience and industry. There was something uncompromising in the religion of Joseph Powell, but it was tempered by the placid disposition of Mrs. Powell.

The growing family strained their resources and increased Father Powell's determination to move farther west where he could purchase or take up a farm. His income scarcely provided for the family, but despite the uncertainties involved, he was determined now to devote his talents to preaching.

Joseph Powell had a good deal of the wanderlust in his character. He found no permanence in these earlier years in America, yet in each instance where some record of his activities is preserved he appears to have had increased success in material ways.

Step by step, Joseph Powell had moved his family across New York by way of the Erie Canal. Now he was close to the wide expanses of Ohio. The achievement of his mission seemed near at hand. Southern Ohio was rapidly being transformed from wilderness to settlement, and the Methodist Church was vigorously engaged in the area. Powell had been considering for some time the possibility of going by flatboat from Olean, New York, at the headwaters of navigation on the Allegheny River, to Pittsburgh and Marietta, but the Ohio Canal, from Cleveland to Portsmouth, seemed now a much more suitable route.

Joseph Powell knew the locations of the Welsh communities in Ohio, and from itinerant preachers and travelers learned all he could concerning the country. In 1836 Reverend Powell had the good fortune to meet Reverend B. W. Chidlaw, a Congregational minister who was journeying from Ohio to visit his native Wales. Powell, after conversing with him and explaining his plans, decided to settle in Jackson County in southern Ohio.

In the late spring of 1838 the Powells went with all of their personal belongings to Buffalo and from there by steamship to Cleveland. According to tradition [3] they traveled by canal packet from Cleveland to Chillicothe, a distance of two hundred and fifty miles to the southwest. The leisurely trip, at only two to four miles an hour, must have seemed endless to the children, but three days later the boat arrived on schedule at Chillicothe and discharged its passengers on the landing.

Water Street, along the canal, was one of the busiest streets in the West; scores of grain wagons and produce carts, farmers, clerks, canal-

---

[3] Three traditional accounts of the journey of the Powell family to Jackson have persisted through the years. Two relate that they came by canal boat, the third "believes" they came by wagon. Specifically acknowledging tradition, I have combined details from all three versions.

men, and bystanders jammed the landing. A great steam flouring mill, two paper mills, saw mills, oil and spinning mills, and other enterprises showed Chillicothe to be energetic and courageous.

The main part of the town was even greater proof of its ambition. The main streets were ninety-nine feet wide and the secondary streets, sixty-six. More than a score of mercantile stores made up the business section. The shops were stocked with delicacies, fine teas, and the best of domestic and foreign liquors. Even the stores dealing in general merchandise had large selections of books at nominal prices. Titles ranging from the Bible to the latest poetry published in England were to be found in the book stalls. Joseph Powell was astonished by the varied fabrics in the dry goods stores—madras, silks, and fine linens, as well as homespun and local cotton weaves. The town for some years had been a center for hog raising and at certain periods of the year large numbers were driven overland to New York and Philadelphia. As many as 20,000 hogs in one year were sent to eastern markets, and this, in addition to the slaughtering and salting of pork, made a very profitable local industry. Chillicothe, one of the oldest settlements in southern Ohio and, for a short time, the state capital, had a considerable number of fine homes and substantial buildings. Luxury and frontier hardship were near neighbors.

Joseph Powell inquired for a dealer in livestock from whom he might obtain a team of horses and a wagon. He purchased a small but sturdy wagon and two horses, one of which, a young black mare, had been selected as a riding horse.

The distance to Jackson could be covered in one day's journey in good weather and the season being favorable, the Powell family approached the farms around Jackson by sundown. They slept in the wagon that night, the children bundled in heavy covers against the chilly dampness. The next day they entered the village.

Joseph Powell, tailor and lay preacher, drove his team up the steep hill to the center of town, fastened the horses, and lifted the children down to the street to stretch their limbs. Welsh faces and Welsh accents greeted the newest arrivals into Jackson. Father, holding Wes by the hand, walked around the village square and went to the courthouse to inquire about local accommodations and a land office. At the door stood an awesome man weighing about 350 pounds. The big fellow, who appeared to be between fifty and sixty years old, smiled and spoke kindly. Reverend Powell introduced himself and inquired as to a suitable clearing where he could encamp with his family for a few days. Half-jovially, half-seriously, the native exchanged introductions, calling himself George Crookham—"Big George" Crookham. He invited the new parson to work among the local citizenry, a lazy, drunken, ignorant, and unruly lot. Powell in his turn explained that he earned a livelihood by tailoring but that he hoped to purchase a small property in or near Jackson. However, not knowing the country about, it might take him some time to select a suitable location. Crookham invited the Powell family to his place with such a show of cordiality that they did not wish to decline. The Powells camped in their wagon on the Crookham land, refusing to sleep in the house lest it be an imposition.

The two men swapped information about themselves as they busied about. Joseph told of his calling to the church and his coming to America. Crookham in turn related how he had come from Pennsylvania to Lick Creek in 1799, had taught school, worked as a salt boiler, became a farmer, and had raised a large family.[4] He was a Calvinist, antiliquor, antislavery, and well-nigh antieverything. He assured Powell that George Crookham was mighty unpopular in these parts, but his hearty laugh seemed to discredit this self-appraisal.

Joseph Powell did not dally long. For two hundred dollars he purchased a town lot on Main Street less than two blocks west of the courthouse.[5] There was no dwelling on the property, but neighbors helped him raise a temporary log cabin. A frame house was constructed before winter set upon them. Within two months Powell purchased additional parcels of land: for forty dollars a part of a four-acre out-lot, and for seventy dollars a full out-lot of four acres. Joseph Powell was now a man of property and he had rooted his family in America.

It was evident that Crookham's opinion of his fellow townsmen, though considerably exaggerated, was not without foundation. Jackson, a community of barely 250 souls, had six stores and three taverns, and liquors were sold at eight of these establishments. Temperance among the old-timers was either unknown or just not practiced; they were a rough crowd. Among the newer families from New York, New England, and Pennsylvania there was perhaps a more objective sense of religion and a smattering of refinement. Many of the older families, having settled from southern states, resented the introduction of this new element. The complexion of the neighborhood was changing and the transformation was not a peaceful one. The intermingling of coonskin and

[4] George L. Crookham, *History of the Hanging Rock Iron Region*, pp. 369–70; *History of the Scioto Valley of Ohio*, p. 471; see also Jackson *Standard*, March 5, 1857.
[5] *Jackson County Court Records*, Book C, 1838, Book E, 1841, and Book G, 1845–1846.

homespun with more stylish woolens and linens was but outward evidence of a deeper social cleavage.

Ever since the close of the Revolution and the opening of the old Northwest Territory, waves of settlers had swept into the Ohio Valley, and by 1830 the frontier had moved far beyond the boundary of Ohio, had cut through Illinois and into Missouri. Land and opportunity had beckoned the ambitious, the adventurous, the restless, the refugee, and the fugitive.

Ohio was the natural highway for three great routes of migration. The stock from the northeast, especially New England Puritan from Massachusetts and Connecticut, found its way across New York State along Lake Erie into the region of Cleveland and the northern counties. Toward the central part, and especially along the Ohio River from Marietta into Cincinnati, strong elements of Scotch-Irish Calvinists and Germans came across roads and trails from Pennsylvania or on flatboats down the Ohio River. Southern Ohio had also been settled by large numbers of southerners, most of them coming from the upland counties of Virginia, Kentucky, and Tennessee. Recent years had brought new immigrants, mostly from the British Isles. Each of these elements introduced its own characteristic traits and attitudes.

The sympathies of the southern element were with slavery and with the rugged independence of the backwoodsman. The migrants from the middle states and the north were more gregarious and of a more religious turn of mind, looking upon slavery as a moral wrong which had to be abolished.

Here was the place, at last, where Joseph Powell could carry the message of grace to the churchless.

The residents of Jackson were aroused over slavery. Bitterness existed among neighbors. Hates were deeply rooted and open violence was frequent. In this agitation George Crookham had long been active, and quite naturally Reverend Powell took part. Crookham, who had been the first professed abolitionist in Jackson County, had stanch friends among leading citizens—Dr. Asa Isham, Rev. Isaac Ford, and Samuel Montgomery. Montgomery had known the bondage of Scotsmen chatteled to the coal pits of Glasgow and who were sold with their families along with mining rights. The friction increased as more and more immigrants from the northeast bid fair to outnumber the old inhabitants, and the agitation was kept in ferment by meetings, pamphlets, and broadsides. Since Joseph Powell had identified himself with the abolitionists, he was no more popular than Crookham.

Long before the Powells came to America, the Methodist Church in England had taken a vigorous stand against slavery, and agitation to abolish servitude throughout the world was highly organized. In fact, in 1833 Great Britain had abolished slavery in all its colonies. Joseph had been somewhat dismayed that in the United States opposition to slavery had been so passive that even in the Methodist Church slavery as an institution had its defenders. There was in 1840 a gathering of forces which threatened an upheaval in the Methodist Church, particularly in western New York. Acrimony over the church's stand on abolition had increased in its ranks. Without question Joseph Powell was on the side of unequivocal rejection of slavery. Had not Wesley himself in his *Thoughts on Slavery* denounced it in the simplest of terms? In 1843 a formal split in the Methodist Church developed and the Wesleyan body separated on the slavery issue.

Jackson was typical of the growing tide of conflict between elements of the South and the more aggressive partisans from the North. The town, despite its small size and rude nature, was the home or stopping place for a notable number of scholars, among them Professor Charles Grandison Finney of Oberlin College, who paid frequent visits to the town to take part in antislavery meetings; Salmon P. Chase, the undisputed leader of the Liberty Party in Ohio; and Joshua Giddings, a Whig representative in Congress. These men were occasional guests in the Powell home and expounded their social and political views. Young Wes, eavesdropping eagerly to the impassioned arguments, was unconsciously exposed to the issues of the time.

Itinerant preaching kept Reverend Powell away from home much of the time. His circuit embraced a large part of sparsely settled southern Ohio and he was expected to cover the assignment on horseback in four weeks. Each day at noon the circuit rider held a service at some convenient location—a village square, a cabin, or even a clearing along the road where a few listeners might gather. Dangers and privation attended these itinerant missions—cold, hunger, and accidents, even abuse at the hands of ruffians. Yet the circuit riders, who, in a real sense, conquered much of the West by earnest devotion and vigilant faith, carried on their work fearlessly and uncomplainingly.

Reverend Powell looked much older than thirty-five or six. His hair had greyed somewhat prematurely and his serious, almost stern, manner, accentuated by somber habit, black waistcoat, high collar, and plain black tie, commanded respect. These were assets, though the circuit rider was much more than a religious preacher. He was expected to use his influence to increase the knowledge and culture of the communities in his circuit. He carried books and newspapers in his saddlebags and loaned them to the people with whom he visited. He would tell of mechanical inventions, agricultural advances, political issues, new styles in dress, and scatter neighborhood gossip.

The children always looked forward to their father's return from the long journeys. Usually he brought back some small gift for each. More than likely, if his calls included Chillicothe or Marietta, there would be some fabric or lace for the girls and books for the boys. But best of all, there would be a fund of new stories. When supper was over and the chores completed, he would gather the family together and relate his experiences, adding to them appropriate moral embellishments.

Reverend Powell was a stern disciplinarian. Genuine levity there was, but the order of the household was strict indeed. Although Mrs. Powell was more gentle by nature, even when the Reverend was absent she did not relax the discipline. As for Reverend Powell, he was far more interested in spiritual pasturing than in dirt farming, and all the burdens of the farm, despite the cares of small children, fell to his wife. Even the tailoring shop which occupied the front room of the house failed to tie down Joseph's restless spirit.

The common school (held wherever rooms were available) which Martha, Mary, and Wes were old enough to attend was, as in most other towns in Ohio, ungraded, the younger children being segregated from the older only for convenience. Not until 1843 did Jackson find it necessary to build a schoolhouse—and then it was a log cabin. The bitterness over the abolition sentiments of their parents caused no end of strife among classmates. Wes was stoned frequently by older boys, though they were somewhat more considerate of his sisters. Mrs. Powell feared for his safety and turned to Mr. Crookham for help.

Crookham, who ridiculed the Reverend in good humor by referring to him as "Great Britain," was a successful farmer and recently had turned over the running of his lands to his sons so that he would be free to devote his energies to the study of science. One of the most learned men of Jackson County, and one of its first commissioners of education, he was self-taught and self-made in every sense. He had compiled a history of Jackson County, had gathered a large collection of Indian relics, maintained a considerable collection of plants and animals, and experimented with chemistry. He had built on his farm a rambling log building, patterned after the typical log house of western Pennsylvania in the earliest eighteen hundreds, consisting of two large rooms separated by a breezeway, but connected by a common roof. One of these cabins was used as a combination library, museum, and workshop. The other was used as a classroom for young men who wished to improve themselves. Crookham never accepted any fee for his teaching, feeling that he would like to make it easier for others to become educated than it had been for him. In his rude sanctuary Crookham read his books, studied his collections, and performed his experiments. Many years before, he had been the first inhabitant of Jackson County to accumulate a library, an excellent collection containing first-rate scientific works in English and Latin. He was proud and enthusiastic about his possessions and shared his knowledge with all who would listen. All of Crookham's students had been mature men, but when the frequent assaults on Wes caused concern for the boy's safety, Crookham offered to take him into his own home and accept him as a pupil.

The method of instruction was unusual for a boy of eight or nine. The old man would read aloud from such books as he thought the lad could understand, and a few hours later discuss the things he had read. Wes, before he was ten, had read David Hume's *History of England*, Edward Gibbon's *The Decline and Fall of the Roman Empire*, and other substantial books; but the intimate instruction which had the greatest influence on him was the field trips and walks through the countryside, during which he was introduced to the elements of geology, archeology, and natural history.

On many occasions, Crookham took the Powell lad with him as a companion for walks along Salt Creek Gorge. Together they hunted crawfish and minnows in the creeks, and fossils in the rocks. Crookham delighted in knowing just where to look for any creature or wild plant in the neighborhood, feigning surprise when his search was rewarded. They dug in the prehistoric mounds of Jackson and Ross Counties, visited the old salt works, the millstone quarry on the road to Athens, the charcoal burners, and the iron furnaces. Mr. Crookham showed Wes the "Crookham Coal" seam, which Dr. William Mather had named in his honor.

Quite by accident Reverend Powell had made a geological discovery by himself. While digging a well near his home, he struck a vein of coal. Crookham pronounced it coal of good value, an opinion in which Dr. Mather concurred. Great excitement followed, and well it might, for the coal industry of Jackson dates from Joseph Powell's discovery in 1842.[6]

William Mather,[7] the first state geologist of Ohio, owned a large farm about a mile from that of Crookham. He had been engaged in a survey of the state and had enlisted the assistance of Crookham because he was intimately familiar with the surface geology of Jackson County. Crookham had aided several of Mather's assistants, Charles Whittlesey, S. P. Hildreth, and Cabot Briggs, during the preceding year and had provided much technical information on salt boiling for Mather's official reports.

Mather, a gentle and modest man of remarkable physical endurance, had resigned from the army in 1836 after serving at West Point as an instructor in artillery and as an assistant professor of chemistry and geology. After leaving the military academy he had made extensive surveys in the West and had recently completed a survey of Wisconsin. Like Crookham, Mather was interested in improving education, agriculture, and the mechanical arts. These men often took Wes with them on their excursions so that the boy became familiar with the professional methods of geology and exploration.

On one of these excursions Crookham inquired whether the lad had ever seen a railroad. When the reply was affirmative, he promised to show him a different kind of railroad. The two worked their way through Salt Creek Gorge, farther than they had ever gone previously, until they came to a ravine where overhanging ledges formed protected caves high above the stream bed. Suddenly, a black man, the first Negro Wes had ever seen, crawled out from one of the caves. He was followed by another man, and then a third. Two of them recognized Crookham as a friend and smiled when he spoke to them. When mentor and pupil had passed beyond view, Crookham explained how these miserable fellows had fled to safety by the "underground railroad" and cautioned him never to speak of what he had seen except with his parents. Indeed, Crookham was familiar with this mysterious railroad because he had been in charge of the local station, and during his lifetime had assisted scores of runaway slaves on their way to Canada. The first of the refuge houses of Jackson was located close by Crookham's farm and he had helped many to reach this station of safety and escape. A large colony of runaway Negroes became established in the more inaccessible branches of Rock Run, Salt Creek Gorge, and West Pigeon Creek.

[6] R. A. Jones, *Early Jackson*, p. 29.
[7] D.A.B., Vol. 8, p. 146.

All the issues were confused with abolition sentiment in the election year of 1844, the stormiest that the town of Jackson had experienced. Each of the political parties had put up a slate of candidates for local and national offices. The Free-soilers, Whig die-hards, and Libertyites electioneered with every device known to the politician.

One day Dr. Mather, Mr. Crookham, and Reverend Powell were walking down the street with a Professor Williams,[8] who had been invited to speak in the town. In front of a tavern a mob had gathered to break up the party. They attacked the quartet and forced them to take refuge in Dr. Isham's house and remain there overnight. Bitterness between factions continued at a high pitch for some time afterwards.

A few days later Crookham hurried up the path of the Powell home, flung open the door and excitedly inquired for "Great Britain." He came through the kitchen where all the children were gathered for breakfast and sat himself solidly upon a chair. "What do you think they've done?" he puffed. "They've burned down my school!" Destroyed were all his collections, his notes, his journal, his manuscripts, and most of his books. Gone were the rewards of his labor of half a century. Reverend Powell came in from the barn and Crookham explained his misfortunes. "It will take more years than I have left to build a cabinet [a collection] over again," he sighed.[9]

Hoodlums had set fire to his school and laboratory when Crookham was away from home. It was a dreadful disillusionment. Crookham consequently gave up his other pupils and devoted all his time to young Powell. It was under Mr. Crookham that Wes acquired his real education, although after a time he returned to the public school.

Crookham was often present at the religious discussions that were always in order in the Powell sitting room. In these discussions the distinction between Wesleyan and Calvinist views was carefully drawn. Reverend Powell was much more biased than Mrs. Powell or Mr. Crookham. And when arguments became heated Mrs. Powell had to act as moderator and quiet her husband. The children were usually present and, though not permitted to join in, were well aware that the dogmatic opinions of their father were not shared by the others. Reverend Powell became annoyed when his wife held to views less orthodox than his, and he taunted her about her taint of mysticism and Swedenborgianism. To this she merely smiled and avoided direct answers to his theological

[8] Professor Williams has not been identified. He was not from Oberlin College. Several abolitionists by the surname of "Williams" appear in the proceedings of the Ohio anti-slavery societies.

[9] J. W. Powell to Mrs. M. D. Lincoln.

questions. Crookham laughed with delight at their differences. It is not surprising that Wes rebelled at the orthodoxy of his father, but he cared for the pessimism of Calvinism even less. The Powell household engaged in lively discussions dealing with politics and the improvement of the country. Like most true liberals, Reverend Powell and Crookham changed their loyalties frequently. They had been Whigs, but with the rise of the Free-soilers they put their weight to the new party to contain slavery in those states and territories where it was already established. Mrs. Powell once chided them, saying that the gentlemen might just as well exchange their religions, whereupon Mr. Crookham slapped his knee and shouted "Amen!"

There were many happier occasions. Soon after settling in Ohio the family purchased a small piano, and singing became one of their greatest pleasures. The Powells [10] spent eight stormy years in Jackson, but the eight children, Martha, Mary, Wes, Bram, Lida, Nell, Walter, and Juliet, were shielded by devoted parents in a secure cheerful home. Though they were not ignorant of stress and strife, they had acquired confidence and courage.

Joseph Powell prospered. When he found time to tailor no one knew, but the suits and coats were finished when promised. He had no personal desire for luxuries but, without denying them to his family, preached their unimportance. What money came his way Powell converted into land. In 1841 he purchased four acres; in 1844 the balance of the out-lot bought in 1838 and an undeveloped farm of eighty acres. In January 1845 he secured another farm of forty acres and in April another choice one-third-acre plot. The total investment amounted to fourteen hundred dollars. The Lord had been good. Material success had come easily; too easily, Joseph Powell said. Satisfaction and greed blind us to our duty. Mary knew what that meant. They were about to move again.

In 1845 Reverend Powell had become convinced that if he were to take up a larger tract of land as the public domain was opened to homesteading, he could better provide for his family and devote full time to the ministry. The lands of the prairie farther west were more fertile than the sandy and gravelly soil of southeastern Ohio. In Wisconsin,

[10] General information about the Powell family is recorded in the U.S. Census of 1840. Incomplete and somewhat inaccurate data appear in C. S. Powell, *History and Genealogies of the Powells in America*. The ages of Joseph and Mary Powell are uncertain. They gave different ages in the censuses of 1840 and 1850. A search of the town and parish records in Shrewsbury, England, did not yield conclusive evidence as to Joseph Powell's birth date. It was between 1802 and 1805. The probable date of Mary Dean's birth was November 11, 1805. They were married on January 31, 1828, in Birmingham.

for a modest sum, he would be able to take a farm of 160 or 320 acres. At one of the annual conferences of the Church in Cleveland, Reverend Powell learned that Indian lands in Walworth County, Wisconsin, were about to be opened to settlement. When informed by a fellow preacher that this region was part open prairie, part woodland, and that the fertility was something to behold, Joseph Powell was convinced. The Jackson properties were sold during the summer of 1846 preparatory to migration to Wisconsin. The town lot and house realized seven hundred dollars. One by one the other parcels were sold to townspeople, yielding a net profit of nearly seven hundred dollars, fifty per cent on the original investment.

2

1846-1853 · Prairie Farmer

REVEREND POWELL's conscience was troubled. "So long as his doctrines comport with the discipline of the Methodist Episcopal Church," he was licensed to preach. Anxiously, he had watched the movement within the Church to purge itself of slavery. When the Wesleyan Connection formally separated in 1843, he hesitated to join it. After all, a man has his obligations, but he has his principles, too. The new Wesleyan discipline included three forthright declarations with which he was in complete sympathy: the buying or selling of human beings with the intention to enslave them, the holding of slaves, or even claiming the right of others to do so, was forbidden; the manufacturing, buying, selling, or use of intoxicating liquors, except for mechanical, chemical, or medicinal purposes, or in any other way knowingly aiding others to do so was prohibited; and the Church and the conference government was to be democratized by giving laymen a greater voice in their affairs. In fact, Joseph Powell was almost smugly satisfied with the outspoken firmness of these declarations. These were all or none measures. So, to the dictates of his conscience, in 1846 Reverend Powell resigned from the Methodist Episcopal Church and joined the Wesleyans.

The Wesleyan Connection had adopted a conference system and a division of territories after the pattern of the parent Methodist Church. Six annual conferences had been organized, and Reverend Powell was assigned immediately to the Miami Conference, which embraced western Ohio, Indiana, Illinois, Iowa, and Wisconsin. He had requested an assignment to Wisconsin.

Reverend Powell lost no time in taking full advantage of his new opportunity. With the help of a fellow minister he arranged for the purchase of 160 acres of land in South Grove, Wisconsin, near the village of Sharon, in Walworth County. The counties of southern Wisconsin adjacent to Illinois were receiving large numbers of settlers. Since most of the towns and villages were less than ten years old, there was a great need for ministers, schoolteachers, and professional men.[1]

Already the self-sufficient frontier farm had given way to a newer agriculture based upon wheat. Wheat was the chief cereal in the American diet and Southport and Racine were doing a thriving business in shipping grain to the cities in the East.

In early September, after the summer sun had well dried the ground, the Powells set out with two carriages and an immigrant wagon loaded with furniture, household goods, and personal belongings. Wes held the reins of one of the carriages.

They followed the well-worn stage roads to Columbus, Fort Wayne, and South Bend, and then took the shore road along Lake Michigan to Chicago. Beyond Chicago no direct route to Walworth was open. Because the road to Beloit was reported in fair condition, they proceeded to Rock County, Wisconsin, and from there turned eastward, picking a way over poor roads, trails, and at times open prairie, until they reached the settlement in South Grove.

The parcel which Reverend Powell had purchased proved to be much more heavily timbered than most of the neighborhood and afforded no quick means of subsistence. Thereupon he decided to buy a smaller partly improved farm close by. The first tenant had made a small clearing in a burr oak opening. Clumps of oak trees capped the summits of gentle swells of land like so many well-spaced orchards. A rivulet meandered through a beautiful grassy meadow into a small wet marshland outlined by tall blades of cattails. The landscape wanted nothing save a lively homestead to give it complete charm.

Reverend Powell examined the land with approval. The timber was of little value except for firewood and fencing, but the meadow soil was fat. Wes and Bram ran to the brook, flushing a family of quail and scattering prairie chickens in their excited haste. From the bank of the brook they tossed green acorns at the trout darting from pool to pool. How much more fun than Jackson!

Mrs. Powell was more interested in the house than in the land. Once again she had to transfer her countless domestic activities to a new location. The cabin was little better than their first cottage in Jackson. Eight children would tax its facilities, but Mrs. Powell was uncomplaining. The outlook from her front door had changed with the years, but

---

[1] A description of Walworth County and contemporary conditions may be found in I. A. Lapham, *Wisconsin: Its Geography and Topography,* p. 136.

inside she cared for her family with slight interruption. Martha, eighteen, and Mary, sixteen, were old enough to help with the younger children.

There was as yet no common school in the vicinity and Mother Powell, as she had before, taught her children. Six days a week there were lessons for Bram, ten, Lida, eight, and Ellen, six. Walter, four, and Juliet, two, were still too young for the traditional "three R's." Wes, twelve, seemed to have learning beyond his years and, except for encouragement to read, received no further schooling.

Joseph Powell had been advised to plant most of the farm in spring wheat, but to put in sufficient dent corn for his livestock and for home use to safeguard against loss of the wheat should the summer be rainy. At the village of Walworth he purchased two Durham cows, four Suffolk hogs, four Merino sheep, and some chickens. A Noah's ark, the Reverend called his stock. Cuttings of grapes and young plum and apple trees were planted and protected against winter kill.

The barn erected by the first owner was barely large enough to hold the animals and only fifteen acres could be planted with wheat, corn, and a little flax. There was no chance for a cash crop the first year. In spring a vegetable garden was planted near the house, and Mother set out her day lilies which she had divided many times since planting them in Palmyra many years before.

Joseph Powell cared little enough for farming. In Ohio he had a few acres and planted a garden, but it was cultivated, weeded, and harvested by his wife and the children. Duties kept him away from home much of the time and tailoring consumed the rest. The Reverend did not manage his land. Indeed he had no intention of becoming any more of a farmer than before, taking for granted that his sons would do most of the work and that two or three hands could be hired for heavy work. At first Mrs. Powell remonstrated because the boys were too young to manage the farm, to which Father lightly replied that Wes was more than twelve and Bram going on eleven; besides, it would be good for them. Wes became the farm manager with all its responsibilities when still in his twelfth year.

During the winter some clearing had been accomplished, but the deep snows and intense cold hindered progress. The trees on five acres were felled, but the stumps remained. To gain a head start for the next year, the trees on eight additional acres were girdled. As soon as the snows melted, five acres of prairie were broken.

Improvement of virgin land, untouched by axe or plow, meant more than felling trees and breaking prairie. Wet land had to be reclaimed by ditching, bare land had to be sodded, weed shrubs had to be uprooted, and equipment had to be improvised.

In off seasons sheds, outbuildings, and even an annex to the house, were constructed. During their second year the barn was enlarged. Every convenience, every comfort, was earned by sweat and brawn which could never be valued in money.

In May of 1847 [2] the Powell family was alarmed by the unheralded arrival of a large band of Winnebago Indians who camped themselves on the farm about a mile from the new house. They came with a few weary horses burdened with packs. The older men and women, mothers with small children on their backs, and tired toddling children, sat down to rest or drop off to sleep. A few of the men and the more vigorous women began preparations for a scanty meal of corn, wild rice, and a little dried fish. Wide-eyed with excitement, Wes watched them from a distance. Neighbors said that in former years many bands of Winnebagos passed by on the trail to Lake Geneva and Buck Lake where they hunted and fished. They were always friendly. The large company now encamped on the farm were on their way to Chicago to meet with federal authorities.

A week later these same Indians returned. The women were dressed in calicoes instead of skins, each man had a cheap bright-colored blanket, and everyone, even the small children, wore new shoes. They were happy and festive. The Winnebagos camped again near the great spring which bubbled from a hill covered by burr oak. It was historic ground to them. The groves had been the traditional hunting grounds of their forefathers, and generations of their people had fished in the brook.

The Indians set up a town of canvas tents, arranged in a great circle, in the center of which they built a campfire. They remained for more than a week on this ground, hunting and fishing by day and feasting and dancing by night.

Wes visited the camp with his mother and elder sisters. From several of the Indians who could speak a little English, his mother learned that the creek, now obstructed by a mill dam, was once set with fish snares, and the strip of land on which young apple trees were planted was once a rabbit preserve. Their new wealth of calicoes, blankets, and shoes was part payment for the very land which the Powells had obtained through the government. The Winnebagos were peaceful, friendly, simple—and

[2] J. W. Powell, *Forum*, Vol. 18, p. 662. I have followed his narrative closely.

dispossessed. For Wes it was an unforgettable introduction to the Indians.

The third year in Wisconsin, after sixty acres of land had been cleared and planted, the Powells built a threshing floor. No longer was it possible to flail the grain by hand. A more efficient method was necessary. A second stable was constructed about twenty-five feet from the first, and the space between was floored over with heavy oak plank. One side was boarded to a height of five or six feet. A center pole was placed in the middle of the floor. A few weeks later, threshing began. The well-dried wheat was brought in and spread in a great circle, the first layer with heads toward the center pole, and a second layer, overlapping the first, with the heads directed outward and the butts pointing toward the center. The two horses were led in harness to the center pole and driven round and round, tramping down the grain. The driver was provided with a switch and the helpers with a rake, a pitchfork, and a useful long-handled pan.

When the wheat was thoroughly threshed, the straw was forked up and pitched into the barn and the loose grain shoveled close to the center post from under the horses' hoofs. The procedure was repeated. In two days' tramping, from ten to twelve bushels of wheat could be recovered, but of this from two to four were lost at the fanning mill; an overall yield of ten bushels was considered to be very profitable.

Now that three or four hundred bushels of wheat could be taken to market, it was necessary to make suitable arrangements to haul them to Racine or Southport. The Powells had two possibilities to market their harvest: to Racine over a plank road under construction from Janesville or over a new road passing to the north of the farm through Delavan and Elkhorn. If the new road were kept in repair, it would be an easier journey than to Racine even though the distance was more than ten miles greater.

Walworth County was a favored wheat-growing region and nearly every farmer had planted most of his lands in spring wheat. It was readily marketable at the lake cities and both of the ports had ample facilities to buy all the grain offered. Oxen hauled the carts to market, and during the harvest season the roads were busy with fellow farmers hauling grain to port. The journey took four or five days in fair weather, but if the roads were bad, six or seven days were not unusual. At times the dirt roads were impassable. The grain usually sold for fifty cents a bushel, though in some years the price fell far below the average. It was Wes's responsibility to haul the wheat to market and to purchase provisions, clothing, and supplies with the proceeds of the sale.[3] If the cash price was low, he was expected to drive as sharp a bargain as possible. It required a good sense of economy to have any money left upon return from the city. More than once, bargaining by barter was more profitable than cash transaction. In a single year as many as fifteen trips were made to the markets.

Most of the drivers were noisy, hilarious, and lusty. They toiled hard and they played rough. Wes associated with them as a matter of course and, though enjoying their company, remained outside the boisterous fun. Stern upbringing prevented him from surrendering to the temptations or experimenting with the pleasures of a wide-open town. Not the least restraint was the sense of responsibility, because, at fourteen, he was steward of the family purse. Reverend Powell was simply too busy with spiritual matters to worry himself about it.

Like every other healthy farm lad, Wes labored long days both summer and winter but, unlike most of them, at night studied from a varied assortment of serious books, reading eagerly anything that was printed. Occasionally his father, returning from conference meetings, brought with him pamphlets on contemporary issues as well as his religious tracts. Wes worked faithfully, but his thoughts were far away with books, collections, and Mr. Crookham.

In southern Wisconsin there were many Indian mounds similar to those which Wes Powell had visited with George Crookham near Chillicothe and Marietta. Most of the farmers in the neighborhood had turned over, when plowing, various Indian implements and ornaments. Some of these were of striking nature, and several collections had been accumulated by local amateurs. Wes began a little museum of his own. After coming in from the fields, driving the cows to their stalls, or bringing in the oxen at the close of the day's work, he would gather wild flowers and curious insects and try to identify them. To a certain extent Wes was encouraged to study his specimens, but Reverend Powell was determined to divert his son's developing interest in natural history.

Returning from trips to Racine, Wes often stopped at Delavan to watch the unusual animals caged at the circus farms. The reptiles and the great cats fascinated him. The Mabie Circus had its headquarters in the village and almost everyone living in the vicinity was engaged, in one way or another, in the circus business.

On one of his trips to Southport, Wes chanced to meet William

[3] M. D. Lincoln, *Open Court*, Vol. 16, p. 709.

Wheeler, an intelligent and well-read young man then about twenty-one. His manner was affable, and they became fast friends. Wheeler was quiet, scholarly, and devoutly Congregationalist. He usually read from a book while his oxen followed the carts ahead. Wes thought it a good idea, followed his example, and afterward kept several books in his wagon box. Wes held to no program. His reading certainly lacked unity or direction, but despite its desultory nature was nonetheless profitable. He reread the books given to him by Mr. Crookham, like Thomas Dick's *Philosophy,* and John Bunyan's *Pilgrim's Progress,* which for a long time was his favorite. His parents approved heartily and urged him to read poetry, especially Milton. They wondered who this new friend was. Being hopeful still that Wes ultimately would prepare for the ministry—though he had shown little inclination in that direction—Reverend Powell in particular wished to nurture such an apparent good influence.

Wes and Wheeler thereafter met frequently on the road to market and Wes in particular found their discussions stimulating. Wheeler urged him to complete his schooling no matter what the hardships and work toward an education in a good college. The sciences, especially mineralogy and chemistry, were the great enterprises of the future, he thought.

Returning from one trip in a heavy downpour, Wes brought his companion home for a visit. In the evening, after the supper was cleared away and the chores done, everyone except the Reverend gathered around the piano for the customary singing. The evening passed quickly and Wheeler enjoyed the friendly occasion. Mary was quite taken with the guest and, as fortune would have it, Will seemed more than slightly interested in her.

Martha too had acquired a suitor, and by a rather unusual circumstance.[4] Late one afternoon, Joe Davis of Decatur, Illinois, and his son John, who were making a long journey on horseback through Illinois and Wisconsin, rode up to the door and, seeking lodging for the night, called according to custom, "Hello the house." The Powells cordially invited the strangers into their home. Joe Davis prided himself in his ability to judge people, especially the ladies, and he did not overlook the qualities and cheerful disposition of Martha. Davis whispered to his son, nodding in Martha's direction, "There's the wife for you." The following morning the men resumed their journey. A few weeks

[4] This anecdote was related to me by two daughters of Martha Powell Davis, Frances (Mrs. L. D. Whittemore) and Winnifred (Mrs. L. T. Schnacke).

later Martha received from John Davis a courteous letter acknowledging the Powell hospitality and politely requesting some further word
from her. She replied with an invitation to continue correspondence,
and before many letters had passed between them, a happy understanding had been reached.

The Powell household hummed with new excitement as Martha and
Mary spent more time than usual on bleaching linens and doing fancy
needlework. The Powell girls had spent most of their childhood near
the frontier, but they were able to hoard chests of homespun, silks,
imported lace, and fine linens decorated with embroidery or drawn work
copied from the sampler which their mother had cherished with her
own linens from England. Mary and Martha had made plans for marriage at nearly the same time. No date for the weddings had been set,
and it was uncertain as to which would marry first. Reverend Powell
mused that he might be called upon to officiate at a double ceremony.
Martha and John were married first, but Mary and William followed
a few months later.

After the festivities attending the weddings were over and the sudden emptiness in the Powell homestead forgotten, Wes decided that he
too would leave home to resume schooling and prepare for admission
to an eastern college. The grain harvest of 1850 had been marketed
with exceptional profit. Bram, fourteen, had proved his ability to make
the trips to Southport and Racine and take over the regular accounts.
Wes felt that he could now be spared from the farm. It was discontent
with farm work as well as thirst for knowledge that impelled him to
leave his family. Reverend Powell's unsympathetic attitude toward
Wes's interest in natural history, rather than in the ministry, was a
constant disappointment and irritation.

In October 1850 John Wesley Powell came out of the oak clearing to
go to school.[5] Janesville, twenty miles distant, seemed to offer the most
promising likelihood of temporary employment and access to an education. He had not been to school since leaving Jackson four years before.

Near the close of day he arrived at a farm barely two miles from
the town. His earthly wealth consisted of a few silver and copper
coins. Wes asked for work, hoping to obtain lodging until he could find
a job. The farmer engaged him at sight to split wood and repair the
farm tools. At the end of two weeks he had completed the tasks which
his employer figured would require two months. With six dollars in his

[5] In the U.S. Census return (Walworth County, Wisconsin, p. 555) J. W. Powell, "age
16," gave his occupation as "farmer."

pocket and a hearty invitation to return he went to the school in Janesville.

The school, a large one-room building, provided for about forty pupils. Most of the students were much younger than he and the teacher was slovenly and indifferent. Although Wes was keenly disappointed at the quality of the school, he decided to enroll anyway.

He returned to the farm at which he had been staying and offered his temporary employer a proposition: could he have board and room in exchange for doing the chores? He would work early mornings and nights, but he must have the daytime for school and study. There was no argument. Hired men were scarce and Wes was a sterling young fellow. The bargain was accepted. He would have to look after the cattle and sheep, and after supper do odd maintenance jobs. The plan worked well. Evening, when the chores were done, he studied his books by feeble firelight, rocking the cradle of the youngest member of the family.

Wes was handicapped by serious deficiencies in mathematics and grammar. In the common school in Jackson he had studied the traditional subjects, but the time spent with Mr. Crookham interrupted a more thorough training in elementary subjects. If he hoped to obtain college entrance, not only would it be necessary to acquire a knowledge of mathematics, but the classic languages as well.

In the five years that the Powells lived in Wisconsin, the population of Walworth County tripled. The demand for wheat increased so that the price, because of threatening war in Europe, had gone above $1.00 a bushel for two consecutive years. The value of good land appreciated accordingly. Commerce in the lake ports had expanded rapidly, largely because of the roads which linked them to the nearby towns. Reverend Powell sensed an opportunity to dispose of his farm at a profit. Moreover he knew where he could purchase undeveloped land—cheap.

In the fall of 1851 the farm in South Grove was sold at a handsome price and Reverend Powell purchased a section of 320 acres on Bonus Prairie,[6] Boone County, across the state line in Illinois. Wes had attended the school in Janesville for a single term when his father appealed to him to come home and help put the new farm in order. In return, he promised to aid Wes to attend Oberlin College but, of course, with the stipulation that he prepare for the ministry.

Wes was too dutiful a son to refuse his father, but the conditions

[6] C. Colby, *Handbook of Illinois*.

laid down were unsatisfactory. Long before this their differences over Wes's vocation—or lack of one—had been a source of contention. Father had no sympathy for science, and Wes had no desire to enter the ministry. As soon as they were together argument piled upon argument.

Nevertheless, Wes went home to Walworth County, and helped to close up the farm and move the family belongings to Bonus Prairie. The toil of the first year was almost as difficult as the work on their Wisconsin farm. There was less clearing but more breaking of prairie. However, it was a good growing season and a reassuring profit was obtained by the end of the year.

Father was willing to make good his offer but Wes refused to commit himself. There were angry words again. The only means by which Wes could further his ambition to attend college would be to earn the money himself. To do that he again turned over the management of the farm to Bram. Teaching offered the greatest opportunity. At home he began to review grammar and arithmetic in preparation for teaching. He was confident that he knew more than his former teacher at Janesville.

After preparing himself to the best of his ability, Wes set out for Jefferson County, Wisconsin, thirty miles away. He walked the distance over frozen rutted roads against a fierce north wind. The region was receiving hundreds of new homesteaders each month and he knew that there would be no difficulty in securing a teaching engagement. However, it would be necessary to secure first a certificate of proficiency. Late in the afternoon of his second day's journey, Wes presented himself for examination at the home of the superintendent of the district schools. The man was out, but his wife welcomed him to the parlor where a cheerful fire was burning in the fireplace. Meanwhile, his hostess served him hot tea and biscuits and talked with him about his family. Wes glanced about the room and admired the fine furniture. He recognized that this was a home of culture and comfort.

At length, the superintendent [7] returned home and insisted that the prospective schoolmaster remain overnight. As the family sat together, they conversed about the school, the pupils, and the subjects being taught there. In a skillful way the superintendent quizzed the prospective teacher and learned a great deal about his background and ambi-

[7] An exhaustive search has failed to identify the superintendent; nor has it been possible to verify the district school in which Powell held his first position. There is substance to the story, however. I have a statement by Powell dated September 12, 1860, saying he had been a "teacher in Jefferson County."

tions. Just before retiring, the superintendent went to a Governor Winthrop desk in the corner of the room and signed a certificate of proficiency which he handed to Wes without ceremony or comment.

The superintendent and his wife were well educated. Together they offered Wes advice and honest encouragement to bend all his effort toward a good education. Their sincerity gave him a feeling of confidence. He went upstairs to bed, happy that he had so easily passed the ordeal, and calculated how long it would take to save a hundred dollars on a salary of $14.00 a month.

Wes Powell's first school was a one-room stone building which, like a thousand others in the prairie, had the barest facilities for the teacher and the classes. The seats were split logs, eight inches in diameter and approximately fifteen feet long, mounted upon four legs. With the flat side up they served their function but were hardly comfortable. In the front of the room benches with shorter legs were arranged for the younger students. Around three walls, boards set up on sturdy pins served as desks. While studying, working, or waiting turn to recite, the pupil was obliged to look at his slate or stare at the bare wall. A pupil faced the teacher only when reciting or when requested to do so. The single door, made of rough boards, hung on great wooden hinges and was fastened by means of a wooden latch.

Each morning classes were opened with the schoolmaster at prayer, and tardy pupils found themselves locked out until the ceremony had been completed. Some of Powell's students were as old as he was and it was necessary to carry on a considerable program of study to keep ahead of them. It was a common sight to see some of the boys sixteen to eighteen years old working over words of one or two syllables while, beside them, youngsters eight or nine years old read from books and engaged in arithmetic well beyond the capacity of most of their parents. So long as a school could draw only twenty or thirty scholars from a wide area, no single class would have more than five or eight pupils. A year before, the Wisconsin legislature had set up a district system of common schools, and the state constitution provided for free schooling for all children between the ages of four and twenty. Wes Powell followed the discussions in the newspapers and had read about new trends in education, but he held independent, if not unconventional, views on how to teach.

In larger towns a real revolution in education was in the making. In fact, the Midwest outstripped more conservative New England and the middle atlantic states in modernizing their curricula. Already, some of the larger cities like Cleveland, Cincinnati, and Chicago had set definite standards and minimum requirements for their teachers, and had specified what constituted classwork for each of the six lower grades. Practically no school in the Midwest offered more than six years of instruction, and yet many of the students in the fifth or sixth grades were well advanced in mathematics, or initiated to Greek and Latin. Such opportunities were dependent upon the skill and willingness of the teacher. The classical languages were not required, but the teacher might interest, or force them upon, older students. A more satisfactory education often could be obtained from the many academies which had been established almost as soon as a county was occupied by homesteaders. Indeed, in Illinois and somewhat later in Iowa, an academy or college was established in every county soon after a church had been erected. Most of the academies were divided into primary, preparatory, and academic or college departments. The so-called college departments did not offer instruction equivalent to that of eastern colleges, but it was the best obtainable and it served the communities well.

Wes Powell taught himself elementary geometry and took his classes about half as far as he had progressed. He worked through four advanced grammars, and continued studies in geology. One night each week he gave a popular lecture on geology or on geography to his older students, and the news of the program attracted many young people from adjoining villages and towns. Often there was an audience of thirty interested persons, and he enjoyed his success genuinely and modestly.

It was the custom for the teacher to "board around" with the families of the pupils; usually it was part of the contract. However, a Mr. Little, one of the trustees, took Wes into his home and insisted that he stay the greater part of the year with him. Mrs. Little had been a schoolteacher in Massachusetts and possessed a library of good books which, in terms of the frontier country, was of substantial proportions. She helped Powell with his public lectures, reading over outlines of his talks before he delivered them. Mrs. Little took also a great interest in his geological work and urged him to stick to his ambition for a scientific education.

In the summer of 1852 Wes worked on the family farm in Bonus Prairie to add to his slow-growing savings. Meanwhile, his father had become interested in the establishment of a college at Wheaton, Illinois. Four years before, plans had been laid for the founding of a Wesleyan college and seminary at Wheaton to prepare young men and women for preaching and teaching. Money was scarce and, after years of difficult work and sacrifice, one college building was under construction. Reverend Joseph Powell was elected a trustee of the college, so he decided to move to Wheaton where all his children could have the advantages of a college education. The family purchased a forty-acre tract of fertile land on which there was a small but very comfortable house. They bought also a five-acre plot near the new college building. In mid-September, Wes, his youngest sister Juliet, and his mother journeyed to Wheaton, looked over their new home, and measured their neighbors. The family agreed that it would be more convenient and congenial to live on the small plot near the village. There was no building on the smaller lot, but Wes assured his mother that the house could be moved from the forty-acre tract without much difficulty. The distance was only a half mile and the road leading into town was well graded so that the house could be set wherever she wanted it. This was Mother Powell's eighth home, but for once she had the pleasure to decide where it should be placed.

Mother and Juliet returned to Bonus Prairie and Wes at once made arrangements to transfer the house. With the help of three husky men, the building was jacked up and eased onto rollers. Then, with six oxen hitched in teams, it was dragged to the southeast corner of the lot. The house was settled where a broad lane joined the main road entering Wheaton from the west. It was soon ready for occupancy and made suitable for winter. Cordwood was piled high against the house. A large shed was erected and staple provisions stored in the pantry. The rest of the family arrived in early November, and the Powells took possession with enthusiasm and anticipation.

3

1853-1861 · Illinois Schoolmaster

EDUCATION now appeared to be within easy reach and Wes Powell awaited expectantly the opening of the new college in Wheaton. The building was completed in September and the workmen removed the litter and tidied up the grounds. Reverend John Cross, the college president, moved into his residence, a faculty was hired, and announcements of the grand opening were published in the newspapers throughout northern Illinois.

Illinois Institute opened its doors on December 14, 1853, and accepted students in its three departments, the elementary, which was open to all Wheaton children, the preparatory, and the college. The school was coeducational and admission was granted to any qualified person. An enrollment of not more than forty students in the two upper departments was expected, so the trustees had proceeded cautiously. The prospectus had stated merely that a full curriculum would not be offered during the first year. There were no courses in the sciences, none in advanced mathematics, none in logic.

Wes Powell was bitterly disappointed. He had left home to further his education, had engaged in teaching to earn money for college, studied industriously, and twice had his work interrupted to return home and move the family. He was further from his ambition than he had been two years before. At nineteen, almost twenty, a young fellow ought to be heading in one direction, not tethered to indecision. Reverend Powell called his son undisciplined and irresponsible. At least there were outward indications that Father was correct, but he had misjudged his boy. Wes had found his greatest strength within himself, and failing to gain a sympathetic understanding, turned more and more self-sufficient. Friendly and optimistic, talkative, yet secretive about his own affairs, Wes Powell showed self-discipline and self-reliance in studying independently and paying little attention to Illinois Institute or the town of Wheaton.

Wheaton was a community of less than two hundred people. Its future, because of the new college, had appeared hopeful, but when the Galena and Chicago Union Railroad surveyed its line through the town, Wheaton's development, at the expense of Naperville, was assured. Streets were laid out and the roads in and out of the village were improved as far as conditions would permit.

Although DuPage County was undergoing rapid development, it was primarily an agricultural district in which the rich prairie soil produced abundant grains and a large variety of fruits. In a very real sense, prosperity of the county and its towns was based upon agriculture.

Almost as soon as the town was founded, the residents organized an agricultural and mechanical society. The first meeting was held on October 19, 1853, and Wes went out of curiosity to see what kind of a constitution and bylaws would be drafted. The chief purpose of the society was to encourage improvement of crops and stock and to increase the use of new mechanical inventions. Besides monthly meetings, an annual county fair was proposed so that exhibits of farm products, livestock, and mechanical inventions could be entered in competition. The womenfolk could display examples of needlework, culinary art, and other domestic skills. In addition to these regular features, prizes would be offered for the best collections illustrating the natural history of the region to encourage the serious study of the plants and animals of Illinois. Wes liked the idea and thought that he could enter several prize-winning collections whenever the fairs were held.

Wes Powell, nevertheless, found little of interest in Wheaton. The college offered him nothing, he was not qualified to teach in any of its departments, and he could find no employment to his liking in the village. Now, four years after he had quit farming for good, a college education seemed as remote as ever. He had prepared himself to the best of his ability to meet entrance requirements, but he had been unable to save enough money to pay even one year's tuition. Father would have paid the tuition gladly if Wes agreed to study for the ministry, but he would not accept help on this condition. Undoubtedly he could have borrowed enough to see his way through, but this would have antagonized his father. Wes chose, therefore, to work for his ambition, no matter how long it took.

John Davis,[1] Martha's husband, was very anxious to see Wes further

[1] For a brief review of John Davis's career see Topeka *Journal*, August 2, 1901. I have had access to family papers in the possession of his daughter, Mrs. L. D. Whittemore, and granddaughter, Miss Margaret Whittemore.

his scientific training. His father, Joe Davis, had allowed his children to have educations of their own choosing. John Davis had been to Springfield Academy and to Illinois College at Jacksonville. His younger brother, Henry, was soon to enter Illinois College and perhaps Wes might be able to go at the same time. John and Martha urged him to come to Decatur to stay with them because they were sure he would find greater opportunity of employment there. John had a large nursery and stock farm close by his father's place in Long Creek township, about eight miles east of the town.

In the early spring of 1854 Wes Powell, now a young man of twenty, went south to Macon County seeking employment as a teacher in one of the district schools. Without difficulty he found an opening at the Emerson School,[2] located on Long Creek about four miles east of Decatur. Bram came with him. He was eighteen and felt keenly the necessity of preparing himself for college entrance. Bram's ambition was to become a teacher, but he did not try to obtain a position until he had carried his studies a little further.

The Long Creek school was a one-room frame building with furnishings slightly better than at Jefferson; the teacher was provided with a sturdy chair, a long pointer, and a good slate blackboard. A lively class of youngsters kept Mr. Powell busy and he earned his monthly salary of $24.00. An evening class in geography,[3] similar to the one he had organized at Jefferson, met once each week at the schoolhouse and all interested persons were welcome. When curious pupils arrived for the first recitation they found the walls lined with large unlettered outline maps. The schoolmaster took his place and announced that this would be a singing geography class. Then, taking his long pointer, he began.

The first lesson was composed of the states and their capitals, each rhyme to be sung to a slow chant, such as "The state of Maine, the capital Augusta," and so on through them all. As Mr. Powell pointed to the outline of one state, and then another, the pupils alertly chanted the proper stanzas. In other meetings he taught them the mountains of Europe to the tune, "From Greenland's Icy Mountains"; even the rivers of Asia were rhymed with appropriate music. But the favorite number sung on every program was:

[2] There is a little confusion over identification of this school building. It is also known as the second Cherry Point or Cherry Grove School. Later, Bram Powell and Ellen Powell taught there.

[3] Rev. William Pinckney Baker, MS, *Early Recollections*. Used with permission of Miss Mary E. Baker, Decatur, Illinois.

Of all the mighty nations,
    In the East or in the West,
Oh, this glorious Yankee nation
    Is the greatest and the best.
From the great Atlantic ocean,
    Where the sun begins to dawn,
Leaps across the Rocky Mountains
    Far away to Oregon—
Come along, come along,
    Make no delay,
Come from every nation—
    Come from every way—
Our lands are broad enough—
    Have no alarm—
For Uncle Sam is rich enough
    To give us all a farm.[4]

It is no wonder that some of those who attended the singing geography class in childhood remembered it many years later in old age.

Decatur in 1854 [5] was a busy town built on the edge of the timber. The town itself was four blocks square; nearly all of the buildings were frame and the sidewalks were plank. The streets were dusty in dry weather and a morass in wet. Already the community had grown to fifteen hundred citizens and was beginning to scatter in all directions over the adjacent countryside. Saturday was a big time and from day-break until after ten at night the town bustled with commotion and celebration, with at least one good fist fight thrown in.

There lived in Decatur a scholarly gentleman, John W. Coleman, who conducted an academy in the basement of the Methodist Church. He anticipated rapid growth of the town and was hoping to develop a high school. Mr. Coleman had a flourishing school of nearly 180 students and, with the assistance of Mrs. Coleman and Miss Maria Ela, was doing a very creditable job in this prairie community. Wes and Bram came to Decatur to study as private pupils under Mr. Coleman because they had advanced beyond the instruction offered in the regular classes. While there the Powell brothers studied mostly Latin and Greek and some mathematics and natural science.

There was much more unrestrained joy in Long Creek and Decatur

[4] The quotation is as given by Rev. Baker. See also Decatur *Herald,* May 14, 1916. It is, of course, a version of the song, "Uncle Sam's Farm," by Jesse Hutchinson, Jr.

[5] See B. M. Lindsey, *Long Creek Township in Macon County;* E. B. Hitchcock, *Story of Decatur;* W. E. Nelson, *City of Decatur and Macon County, Illinois.* Data also provided by Mrs. L. D. Whittemore, daughter of John Davis, and Mrs. Mabel E. Wilson, a grand-niece of John Davis.

than Wes had experienced in his strict Methodist home. There were dances, parties, and other merrymaking. Holidays were events for everybody. The Glorious Fourth began with a parade to the bandstand for a spread-eagle speech and ended with a barbecue on the edge of town. With whiskey at forty cents a quart, it was possible to get comfortably mellow on a very small investment. Wes and Bram did not drink alcoholic liquor, but they were amused at the fleeting hilarity of those who did. In all of the social life of the town these two young handsome fellows joined heartily. Although the Powell brothers had very different personalities, Bram quiet and shy, and Wes confident and forward, both were welcomed into local activities.

Dances were usually held in the brick courthouse which stood on the southwest corner of the town square. Matt Johnson, the fiddler, sitting on the judge's bench with a little brown jug at his side, furnished the music. The men wore cowhide boots with trousers tucked in, while the girls were more stylishly adorned. For festive occasions Jim Schoaf, who published the *Weekly Gazette,* served as caller and master of the dance. The Christmas ball outshone all others of the year. After the celebration the entire crowd bulged the facilities of Mrs. Harrel's Social Hall where a substantial supper awaited them.

These were happy months and Wes found the romantic and lighter side of his nature. He became infatuated with a belle of Decatur,[6] but they disagreed over differences in religion, and at the insistence of both families the brief engagement was broken.

Sometime during 1855 Mrs. Powell was startled by a letter from Joseph Dean, her long-lost brother, who twenty-five years before had planned to come to America on the same boat as she. Joseph Dean [7] now was living in Detroit with his own family. There was great excitement, and as soon as she was able, Mrs. Powell made a trip to Detroit for a happy reunion.

The following year Wes made a trek across Michigan to collect shells and reptiles, and he made the acquaintance of his Uncle Joseph, Aunt Harriet, Cousin Emma, and Cousin Charlie. Emma, two years

[6] I have been unable to identify the "belle of Decatur." There is a hazy tradition concerning this young lady, but accounts differ. One account says she was a Catholic, another says Unitarian. Either would have been unacceptable to Rev. Joseph Powell.

[7] I have not been able to learn when Joseph Dean came to America. See note 8 below. In 1840, he was employed as a hatter in New York City. Dean followed the same trade in Detroit in the firm of F. Buhl. Later he became an executive with the Buhls and in other business enterprises.

his junior, was a pretty lass who wore her hair braided elaborately.[8] She was engrossed with his stories of travel and adventure and he thought she was the most beautiful girl he had ever seen.

John Davis was at this time considering enlarging his stock farm and nursery. Wes borrowed several hundred dollars, put up his own savings, and assumed partnership in the Davis sheep farm. Regardless of the bright prospect for a fair profit the first year, Reverend Powell demanded that his son get out of the business at once. He wrote Wes an angry and intemperate letter insisting "that the borrowing of money to make money is not one whit better than highway robbery." [9] Wes resented the implications with equal bitterness; his feelings were hurt. Mrs. Powell disapproved too, but her softer objections were essentially that a business project would delay rather than hasten a college education. In deference to Mother rather than to Father, Wes withdrew, repaid the borrowed money gradually, and lost his own savings, refusing to let John liquidate any of his share. All this Wes accepted philosophically; another dream had evaporated.

A few weeks later Wes left the Davis farm to go to Decatur. With but sufficient money to rent simple quarters, he set up housekeeping in a vacant one-room building which had been a cobbler's shop, sharing it with a large family of rats. The place reeked with the smells of grease and leather. Not only was it unheated, but the light was poor. Here he lived for nearly five months on bread, milk, cheese, and such other provisions that required no cooking. When John came to town, Martha would send with him a smoked sausage, a roasted joint of mutton, or boiled eggs, to augment his meager fare. He resumed studies on his own, visiting Mr. Coleman socially, having no funds to engage him as a tutor. Coleman understood and nicely avoided the situation by lending books from his private library and inviting his former pupil for frequent friendly discussions.

There were but two alternatives, farming or teaching. Wes had given up farming for good, so once again he decided to teach. Now John Davis came forward with another idea. If Wes could earn thirty dollars to cover tuition, attendance at Illinois College could be arranged. It was just the thing.

[8] Emma Dean was born in New York City in 1836. My description is based upon a photograph made in 1859 or 1860.

[9] This quotation is rarely given in its full meaning, "the borrowing of money *to make money. . . .*" The aversion to debt among the English, Scotch, and Welsh should not be overlooked. Joseph Powell, March 4 (7?), 1855,

In 1855 Wes entered the scientific department of Illinois College at Jacksonville and took up residence with Henry Davis in Grove House.[10] The tuition was only thirty dollars, but the estimated living expenses about a hundred dollars more. There were a few more than a hundred students in attendance, eighty of whom were in the college department, and twenty-seven, including Henry Davis, in the preparatory department. Many like Wes had paid the tuition but lacked funds to pay the other expenses. The school permitted payment by note, provided that the student was willing to redeem it by labor whenever called upon to do so. John Davis signed this note for him.

Early during the first term Wes became a member of Sigma Pi society which had a slight element of secrecy to it. The society's motto was "Let there be light," and lecture programs and debates, as well as the usual social gatherings, fulfilled its lofty literary purpose.

The courses seem to have been lightweight—Jeremiah Day's *Algebra to the Binomial Theorem* and English grammar (Wes declined to take optional French) in the first term; John Playfair's *Euclid,* six books of geometry and Day's *Elocution* (still no French) in the second term; and in the third term, the conclusion of algebra and geometry and select English classics.

John Davis had attended Illinois College in 1848–1849 and while there became intimately acquainted with Jonathan B. Turner.[11] Although still known as "Professor," Turner had resigned from the faculty of the college some months earlier. He had had a brilliant but stormy association with the institution extending for more than thirteen years—stormy because of apprehension caused by his liberal views on slavery and religion. Turner had been worn down by anxiety, bickering, and debt. Nevertheless, he resigned to uphold his ideals, and then, without capital, began to experiment with horticulture in a modest way. By 1850 Turner had achieved unexpected success when he solved the fencing problem of the prairie with the shrub, osage orange. Education and osage orange were closely interrelated. For some years he had tried to introduce into Illinois a common-school system patterned after that of New England, but this proved to be impossible because farmers had located their houses at the edge of timber so that it would be easier

[10] Illinois College, *Cat.* for 1855–1856 and 1856–1857, and *Alumni Records.* For background material see C. H. Rammelkamp, *Illinois College: A Centennial History.*

[11] Jonathan Baldwin Turner was a truly remarkable man. See C. H. Rammelkamp, *Illinois College: A Centennial History,* and M. T. Carriel, *Jonathan Baldwin Turner.* John Davis named one of his children Buel Turner Davis after his mentor. I am indebted to "The Club" of Jacksonville, of which Turner was a member, for additional information.

to fence in their lands with the handy supply of wood. For this reason, farms were at great distances from one another. Turner hit upon the idea that some fast-growing shrub might literally fence in the prairie and make it possible for a farmer to separate his fields and build his homestead at whatever point he wished. After experimenting with many kinds of plants for hedging, he found success with osage orange. This shrub grows rapidly, is well covered with thorns, and is resistant to intense cold and the rigors of winter. Within a few years it became popular, and hundreds of miles of osage hedges stretched across the prairie. Thus, from his experiments it was possible to locate a village in the very heart of the prairie with farms extending outward from the compact settlement. The village could then support schools and churches.

The work earned for Turner both reputation and financial reward. However, his fame rested not so much on his technical and scientific work, as on his political liberalism. It was this liberalism that had attracted John Davis in 1849 and which had nurtured their lasting friendship. John insisted that Wes must call upon Professor Turner and make his acquaintance, and wrote a warm letter of introduction on behalf of his brother-in-law.

Soon after Wes arrived at Jacksonville, he called one Sunday afternoon upon the professor. The letter of introduction was indeed unnecessary. His enthusiastic host guided him over the experimental farm, pointed out the prize plots, and talked of natural history. Turner explained that he never missed a county agricultural fair, and lectured before any audience that would give him ear. Turner loved his large family and had great pride in his farm, but he was not satisfied with this success. He devoted his energies passionately to the liberalization of education, the improvement of agriculture, and the advancement of the rights of the farmer. And thus, Turner became the second of Powell's great teachers.

Wes Powell completed the year at Illinois College with marks between 90 and 100. He then decided to interrupt his schooling, first by making a long collecting trip, and then by filling a teaching position at Clinton in De Witt County at a salary of sixty dollars a month. Certainly, with this income he would at last be able to save enough to take him to Oberlin.

During 1855 [12] Powell made his first long journey to study mollusks

[12] It is unfortunate that so little is known of the river trips of John Wesley Powell. Aside from two letters to his mother, two newspaper notices, and records of a few specimens, I

of the Mississippi drainage system. He purchased a small skiff and rowed up the Mississippi River to St. Paul, sold his boat, and walked across Wisconsin to Mackinaw. Alone, and with almost no burden, he spent four months gathering specimens and sending them back by post to his home at Wheaton. From this year on, Powell spent every summer making journeys by rowboat on the tributaries of the Mississippi. In 1856 he descended the Mississippi from the falls of St. Anthony to New Orleans, making collections all the way, and as before sending them back for safekeeping. It is disappointing that no complete record or journal of any of these trips has been found. Very likely at this time Powell had no desire to keep such a record. Apparently his only notes consisted of lists of the specimens collected and the localities visited.

Powell had reached the age of twenty-two. He was thin, spare, and of average height. He had allowed his beard to grow, but cropped it close. The roustabouts and ruffians engaged in the river traffic from Pittsburgh to the Gulf were notorious for their pugnacity and their troublemaking, but he was never molested nor did a sense of personal danger disturb him. A skiff, pencils, a notebook, food, and a little pocket money—the latter often extremely limited—were all he needed to be on his way.

In the fall of 1857, when the next academic year commenced, Wes was not at Oberlin, but at Illinois Institute in Wheaton.[13] Regular instruction in the sciences was now offered and he could live at home and hoard his earnings. He had made a tidy sum at Clinton, but alas, had spent most of it during his trip to New Orleans.

From the very beginning, the college in Wheaton had financial difficulties, contracting debts far beyond its power to pay. The income from tuition was so small that the trustees had to seek assistance outside the denomination. Locally, the Methodists had been losing ground, many of their number joining the Congregational Church, which was gaining influence throughout the Midwest. The presidency of the college had been held by Rev. John Cross for only a few months, and he was succeeded by Rev. L. C. Matlack, one of the great figures in the Wesleyan movement in America. It was assumed that his prestige would make it much easier to obtain support for the shaky institution. Matlack did not remain long in Wheaton. He resigned to become

have been unable to locate anything substantial. Powell was preparing himself unconsciously for later explorations.

[13] Wheaton College, *Archives;* Illinois Institute, *Cat.* for 1856–1857, 1857–1858, and 1860–1861. Copies of catalogues for the two intervening years are missing.

director of the book division of the Wesleyan Church, believing that in the new position he could do more missionary work.

During these years all the Powell children attended the Institute. Wes was officially connected with the school for only one term, in 1857–1858. The younger Powell children and their cousins,[14] the children of Walter Scott Powell—Morris, Walter (usually called "Clem"), and Ada—were members of the preparatory department. Financial matters went from bad to worse and finally, in 1860, the school was reorganized as Wheaton College under the control of the Congregational Church with the willing cooperation of the Wesleyans. The new trustees were, of course, prominent Congregational gentlemen. Rev. Jonathan Blanchard assumed the presidency.

In 1858 Powell entered Oberlin,[15] and because of his previous work in other schools, was enrolled with the class of 1861. Being given an advanced standing, he found it possible to study Greek and Latin and continue work in botany. Reverend Powell had always desired that Wes should attend Oberlin, not only because of its leadership in western education, but because of its orthodoxy and its devotion to Christian service. If his son would not enter the ministry, he might at least preserve his Christian upbringing.

Among his classmates Powell found a friend in Carlos Kenaston,[16] who lived not far from the school on East College Street. Almost every morning after classes they would meet and walk together back to their rooms. Wes had obtained a small room with the Haines family across from the campus, and from his window over the front hall was able to see the school buildings while he studied.

No student who came under the influence of Oberlin in the 1850's could remain untouched by its militant Christianity and stern morality, much less its social liberalism. Oberlin's stand against slavery was known throughout the country. In 1854 the Missouri Compromise was repealed in Congress and all of the territories were potentially opened to slavery. Gradually, as new states in the West became organized, slave states might well outnumber the free states. Though this measure

[14] The children of Joseph and Mary Powell attended Illinois Institute as did those of his younger brother, Walter Scott Powell, a watchmaker. He was living with Joseph and Mary Powell in Jackson in 1840, married in Ohio a few years later, and migrated from state to state with the Reverend. There were at least six children—Morris, Ada, Walter (Clem), Minnie, Isabel, and Lucy. Walter S. and his wife Ellen died suddenly of fever during the Civil War period.

[15] Oberlin College, *Gen. Cat.*, 1858–1859. See also R. S. Fletcher, *A History of Oberlin College* (2 vols.).

[16] C. A. Kenaston, letter to Oberlin College, 1903. Transcript provided by alumni office.

had been a political issue for some years, it was still a heated controversy and, if anything, caused redoubled efforts among liberals to further abolition in every possible manner. Nearly all of the student societies at the college had identified themselves with abolition work.

There were other attractions at Oberlin. The chapel contained one of the finest organs west of the Allegheny Mountains and a large student chorus, which prepared oratorios for public appearances, practicing daily for many weeks. Not only the students who were interested in music, but all others were welcome. Yet in all of these activities Wes took little part. Despite his political sympathies and his enjoyment of music, his chief interests were in the outdoors. On his own, he studied botany, gathering an extensive collection of the wild plants found in the vicinity and enlisting the aid of fellow students to make a complete survey of the local flora.

Among the books and papers which interested Powell during his term at Oberlin was a curious poem then being published in a new American edition, P. J. Bailey's *Festus*. Some of the fellows joined with Kenaston and Wes to discuss it after morning recitations. *Festus* was a semireligious and philosophical work, in some respects not unlike *Faust*. It is difficult to see now why this little book enjoyed the popularity of several generations, but it made a deep mark on many of the students in colleges at the time.

Powell attended numerous lectures on missionary work among the Indians of the Lake Superior region and Oregon. Under Oberlin's plan the Indians were being taught to grow vegetables, to wear clothes, and to read and write. He noticed Turner's osage orange hedges around the college grounds. But regardless of these diversions, his interests were elsewhere. He simply did not find enough to fill them and even with his extracurricular avocations, there had been insufficient activity. As unobtrusively as Powell came to Oberlin, he left it. Most of his classmates did not know the reason for his going, attributing it to some personal misfortune.[17]

About the same time there was organized at Bloomington a state natural history society having as its immediate objective a thorough exploration of the State of Illinois to enumerate every kind of plant, animal, or mineral found within its boundaries. Professor Turner had been its guiding spirit and, after preliminary planning at Decatur, the society was founded in June 1858. Wes Powell had been unable to

[17] Powell had merely lost interest; a rumor implied his father had died and left him with the responsibility of supporting the family (Kenaston).

attend the organizing meeting, but he joined the group shortly thereafter.

Volunteer curators, serving without remuneration, made collections in whatever branches of natural history were most interesting to them. The results of these labors were accumulated into systematic collections and housed in the Illinois State Normal University at Normal. The society planned to prepare small representative collections and distribute them through the public school system to awaken an interest in natural history among younger people. To encourage the survey, cooperation of railroad and steamship companies had been obtained, and passes for free transportation had been issued to each curator. Wes was elected to the curatorship in conchology, and later to the secretaryship.[18]

For a number of years Powell had followed his bent for natural history with persistence. He had gathered an herbarium of almost six thousand plants and a large collection of land and river mollusks. The shells were kept in wooden boxes which he had made himself. In addition to botanical specimens and shells, Wes had creditable collections of snakes, fossils, and minerals.

Conchology, the study of shells, was not an unusual avocation at this time but was in fact a popular diversion of many college students and amateurs. College courses in conchology were offered to young ladies as a fitting leisure activity. But Powell's interest was scientific, not dilettante. He made his collections in river drainage systems, and had much less interest in gathering rarities than acquiring representative local collections.

Every farmer knew the resident birds and the more conspicuous migrating species, and was more or less familiar with the common animals, but there were few accomplished naturalists in the prairie. The seemingly endless variety of living things was well appreciated and a person versed in the habits of plants and animals was respected. Local legends endowed Powell with phenomenal knowledge and fantastic skills as a naturalist.

One warm day in early May he passed through the square in Wheaton with a basket containing a half-dozen large fruit jars. Inquisitive neighbors joshed him, saying that the cherries were not yet ripe. With mock seriousness he replied that he was going to the woods to find a rattlesnake. It happened that he did find a rattlesnake, and returning through

---

[18] For a history of the Illinois State Natural History Society, see Ill. State Agric. Soc., *Trans.*, Vol. 4, 1859–1860.

the town chanced to meet three of the fellows who had stopped him earlier in the day. They crowded around to see the live reptile in the jar—nine rattles and a button!

"How did you catch him?" one asked.

"I just picked him up," was the reply.

This incident gave rise to an exaggerated yarn, that made the rounds of county newspapers, to the effect that Powell was acquainted with the homes and habits of all of the animals of the state and, being thoroughly familiar with their haunts, he could find any animal any time he desired. "When last repeated he learned for the first time that he had appropriated the upper story of his father's house for a museum and had it full of all sorts of reptiles. . . ." Although he did have a large collection, the story was much larger than the collection.[19]

Gradually his main interest shifted from plants to reptiles to mollusks. He had collected abundant materials in the Great Lakes and in the smaller lakes of Wisconsin. Now he made a specialty of river shells from the Mississippi and most of the streams of Illinois, Iowa, Missouri, and Indiana. His greatest difficulty was in obtaining books with which he could identify his finds; actually, there were no comprehensive books covering this region in which he had been the first to make large systematic collections. Consequently it is no wonder that Powell had been unable to identify properly many of his specimens. When a search through the available books failed to give a clue, he bestowed locality names to the specimens in addition to descriptive names of his own invention.

He had collected some fossils too, both of plants and animals, and had gathered a considerable collection of minerals. He built up a far larger museum than Mr. Crookham had and investigated his collections scientifically. These collections were the reward of diligent field work. Wes had made excursions every summer in search of interesting specimens in 1855 up the Mississippi River to St. Paul and then overland across Wisconsin; in 1856 down the Mississippi to the mouth of the great river below New Orleans—not to mention the many short trips to nearby streams.

The river trips afforded a means of collecting mollusks, but in a larger sense they were sightseeing journeys. The wanderlust of Joseph Powell flowed in the blood of his son.

Every winter John Wesley Powell taught school to earn money to

[19] This anecdote is related by Mrs. M. D. Lincoln, *Open Court,* Dec. 1902, pp. 713–14.

attend a university, but with each reawakening of spring, with bursting buds, singing birds, and crawling insects, he had been seduced from the classroom into the limitless fields of nature.

In 1857, in late spring, Powell went by train to the industrious city of Pittsburgh and made preparations for a trip down the Ohio River. From the station he crossed the Monongahela River and climbed the road to the top of Mount Washington to look out upon the green landscape with two great rivers, the Allegheny and the Monongahela, joining to form the Ohio. The Allegheny was blue and slow, the Monongahela yellow and swift. Below, along all of the shores near the point, the bustle of river traffic—ornately decorated steamers, flatboats, barges, smaller craft of every description—fascinated his imagination.

He rented a room on the hill and sat on the porch at night to watch the busy river. As scores, then hundreds of small lights dotted the valleys, he marveled at this metropolis. Never before had he been able to look down upon such a landscape as that below.[20]

In the fall of the same year, Wes went to the Iron Mountain region of Missouri south of St. Louis to collect minerals. He found the country so full of new and interesting things that he remained there until his money was nearly gone. When at last he had just enough to return to St. Louis and pay for a few meals or a night's lodging, he left Ironton for the city. He had assumed that it would be possible to find work in St. Louis and earn enough to pay expenses home. He searched for a day, then, with less than a half-dollar left, and failing to find employment, pawned his gold watch and returned to Decatur.

In January of 1858 Powell, now twenty-four, became the newest teacher in the town of Hennepin, Illinois, at a salary of one hundred dollars a month. Slender, handsome—except for a prominent roundish nose—this young man with auburn hair brushed flat, to add to his dignity grew a stylish beard which covered most of his face.[21]

When Wes Powell came to Hennepin, he found a small agricultural community of some seven hundred people situated on bluffs overlooking the Illinois River. The town had a considerable business drawn from all of Putnam County, the smallest one with respect to population in the state. There were seven groceries, five dry goods stores, three drugstores, two hotels, a flour mill, one distillery in operation, and

[20] J. W. Powell, letter to Mary Dean Powell, May 14 [1857].

[21] Mrs. W. A. Boyle, a daughter of Lyle Durley, has searched court records and local newspapers for Powell's activities in Hennepin. The description of Powell is based upon a tintype made by William O. Bowman in Hennepin in 1859.

another under construction. There were two public schools with a few more than a hundred pupils, and it was Powell's job to teach the higher classes.

The Illinois River, a placid stream during most of the year, extended along the borders of the township for about twelve miles. To the east the fertile rolling prairie was intensively cultivated in corn as the major crop, and with wheat, barley, and oats, as secondary crops. To the south the hilly land was cut by ravines and heavily wooded with oak, hickory, and maple. On some of the hills, cleared years before, fine apple orchards had been developed. The apple, providing cider, cider vinegar, applejack, apple butter, and dried snitz, as well as fresh eating, had been introduced early into the region. The Pennsylvania Germans, who came to Hennepin in the 1840's, had brought with them their traditional apple recipes as well as their favorite varieties.

The country about offered many features interesting to a naturalist. Powell continued to collect mollusks and plants, but his curiosity was stimulated by the geology of the region. Rocks of Carboniferous age outcropped to the surface not far from town. Several shafts had been sunk to mine a good seam of coal, and Powell walked over the gob piles in search of fossils. He was intrigued also by the glacial drift, evidenced by sands and gravel, which covered all of the region. Powell made a careful study of this drift over an extensive area, and although he had seen similar deposits on his earlier travels, he could not untangle its complex history. No longer were his excursions primarily to gather specimens; he was observing and investigating larger problems.

When spring came the fragrance enveloped him and swept him into the outdoors again. As soon as classes were over for the season, he purchased a good skiff and a few supplies. Starting from Ottawa, he rowed to the mouth of the Illinois River, and from there ascended the Des Moines River in Iowa to the mouth of Raccoon Creek. Observing how soils and natural vegetation follow the drift and the rock formations, he was impressed by the importance of applying this kind of knowledge to agriculture.

In the fall Powell returned to his teaching in Hennepin and began a barnstorming tour to urge the inclusion of science in the common school studies. This work took him over most of the counties in Illinois and brought him into contact with many politicians and educators.

At the eighth annual fair of the Illinois State Agricultural Society held in September 1860 at Jacksonville, Powell's collection of mollusks won a premium of twenty-five dollars as the "Best collection illustrating the zoology of Illinois." [22] With the money Wes made a trip to Detroit to visit Emma Dean. He had corresponded regularly and had gone to Detroit several times before to see her. The Deans and the Powells were anxious lest Wes and Emma, first cousins, would want to marry. Parental objections were undisguised.

There was very little of the dreamy suitor in Wes. He was serious and scholarly and had shown little interest in the young ladies. Emma, for her part, excluded other men from her thoughts. When they were together Wes recounted stories of his experiences, while she listened approvingly and wished that she might join in his adventures. Wes Powell was in no financial situation to woo a lady, not even one who understood him. He had a respectable teaching position, but wanderlust kept him penniless.

In the spring of 1860 Powell had engaged in a lecturing tour on a backwoods lyceum circuit through Tennessee, Kentucky, and Mississippi, speaking on geography and geology. He observed the sentiment of the natives toward slavery and studied the position of the slave in the southern agricultural system. Returning to Hennepin, he wrote a letter to his father expressing the opinion that only war could settle the slavery problem.[23] It would be impossible to disentangle the uneducated and unskilled slave from the economy and relative protection of the plantations. Yet the moral issue was tantamount.

That summer Powell was made principal of the public schools at Hennepin. He set at once upon reorganizing and grading the classes, selecting modern textbooks, and preparing himself for teaching science and mathematics to the upper grades.

On March 4, 1861, the members of the State Natural History Society, chartered by act of the state assembly only two weeks before, met in the society's rooms at Normal to elect officers and organize a technical staff. J. B. Turner was unanimously elected president and C. D. Wilbur replaced J. W. Powell as secretary. Ira Moore became the librarian and George Vasey was elected as a member of the executive council. Eleven commissioners, each assigned to a different department, were appointed, including Vasey in botany, Powell in conchology, Wilbur

[22] Ill. State Agric. Soc., *Trans.*, Vol. 4, 1859–1860. Powell gave his legal residence as Wheaton, not Hennepin. This is borne out by the 1860 U.S. Census, in which Powell is listed as a "naturalist" in Wheaton.

[23] The lecture tour was arranged by the Janesville (Wisconsin) Lyceum Bureau. Aside from the fact that the engagement took Powell to Tennessee, Kentucky, and Mississippi, I have no other information. The letter from Powell to his father is mentioned by Mrs. Lincoln. I have been unable to trace the original.

in geology and mineralogy, A. H. Worthen in paleontology, and Joseph Sewall in entomology. The officers were installed and the president and his advisers canvassed the scientific needs of Illinois. On that same day a thousand miles away, another president, Abraham Lincoln of Springfield, well known in Normal, Bloomington, and Decatur, also took office and weighed his responsibilities.

Wes Powell was convinced that war was inevitable. To utilize his knowledge of topography and mapping, he began to study military tactics and engineering, especially bridge building. He knew how to travel on rivers; now he wanted to learn how to cross over them. He felt sure that the North would take the offensive and wage war in the South. He would be ready.

On Sunday, April 14, 1861, the citizens of Hennepin were stunned by the news that at Fort Sumter the American flag had been fired upon by other Americans. Wes wrote to Bram to hurry to Hennepin at once. The next day President Lincoln's call for troops was proclaimed to the people and the courthouse opened for enlistments.

4

1861-1865 · An Arm for Union

THE citizens of Hennepin followed the news of threatening hostilities anxiously. President Lincoln had called for the enlistment of troops for three months' service as home guards, and there were many who believed that a mere show of determination would be sufficient to prevent actual warfare between the North and the South. But as the days passed and preparations in the South became even more vigorous, a struggle seemed assured.

On May 3, 1861, President Lincoln issued a call for 42,000 volunteers for three years' service, and authorized the raising of ten new regiments in the regular army. By now Bram had arrived from Decatur and had been hired to succeed Wes as superintendent of schools. Walter had already joined the home guard in Decatur.

Answering the call for troops, Wes Powell and a small party of other young men assembled at the courthouse and filed down to the station. It was the eighth of May. The newspapers had announced the departure of a local company, and a goodly crowd of friends and neighbors came in farm wagons and on foot to see them off. The men from Hennepin enlisted in the Granville company and left on the same day for Joliet, where the Twentieth Illinois Volunteer Infantry was being organized under the ten-regiment bill.[1]

John Wesley Powell was sworn in and listed as private, Company H. He passed the casual medical examination, and the orderly entered into the record book, "Age 27, height 5' 6-1/2" tall, light complected, gray eyes, auburn hair, occupation—teacher."[2] Slim but wiry and strong, Powell weighed scarcely 120 pounds. Wes Powell held the rank of private for only a few days. His comrades elected him sergeant

[1] U.S. War Dept., *Records*, 1861–1865. The files on Powell in the War Department archives are considerable. I shall indicate only the most important; company muster rolls, "Service Record," and "Claim and Affidavits for Invalid Pension."

[2] U.S. War Dept., *Records*, 1861–1865, "Company Descriptive Book, Company H, 20th Reg't. Illinois Volunteer Infantry."

major in recognition of his superior education. A month later, on June 13th, he was promoted to the rank of second lieutenant to fill a vacancy caused by the resignation of the company commander. The same day the "Twentieth" was mustered into the United States service and ordered to Alton, Illinois.

While still stationed at Joliet Powell had requested permission to visit Chicago, sixty miles to the north, to obtain an officer's uniform and to purchase a few books on military science. Col. C. Carroll Marsh granted him three days' leave for the trip. While in Chicago Wes located handbooks by Dennis Hart Mahan and Sebastien Vauban on military engineering, a subject which he had been studying for nearly a year. He was fitted for a uniform and spent the remaining few hours of his furlough with Emma in Detroit.

There was wild excitement on July 6th when the men were assembled and were told to prepare for active service and to be ready to move to the front on one hour's notice. In the early forenoon, the troops were lined up and marched to the landing, embarked on small steamers, and taken down the Mississippi.

The regiment had been ordered to St. Louis, the gathering point for a great army which, it was hoped, would break the South in two. The men were billeted in tents on the outskirts of the city, and a few uneventful days passed before any new orders were issued. On July 10th three brigades, including the Twentieth Illinois Infantry, were assembled, lined up, marched to the river landing, boarded on boats, and moved a few miles farther downstream to Cape Girardeau.

The town of Cape Girardeau was a pretty little community of somewhat less than two thousand inhabitants. It had a considerable river commerce and served as a port for a number of inland villages. The streets were laid out on the bluffs about 150 feet above the river. In ordinary times life must have moved leisurely and comfortably. The contingent of three hundred soldiers to which Powell's company had been assigned were marched to the public square and ordered to pitch camp. Within a few hours rows of Sibley tents were erected and the men assigned to messes of four each. So this was war!

Because of its prominence overlooking the Mississippi River, Cape Girardeau appeared to be a likely objective of roving Confederate forces, and the citizens were badly frightened. Most of the natives were loyal to the northern cause, although throughout Missouri and the border states there were many southern sympathizers. No enemy troops were to be found close to the town, and there being little to do,

Powell took short trips on foot or on horseback in each direction from camp, exploring the country and trying to apply principles of defensive tactics against an imaginary enemy. On some of these walks he was accompanied by Lt. Col. William Erwin, who discussed with him problems of fortifications, entrenchments, and bridges.

Although no action occurred during the first few weeks at Cape Girardeau, an attack seemed imminent. Lieutenant Powell was detached from his regiment in order to plan a more elaborate camp site and to construct works to fortify the city.[3] He had already estimated altitudes and paced distances for practice, so now he prepared a map indicating vulnerable approaches and proposed defense works. When this preliminary work was completed, because there had been no further indication of an attack, the commanding officers lost interest in fortification and would not even authorize execution of the project. This was a disappointment to Powell, but then, the work had engaged his interest during what would otherwise have been very dull moments.

Early in August Gen. John C. Frémont, with his dazzling coterie of foreign officers, arrived at Cape Girardeau for a tour of inspection. Finding the town unfortified, Frémont ordered that immediate steps be taken to throw up defensive works. Colonel Marsh informed the General that a junior officer had already been assigned to that task and sent for Powell. The plans were examined, found to be satisfactory, and orders issued that they be carried out without further delay. For the remaining part of the summer and fall Wes was largely occupied with this task. At first a few hundred men were employed to construct earthworks, but as the summer drew to a close several thousands of soldiers and civilians were engaged in the digging. Powell's plan called for the construction of four triangular forts, each with six heavy guns guarding the four corners of the town—Fort "A" on the north corner overlooking the Mississippi River, Fort "B" on the knolls to the northwest of the town, "C" to the southwest, and "D" to the southeast on the highest prominence overlooking the river.[4] Two of the forts guarded land approaches, the other two, river approaches. They were connected by earthworks and parapets sufficient to withstand any reasonable musket or light artillery fire.

For a short time General Frémont had dispatched an aged Prussian

[3] U.S. War Dept., *Records*, 1861–1865, "Company H Muster Rolls." They record Powell's detachment on fortification duties, and his early promotions.

[4] A map of Fort "D" was published in the Cape Girardeau *Community*, August 27, 1936.

officer who spoke almost no English to oversee the construction, but the old fellow contented himself with the building of a small fort while Powell, unhindered, proceeded with his plan to enclose the entire town. Soon after, the Prussian was recalled and Capt. Henry Flad, who had supervised the construction of the fortifications at St. Louis, came down to assume charge of the partially constructed works at Girardeau. Powell found his new superior officer a genial and instructive friend.

The garrison at Cape Girardeau engaged in several minor operations in southeastern Missouri. Although Lieutenant Powell was still detached from his company, he was ordered to participate in the expedition to Price's Landing and Hamburg early in August. At the siege of Lexington, Missouri, a section of the regiment was dispatched to relieve Mulligan's brigade, but from a distance they watched the Confederates successfully storm the town and capture the Union positions. Powell and his boys had been under fire in some of these skirmishes, and almost without realization they were slowly becoming seasoned soldiers.

On August 28th Brig. Gen. Ulysses S. Grant was placed in command of the troops in southeastern Missouri, and the men heard that their new commander was on his way to establish headquarters at Cape Girardeau. Grant remained there for only a few days because he had already decided to move his headquarters closer to Confederate concentrations. When General Grant took command of the department, he planned early offensive operations in place of the watching and waiting which had characterized Frémont's actions. Some work on the fortifications was continued, but the grand plan of enclosing the whole town was abandoned.

Finding his services as an engineer more or less unnecessary, Powell expressed a desire to return to his regiment. The request was summarily refused. A week later he tried again, with no better luck. Then a third appeal, but it too was refused. Without further authority, he began to instruct a group of Missouri home guards in engineering and artillery practice, and interested them in the formation of an embryonic light battery. On October 8, 1861, John Wesley Powell became acting captain of artillery—captain of an unofficial battery without field pieces.

General Grant ordered this little company of men on September 17th to take charge of Fort "B," which mounted six twenty-four-pounders. There were by now forty men in the company, but it had no official standing whatsoever. Guard duty offered little excitement, but it did provide some break in the monotony which was their lot. New recruits signed up and the roll grew quickly. The men assigned to the several forts soon devised competitive games of skill. Next in popularity to cards was bowling with twenty-four-pounder cannon balls. Alleys of heavy planking were laid down the narrow aisles of the forts, and pins eighteen inches tall and three inches in diameter were carved of hardwood. Fort "B" became proficient with thirty-two-pounders, though they were second-best with lighter balls.[5]

As more miserable weather came upon them in November some of the men dug small caves in the terraces above the river, but most of the soldiers were unable to abandon their chilly tents. The weeks and months of inactivity and the impression that the war was moving away from them increased the boredom and grumbling. In mid-November General Grant came again from Cairo to inspect the camp, and Lieutenant Powell was assigned to accompany him around the fortifications. They rode together for three hours, and after the inspection trip Grant invited Powell to come on board his boat and have supper. Afterward, while they were smoking cigars, Powell asked a personal favor. He wished leave of absence for one week. He had been engaged for a long time to a young lady in Detroit and wished to get married. Demurring but a moment, the General granted him leave to go.

Wes dispatched a letter to Emma telling her to make all of the arrangements by the time he would arrive in Detroit, on November 28th. Wes arrived in the late afternoon of the 28th, hurried over to Emma's home, had a hasty supper in the kitchen, and talked with Cousin Charlie while the womenfolk rushed the final preparations.

Rev. John H. Griffiths, pastor of the First Baptist Church, arrived at 7:30, shook the bridegroom's hand, and chatted about army life. The Dean family, Mrs. Griffiths, and George and Annie Willson gathered for the simple marriage ceremony.[6] Vows were exchanged, and with happy greetings and tearful partings the bride and her soldier-husband, accompanied by the wedding party as far as the station, boarded the train for Chicago. The next day they went to Wheaton for a brief visit with Father and Mother Powell, then returned to Chicago and retraced the miles to camp. Emma now had her wish—to join Wes on his adventures—a wish she had nurtured for almost five years. He had promised her that she could join him in these travels and studies, al-

[5] Related by Mrs. M. D. Lincoln.
[6] The correct wedding date is November 28, 1861. The marriage certificate is preserved with Powell's pension claims. A manuscript list of marriages performed by Rev. John H. Griffiths is in the New Eng. Hist. and Gen. Soc. Lib. See also Detroit *Free Press*, Dec. 1, 1861.

though the possibility that they would share their first years in the army had not entered their thoughts.

General Grant arrived at Cape Girardeau again on the last day of November before Powell and his wife returned to the post. Powell appealed to be reassigned to the Twentieth, which had left the day before for Bird's Point, but General Grant would not consent. Instead, Grant handed him a commission as captain of artillery. The General had already written to Gov. Richard Yates of Illinois informing him that, since his state was actively organizing batteries of artillery, Lieutenant Powell could make up a battery of Missouri soldiers who had been enlisted by Frémont without authority. The Governor was informed that Powell had been drilling these men for months and that, if a few more men from Illinois could be enlisted, the battery would be organized at once. Meanwhile, Grant submitted the following statement on December 2nd to the Secretary of War:

> There seems to have been no provision made in the acts of Congress organizing our soldier system for manning our siege batteries other than to take companies authorized as light artillery companies. All these manifest a great desire to get their batteries and do not like to remain in fortifications. In view of these facts I authorized Lt. Powell, as acting engineer on the works at Cape Girardeau, to raise a siege company out of the Missouri Home Guards that were on duty there.[7]

On December 11, 1861, Battery "F," Second Illinois Light Artillery, was mustered in at maximum strength. There were 132 men on its roll. With the recruits from Illinois came ten six-pounders with complete equipage. The men admired the pieces, thrilled at the sight of their finish, their perfection. The cannon were unloaded from the boat and wheeled onshore. Unfortunately, no mention of the assignment of the cannon was made, and to their disappointment the cannon were placed in storage and the battery remained in Fort "B" with the fixed guns. The boys grumbled a little, especially when, on New Year's Day, Captain Powell read an order that a detail of fifty-four men would stand guard and command the four twenty-four-pound siege guns at Fort "A." Assurances by Col. Leonard F. Ross, commander of the Seventeenth Infantry, that this was purely a temporary assignment did not count for much.

Nevertheless, little by little, tension was mounting. Horses, cannon, caissons, and provisions were being piled up and military traffic on the river increased with each succeeding day. Now that armament was

---

[7] U. S. Grant, letter dated Cairo, Illinois, Dec. 2, 1861.

on hand and transportation was provided, it would not be long, they hoped, before something would happen. The war was nearly a year spent, and nothing of consequence had happened in the Mississippi Valley.

Suddenly, on February 6th, the news that Fort Henry had surrendered to the Union Army was telegraphed to the world; the troops, long in garrison, were beside themselves with nervous excitement.

On February 9, 1862, by order of General Grant, six six-pounders were transferred to Battery "F" as equipment for the field battery. Finally—action! The men were elated. Intensive drill, consuming half the day, was begun at once.

Three days later the encampment was thrilled by the report that an assault on Fort Donelson had begun, and after anxious days the glorious tidings of victory, and of fifteen thousand prisoners taken, cheered them to eager impatience.

The days wore on; forces were gathering; more supplies were piling up. Powell, a disciplinarian, drilled his battery with monotonous regularity. There were as yet no orders to move, but they were not long in coming.

On March 11th Battery "F," in full battle regalia, marched to Bird's Point where they boarded a transport which took them up the river. Savannah, Tennessee, it was whispered, was their destination.

Battery "F" arrived on March 14th at Pittsburg Landing, Tennessee, on the westerly bank of the Tennessee River with 156 men, their six six-pounders, and a complement of fine horses. The battery, organized only three months before, was well drilled, disciplined, and resourceful. Walter Powell had reenlisted and joined the battery as a second lieutenant just in time to make the trip from Bird's Point.

Captain Powell ordered his men into park on the bluffs above the Landing. He rode with his brother to the high ground, selected the camp site personally, and eyed the countryside carefully.

It was rolling tableland, for miles around covered with dense forest. In some places it was open red-oak forest, in other places mixed hardwoods with extremely heavy underbrush. The tableland was traversed by many moderate ridges cloven by a series of steep densely wooded ravines. The main road to Corinth followed through one of these ravines. A few cleared fields broke the continuity of the forest. Most of the clearings were near the river—the farther inland, the rougher the country. Most of the fields were about eighty acres in extent and cultivated in cotton, but some were in oats and indigo. There were also frequent small peach and apple orchards neatly rowed. The fields were bordered with sassafras and blackberry.

To an officer like Powell, well-disciplined and already tried under fire, though inexperienced in heavy combat, the indifference of brigade commanders and their men to mortal peril was appalling. At Cape Girardeau Frémont had ordered strong and adequate fortifications against a distant enemy. True, they had been discontinued, but only after the danger of assault had dissipated. Here at Pittsburg Landing no earthworks were thrown up, hardly a tree was felled for defense, and not a single brigade had built an abatis to guard its approaches. Yet, day by day new rumors of Confederate pickets observed close to the Union camps made the rounds of the campfires.

Meanwhile, Grant had established headquarters at Savannah, a small town with barely two hundred inhabitants. His headquarters were to be transferred to the Landing. As yet he had not moved his office, although almost daily he made a trip there. Emma was staying at Savannah, and as it was only eight miles down the river, Wes could arrange to visit her nearly every day, usually by hopping a ride on the *Tigress,* Grant's boat, or on one of the innumerable boats plying traffic between Savannah and the Landing.

By the first of April the impression was pretty general that a great battle was imminent. Apprehension pervaded some of the outermost camps, and a crude defensive field organization was set up. In case of a rebel attack, Brig. Gen. William T. Sherman's division was considered an outlying picket, while the divisions of Maj. Gen. John A. McClernand and Maj. Gen. B. M. Prentiss would form a first line of battle. Maj. Gen. W. H. L. Wallace's division would support the right wing and Brig. Gen. Stephen A. Hurlbut's, the left wing.

The reserve artillery, parked above the Landing, was assigned but the orders were changed and countermanded the same day. Within one day Battery "F" had been assigned successively to Wallace, Hurlbut, and Sherman, and then returned to "unassigned." It was discouraging. Something was stirring, but the men did not know what.

On Saturday afternoon, April 5th, General Prentiss held the first dress review of his division. After the review a guard reported that he had seen about a dozen "butternuts" watching the parade through the underbrush. About 8:30 p.m. it was reported from the outposts that guards had seen long lines of distant campfires, and faint bugle calls and drums had been heard. Both of these occurrences were reported to Prentiss, who promptly sent out additional pickets.

That night, as on every Saturday night, there was frivolity and revelry around the campfires. For almost three weeks the Union troops had occupied this rolling tableland, now with some 34,000 men.

There was no warning that not mere raiding parties and pickets, but 40,000 Confederate soldiers, had been drawing nearer for two days and had approached to within one mile of the outermost federal posts. During the night the deployment around the sleeping Union camps was completed, and the attacking army halted for a brief rest before giving battle.

Sunday dawned with a blue and warm cloudless sky. Some of the men of Battery "F" were waiting for the early risers to finish cooking breakfast when, scarcely audible, a long roll ruffled the morning calm. Again! The distant roll of drums mingled with the discharge of muskets and faint bugle calls. But other regiments, closer, had taken up the alarm. Every drummer in turn beat out the call. Officers shouted to their men. Almost at once the roar of artillery dispelled all doubt—the deadly cannonading meant that heavy fighting, not a skirmish, was in progress. Closer and closer the sound of artillery fire, and more and more the rattle of small arms, came toward the Landing. The rebels had attacked.[8]

The greatest commotion was near the center held by Prentiss. Breakfast was finished, the fires stamped out, and the men alerted for orders. The horses were harnessed and the guns limbered. A fire was built for the forge. Battery "F" was ready to engage the enemy but—no orders! In front of headquarters on the bluff general agitation made clear the fact that the troops of Wallace and Hurlbut were preparing to move out to the battle line. Seven-thirty o'clock—eight o'clock—eight-thirty— still no orders. With angry impatience Captain Powell listened to the sounds of battle and, not receiving instructions, rode about looking for someone in authority who could assign him.

Finally, on his own, he decided to take his battery to McClernand's front. He knew every yard of the road well beyond Shiloh meetinghouse. The battery had been in readiness for nearly two hours and the men were cursing at the delay. It was self-evident that the rebels were getting the better of the fighting.

[8] Two brief published notes give the bare facts of the action of Battery "F" in the battle of Shiloh on April 6, 1862: D. W. Reed, *Battle of Shiloh*, p. 61; and George Mason, *Illinois at Shiloh*, p. 161. Three markers on the battlefield indicate the positions of the battery on April 6th and the location of the camp. General Prentiss, owing to his capture, did not submit a report to the War Department until nearly a year later. Gen. W. H. L. Wallace was mortally wounded. These two circumstances have shrouded the events in the "Hornet's Nest."

Powell could wait no longer. With his right hand held high he signaled his battery to mount and then to advance, shouting at the same time, "Forward, boys." Out past Gen. T. W. Sweeney's regiments they galloped at full speed and, as they dashed through, the men scrambled to the sides of the road, cheering the artillery. They too were headed for the front. By now the din was intense and it appeared that there was fighting near Duncan's field. Powell rode in haste until he could see the skirmish line, long bayonets glistening in the morning sun. He hurried back and rejoined the battery, encouraging them to hurry and take position to the north of Duncan's field. The open field would give them a wide sweep against the enemy. Battery "F" arrived at the spot only to find that the Union line had fallen back to the south edge of the field, the men retreating into the woods. The Confederates were hotly pursuing in force. This was no place to make a stand, and the Powell battery wheeled and retired, upsetting and abandoning one gun at the pivot. The straps of the harness were cut just in time to save the horses. The battery was now incomplete.

Without delay the battery headed for the lines of Generals Wallace and Prentiss and reported for duty. They had come the half mile with full equipment over rough roads in less than six minutes. Powell, at Sherman's left, took position on an open hillock in front of three tall hickory trees. He looked at his watch; it was twelve minutes past nine.

Prentiss had posted his battery, Capt. Andrew Hickenlooper's Fifth Ohio, to the right of Corinth road, but after a short gallant struggle, his lines buckled and gave way, the men retreating through their camp site, leaving behind two of the guns, of which all the horses had been killed. Prentiss, in person, put the remainder of the battery in position immediately to the right of Corinth road intersection, while the infantrymen used the sunken roadcut as a defense. General Grant, making a quick survey of the field, passed a compliment to Powell and ordered Prentiss to hold this new position at all costs. At ten o'clock the line was assailed by a yelling determined foe.

Prentiss appealed for help. His command was badly shaken and seriously reduced both by casualties and the defection of many men who were facing fire for the first time. In reply Col. J. G. Geddes arrived with the Eighth Iowa and took the ground on the extreme right. About one p.m. the Powell battery was placed immediately in front of the regiment with instructions to hold the position to the last.

The precision of its fire wreaked havoc in the advancing Confederate columns, first at six hundred yards, then five hundred yards, finally concentrated in a three hundred-yard arc. Battery "F" and its protecting infantry became a target of strategic importance. Meanwhile, ghastly casualties were being inflicted on the Eighth Iowa, more from enemy shellfire than the hail of minie-balls that stripped the branches from the treetops.

A runner reported to Prentiss that all direct communications with the rear had been severed, but that small units might still filter through and reach the Landing safely.

The sounds of battle were diminishing. There could be but one meaning—the division was being surrounded. The Confederates were massing artillery to bombard the "Hornet's Nest," as they had named the peach orchard near the sunken road.

Shortly after four o'clock Captain Powell raised his right arm to signal "Fire." As the hand went up, a half-spent minie-ball struck the wrist, glanced toward the elbow, and buried itself in the flesh. Stunned, he sat down. He grasped the fingers of the injured arm. Walter hurried over to see what had happened. It was a bad wound. Blood spurted from the gash and the region of the wound was bruised. Throbbing pain, experienced for a few minutes, gave way to awful numbness.

"A couple of bones are smashed," Wes told the men who had gathered around him. "Man the guns." Walter tied on a tourniquet, helped his brother to a large tree, and sat him down.

General Wallace, who had been nearby, rode over and spoke to Walter. Then, turning to Captain Powell, said, "We are almost surrounded and I shall be captured with my men. You may have time to escape. Take my horse and ride to the Landing. Hospital boats are there, and you will be cared for." [9]

The General dismounted, lifted Powell, and placed him on his fine horse. Wes was sick at heart, fearful that the day was lost. He said farewell to the men, thanked Wallace, and rode off. He raced as fast as he could, checking the speed only when his arm ached beyond endurance. There were many wounded on the way back, some walking, some being carried on litters, others just sitting and waiting, and there were many dead.

At the Landing the scene was grotesque. Thousands of beaten frightened men cowered along the river. Many of them were muttering and weeping about disaster. Powell vaguely remembered being taken from the horse and helped up a gangplank onto an Illinois boat.

[9] Marcus Baker, *Open Court*, Vol. 17, p. 348. Powell described this incident to many persons.

Dr. William H. Medcalfe,[10] who had been ordered to Savannah to aid in caring for the casualties, came by, loosened the bandage, and called for a wound dresser. An orderly brought hot water and clean cotton cloth, and tenderly bathed the arm. At the bruised and swollen wrist a little blood oozed out, but further up the arm the furrow cut by the ball bled freely again. A little disinfectant was placed on the rags and the wound bound again.

A red spring sun was setting when the boat tied up at the town landing of Savannah. Wes heard the deck hands about as they threw a line to shore. It was only a short run to Savannah—how many times he had made it in the past weeks!—but this time it seemed a thousand miles from the battlefront. Two soldiers came in, placed him on a litter, and carried him to shore. Emma was on the landing—waiting. Her eyes were misted. Wes studied her face as best he could. "Now, now," he assured, "everything is going to be all right." [11] It was only a short distance to the general hospital. Emma hurried along by his side, carrying his hat. In the town hall, commandeered as a hospital, his case was registered and he was assigned to a bed on the second floor.

Five empty cots were placed in a small room which must have served as an office. Before long the other four beds were occupied by men who like himself had extremities struck by canister or minie-balls. "They're classifying us into varieties," he joked to Emma.

An attendant came in and gave a dose of laudanum to each of the patients, and Emma remained by her husband's side until she had satisfied herself by his heavy breathing that he was asleep.

Monday was a day of anxiety. Throbbing pain was incessant. As yet there was little pus, but by afternoon it was evident that the wound would never heal. The bruise had clotted and swelled. Dr. Medcalfe came several times to examine the arm and finally decided that he could not remove the ball.

Fretful, half-awake, feverish, weak from loss of blood, Powell remembered little and cared less. He took nothing but strong tea all day. There was much to do and Emma, serving as a nurse, came frequently and stayed for a few moments.

---

[10] William H. Medcalfe, Surgeon of the 49th Ill. Vol. Inf. In civilian life he was a druggist, which explains, at least in part, why the surgery on Powell's arm was poorly done.

[11] Emma Powell related to her friends a fair number of personal experiences during the Civil War years. Most of these are known to me on hearsay, although vivid recollections of those used in this chapter have been communicated by Mrs. Klotho McGee Lattin, Mr. Eric Parson, and Miss Margaret Whittemore. Mrs. M. D. Lincoln, G. K. Gilbert, and C. D. Walcott have published other details.

On April 8th, Tuesday, Dr. Medcalfe returned again, and after an examination of the wound decided to amputate.[12] Wes was conscious and a little chloroform was administered. The surgery was quickly done. Early in the evening Wes recognized his wife, and then fell off into troubled stupor. She remained by his side all night.

Joseph Mitchell, the second lieutenant of Battery "F," came to the hospital on Wednesday morning to see his captain. Powell's boys had been worried too, but now they would be reassured. His fever was not dangerous.

Powell asked many questions about the battle. General Wallace had been mortally wounded and left on the field, though next morning had been brought in still living. Prentiss had been captured with two thousand men, but when the enemy concentration of fire beat upon them, he had ordered the batteries back to their original camp to protect the Landing. Battery "F" had slipped through about five o'clock. The carnage had been awful. Powell inquired about casualties in the battery, but Mitchell avoided a definite reply, admitting only that they were light. They had lost one killed, three missing—later known to have been killed—and six wounded, but they had lost a score of horses.

Wes's fever continued, his body wasted, but ultimate recovery was assured. The days that followed were bitter days. Wes stared at the bandaged stump and imagined he felt a hand that wasn't there. Emma patiently nursed him back to health, assured him that he would rejoin his battery—but to herself prayed that he would resign—declared her devotion, and talked of old times.

Captain Powell determined to remain in active service on one condition, that Emma, his bride of six months, could accompany him wherever he went. He addressed a simple personal request to General Grant. In a few days the General replied by enclosing a "perpetual pass" which permitted Mrs. Emma Dean Powell to enter and leave all military lines without further authority.

On June 30th Wes and Emma went to Corinth to rejoin Battery "F." A few of the men had been able to visit their captain during his convalescence, but for most of them his return was a signal for celebration. A round of three cheers brought tears to his eyes. One by

[12] Powell's arm was not shot off as is commonly stated. Another misstatement is Emma's presence on the battlefield. Powell, wounded, "was brought on the Hospital Boat in my charge at Pittsburg Landing . . . with his right forearm badly shattered . . . and conveyed to Savannah, Tenn., and placed in General Hospital." (Affidavit, Wm. H. Medcalfe, Jan. 3, 1865.) Emma was staying in Savannah, although she was a frequent visitor to the battery camp above Pittsburg Landing.

one the boys shook his left hand and wished him well. Despite the long rest, fever had taken its toll. Thin even in good health, their captain was now lean indeed.

Captain Powell received orders to leave his outfit to go to Chicago, Springfield, and Bloomington on recruiting duty for six months. Emma was happy, but her husband was restless for activity. The recruiting assignment covered the long period from August 31, 1862, to February 28, 1863, even though travel proved to be almost unbearable. The stump of the arm pained him continuously. He tried to convince himself either that he would get used to it, or that the wound would gradually heal.

During the fall and early winter of 1862 nothing of importance happened in the Corinth area. In November a section of the battery under the command of Lieutenant Mitchell was detached to take part in the northern Mississippi campaign in Grant's first attempt to capture Vicksburg, advancing as far as the Yocona River. After the fall of Holly Springs they proceeded to Memphis. The rest of the battery remained in camp until early February when Powell received orders to proceed to Lake Providence, Louisiana, situated on the west bank of the Mississippi River about 120 miles by water above Vicksburg.

Ever since early February 1863 the contingents assigned to the Seventeenth Army Corps were assembling at Lake Providence in preparation for the campaign against Vicksburg. Powell arrived with his battery and his wife on Saint Valentine's Day and found his headquarters in a handsome mansion which had been vacated a year before. Battery "F" had been at the lake for nearly a month drilling daily, defiling the lawns of the manor. They were now equipped with twelve-pounders and had a complement of new horses to replace those that had been lost at Shiloh.

In April General Grant began to move his forces. The Second Brigade of the Seventeenth Corps received its marching orders on April 19th. By boat they were taken to Milliken's Bend and then, since the roads on the Louisiana side were considered to be sufficiently dried out despite a long period of inundation, began travel by land.

On April 26th the march was begun, without tents, without blankets, without baggage of any kind. The road to Richmond was tolerable, but the mud, furrowed by a million footprints and the wheels of caissons, slowed progress to an evil degree. To Perkins Landing the roads, which were poor in the best of weather, were miserable, at times nothing more than quagmires. Every rod of advance of the caissons and the wagons required backbreaking work through deep mud and stinking muck. The artillery batteries had to construct mile upon mile of corduroy road not only to move their cannon, but to make way for the supply trains which followed behind. The country was alive with unexpected enemies. Myriads of gnats swarmed through the swamps, flew into eyes, crawled into ears. Mosquitoes tormented every hour of the day and night. Crawling snakes and croaking frogs made restful sleep without protection impossible. Day after day the army pushed and dragged itself southward. Fever and dysentery added to the misery. After six weeks of forced marches the brigade reached Grand Gulf. From that point they were ferried across the river, a few hundred at a time.

The Confederates, from their positions on high ground, were able to watch the entire movement of the Union army and to have complete information of the proceedings. The movement could not be concealed; indeed, its very magnitude had been calculated to frighten the enemy. The advance troops skirmished with a rebel guard at Bruinsburg and after a short stand the Confederates retreated with the Federals pursuing close on their heels. At every naturally protected location the Confederates would halt, throw up hasty defenses, and stand for combat to delay the advance of the Union forces.

General Grant now ordered an audacious pursuit. All personal belongings were discarded and each man was allowed one spare shirt in which he was permitted to roll one pair of trousers. The commissary issued five days' rations. More than twenty thousand men had gathered at Grand Gulf, and the Confederate forces redoubled their efforts to retreat. The Union brigades and batteries passed through Rocky Springs, Utica, and Raymond. Two miles from Raymond they had a lively brush with the rebels, who had to leave nearly two hundred wounded on the field. Jackson had already fallen, and although the Second Brigade had hastened toward the sounds of cannonading and musketry, arrived too late to participate in the battle of Champion's Hill.[13]

At two o'clock in the afternoon of May 17th the brigade reached the Big Black River, just north of the railroad bridge and three miles above McClernand's corps. The enemy had set the bridge afire a few minutes before and the trestle was burning fiercely. On the opposite shore the Confederates had thrown up earthworks, apparently intending to defend the bridgehead. However, after a brief engagement, they retired, abandoning virtually all of their artillery. Fording the river

[13] There is an amusing experience of Powell's in the battle of Champion's Hill which he related to Mrs. M. D. Lincoln. See *Open Court,* Vol. 17, p. 20.

was impossible. Two volunteers attempting to walk across were trapped in the soft bottom and drowned. Gen. James B. MacPherson sent for Powell, who was the ranking engineer present, and ordered him to construct two bridges across the stream. The regular pioneer corpsmen were with McClernand; no time could be lost. During the remainder of the day and far into the night, by the light of great bonfires, two bridges were constructed. One solid bridge was built of heavy timber obtained by dismantling a nearby cotton gin, while the other was a pontoon affair of timber cribs filled with cotton bales. The flooring was obtained by tearing down a small shed several hundred yards from the shore. By dawn two full divisions and four batteries had crossed the river over these improvised structures.

Powell, who had gone without sleep, was eating a breakfast of beans, bacon, and coffee when orders to move stirred the tired line to action. For eighteen days Powell and his men, indeed the whole army in this gathering force, had lived on five days' rations. They had marched more than three hundred miles without a change of clothing and without shelter. Most of them had taken part in six battles, four of them in six days, had inflicted five thousand casualties on the enemy and so hurried them that they had left behind eighty-eight pieces of artillery. It had been Port Gibson May 1st, Grand Gulf May 3rd, Raymond May 12th, Jackson May 14th, Champion's Hill May 16th, and the Big Black River May 17th. The artillery had comparatively little to do in the fighting, but in the unspectacular engineering it had done heroic work.

Battery "F" arrived, nearly exhausted, behind Vicksburg on the evening of May 18th. They halted temporarily in a cotton field waiting for assignment to a camp site. An assault for the following morning had been ordered. Already the Union forces had almost completely invested Vicksburg by land. Powell wrote to Emma suggesting that she come to Vicksburg as soon as possible because they would likely remain at this place for several months.

On Tuesday, May 19th, the real battle for Vicksburg began.[14] Throughout the morning the artillery bombarded the rebel forces

[14] Ransom's brigade on the first of May was "one of the strongest and best in the whole army being composed of the 11th, 72nd, and 95th Illinois, and the 14th and 17th Wisconsin and Major Powell's Battery F, 2nd Ill. Artillery." (*Hist. of the 95th Ill. Vol. Inf. Reg.*) I have transcripts of two unpublished reports of the First Minnesota Battery (Lt. Henry Hurter to Adj. Gen. Minn., June 4th, and Capt. Wm. Z. Clayton to Adj. Gen. Minn., July 16th), which was also under Powell's command. Powell was a captain, not major, at this time. The regimental history, being written after the war, uses the higher rank.

mercilessly and drove them into the fortifications. Battery "F" stood in reserve but did not take part in this action, being too far from the point of concentration to be effective. At two o'clock in the afternoon General Grant ordered a charge in order to seize more favorable positions for his advance troops. It was a murderous onslaught with far heavier casualties in the ranks of the Union troops than of the Confederate. Although some of the companies managed to gain advantageous locations and forward placements, they found themselves isolated from support, and at nightfall nearly all of them retreated. Little was gained in the attempt. There had been insufficient time for the Union troops to fill in their ranks, consolidate positions, and completely invest the city. After two days of intense activity Grant was ready to order another assault. On the night of May 21st Powell inspected the works which had sheltered Gen. John C. Pemberton's defenders of the city. About daylight he returned from his assignment. The Illinois troops in the Seventeenth Army were on the far side of a steep ravine. It would be necessary for the infantry to lunge down the slope, cross a small stream, and then attempt to climb the opposite bank of the ravine. It was an impossible task. Only at a few points, where roads entered the city of Vicksburg, was there any likelihood of substantial success. Throughout the night Powell directed the digging of earthworks to cover his batteries. All of the commanders had received orders that an assault would begin at daybreak.

The action of May 22nd began with a simultaneous charge by the three corps at ten o'clock. For four hours the men had stood in readiness, impatient for the command to go forward. Gen. Thomas S. G. Ransom's brigade was placed in the ravine south of the Graveyard Road and Glass Bayou, while the cannon of Battery "F" supported them, firing round after round of canister over their heads until the blue uniforms of the Union troops neared the rebel parapets. Dense white clouds of sulphurous smoke filled the hollow, and as the smoke cleared and the cannonading was temporarily halted, the Union men fell back from the crests of the Confederate works and sought refuge in protected crannies. The batteries reopened fire with shrapnel to prevent a countercharge and to give their comrades a better chance to retreat. The assault of May 22nd was no more successful than the first one. Ransom's brigade suffered catastrophic losses—484 killed and missing.

It was evident now that the Confederate defenders of Vicksburg would have to be starved out. Grant faced an enemy of 60,000 troops with only 43,000, and some of these had not arrived in time to take part in either the actions of May 19th or 22nd. With this disparity in numbers, he ordered a halt to await the arrival of reinforcements. The only course left was to lay siege, and now was to begin, in Powell's words, "the forty hardest days of my life."

The immediate objective was to worm forward under cover of darkness and move the cannon close enough to the parapets of the rebels to do effective damage. Each night a plan of work was mapped out for the succeeding night. Furiously, using shovels, tin cups, and even bare hands, the troops dug open runways through which they would later be able to drag the cannon. They gathered twigs, cotton, cane, and burlap, and any other material which might be used, to build defensive structures. Dense jungles of cane grew everywhere in the ravines. The stems were cut and tied into fascines.

Someone suggested that telegraph wire would make a good binder, and three hundred men volunteered to cut down all of the telegraph lines strung eastward toward Jackson. The detail was a lark, a welcome diversion in the monotony of siege. Miles of wire were brought in. Each morning the digging would be discontinued because of the effectiveness of Confederate sharpshooters and pickets. Powell would turn in for a few hours' sleep. His wounded arm bothered him continuously. Emma pleaded with him to resign after the close of this campaign, but he would not give in. Instead he argued that the surgery had been poorly done and that a second operation would alleviate all his sufferings. Thereupon Emma cheerfully did her best to make him comfortable, sharing privations and months of weary waiting with unselfish devotion.

During lulls in the fighting—and there were long periods of inactivity—Powell studied the hills in the Vicksburg neighborhood. The terrain, which nature had made so formidable against violent assault by man, could little withstand the more gentle assaults of wind and rain. The country about had, in ages past, been a plateau of soft rock, but time had incised it with deep ravines and valleys, leaving behind steep hills. The Confederates had cut down the trees in front of their works so that they would have a clear view of attacking forces. The cannonading had stripped the foliage for miles around. The hot dry summer air had desiccated the ground and powdered the light soil. Choking dust set in motion by the infernal turmoil sifted into every fold and crevice. Powell observed this man-made desert over which they were fighting, studied the economy of water and the profound influence of water at work. In a little pocket notebook he jotted down some of his observations and sketched a profile of the river at Vicksburg.[15] Day by day the artillery batteries were enlarged and moved into more advantageous positions. The embrasures of batteries close to the Confederate line were protected against rifle balls by planks, shutters, and burlap bags filled with cotton.

The slow progress of digging gave Powell ample opportunity to examine the rocks of the area, especially because fossil seashells were uncovered in the trenches. During periods of inactivity Wes and Emma collected specimens of these fossil mollusks, discarding inferior examples as better ones came to light. He treasured this little collection and, before the final assault, carefully wrapped each piece in cotton scraps and sent them by post to Wheaton for safekeeping.

By the middle of June 1863 the troops had extended earthworks across the stream. Now, digging an ascent on the Confederate side had to be undertaken. The Powell sap was but one segment of a system. The project was started by opening a parallel or trench to the besieged line. Three of these parallels were developed simultaneously. Connecting these parallels were many zig-zag approaches or saps. Sixteen principal saps were begun, eleven of which were continued and carried close to the Confederate line. On June 19th three of the saps were closer than one hundred yards to the Confederate parapets. Powell's "graveyard sap" was within seventy yards, and the Jackson Road and Baldwin's Road saps were nearly as close.[16]

At sundown on June 20th Powell called his men together and asked for volunteers to drag the guns 140 yards up the slope through the sap. Two heavy twenty-four-pounders would have to be dismounted from their carriages and moved the distance with darkness the only protection. Rebels could be counted on to resist their advance with grenades and shellfire. He need not have asked for volunteers; his own men and a score of others from Ransom's brigade lent willing hands. At ten o'clock that night the men took their positions wherever there was

[15] A few of Powell's geological notes have survived. The catalogues of the Illinois State Normal University Museum record specimens of fossils from Vicksburg and Nashville, but the specimens themselves have been separated from their original labels. The profile sketch of the river at Vicksburg was used by Powell in some of his later geological publications.

[16] The progress of work is indicated by Chief Engineer Andrew Hickenlooper's official return filed October 23, 1863 (*War Rebellion Records,* ser. 1, Vol. 24, part 2, pp. 197–203). A monument on the battlefield marks the most advanced position of the approach. Battery "F" faced the Thirty-seventh and Thirty-eighth Mississippi Infantry Volunteers. Numerous references to this portion of the field, from the Confederate viewpoint, may be found in Miss. Hist. Soc., *Publ.,* Vols. iii–x,

space enough on the wheel or barrel for a hold. Ropes were fastened to the cannon to give more power. Thus, by hand these two guns were dragged and placed in position, seventy yards from the enemy's works. With pick and shovel, with brawn and courage, they had moled their way to the head of the sap. Except for occasional pot shots from the rebels, their ascent had not been interrupted. Now that the head of Powell's sap was armed, it was widened to permit four men to stand abreast.

Meanwhile rumors were passed about the troops that orders would be issued for a grand attack on either July 5th or 6th. It was known that the defenders of the city and the civilians trapped with them were near starvation. Capitulation would soon come even if an assault were delayed. Grant was convinced, however, that he could hasten a decision by striking at an early date. During the forenoon of July 3rd General MacPherson and General Ransom called on Captain Powell.[17] They inquired if, in his opinion, the enemy redoubts could be stormed successfully in front of his sap. Powell replied that he was confident it could be accomplished. In a few minutes MacPherson came back to Powell's headquarters and requested pen and ink from an orderly. He then wrote out an order that Powell's batteries should "Open fire on the enemy lines with a national salute at daybreak on the Fourth."

There was no assault. At daybreak a hundred white flags of surrender fluttered from the enemy's ramparts. A cheer went up, then wild hurrahs rent the morning calm. At three o'clock the day before General Pemberton had met with General Grant and arranged terms of surrender. It was a sad day for the Confederacy. At that very hour, a thousand miles away at Gettysburg, another southern army met disaster.

Logan's division with Ransom's brigade, which had approached nearest to the enemy's works, were selected as the first to march into the city. The artillery remained at their emplacements until July 7th when they went into park in the town. Meanwhile the scattered rebel forces to the south were trying to retrieve what supplies they could and concentrate for a stand somewhere to the east. A few days after the battle General MacPherson was informed by his intelligence that the rebels were trying to transfer a large body of Texan cattle and horses over the Mississippi. Ransom was ordered to take three boats, descend the river with utmost speed and, if possible, capture the cattle. Battery "F" was one of the three detached for this assignment.

---

[17] This account was related to Mrs. Lincoln by Powell himself. There is no other confirmation.

When the expedition reached Natchez the division was landed and hurriedly deployed so as to encircle the city and a considerable adjacent area. The snare was drawn tighter and closer until five thousand head of cattle were trapped in the northwest corner of the town. A goodly number of the animals were sent back to augment the slim food supply at Vicksburg while the remainder was transported to New Orleans to provision Union troops garrisoned there.[18] Powell went down to New Orleans with the troops and cattle and returned after a week to Natchez.[19]

During the siege of Vicksburg, with the excessive physical work and, at times, inadequate food supply, he had lost a great deal of weight. He guessed he was down to 110 pounds, perhaps less. The wounded arm caused him severe pain and the surgeons in the base hospital recommended a resection of the stump. The trouble was caused by the regeneration of nerves which had increased the sensitivity of the arm to the slightest touch or irritation. Powell requested sick leave for two months so that he might undergo a second operation on the stump of his arm. Few preparations were necessary. Personal belongings were placed in storage, and Wes and Emma were given passage on a transport going north to Cairo. After a few days' visit with his parents in Wheaton Wes went to Emma's home in Detroit.

The second operation was performed on his arm. A little more flesh was removed so that the stump could heal without the annoying complications which had developed after the original amputation.[20] While convalescing in Detroit he received notice of his promotion to chief of artillery with the rank of major in the Seventeenth Army Corps with orders to report to headquarters at Natchez on September 1st.[21] Emma insisted that she return with him to his command.

Shortly after Major Powell's return to active duty he was sent to the village of Hebron, where winter quarters were established. There would be no activity for some months, the Confederates being too dispersed to launch any serious counterassault. The batteries were parked

[18] The extent to which citizens of the North responded to appeals to augment the inadequate food supply is seldom realized. Martha Powell Davis was active in the Long Creek Methodist Church's effort to send preserved fruit, sauerkraut, dried apples, etc.

[19] The official reports of the Natchez expedition are very scanty. It was, of course, a minor assignment. See *War Rebellion Records,* Vol. 24.

[20] Powell was on sick leave (Special order 157, Hqrs. 17th Army Corps) during July and August. I have not been able to determine who performed the resection of his stump arm.

[21] Powell was officially promoted to major and "Inspector of Artillery for the Department, and Army of the Tennessee" on September 18, 1864, but recognized by the military service as a major from May 29, 1864.

on the beautiful grass-covered lawns of the estates, and the sod was soon marred by the drilling and routine camp work. The weeks that followed were spent in recruiting replacements and scouring the countryside for horses and mules.

The easygoing camp life was interrupted by orders to accompany General Sherman on a raid of destruction. This was to be a fast and wily expedition to attack savagely a small body of Confederate troops that had occupied the country to the east not far from Jackson, drive them back into Georgia, and, most important of all, to destroy all railroad communications with Vicksburg. Once this objective was accomplished a very small garrison stationed in the city could hold it even though the main body of troops was withdrawn and shifted for operations elsewhere. Major Powell was ordered to accompany his batteries, so Emma remained at Hebron until his return. On November 13th the raid was set in motion. On the way to Meridian the expedition encountered virtually no opposition. Some skirmishing with trifling losses took place nearly every day, but there were no important engagements. With boisterous glee the troops tore up the railroads, whole sections being lifted up with crowbars and pitched over. The ties were piled and burned; the rails were heated white hot and wrapped around nearby trees in "Jeff Davis neckties." Everything that the enemy might use in support of troops was callously destroyed. The invading Union army ravaged the countryside like a plague of locusts.

Gen. Marcellus M. Crocker's division went into winter camp at Hebron and Powell was reunited with his wife. Major Powell was detached from his command to organize and train a regiment of Negro troops at Vicksburg, partly to make use of the able-bodied Negroes who were scattered in the vicinity, and partly to obtain guards for positions far behind battle lines.[22] He surmised quite correctly that these troops would be kept behind for garrison duty, and that should he remain with them, he would see no more front-line service. His restless nature would hardly tolerate that kind of confinement. The organizational work of the Negro regiment consumed most of the spring and summer of 1864. Major Powell had undertaken the assignment only because of the personal request of Gen. G. H. Thomas, but he declined the rank of lieutenant colonel despite the fact that the commission had already been given him by General Grant. As soon as the regiment reached

[22] For this duty Powell was detached from his battery from early April to September 18, 1864. Mrs. Lincoln says that Powell was promoted to the rank of colonel upon completion of the organization of the regiment, but that he refused the commission. Although this is highly probable, I have found no evidence to substantiate the promotion.

full strength and had been adequately equipped and broken in, Powell obtained permission to return to the Fourth Division.

Meanwhile, at Atlanta, a section of Battery "F" under the command of Lt. Walter Powell fought and suffered heavy losses in that bloody campaign. On July 22nd part of the battery was captured and with it, Walter. When the field returns came in he was listed as "missing in action." For two months there was no definite word of his whereabouts or safety. Finally information came through official channels that he was convalescing from fever at Camp Sorghum, South Carolina, where he had been imprisoned. Emma wrote to her father in Detroit, and Joseph Dean sent five pounds sterling through the War Department to buy his nephew needed food. Packages failed to reach prisoners of war housed in the worst of the Confederate prisons. During Walter Powell's confinement he escaped from the hospital, stark mad, and after wandering two days in a no man's land met some of his comrades, fellow prisoners, and was returned to the hospital.

On September 18th Major Powell received his appointment as chief of artillery of the Seventeenth Army Corps.[23] Perhaps now, at long last, he would have an opportunity to witness an entire battle, not merely some restricted action on the field. He might plan strategy and deploy forces. This was the kind of military science he had studied.

The first field assignment in his new office was far less exciting than he had counted on. There was plenty of action, but he saw none of it. When the Confederates under Lt. Gen. John B. Hood turned back toward Nashville, Powell was out with Sherman's pursuing army looking after supplies and equipment. In rapid sequence there had been engagements at Alatoona, Kenesaw Mountain, and a drive toward Rome, but Powell reached each battlefield a day after the fighting. During this difficult campaign the artillery lost most of its best horses, and many others had to be destroyed because of broken bones or severe wounds. Their places had to be filled by sorry specimens of nags and broken-down mules.

A few days before the railroad connection with Nashville was severed, General Sherman ordered Powell to move his sixteen batteries, without animals, by railroad to Nashville and ship them around to Savannah. Sherman needed the animals, miserable beasts though many of them were, for the quartermaster's train, because nothing this side of hell was going to stop him in pursuit of the rebels to the sea. More guns he

[23] Major General O. O. Howard designated Powell his chief of artillery (Dallas, Georgia, Nov. 3, 1864). "You will find him a straightforward and attentive officer."

could do without; horses he could not. Powell reached Nashville with the guns while preparations were being made for the battle of Franklin. There he received instructions to report to Maj. George H. Thomas.[24] Thus, by coincidence, he participated in the battle of Nashville and realized one of his consuming desires—to observe the progress of an entire battle. For some days Powell was assigned to superintend the construction of defenses, the throwing up of earthworks, and making of gabions.

On the morning of the battle, under General Thomas's instructions, Powell arranged the sixteen batteries into four equal divisions placed in four sections to the rear of the army. As the opposing forces were engaged the batteries galloped at full speed to the front of the fighting, took on the enemy at murderously close range, and then darted to another position on the field before the Confederate batteries could mass their guns and counter at close range. From the new position, the Union batteries would fire another round of canister, then take still another position on the field. Powell rode from battery to battery, periodically reporting to Thomas for instructions and orders. This was the kind of line fighting he had hoped for, and during the first two days of battle Powell witnessed all of the important engagements.

Brig. Gen. Edward Hatch's mounted artillery attacked the rebels on the extreme right with two batteries. Early in the morning mists Powell, standing by the side of Thomas, watched this isolated conflict through field glasses. The Union infantry behind the batteries charged to the top of the hill and to the enemies' works. As they reached the parapets, a thin cloud of mist obscured the view. Suddenly a gentle northwest wind pushed the clouds away, and they saw the Union standards mounted over the Confederate forts two miles distant. General Thomas was now satisfied and said that they need have no further fear of the outcome. After the destruction of General Hood's forces Major Powell remained in Nashville until the batteries under his command were again equipped with horses, munitions, and tools. He saw to it that his men were well rested and restored to health.

On December 28th Major Powell received instructions to proceed to Springfield to attend the reenlistment and reorganization of his regiment, which had served its full three years. Despite the second operation on his arm, he had not been free from frequent and intense pain.

---

[24] On October 31st Powell received orders to move his command and report to General Thomas at Nashville. I rely upon Powell's own recollection of the battle of Nashville. See *Open Court*, Vol. 17, pp. 24–25.

He had endured it stoically, knowing that nothing could hasten healing. The war was fast drawing to a close. The progressive collapse of Confederate resistance in the west, though slow, had been disastrous. He had been a participant in the extension of federal control to the Deep South and far to the southeast, and had left Sherman when he started his "march to the sea," patterned on a grand scale after the Meridian raid. Far into the night Wes and Emma discussed their plans. Finally he decided to resign from the army for reasons of ill health and disability.

The regiment arrived in Springfield on January 2, 1865, and the following day, Major Powell went to the general headquarters of the adjutant general, State of Illinois, to obtain certification of his injury at the battle of Shiloh. Dr. Medcalfe, the surgeon who had performed the original amputation, was there waiting the reorganization of his own regiment, and he wrote a brief statement concerning the wound and surgical operation.[25] On January 4th Powell submitted a letter requesting discharge as of that date.[26] The request was granted and he was mustered out immediately, receiving payment of accrued sums amounting to $228.00. The summer before, he had deposited a modest sum in a bank in Detroit and, although a part of his savings had been used to pay for his operation and subsequent medical care, he had adequate means to take his time before seeking civilian employment.

On the last day of February, in company with his father-in-law, Joseph Dean, and Joseph Sparks, a fellow worker with Mr. Dean, Powell went to the office of the pension agency in Detroit and filed a declaration of "total and permanent disability." He acknowledged Alexander G. Noyes as his authorized agent. Powell signed his name in great letters with his left hand. During the past three years he had written as little as necessary. Although it was a legible hand, he would have to do some practicing.

The following week Wes and Emma were off to Wheaton to visit his parents. They spent hours of affectionate reminiscing of Oberlin,

[25] Medcalfe had experienced unwarranted disgrace following the battle of Shiloh. He had been ordered from the field on April 6th to duty on a hospital boat, sent to Savannah and placed in charge of Hospital No. 3. Meanwhile his commanding officer, Col. William R. Morrison, reported that he "without orders, in great haste . . . betook himself (if not to flight) to the river; and thence, whether with or without orders I am not advised, to Savannah. . . ." Medcalfe was accordingly mustered out dishonorably, but subsequently reinstated. This incident suggests the disorganized state of affairs prevailing on the first day of the battle.

[26] Powell was honorably discharged (S.O. 22, War Dept. Adj. Gen. Office, Jan. 14, 1865). Actual discharge was on Jan. 4, 1865, at Springfield "by reason of expired time."

Hennepin, and of his sisters and their families. The conversation finally drifted to Wes's plans for the future. He had none—that is, he had many. Reverend Powell insisted, "Wes, you are a maimed man. Settle down at teaching. It is a noble profession. Get this nonsense of science and adventure out of your mind." [27] Wes listened. It sounded like old times.

On March 1st Walter Powell was exchanged as a prisoner of war and moved by train to Wheaton.[28] He was a sorry sight. He was still emaciated from his long illness and, though overjoyed at his freedom and safety with his family, was moody and at times disagreeable. Five feet ten inches tall, and never very heavy, he was now skin and bones. Walter had begun teaching school when he was sixteen and had spent his winters in various public schools in central Illinois. In his present condition he was unfit for any work requiring patience.

While at Wheaton, Powell received a letter notifying him that his claim for disability pension had been denied, that he had been absent from duty without leave on the day of the battle of Shiloh and for six weeks thereafter! Investigation of regimental records had shown that John Wesley Powell had deserted, "Away without leave," from April 6th to August 6, 1862. To be classed as a deserter with those hundreds of cowards who huddled together at Pittsburg Landing and stole away to safety at home! The thought rankled him for days. Fortunately, the statement of Dr. Medcalfe, which had been written at the time of Powell's mustering out, ultimately was accepted as evidence in substantiation of the disability claim, and a few months later, on May 22, 1865, the pension was granted, and payments were made retroactive to January 4, 1865.

Powell's career as a soldier was over. He had loved the discipline of the army, the red trappings of the artillery, and the title of a volunteer officer.

[27] J. W. Powell to Mrs. M. D. Lincoln.
[28] Walter H. Powell was delivered as a "paroled prisoner" on March 1, 1865, at Wilmington, N.C. He was mustered out at Camp Chase, Ohio, April 30, 1865. However, by S.O. 35AGO Feb. 11, 1889, his service record was amended to read, "captain," instead of first lieutenant, "from May 29, 1864 to honorable discharge on May 15, 1865."

5

1865-1867 · Up Pike's Peak

AT WHEATON, Powell picked up the loose threads of his scientific work, not an easy task after a lapse of four years. He rummaged through his collections in the attic of his parents' house and discovered that the beetles had gotten the best of the dried plants and the insects. At least the minerals, the fossils, and the mollusks were undamaged. He spent hours thumbing through old companions among his books, gritty with prairie dust.

The collections sent home during the war were unpacked and sorted. At leisure he identified the mollusks gathered at Lake Providence and other localities in Louisiana and selected the best specimens for his private collection. The fossils from Nashville and Vicksburg were cleaned and sorted, but they were too unfamiliar to identify. Science, geology especially, still held his interest.

Major Powell visited frequently at the college, which was now called "Wheaton." Illinois Institute had suffered lean years and had been reorganized under the auspices of the Congregational Church with the cooperation of Wesleyan friends. Powell offered to arrange a collection of rocks, minerals, and fossils, "illustrating the geology of the west," and went about selecting and exchanging specimens to make an attractive cabinet for the scientific department of the college.[1]

On April 14, 1865, after most of the Wheaton townspeople had retired for the night, excited criers hurried up and down the streets shouting the news that President Lincoln had been shot. Almost before they could realize what had happened, word of Lincoln's death stunned and overpowered them with grief.

Abraham Lincoln had abolished slavery and preserved the Union, causes to which the Powells gave their unstinted support. Not once

[1] "Major J. W. Powell, prompted by his love of Science, and friendship for the Institution where he received part of his education, proposes to put up, during the summer a cabinet illustrating the geology of the west. . . ." Wheaton College, *Cat.*, 1865. The catalogue for 1866 announced completion of the exhibit.

had Reverend Powell raised his voice in criticism of the President, even when countless others, honest citizens, shouted disapproval of Lincoln's rash and unrestrained use of the unlimited executive war powers. Now Lincoln was gone. "His work was finished," Reverend Powell said.[2]

In the early hours of May 1st the whole family went to Chicago to await the arrival of the funeral train bearing Lincoln's body on its journey to Springfield for burial. They stood for hours at the station until a volley from a battery of minute guns in the yard burst the silence. A mournful cadence boomed over the hushed multitude while the black-draped train drew slowly into the station. For twenty-four hours thousands, Major Powell and Mrs. Powell among them, passed by the bier to pay their last respects to the great Lincoln, lying in state.

A few weeks passed and with them, it seemed, an age. Out of the deluge of war, peace—a vindictive peace—returned. Times were uncertain. Wes Powell had to resume civilian life; indeed, Emma had been a little impatient with her husband, for he had not yet made up his mind about the future. His ambition was hazy, although his confidence was as sure as ever.

Powell had several opportunities for employment, two of which were interesting. He had been offered the nomination for the clerkship of DuPage County on the Republican ticket. Nomination was assurance of election. The position, though carrying a modest salary, would with fees give him an income of several thousand dollars.[3] In addition to this very tempting offer he had been invited by Dr. O. S. Munsell, president of Illinois Wesleyan University, to a professorship in geology at an annual salary of one thousand dollars.

Illinois Wesleyan University,[4] established in 1850, was a struggling Methodist college at Bloomington. Owing to financial difficulties, the college had suspended operations during 1855 and 1857. Reorganization and a drive for funds put the university on a fairly sound foundation. Dr. Munsell held out the possibility that a supplementary sum would be added to the salary if conditions allowed. There were other considerations. Illinois State Normal University was located nearby at

[2] Quoted by Mrs. F. D. Whittemore.

[3] Powell says he was "offered" the nomination, which implies he was approached by the Republican county organization. The presumed income, at first glance, appears to be exaggerated, but this figure during the postwar period of land speculation and development is within reason.

[4] Dr. Elmo Scott Watson has provided extensive information about Illinois Wesleyan University. See *Historical Sketch and Alumni Record 1853–1895* and faculty minutes for 1865–1868.

Normal, a town adjacent to Bloomington. The collections of the Illinois State Natural History Society were housed in the Normal University building. Many of Powell's own collections had been presented to the society and as curator of conchology he had certain responsibilities to identify and classify specimens which were submitted for examination.

During the war Powell had met many of the men in the "Normal Regiment," the Thirty-third Illinois, an outfit largely recruited from the students and faculty of Illinois State Normal University. Maj. Gen. Charles E. Hovey and Col. Ira Moore had been principal and assistant of Illinois Normal in its early days when classes were held in Bloomington. They were fellow members of the Natural History Society, too. Powell already had friends there, and he knew the towns from previous visits. The communities of Bloomington and Normal were neighborly and prosperous towns, surprisingly self-contained, and offered a delightful environment for the complacent securities of college teaching. The Normal University had been awarded to Bloomington in 1857, and the section known as North Bloomington, where the university was located, promptly changed its name to "Normal." [5] In view of all of these factors, a decision was not very difficult. The county clerkship would be too confining and would, undoubtedly, interfere with his scientific interests. So, without misgivings, Powell declined the political office and accepted the professorship at Wesleyan. Personal remuneration was never a primary consideration in Powell's decisions.

Powell, during his first term at Wesleyan as professor of geology, had a limited number of students drawn mostly from the senior class, but his enthusiasm and his personality soon attracted many others to his lectures. Called upon frequently to address various civic organizations, Professor Powell rapidly gained popularity and publicity.[6] Illinois Wesleyan had been prosperous beyond anticipation, and at the close of the first term of the school year the trustees, recognizing Professor Powell's talents, voted to him an increase in salary of five hundred dollars.

Instruction in the natural sciences when Powell began college teach-

[5] A reminiscent account of the town life of Normal is given by H. F. Richardson in *Quaker Pioneers*. Normal and Bloomington are described fully in E. Duis, *Good Old Times in McLean County*.

[6] The files of the *Daily Pantagraph* from November 1865 to January 1873 contain many references to Major Powell, not only about his activities at the colleges, his explorations, and lectures, but also about his more personal affairs.

ing was generally uninspired and insipid, depending upon the traditional textbook and recitation method. Louis Agassiz was instigating a one-man revolution in the teaching of zoology at Harvard; independent of his efforts, it fell to Wes Powell to do the same for geology.

Within a year Powell became professor of natural science and, according to Wesleyan's catalogue for 1866, the college offered special facilities for the "practical study of natural science, extensive and thorough." Professor Powell carried a Herculean load: "Botany, Lectures of Cellular Histology, Comparative Anatomy and Physiology, Lectures on the Vertebrate Skeleton, Systematic Zoology, Lectures on Insects Injurious to Vegetation, Natural Philosophy, the Logic of Natural Science, Geology, and Mineralogy."

Who contrived this professorial man's eye view of the world and all that therein dwells? None other than Professor Powell himself. All his life Rev. Joseph Powell had preached and lived the ideal, "the world is my parish." To his scientist son, the world was his parish.

Now Wes Powell had the opportunity to introduce the kind of instruction he wanted—to have the student learn about his environment at firsthand. In the laboratory classes the students studied minerals with the blowpipe and a block of charcoal, thus performing chemical experiments to augment their observations on visual properties of the specimens. They reduced galena on the charcoal, extracted a little pellet of lead, beat the metal with a hammer, and played with it. Ores of iron, copper, and zinc, were studied in the same manner. In botany Powell took his students over the flowering prairie and along the streams bordered with woods to examine plants and to collect specimens. The classes gathered a representative herbarium. They dried and mounted plants; they planted seeds and watched their germination; they dissected fruits; with their professor's personal microscope, they examined the minute structure of plants and animals. In zoology the students searched for animals in nearby streams, in rotting wood, even in manure piles. Powell moved among his pupils while they examined the stomach contents of the crow, the brown owl, and the blacksnake, encouraging the squeamish or fastidious ones to mess things up a bit.

Professor Powell believed that the prevailing college curriculum could be liberalized a great deal by the introduction of more of the natural sciences. Enthusiastically he explained his pet projects to fellow instructors. Before long Powell found himself speaking to larger audiences, chiefly professional organizations, trying to create sentiment in support of this project. Natural science, in Powell's view, should not be limited to classified knowledge; equally important is the practical use of that knowledge.

Almost as soon as the prairies had been transformed into the granary of the nation, farmers found themselves victims of the wheat rust and other disastrous plant diseases, hordes of cinch bugs, corn borers, and similar pests—many of these presenting new problems which eastern and Old World farmers had not faced. To find means to control or eradicate such diseases and pests was an earnest hope. The homesteaders, who made sacrifices to build academies and colleges as soon as they established communities and churches, did so not only to educate their children in the Christian tradition and to become familiar with the knowledge of the past, but also to prepare them for the very difficult problems of the times. What good was education if it did not lighten the toil and burdens of the people?

They were friendly audiences, then, when Professor Powell barnstormed the state to gain sentiment in favor of more practical science in the college curriculum. On this issue, prejudices within the colleges were far more difficult to overcome than those outside the cloistered halls. Powell, for his part, thoroughly enjoyed giving these lectures. Nearing thirty-two, he had lost his youthful figure but not his enthusiasm. When he strode upon the platform, his large head with its thick crop of reddish hair brushed back carelessly obscured his short stature. Powell's beard was trimmed to sideburns; he wore no mustache. His clothes were of good quality and in good taste, but otherwise he paid little attention to them—an indifference from which Emma could never move him. His voice was not strong. To compensate, Powell pronounced his words slowly and deliberately. Never did he read a prepared speech though he would read resolutions and quotations for accuracy and emphasis. Gifted with an uncommon memory, he could dazzle most audiences with a fund of detail.

Powell was always master of the situation. His manner was one of unmistakable self-assurance. This versatility was readily recognized by the college administration. When it was necessary to seek support, especially in a financial way, he was called upon to do his share.

Shortly after Powell came to Wesleyan he set out to form a local chapter of the State Natural History Society in Bloomington. Within two months after assuming his professorship, with the willing help of R. Holder and Dr. C. R. Parke, Powell organized a Bloomington branch chapter. The collections of the society housed at Normal were in such a haphazard condition as to be both an embarrassment and a problem. When the society had been chartered by the legislature no provisions for the care of the collections had been made. All work was voluntary, depending upon the cooperation of the members, not upon any state aid. Prof. C. D. Wilber had been the unofficial curator, devoting as much time as he could to the task.

When the state society held its annual meeting in Bloomington on July 30, 1866, Powell moved that a committee be appointed to confer with the state board of education concerning the possibility of securing an appropriation for the museum. Wes Powell was promptly appointed chairman of the committee.

Meanwhile the Professor had been pursuing his classroom work energetically. He was in the field every holiday increasing the collections used in his laboratories. The old wanderlust was unsatiated. From reading, conversations with Frémont, and correspondence with fellow scientists about the vast western territories and their unexplored mountain ranges, his imagination was stirred. He had never studied deserts or mountains. The classes were pleasant, the students appreciative, but the academic atmosphere was much too quiet, too restrained. He craved action.

At home he talked to Emma about an exploring trip to the Rocky Mountains. She was willing. The expedition would be costly, beyond their limited means, but perhaps in a year or so they could raise funds to augment whatever savings could be spared while reducing the mortgage on their home in Normal. Meanwhile they would learn all they could about the country.

Little by little these dreams took substance and Powell baited his maneuvers with a bit of promotion. His plan was to gain a measure of independence, yet remain affixed to the colleges. Normal University, as a state institution, would better serve his interests than Wesleyan, a denominational college with the usual financial anxieties and with a more rigid interpretation of the duties and obligations of its faculty.

The first move was simple. He would suggest that he give a course of lectures in geology at Normal. The next step was to encourage the establishment of a paid curatorship of the Illinois Natural History Society collections and then obtain that position himself. Indeed, it never occurred to Powell that anyone else would be a competitor for the job. Joseph A. Sewall, who was professor of natural science at Normal, was acting curator of the museum, but he was a quiet scholar who was not of a disposition to promote the museum. Moreover, he hoped to be relieved of the burden.

Powell's name first appeared in Normal's register in 1866.[7] During his first year 206 ladies and 121 men were in his department; of these, only seven young ladies and six men were seniors. This gave Powell an even greater opportunity to experiment with his methods of instruction.

The faculty of Normal was a New England stronghold: Professor Sewall, a native of Maine, was graduated from Harvard in 1852 and completed his medical degree there in 1860; Thomas Metcalf, professor of mathematics, was graduated from Bridgewater Teachers College in Massachusetts and came to Normal after several years of teaching in public schools; Edwin Hewett, professor of geography and history, was another alumnus of Bridgewater; Albert Stetson, professor of languages, had attended both Bridgewater and Harvard, graduating from the latter in 1861 (Stetson achieved recognition as the editor of the *Illinois Schoolmaster*); Dr. Richard Edwards, president of the college and professor of mental science, had studied at Harvard but was graduated from Bridgewater. Powell was cast from a different mold and, though recognizing the scholarly bearing of his colleagues, took satisfaction in his own achievements.

During this period Powell was secretary of the Illinois Natural History Society. The collections of the society were displayed in many instructive exhibits in the museum rooms on the top floor of the college building, but adequate funds for maintaining them were not available.

Powell went to work, persuading the faculty members to recognize the value of the collections and convincing the administration of the prestige and public recognition which would accrue from such a museum. Not once did he hint that he wanted the curatorship, giving praise at all times to Sewall and to his predecessor, Dr. Wilber. In November 1866 the officers of all three institutions—the Natural History Society, Normal, and Wesleyan—agreed to send Powell to Springfield to plead for a small endowment for the museum at the State Normal University.[8]

On three occasions Professor Powell appeared before the legislature to present his recommendations on behalf of the Natural History Society.

[7] J. W. Cook and J. McHugh, *A History of the Illinois State Normal University*, 1882, and *Proc. Bd. of Ed.*, 1858–1875.

[8] The 25th Illinois General Assembly, "An Act concerning the board of education and the Illinois Natural History Society," *Illinois Laws*, 1867, pp. 21–22; also *House Jour. 1867*, Vol. 1, p. 178; Vol. 2, pp. 227–28; *Sen. Jour. 1867*, pp. 767, 1093.

He explained the three chief functions of the society: to conduct a thorough survey of the natural history of Illinois; to initiate original research; and to maintain a museum in which study collections could be prepared for any interested colleges and high schools. All of the work, he stated, was volunteered by the members and cooperating organizations, and some coordination was urgently needed. Summing his arguments, Powell cited many examples to show that all civilized nations considered it wise to support such museums—the Royal Societies of London and Edinburgh in Great Britain and those of Russia, Belgium, and Sweden, and the numerous government-sponsored academies of science. Even in the United States, the Smithsonian Institution enjoyed governmental support. In a new state like Illinois, a museum such as the Natural History Society was contemplating would be of inestimable value to the people. Then, to close his words, Powell offered a concrete proposal:

> In order that the Society may carry out its purposes, it should have a general commissioner and curator, who can give his whole time to the work of the society; and whose duty it would be to superintend the researches and collections, take charge of the museum, carry on the exchanges, and make the distributions.

Then, referring to the actual appropriation:

> The aggregate of this expenditure would be about twenty-five hundred dollars; fifteen hundred dollars for the salary of the general commissioner and curator, and one thousand dollars for books, apparatus, etc.[9]

These efforts achieved complete success. On February 15, 1867, the Illinois house of representatives passed by unanimous vote a bill incorporating Powell's exact words. The senate concurred on February 26th. Fifteen hundred dollars for a curator and a thousand dollars to enhance the value of the museum were thereby authorized.

A special meeting of the Illinois board of education was called at the Normal University on March 26, 1867, to consider the appointment of a curator. Powell was appointed, as expected, by unanimous vote of the board. Privately he had been assured of the decision and was asked to have a little speech ready. That same day he was officially notified and invited to give his views on the interests of the museum.

Powell explained that prior to his appointment as curator he had planned an expedition to be undertaken during the present season to the Rocky Mountains for the purpose of exploring the park country of Colorado. In his opinion the interests of the museum could not be served

---

9 *Ill. Gen. Assembly Reps. 25th Sess.,* Vol. 2, p. 242.

better than by enriching its collections with material from that little-known territory. He requested that a portion of the thousand-dollar appropriation be devoted to exploration. The board promptly allocated five hundred dollars, half of the total fund, to help defray the field expenses.

The Professor was an experienced organizer. What had been a dusty reference collection for amateur and professional naturalists he hoped to transform into the "biggest" and "best." The first objective was to increase the collections by his expedition to the Rocky Mountains. It was to be a teacher and student affair, with each member of the party responsible for his own personal expenses.

The summer of 1866 had passed by with no greater diversion or excitement for the Powells than a visit to the family at Wheaton and Detroit, with stopovers with Martha and John Davis and Bram. With a mortgage on a new house in Normal, family finances hardly permitted a more extensive tour.

As for the Colorado expedition, the first obstacle was money. The museum appropriation of five hundred dollars was but the beginning. During the latter part of April Professor Powell went to Washington and called on his old commander, General Grant, to obtain the support of the War Department. Grant advised him to present a written request and promised to issue orders authorizing the commissary department to furnish rations at government rates for a party of twelve persons, and the military department of the Platte to furnish an escort of soldiers from Fort Laramie through the Bad Lands.

Next, Powell approached the officials of various railroads to ask for free transportation for his men. The response was complete: four lines—the Pacific Railroad; the Chicago, Alton and St. Louis; the Pittsburgh, Fort Wayne and Chicago; and the Chicago and Rock Island line—issued passes valued at more than seventeen hundred dollars. A similar petition brought promises of free transportation for parcels from the American Express Company and Wells, Fargo and Company.

Even with this substantial aid the funds were insufficient to meet the expenses which would be involved. Thereupon Powell applied to several scientific and educational institutions for additional support. In return he agreed to distribute duplicate series of specimens to the contributing institutions. Under these arrangements the trustees of the Illinois Industrial University (later the University of Illinois) appropriated five hundred dollars, and the Chicago Academy of Sciences appropriated one hundred dollars and loaned numerous tools and materials.

Nor were these efforts enough. Still needed were various scientific instruments, some of which were quite costly. Inquiries to the Smithsonian Institution led him to the secretary, Joseph Henry, who willingly loaned the necessary scientific equipment. In return Powell was to deposit with the institution the topographic measurements made by his party.

Recruiting personnel was a much easier problem. Fifteen persons agreed to join him on the expedition although the number diminished to eleven as the time for departure drew near. The final group totaled twelve: A. H. Thompson of Bloomington and Rev. William E. Spencer of Rock Island, entomologists; T. J. Burrill of Urbana, botanist; Rev. J. C. Hartzell of Bloomington and F. M. Bishop of Marquette, Michigan, zoologists; E. W. Spencer of Rock Island, S. H. Huse of Evanston and Mrs. Powell, ornithologists; M. Titterington of Rock Island, herpetologist; S. H. Kerrick of Bloomington, mineralogist; George D. Platte of Rock Island, artist; and twelfth, the Professor, who listed himself as geologist. Three of the men were college seniors, the others were amateur naturalists. Dr. J. A. Sewall and Dr. George Vasey, during the early stages of planning, had expected to join the party, but later found it impossible to go along.

During the latter part of May, Powell proceeded to Council Bluffs, Iowa, which was to be used as an outfitting base, and presented his credentials to Gen. William T. Sherman. General Sherman advised him, because of the danger of Indian raids, to avoid passing through the Bad Lands and follow a more southerly route into Colorado. The Indians in the territories were in an ugly mood. During the recent war when the federal government had withdrawn its western garrisons, the more warlike tribes assumed that the white men were frightened. Certainly the wiser elders among the tribes knew that this was not so and that the absence of soldiers was merely a temporary lull in the encroachments against the Indians. For years the increased migration of whites, not only for permanent settlement but for exploitation of the country, had forced the Indians into greater resistance. They took advantage of this temporary weakness. At the moment the advance of the transcontinental railroads meant the destruction of favorite hunting grounds and traditional tribal homes. The more restless and troublesome tribes, like the Apaches, Sioux, Comanches, and Utes, stepped up their depredations and broke into open rebellion. Scarcely a day passed that the newspapers of large eastern cities did not note at least one killing.

On June 1, 1867, the expedition [10] gathered on the south bank of the

[10] There is extensive material on the Rocky Mountain expedition. The principal sources used in the following account are: "Report of Professor Powell," in *Proc. Bd. of Ed.*, 1867,

Platte River near Council Bluffs and began their journey. They were outfitted with a dozen riding animals, teams, and two heavy wagons loaded with axes, picks and other tools, heavy clothing, and ample collecting equipment. Travel across the plains was very leisurely.

Just after dusk on June 10th they were surprised by a distant glow which appeared to be located on the trail directly ahead of them. As they approached nearer, an American flag hung silhouetted against the sky, reddened by the dancing light of a great bonfire. The wagon train had reached Fort Kearney. The flag marked the parade ground. The caravan had made sixteen miles that day, which proved to be their average rate of progress.

Each member of the party was assigned a specific share of the scientific work. They set traps to capture small animals, shot specimens of larger beasts. They collected beetles, butterflies, and other insects and gathered plants, which had to be dried and pressed in camp. Powell, while directing the operation, devoted most of his time to the study of geology. By day the camp was busy preparing specimens—salting and stretching skins, cleaning skeletons, wrapping minerals, extracting fossils, drying mushrooms, pressing plants, and performing the countless other tasks of field preparation.

Every evening the small cooking fires, one for every four persons, were extinguished and a cheerful bonfire built in the center of the camp. By night the camp was merry with singing and storytelling, occasionally serious with scientific discussions.

The party had to be on constant alert for Indians. Army scouts moved ahead of the main party and at night posted guards against possible surprise attacks. For most of the route they had hugged close to the Platte, a broad, muddy, shallow stream along which cottonwood groves at occasional intervals broke the monotony of otherwise treeless plains. Short distances away from the banks of the river the rolling prairie, alternating with bleak sand hills and seminaked cactus fields, was a checkered landscape as far as the eye could see.

As the party neared Fort McPherson they overtook and joined up with a train of fifty-two wagons with more than 350 animals and 250 men, women, and children. These pioneers represented every economic level and virtually all of the common occupations. Each night the wagons were drawn into an ellipse and chained together, and guards posted to warn of any approaching raiders. Inside this great circle the travelers

pp. 9–13; Chicago *Tribune,* Chicago *Republican,* Bloomington *Daily Pantagraph,* June–Nov. 1867.

gathered for gaming and for conversation, enjoying the companion-
ships which were theirs for a few fleeting hours. The majority of these
pioneers were farmers seeking new homesteads; the others were floaters
or hangers-on hoping to strike it rich in the fabulous country to the west.
On the fourteenth of June the expedition reached Fort McPherson and
halted for a good rest while the great wagon train they had joined for a
few days proceeded without them.

On June 23rd the Powell party, after completing another leg of
their journey, left Fort Sedgwick and followed the trail to Fort Morgan,
which was situated eighty miles east of Denver. Crossing the Bijou
Basin about fifty miles from Denver, the men had their first thrilling
glimpse of the Rocky Mountains. They remained at Fort Morgan three
days to replenish supplies and to rest their animals. For nearly six weeks
they had been trundled along in the swaying wagons.

On July 1st Powell rode ahead to visit Denver and to pay his respects to some of the prominent people in town. He called upon William
N. Byers, editor of the *Rocky Mountain News,* and there made the
acquaintance of O. G. Howland, who was employed by the newspaper.
After Powell had explained his mission, particularly his desire to visit
Middle Park, Byers recommended his brother-in-law, Jack Sumner,
who had a small outfitting shack in the park, as a competent and willing guide. With a letter of introduction from Byers, Professor Powell
completed preparations.

The main body of the expedition arrived at Denver on July 3rd and
the newspapers were expecting them. Denver, to the amazement of a
visitor from the States, was a city of nearly five thousand citizens, with
three-story brick stores on the main business streets, and much more
modern and prosperous than many cities back east.

From Denver the party had planned to follow the beaten road by
way of Colorado City to Pike's Peak, a distance of approximately eighty
miles. However, Byers suggested that it might be possible to reach the
peak by a much shorter route over a mountain range, subsequently
named Rampart Range, into the valley known as Bergen's Park. Only
one stout wagon, pulled by an ox team, traversed the route the year
before to haul provisions to herders who had driven their cattle into the
park to winter in the fine pasturage there. Owing to an accident the
wagon was burned, so it had been a one-way trip.

That the shorter route was beset with difficulties Powell was certain,
but it would give them an opportunity to examine the mountains. Thus
far all of their travel had been limited to easy driving along foothills or

valleys, and only a few side trips into the mountains had been ventured either with ponies or on foot.

It promised to be an interesting venture, so Powell took a southwestern course, keeping to the Colorado City road as far as the canyon of the South Platte, halting there for nearly a week to make huge collections which were packed and sent back to Denver for shipment east. Nearly the whole of this valley, running through a range of mountains for twenty miles, is a small canyon through which the Platte River descends with turbulent force, coming down from the mountains to the plain with tremendous velocity. This canyon, in a direction a little east of south, terminates just east of Pike's Peak. The river in its lower portions was used to irrigate the plain, which was under fairly intense cultivation.

From the canyon, the party worked its way into a park which hedges on the slope of the foothills of Pike's Peak and extends to the north for a distance of more than thirty miles to the base of Devil's Head.

The Professor sent out three scouts to pass over the route and appraise it. They reported that it was barely passable for the wagons. The chief obstacle between Denver and the valley twenty miles distant was a range of rugged mountains which averaged fifteen hundred feet above the base. The route proved to be nothing more than a trail. Trees had been blazed to mark the way and the road, if it could be called such, had been partially cleared of logs and underbrush. The ox team which had preceded them the year before had by brute force pushed its way through thick undergrowth of pine, poplar, and scrub oak. Anticipating a difficult two-day journey, the Powell party set out.

The expedition broke camp at Jackson's Creek, and at daybreak began their first real mountain travel. At the start of the trail they left one wagon with twelve hundred pounds of freight and put six mules to the other wagon with its load of one thousand pounds. Two other mules and four ponies were burdened with packs of a hundred pounds each.

The party ascended fifteen hundred feet in the first three miles over a tortuous course which turned to all points of the compass as well as uphill, downhill, and sidehill. The road was so steeply inclined in some places that their prairie-accustomed eyes were unbelieving. Safety seemed impossible. Had not the baggage been fastened securely with ropes, it would have slid endwise from the wagon. Sometimes it seemed that the animals needed claws instead of hoofs to keep their footing.

Three of the men went ahead as pilots and to clear the way, and others followed the wagon, chocking the wheels—blocking them with large pieces of wood when at rest. The mules proved to be docile, unperturbable, and hardy servants as they toiled on the steep trail. At one point the wagon had to be unloaded and taken apart, the pieces lugged over huge rocks, and reassembled on the other side. Major Powell, with mock military commands, ordered his "artillery" forward.

The descents were precarious. The wheels of the wagon had to be locked so that they could not turn, log chains were wrapped around the tire in such a way as to cut deep into the ground, or catch into bushes and rocks, to retard the velocity of descent. A long rope was hitched to the axletree and five or six men strained on the line with all their strength while the driver checked the reins and the mules settled back on their haunches, plowing up the dirt and smaller stones with their feet. Five hours were required to reach the summit of the range, and then the men and teams had to return for the other wagon. In all, it took twelve hours of exhausting labor to transport the two wagons the three-mile distance.

Far to the east stretched a variegated landscape of hills and valleys checkered with belts of deep green timber and plains studded with small groves. To the south rose the snowcapped and cloud-crested peak toward which they were traveling, and on the horizon the snowy peaks of a still higher range beyond glimmered in the sinking summer sun. The north was lost in impenetrable forests.

That night the party camped on the top of the ridge in a dense forest of pine and fir. For beds, boughs were cut from the pine trees, spread carefully upon the ground, and blankets thrown over them. It afforded luxurious slumber for weary bodies.

The next morning at sunrise the journey was resumed with both wagons, up-and-down travel being somewhat less difficult. An advance of fifteen miles by the trail was made. The party skirted deep chasms and by-passed piles of great granite boulders, each weighing hundreds of tons, heaped like so many toy blocks one upon another. They had expected to reach their objective in two days, but seven mountainous miles stretched between them and Bergen's Park. Camp was pitched again in the mountains and the next day, though Sunday, they covered the remaining distance. The grass had been so scanty that the animals fared badly and completion of the trip could not be delayed longer. The weary men reached the park about noon.

The valley known as Bergen's Park held a pleasant surprise for them. It was an enclosed verdant park twenty miles long and from one half to three miles wide. Opening into it from the flanks of surrounding mountains were numerous other smaller fertile parks, each with a sparkling

stream of cold pure water. A few settlers had already moved in and secured land under the Homestead Act. Grass was abundant and grazing
was profitable, virtually without investment or expense. Cattle were
driven in from the plains to winter on the grass. The soil was fertile but
the climate too cool for corn, though small grains grew well on selected
spots and potatoes flourished remarkably.

Even in late July woolen clothes were worn comfortably, and at night
heavy blankets were a necessity. Light summer showers were an almost
daily occurrence, and in the evenings heavy dew dampened every object.

They remained in Bergen's Park nearly a month collecting plants, insects, and birds from the vicinity, while the Major sketched the mountain profile and made other geological observations.

Long before daybreak on the morning of July 27th preparations were
made for the ascent of Pike's Peak. The climb could be undertaken only
in good weather and an adventurer might be caught unawares by a sudden tempestuous storm of rain and hail. When the first streaks of dawn
from the east spread into a clear rosy morning eight of the party, including Mrs. Powell, started out to make the ascent. Emma was mounted
as usual on her white-eyed Indian pony. The distance from the summit
was about seven miles as the crow flies. The peak, being much higher
than the surrounding ranges, was always in view.

There was no trail and the Major went ahead to select a likely
approach. The ascent was more laborious than they had expected. The
climb, winding about fire-fallen timber, over jagged rocks, up and down
precipitous walls, and crossing mired sloughs at the bottoms of steep
ravines, covered nearly twenty miles. At the foot of the first ridge the
party dismounted and, leading the animals, worked their way up the
rugged ascent. The altitude was nine thousand feet and the air so rare-
fied that they tired frequently. Gaining the top of this ridge, the party
rode as far as possible, then dismounted to climb a second ridge and
follow its serpentine outcrop. About eleven o'clock they paused for a
quick lunch of hardtack and cold beef and to allow the ponies to feed
on the grass of a small valley. They had reached one of the spurs of
the peak itself. Powell estimated that they should be able to eat dinner
on the summit at about two o'clock.

The climb was resumed. They had nearly reached the top of one of
the lesser peaks when they encountered a great rockslide. Footing was
precarious, but they attempted to cross it anyway. It proved to be perilous, the men and animals bruised by falls. The only alternative was
to descend and find another point more suitable for a climb. Finally,

another approach offering comparative safety was located and they stopped for a second lunch of hardtack and cold meat.

This time progress was easier, and by two o'clock they reached the flat top of a ridge from which the snowcap of the main ridge could be gained easily. It was obvious by now that they could not reach the summit and return to camp the same day. They had brought along a few blankets and ponchos, but sufficient food they did not have. The situation was discussed and it was agreed that here at the upper limit of timber they would leave the animals, scale the summit by foot, and return to camp for the night. What little hardtack remained would be eaten for supper and they would descend in the morning without breakfast.

The summit was mounted without as much difficulty as had been expected, and the party reached the top about three o'clock. Enchanted, they gazed over the picturesque landscape which spread for hundreds of miles beneath them. It was a novel experience, for not one of them had ever been above tree line before. They inspected the dwarfed and wind-blown evergreens that clung to life on the weather-beaten slopes. Perpetual snow covered the summit. They spent only an hour on the glorious spot, scanning the lands below.

The day was beautifully clear, and we felt favored and grateful that so rare an occurrence was ours to enjoy. Among those grand old monuments of the ages, with a picturesque landscape of hundreds of miles in extent spread out beneath us, the clear, blue arch of heaven above, no wonder that it seemed to our rapt vision something like enchantment. Surely the Creator intended the grandeur and beauty of the world as foretastes of the hereafter. What a prediction of the Unknown. Eternity itself may easily seem short.[11]

Having had no previous experience in mountain climbing, they lingered too long and the descent began at an alarmingly late hour. Night overtook them, with bitter cold and cutting wind adding discomfort and danger to the darkness. They inched their way over rocks and steep drops until they reached timber line. With this encouragement they built a great campfire, and spent the remainder of the night facing a scorching fire for a few moments and then turning around—to keep warm more evenly. There was no shelter; they had to stay awake to keep warm. The following noon the climbers returned to the base camp, nearly exhausted but joyous at their success. The ascent and descent required three days, and it is believed that the route had never before or since been taken.

Emma Powell was the first woman to climb Pike's Peak. Her field

[11] *Daily Pantagraph*, Aug. 26, 1867.

costume should not go unremembered. Her one-piece dress was of plain waterproof cloth reaching to the top of sturdy buttoned shoes, and she usually wore an English felt hat held in place by a green veil. The petticoats were of sufficient number for service and decorum.

Having rested after the ascent of Pike's Peak, the expedition wandered slowly among the mountains into South Park and explored the South Platte River. In a little park, with Mount Lincoln on the left and Triaquial, a spur of Mount Lincoln, on the right, they found its source. This little meadow of barely 150 acres was of exceptional beauty. The stream which ran through it was traced to two snow-fed lakes, the higher of which cascaded into the lower.

On this side trip they made fine collections of bear, elk, and wolverine. Heavy snows finally drove them from the mountains and they tracked back toward Denver, crossing the range once more by way of Berthoud's Pass in snow two to three feet deep. The return from Pike's Peak to South Park required only two days even though the trip was pushed through a sudden heavy snowstorm. They camped in South Park for three weeks, but the time had come to terminate the expedition and most of the members were compelled to return east.

The party reentered Denver by way of the gold and silver region about Central City. They stopped long enough to make an extensive collection of minerals and to watch the processing of the ores.

The Professor and Mrs. Powell remained behind to explore the Grand River, as the headwaters of the Colorado River are usually called. Powell was determined to descend the Grand River to its junction with the Colorado in the following summer. For two months, during September and October, Powell examined the topography, the canyons and arroyos, and the rock formations, formulating a plan for a survey of the Colorado. He secured the promises of Jack Sumner, O. G. Howland, Billy Rhodes Hawkins, and Bill Dunn to rejoin him in the following season. These four men, who had served him as guides and assistants, were familiar with the country and had shown their interest and dependability. They were the nucleus around which he could build a much larger organization.

On the first of November Professor Powell returned to Denver, stored some of his equipment, and made a few public appearances, announcing his determination to continue his explorations in 1868 with a larger party.

During this brief stay Powell gave the third lecture of a series before the Young Men's Christian Association of Denver, speaking on "The Peaks, The Parks, and The Plains." He explained the origin of Mammoth Cave in Kentucky and the long time required for its formation and, using this as an example, tried to indicate the vast expanses of time involved in geological processes. He discussed the age of the Rocky Mountains, the origin of coal beds, gold and silver lodes, and mountains and plains. The advance press notices failed to attract a large audience, but those who came were entertained by a most enthusiastic and persuasive speaker.[12]

Early in the morning of November 6th the Professor and Mrs. Powell left by stage for the East filled with determination to return to the Colorado country.

[12] *Daily Colorado Tribune* and *Daily Rocky Mountain News,* Nov. 6, 1867. The lecture was given on November 4th.

6

1868 · Across the Continental Divide

POWELL spent the winter of 1867–1868 making preparations for a more ambitious expedition to culminate in a passage of the Grand River to its junction with the Colorado. Barely two weeks after returning to Normal, he appeared before the annual meeting of the board of education and with characteristic enthusiasm stated that his explorations and collecting had been successful beyond expectations. The total expenses amounted to more than $2,100, more than half of which Powell paid himself. The board, considering its financial support judiciously expended and efficiently used, promptly appropriated six hundred dollars to finance a second trip, and promised further aid in the prosecution of the Professor's Rocky Mountain explorations.

The many boxes and parcels of specimens which had been shipped back to the museum were opened and rough sorted, but only a general inventory could be made in the limited time available.[1] As many duplicates as possible had been collected so that they could be distributed among the various cooperating institutions. By agreement, any unique specimen of a given kind was retained for the Normal Museum. The field catalogue showed that they had found nine hundred birds, several hundred plants, and thousands of insects. There were smaller series of rocks, minerals, and fossils, and reptiles and skeletons of mammals. It had been a successful summer.

Powell discharged his obligation to lecture in geology with scintillating enthusiasm. He had large classes of eager students who wanted to hear of his adventures and firsthand observations. His descriptions of Pike's Peak, Mount Lincoln, and the mountain parks were eloquent and vivid. There were few photographs or stereopticon slides in those days,

---

[1] "We confess our surprise at the amount of material there collected. . . . The Professor and four assistants were busy unpacking and preparing the various specimens. . . . Too much credit cannot be given to Prof. Powell. He works sixteen hours a day and pays his assistants out of his own meager salary." *Daily Pantagraph*, Jan. 25, 1868.

and a lecturer had to rely on words and crayon sketches to capture the imagination of his listeners.

Although Powell enjoyed his lecturing and teaching, apparently he was not satisfied. Perhaps he mused on the profession of teaching students, many of whom would return to their farms or in a few years enter business and give up the intellectual pursuits for which they had come to college—a thought which must arise eternally in the minds of teachers. Never bored, Powell was nevertheless searching passionately for something else to engage his energy.

In March, Major Powell spoke before the annual meeting of the board of the Illinois Industrial University on his Rocky Mountain expedition. The immediate purpose was to appeal for additional aid, but it so happened—probably after preliminary negotiations of which there are no records—that John Wesley Powell "was unanimously elected to the Professorship of Natural History, his term of service to commence at such time as may be agreed upon between himself and the committee on Faculty and Courses of Study." [2] This offer and his tentative acceptance was not announced because the Major was in no position to leave Normal, not only for his prior commitment there, but also because of his advanced plans to return to the mountain country.

In April, Powell went to Washington and consulted General Grant concerning the possibility of drawing rations again from western outposts, this time for a party of twenty-five men. The General suggested that he put his request in writing and state the purpose of the proposed expedition. The letter, dated April 2nd, was a routine request except that in it Powell mentioned two significant ideas: [3]

It is believed that the Grand Canyon of the Colorado will give the best geological section on the continent. . . .

And the other:

Nor is it necessary to plead the value to the War Department of a survey of that wonderful region, inhabited as it is by powerful tribes of Indians that will doubtless become hostile as the prospector and the pioneer encroach upon their hunting grounds.

Grant gave his approval and sent Powell's letter with one of his own to Gen. A. B. Eaton, who was commissary general of subsistence. To their mutual surprise, General Eaton declined to give his consent, assuming that it would be illegal to issue such rations since Powell was

[2] Ill. Ind. Univ., *1st Ann. Rep. Trust.*, 1867–1868, p. 127.
[3] J. W. Powell to Gen. U. S. Grant, April 2, 1868.

neither a civilian employee of the government nor a member of the military service of the United States. Eaton in turn suggested that Professor Powell obtain the enactment of a law which would accord him the aid that he desired. It was far more difficult to gain congressional approval for a private venture than to obtain the consent of a general or even the Secretary of War to certain privileges at army outposts. Nevertheless, Powell called on Rep. Shelby M. Cullom and Sen. Lyman Trumbull, both of Illinois, to gain their support.

On April 15th Mr. Cullom introduced in the House a joint resolution which would authorize the Secretary of War to furnish supplies to the Powell expedition. There was little opposition in the House though considerable antagonism was encountered in the Senate. Accordingly, Joseph Henry, secretary of the Smithsonian Institution, wrote a letter of introduction for Powell to James A. Garfield, then Representative from Ohio and a most influential member of the House. Secretary Henry explained that no personal or pecuniary interests were involved and that the venture was to be a survey of little-known country in one of the most interesting regions of our continent. He noted that Professor Powell intended to give special attention to the hydrology of the mountain system in relation to agriculture and that the water might be reclaimed for use in agriculture by a judicious system of irrigation founded on a critical knowledge of such hydrology.

Although the Smithsonian Institution had no funds to give support to Powell's party, Secretary Henry did provide various scientific instruments. Mr. Garfield was a useful ally and, although a member of the House, was able to gain the cooperation of various members of the Senate. Finally on May 25th, while Powell was anxiously awaiting some answer to his request and was forced to delay final preparations for the expedition, the Senate took up the joint resolution and began the debate. After the usual questions concerning Powell's identity and the objectives of the expedition, the main criticisms of the bill crystallized. The objection was that such a precedent might invite other individuals to seek financial support from the federal government for projects which were equally deserving and equally costly. Admittedly, as Mr. Trumbull stated, the area that the Professor intended to explore—six or seven hundred miles along the Colorado River—was marked upon the federal maps as unknown and perhaps never before seen by a civilized man. He called to the attention of his colleagues that Powell did not ask for a military guard, such as many other parties had required, because "his knowledge of the Indians and his acquaintance with the country is such that he is willing to take care of himself."

Finally the opposition was reduced to the single objection that the bill was not limited—that the Professor by asking a carte blanche might obtain support for a hundred men—whereupon an amendment was offered limiting the supplies to twenty-five persons. Then, without further restrictive amendments, a vote was taken and the measure passed, twenty-five to seven, with twenty Senators absent. Inasmuch as the presidential signature was assured, Powell returned to Normal even though final passage did not take place until President Johnson signed the bill on June 11th.[4]

Powell organized a larger party, again representing different branches of natural science, especially geology, botany, ornithology, and entomology. The Smithsonian Institution had furnished a sextant, barometers and chronometers, and a few other facilities. All personal expenses were to be borne by individual members of the party. The main purpose of the expedition was to gather a large collection of specimens representing the different sciences and illustrating the resources of the country. Also, before leaving Illinois it was understood that whatever else might or might not be accomplished, ascent of Long's Peak would be attempted. Repeated efforts to climb this fourteen-thousand-foot peak had failed. In fact, some argued that Long's Peak would never be ascended.

The party for the 1868 expedition included twenty-one persons. Two or three were professional biologists; the remainder were amateurs and upperclassmen at Normal and Wesleyan. Rev. George Smith accompanied the party as an ethnologist and Dr. George Vasey as a botanist. Dr. Henry Wing, a physician going west for his health, and Mr. J. B. Taylor were interested amateurs. Rev. J. W. Healy and Rev. W. H. Daniels, both from Chicago, joined as historians and correspondents to keep the newspapers informed of the progress of the expedition. Mrs. Powell was the only woman member, as in the first trip. Walter Powell, the Professor's younger brother, was taken along as a zoologist. The other members were E. D. Poston, John Aiken, Henry Wood, Rhodes C. Allen, W. H. Bishop, S. M. Garman, L. W. Keplinger, Lyle Durley, Ned E. Farrell, William Woodward, John Wheeler, and —— Chamberlain.

Just before taking leave of the college to begin the trip, Powell appeared before the board on the evening of its spring meeting on June 24th to give an account of his past work and a description of the pro-

---

[4] The essential documents and correspondence, including Powell's letter to Grant, are reprinted in the *Congressional Globe*, 40th Congr., 2nd Sess., pp. 2304, 2417, 2433, 2563, 2564, *et al.*

posed route of his second expedition. Following a short address he took the members of the board to the museum and explained briefly the many additions to the collections which had been made during the preceding season. Much of the material had not yet been prepared nor classified, but the size of the museum's collections had already been doubled.

The board of education of the State of Illinois appropriated an additional four hundred dollars to purchase instruments which could well be used in the expedition to the Colorado River. This appropriation came too late to benefit the 1868 party, but it did enable Powell to place orders for valuable instruments which could be used in subsequent expeditions.

Before daybreak on Monday, June 29th, the party of twenty men and Mrs. Powell left Normal for Chicago, arriving there at five o'clock in the morning.[5] Almost the entire day was idled away waiting for a special car on the Chicago and Northwestern Railroad which was to take them to Omaha, Nebraska. After a tedious delay, during which a large banner lettered "Colorado Scientific Exploring Expedition" was nailed to the side of the railroad car, they boarded the train, which pulled out at three o'clock in the afternoon. They traveled all night by luxurious Pullman car and next day passed over the fertile Iowa prairie. They reached the river opposite Omaha at four o'clock in the afternoon. After unloading the luggage and supplies the boys took a swim in the Missouri River and practiced shooting with their firearms. That night the men spread their blankets on the floor of the depot, but mosquitoes kept them from sleep. The Professor and Mrs. Powell went over to the city and stayed the night at a hotel. The next morning they boarded the Union Pacific for Cheyenne, Wyoming.

Three hundred miles west of Omaha the country became sandy and level without a tree or house visible as far as the eye could see. They had left the rich prairie behind them. The sandy terrain gradually grew more hilly and wilder as the party approached Cheyenne. It was unbroken wilderness except for a small station with a few soldiers posted as railroad guards.

They crossed the North Platte River on July 2nd at a point where one hundred Indians were camped with a large herd of cattle and horses. They were a miserable, dirty, homely looking people, and this first in-

---

[5] There are extensive source materials on the 1868 expedition: there are manuscript diaries of Rhodes Allen and Lyle Durley; the Chicago *Tribune, Rocky Mountain Daily News,* and *Daily Pantagraph* printed many dispatches; there are letters by Keplinger, Garman, and Powell; several published accounts are referred to in nn. 10 and 15, which follow.

troduction to the Indians for most of these Illinois students was a disappointment. The only costume worn by the natives was a blanket which left the arms, legs, and neck bare.

Cheyenne was a town of four thousand people situated on a level piece of prairie surrounded on all sides by barren hills. At first sight the land appeared to be destitute, certainly too dry for agriculture. Yet the grass, which seemed only tolerably good, supported vast herds of cattle and horses. There was some excitement in the town because large bands of Indians were roaming about, and four hundred of them were camped about a mile from the city. The members of the expedition pitched army tents on the common near the depot. The party was split into three-man teams to stand guard, each group taking a three-hour watch. Their caution was needless; no redskins even approached the town during the night. The only alarm was caused the next morning by two Indians on an antelope chase.

The expedition remained in Cheyenne for a week to outfit themselves with good horses and mules. In a body they went over to a corral to select suitable animals. The dealer showed them a herd of wild horses, not one of which had ever been lassoed or backed. The Professor insisted that one of the cowboys employed at the corral back, in the presence of members of the party, each animal purchased. A wiry broncobuster backed them one by one with very disturbing results. Each of the boys was able to ride a horse, and a few had been in the army long enough to become acquainted with mules, but none of them had broken in an animal before or had even been in the cavalry. The saddle animals, broncos fresh from the plains of California, where they had been permitted to run wild, provided the initial adventure of the expedition. The Major took first pick, a spirited mare. With help from three of the boys—two holding and one pushing—he mounted without mishap.

After the animals were shod the next procedure was to saddle them. All of the men except the Professor were thrown, the only consolation being the antics of fellow victims. Rhodes Allen, the ornithologist, was tossed into a cactus bush and suffered the effects for several weeks. Reverend Daniels had a close call when, as he was thrown, his foot became tangled in the stirrup. He called to those standing near, "Take hold of her, boys, take hold of her," and to the horse, "Whoa, whoa, you sweet little angel." [6] This was the mildest rebuke heard. Although profanity was rarely used, more than one beast ragged the patience of

[6] L. W. Keplinger, *Kans. Hist. Coll.*, Vol. 14, p. 341.

its rider until unexpected epithets issued forth. The fellows were proud of their broncobusting and regarded the initiation as complete.

The mules were no less spirited, being not only balky but treacherous. Reverend Daniels wrote in his diary, "Until I had this experience did I understand the meaning of the word 'mulish.' " [7] The rugged country was painful to unshod horses, but a few of them were too cussed to shoe, no smith in Cheyenne being equal to the contest.

Outfitted with animals, and with supplies replenished at the post, the party set out by pack train toward Denver, a distance of 150 miles. Eleven miles south of Cheyenne they passed through Lone Tree, a one-store, one dwelling, one-woman town. Lone Tree was noted for its garden, a plot of five acres fenced in by willow bushes, with its fine crop of potatoes and other vegetables. On the frontier this produce was worth fifteen hundred dollars.

They were scarcely one day's journey out of Cheyenne when a government detective overhauled the train at Box Alder and claimed a mule, the best in the outfit. Major Powell went back to Cheyenne with the detective to counterclaim the mule. The government had seized the animal on the assumption that it was army property, but Powell insisted that it was unbranded and that he had bought the animal in good faith. That evening he returned to camp with the mule. As if minor troubles were not enough, just before twilight twelve or fourteen Indians came to the camp, presumably to beg, but they were very soon sent away with firm words from the Major.

The journey to Denver took six days of fairly rapid travel, camping out by night to let the ponies rest and eat, and by day continuing the exploration of the country. Usually the men scattered in pairs so that it was possible to scour for miles around to see what could be collected. As the trail led to rougher country and to lesser-known areas exploration was made for fifteen or twenty miles on each side of the trail.

They remained in Denver overnight and proceeded next morning through Bear Creek Canyon to Empire City where W. N. Byers joined them. Leaving Empire City they crossed the main range by Berthoud Pass and halted at Hot Sulphur Springs on the Grand River in North Park, where a general headquarters for the expedition was to be established. Here they were joined by the small group of mountaineers, expert trappers and experienced guides who had promised Powell the year before to join the expedition: Jack Sumner; Gus Lanken; O. G.

[7] Chicago *Tribune,* Aug. 3, 1868.

Howland; and Bill Rhodes, who for personal reasons preferred his middle name to "Hawkins," his surname.

For three months the Powell party collected diligently, acquiring considerable material not found during the previous season. Keplinger was assigned to the measurement of altitude, latitude, and longitude with the Smithsonian sextant, chronometers, and barometers. This youthful student and several of his classmates were making permanent geographical records—measurements of an unknown country.

During August the camp was visited by Schuyler Colfax from Springfield, Massachusetts, who was on a junket to convince the territories in general, and Colorado in particular, that the Republican party and Mr. Colfax were interested in the future of the West.[8] Mrs. Powell, Mr. and Mrs. Byers, and the Major met the Colfax party, which included W. H. Blodgett, J. D. Ward, and Samuel Bowles, the chronicler and campaign manager for Colfax, and received them cordially. The guests were treated to a sample of camp life and mountain climbing just above timber line "to get the view." Colfax a few months later received the nomination for Vice-president, and was subsequently elected with Ulysses S. Grant. Before leaving, Colfax crossed the divide over a trail blazed by Powell. He complimented the Major on his accomplishment, but not without adding that the trail was so difficult he hoped that the Major had not overlooked an easier one.

Sunday was just another day on the frontier. There was no interruption in the routine activities—trappers hunted their prey, stages ran on schedule, mines were tunneled for wealth, stamp mills crushed ore, stores were open, mule whackers drove their teams, and honky-tonks did their usual business. But to the group of students—mostly Methodists and Quakers—the Sabbath was still a day of observance. The first Sunday in camp they "erected a preaching tent" and notified neighboring ranches that Protestant services would be held. At the beckoning of a cowbell, rung solemnly by Reverend Daniels, the neighbors gathered together. A goodly number of people turned out to worship with the members of the expedition. Each man had been given a *Soldier's Hymnal* and these were shared for the services. The selections, "I'm a Pilgrim and I'm a Stranger," and "Sweet Home," were sung unaccompanied. Of this service Reverend Healy wrote:

Though less formal and precise than our service at home, yet we believe it was as acceptable to Him Who seeks to be worshipped in spirit and in truth, and

[8] Chicago *Tribune*, Aug. 21, 1868. Colfax's and Bowles' impressions of Powell are given in S. Bowles, *The Switzerland of America, Colorado*, pp. 81–86.

more prophetic of the millennial Sabbath when there shall be no Protestant nor Catholic, no Jew or Gentile.[9]

Although a well-provisioned headquarters was maintained in the park, the men moved away from time to time leaving not more than two or three of their number on guard. They scattered over a wide area gathering specimens, sketching the geology of the country, and hunting food.

The chief objective of the expedition was mountain exploring. Powell busied himself with a study of high altitudes and mountain structure. He made a traverse of the Colorado Range from Lincoln's Peak to the South Platte, camping whenever possible at timber line, sheltered by rocks and near to firewood. He observed the Gore Mountains, a wonderfully picturesque range which up to this time had been unexplored. Later the people of Colorado named the highest peak of the Gore Range "Mount Powell."

On August 20th a party of seven—the Major, Walter Powell, L. W. Keplinger, Samuel Garman, Jack Sumner, Ned Farrell, and William Byers—left their camp on the west side of Grand Lake for the ascent of Long's Peak.[10] Each man was mounted and one mule was packed with rations for a ten-day trip. They were armed with pistols and those not encumbered by instruments took their rifles.

The first four miles led over a very steep rock ridge made almost impassable by entangled fallen timber. Three hours were required to cover this first stretch, but then, entering green timber, more rapid progress was possible. Seven miles from the starting point they reached timber line and picked a trail along the crest of a rocky ridge. Five miles farther the Major halted the expedition. After a discussion of their progress the party decided to return down to the edge of the timber and camp for the night. The barometer recorded the altitude at 11,500 feet.

On August 22nd at about seven o'clock a fresh start was made on horse. Each man carried bacon and biscuits—sufficient for two days' rations—in his pockets. Firearms were left behind and only two of the party took blankets, the others not wishing to be bothered with them. The terrain was tortuous and discouraging. The party circumvented several impassable ledges by dropping to lower levels. Two snow banks were crossed easily, but at the end of a mile they reached a precipice

[9] W. H. Daniels, ["Historicus"] Chicago *Tribune,* Nov. 10, 1868.
[10] On this first ascent of Long's Peak, see L. W. Keplinger, *Kan. Hist. Coll.,* Vol. 14, pp. 340–53, and *The Trail,* Vol. 7, No. 8, Jan. 1915. See also W. N. Byers, *Daily Rocky Mountain News,* Sept. 1, 1868.

which could not be passed, at least on horse. The entire day was spent in trying to locate a detour, but without success. The men back-tracked to camp again at timber line. By now it was clear that better progress could be made on foot, so the animals were turned loose on a patch of short grass and corralled by blocking the narrow trail with stones and poles in such a manner as to make escape impossible. At the bottom they crossed a little valley just at timber line and began the ascent of a range which appeared to join Long's Peak. Reaching the summit the men were chagrined to discover that they were still farther from their destination than they were the day before, and what was more disconcerting, after a whole day's effort they had to descend to the valley and reclimb the same trail for a third time. With extreme difficulty—a slip would have meant death—they descended the precipice and returned again to timber line. There were some hours of daylight remaining and Keplinger offered to make a preparatory exploration over the hazardous ground for a route for the morrow's ascent.

"Kep" failed to return by twilight and the men in camp became uneasy for his safety. When night fell and a thunderstorm broke over their heads, the Major sent Jack Sumner above to light beacon fires and the rest holloed in the darkness. About ten o'clock, hours after full darkness, Kep and Jack returned with the news that an ascent was possible. Keplinger had reached within several hundred feet of the summit himself.

The night was uncomfortable and wearisome. Chilly rain showers driven by gusts of high winds forced the men to take shelter under the rocks. They shivered the whole night through, hoping for more favorable weather in the morning.

The day dawned fair and by six o'clock the supreme attempt was under way. They crossed diagonally over a great rockslide of loose boulders. Progress was laborious and uncertain. No extraordinary obstacles were encountered until they reached a point about seven hundred feet from the summit which appeared to be a great block of granite, smooth and unbroken. This fortunately proved to be an illusion and the men were able to climb the precipitous walls, "life depending often upon a grasp of the fingers in a crevice that would hardly admit them." Before ten o'clock the entire party reached the extreme summit without mishap— Keplinger crawled up first, the Major second, Jack Sumner third, then Byers and the others. A few distant white clouds floated in a sky of deep blue. They were astride a continent in a universe of sky. The Major shouted, "Glory to God!" [11] and the men gave three cheers for their success.

For nearly three hours they remained on the top of the bare granite peak, a nearly flat rectangular surface five to six acres in extent, bare of all vegetation except a small gray lichen and a pretty little moss which grew in the shadowed crevices of some of the large rocks. On the eastern end a few large boulders made a slight promontory ten to fifteen feet higher than the remainder of the surface. Although it was August 23rd, small patches of snow remained in protected crags. The summit was swept with a fierce wind giving a sensation of exhilaration and fear to those struggling to maintain a balance.

As they gazed into the distance they could see Denver clearly, also the hot springs in Middle Park, and vast expanses of plains to the east. Pike's Peak was up to the south, the Sahwatch ranges southwest, the Gore Range and Elkhorn Mountains to the west, and the Medicine Bow and Sweetwater ranges to the north. They counted more than thirty alpine lakes from the summit.

Keplinger and Farrell made barometric and thermometric observations while the others built a monument of small loose stones. Each man wrote his name on a sheet of paper and placed it, along with a copy of the data observed, in a small tin baking-soda can in the monument.

An American flag was unfurled and left upon the summit and the Major delivered a little speech, complimenting the men on their achievement and reminding them of the importance of such work. At the close of this ceremony a bottle of dixie wine was opened, a little sprinkled on the monument, and the remainder disposed of in the usual manner. Two of the party, Garman and Keplinger, refused despite friendly entreaties to drink—"whatever the newspapers may say to the contrary." [12]

The descent was somewhat less difficult and though the party was enveloped in a brief snow squall on the way down, in two hours they crossed three branches of the headwaters of the St. Vrain. Each valley was filled with lakes, which they skirted. Among them were great fields of snow strewn with grasshoppers which literally could have been gathered in wagonloads. Two bears were feeding on the insects, numbed by the cold.

Darkness was nearing and the men stopped for the night on the most

[11] Chicago *Tribune,* Sept. 10, 1868.

[12] Letter, S. Garman to Gertrude Lewis, Aug. 28, 1868. With permission of Mrs. Florence Fifer Bohrer.

westerly branch of the St. Vrain. It was a cheerless night without blankets, and made more unpleasant because they were out of food.

The next morning, on the 24th, with the first streaks of dawn the men worked their way back to the old camp at the head of the Grand where the animals had been corralled. After a hearty hurried breakfast they saddled up, retraced the trail to the main camp, and rejoined the main party.

Keplinger and Garman were left above timber line at the thirteen thousand foot elevation to take barometric measurements and weather data at every hour, day and night, for two weeks while the rest returned to the base and continued to Grand Lake to enjoy the scenery and do a little trout fishing in the lake. Time played strange pranks, for one of the climbers, Garman, discovered to his chagrin that they had made the ascent on the Sabbath. Had he known, he most certainly would have refused to engage in the labor.

On August 24th Powell returned to Hot Sulphur Springs and found nearly a hundred visitors who had come in during their nine days' absence. The Indians had pulled down their lodges very suddenly that same morning and departed, apparently in the direction of South Park. There were rumors of marauding bands but none came near.

The Ute Indians had a small village near Hot Sulphur Springs. From the few natives who knew a little English the Major and some of his students endeavored to prepare a vocabulary of Ute words. These Indians were among the laziest they had thus far encountered; they were content to beg what little could be obtained from trappers and from travelers, who in increasing numbers were beating a path to these famous springs. The members of the expedition had not yet learned to ignore their persistent begging and found themselves each day besieged by a greater number of beggars than they had turned away the day before.

The most onerous job was to keep the headquarters replenished with supplies and it fell to Bishop to take the pack train back and forth over Berthoud Pass and haul supplies from Empire City at the eastern base of the pass. In this capacity Bishop made eleven trips across the Continental Divide before the party moved on to the west in preparation for the winter camp. He had with him two assistants who were picked up in Colorado. Before breaking their summer camp, Powell wrote an account of his summer's work which he mailed to Normal for safekeeping.

Powell had brought with him from the East a sketch of Berthoud's old trail across the Continental Divide.[13] He hoped to follow this old trail into the White River country. The plan was to send a small portion of the party ahead to explore the route and to take the pack train as heavily laden as possible, and then return with the pack animals for the rest of the party. Walter Powell was in charge of this group. It proved to be exceedingly difficult to follow Berthoud's route. In many places they lost the trail and the going was hazardous. At times detours had to be made around impassable barriers.

Some of the mule packers grumbled against this unanticipated hardship and one of them, Gus Lanken, absconded with two of the best pack animals, heavily laden with provisions. Billy Hawkins, who had been Gus's bunkmate, when questioned refused to say much except to express the opinion that Lanken had quit the party. Walter Powell decided to spend the day hunting for Gus, who, being familiar with the country, was undoubtedly in hiding. Hawkins now volunteered the information that Lanken had a cabin nearby where he and a pal had previously passed a winter of trapping. Walter Powell divided his small group into two sections, each group going up separate sides of a ravine. Before long they found Gus, or rather the gulch in which he was hiding. A bullet shot from behind a well-covered rockfall sped past Rhodes Allen.

To avoid bloodshed, it was decided to let Gus and the mules go for good, but not before Keplinger carved on a poplar tree, "Gus Lanken is a mule thief. Keplinger says so, this 14th day of September, 1868." [14]

With Gus gone, Billy Hawkins was under a cloud of suspicion. He had been a friend of Lanken's and his own behavior was not entirely aboveboard. It was Keplinger's job to watch Hawkins. He carried out his assignment by sleeping with Billy, keeping by his blanket roll a double-barreled loaded shotgun. He was ordered to "shoot to kill" at the first unmistakable signs of treachery. The trappers had every advantage; the boys from Illinois had little or no familiarity with the country and no experience fighting it out with desperadoes. However, the suspicions against Hawkins were utterly unfounded; he served the Major well.

Finally the pack train passed over the Berthoud trail for a distance of two hundred miles west of the Great Divide. Then, as agreed, the men

[13] Powell had a map of Berthoud's westward wagon route of 1861, but found the trail so obscure that he repeatedly lost it. The diary of Rhodes Allen alludes frequently to the tribulations encountered in the 150-mile trek.

[14] Rhodes Allen, MS, Diary; also described briefly by L. Keplinger, Kan. Hist. Coll., Vol. 14, cf. note 10.

unpacked the mules and sent the animals back for the main party and the remainder of the provisions. Walter Powell, Keplinger, and Allen remained behind to guard the stores until a new camp was established.

When the party started westward for White River Bishop had been sent to make one more trip for supplies. On his return to Hot Sulphur Springs he was to follow the main party and rejoin them at the new camp. Days and weeks had passed without any word from Bishop. Some of the men thought that he had been killed in an accident or by Indians, and others that he simply had quit the party. To their elation and amazement Bishop appeared five weeks later in a sorry ragged condition, long without food.[15] He had been lost. The original plan which had been made with Bishop assumed that the first camp of the main party would be on White River. Actually, a stop had been made on Bear River and Bishop, upon returning, found the signs of the first camp and followed the Bear River, but failed to locate the trail on White River. He had fought his way through blizzards and heavy snowfalls and it was a miracle that he returned alive. He had not even been warmly clad, and although he had a Maynard rifle, he had only one occasion to use it.

Not long after Bishop's return the whole party moved down the White River toward its mouth. The Major had by now completed his plans for the exploration of the canyons in 1869 and he wanted to be near Green River to prepare for the undertaking. The winter camp was established in the bottoms of the lower White River.

It was now time to begin preparations for winter. Three log cabins were erected and fitted out as comfortably as possible. Natural hay was cut and dried and wood was chopped and split for fuel. It had been agreed previously that early in the winter several of the party would leave in order to reduce the demands on the food stores. Much of the exploration had been accomplished and deep snows blanketed the ground, making further studies impossible.

In December while some of the party remained behind in winter quarters the Major, with several hunters and those returning east, went northwestward to the point where the Union Pacific Railroad now crosses the Green River. At this time the whole journey was through a region unknown and without roads or trails. They had traveled to within fifty miles of Green River when a severe storm overtook them. They went into camp at the foot of Aspen Mountain while the storm raged for three days. When it finally did subside the heavy snowfall

15 T. F. Dawson, *The Trail,* Vol. 11, No. 2, 1918.

made travel difficult. They toiled through deep drifts and reached Green River three days later.

Most of the party from the East returned home, but Mrs. Powell, Walter Powell, the Major, Garman, and Bishop remained in the wilderness.[16] They loaded the pack animals with supplies at Gosio and trekked back to the valley. The trio and several mountaineers, including the Howland brothers, Bill Dunn, and William Hawkins, crossed the range and made their way to White River. They followed down the valley of the Green to the Uinta Mountains, then eastward to Brown's Hole. From this rendezvous Major Powell explored the upper canyons of the Green River, then going eastward he explored the Yampa and from there moved southward, arriving at the camp on New Year's Day, 1869.

Just before they had arrived near the camp ground the Major, Walter, and Jack, riding in advance of the others, sighted two grizzly bears and shot them. This unexpected good fortune provided the party with two warm robes for the bitter cold winter and sufficient oil to light their cabins during the long nights.

Not far from the cabins on the White River, a band of Ute Indians had camped until spring, and the Major made the acquaintance of Chief Douglas. The Major spent most of the long winter evenings visiting these Indians, learning something of their language and recording their myths and customs. Mrs. Powell took an active interest in these ethnologic studies and made many small sketches for her husband. The festivities of the Indians, who proved to be very friendly, added entertainment for all. In return the hunters from the Powell party supplied abundant game for the Utes. These Indians as yet had no firearms and killed game only with their primitive bows and arrows, though in this region of heavy snows, in winter at least, this was an easy task. Nevertheless the bountiful gifts of meat were appreciated by their red neighbors. On one trip the hunters, within a radius of twenty miles of the camp, brought down twenty-three deer, enough to serve them for weeks.

Powell had seen comparatively little of the Indians on his first exploring trip. He was more like a tourist among them. The few Indians he saw interested him sufficiently to plan to engage an ethnologist for the next expedition. The Indians who huddled around the white settlements were reduced to begging and were degraded in strength and body. Most of them were filthy and unhealthy. But when found in his native

[16] On the winter camp, see Chicago *Tribune,* Sept. 24, 1868, and Oct. 26, 1868; T. F. Dawson, *op. cit.*

country, still left to his own resources, the Ute Indian in particular was a noble fellow.

Never once did Powell hesitate to travel through land inhabited by hostile Indians. He moved about utterly unarmed to the surprise not only of the military authorities, but also of the Indians he met on the trail. Not once was Powell molested during many years of exploring in country regarded as unsafe for intruders.

Thus by the close of 1868 Powell had added a new interest to his expanding program. He had become an ethnologist and through mere circumstance had come upon these unspoiled and almost unvisited primitives who retained a nearly pure culture. Powell's vocabularies of Ute words were the first that were ever recorded, and his systematic collections of their handicraft were a revelation to the Smithsonian Institution.

During the late winter months Powell explored the canyons of the White River and the country far up and down the Green to familiarize himself with canyon geography and to devise methods for traversing the Colorado River.

When in early spring a sudden thaw accompanied by heavy rains flooded the valley of the White, the whole river bottom was submerged. The camp stood in three feet of water and the distance to higher ground was so far that it was impracticable to take down all the cabins and move them. Nevertheless, they rebuilt one cabin on high ground. When it was reconstructed Mrs. Powell moved in with the result that the male members of the party were forced to sleep in the open.

The weather soon turned cold again and the men suffered unduly from exposure. This was the final hardship which led Bishop to leave the party although he had previously agreed to descend the canyons with the rest. It had been a summer of hard work and a winter of privation, and he had had enough of roughing it.

Mrs. Powell was a capable member of the expedition. Her fortitude and cheerfulness were respected by all the men, but one trait was a bitter annoyance.[17] Emma resented the independence of some of the young men who, paying their own way and receiving no remuneration for their services, were willing to do only those tasks to which they had been assigned. Samuel Garman felt the imposition when Powell requested him to do all sorts of nuisance jobs about the camp. Naturally, he ob-

[17] Members of the expedition were unanimous in their respect for Emma's fortitude and ability. Those who expressed themselves—Bishop, Garman, and Allen—were equally unanimous in their resentment of her imperious manner.

jected and threatened to leave. Mrs. Powell reminded Garman that she and Major Powell commanded the expedition and the members of the party, and that he was to obey willingly. This little incident brought into words what had long been evident but unspoken—Mrs. Powell had assumed the authority to order the men about. Garman went to Powell and informed him of his intention to leave and collect butterflies on an independent expedition. The Professor attempted to persuade him to remain with the party, but it was too late.[18] Garman traveled with the expedition several weeks longer, but his very presence was a gentle reminder that, despite the friendly terms, others would follow his example if Mrs. Powell interfered again.

Having made three preliminary land explorations—one as far south as Grand River, a second following the White River to its junction with the Green, and the third northward around the eastern base of the Uinta Mountains, skirting several deep gorges—Powell was satisfied. The string of chasms, virtually inaccessible by land, could be traversed in boats—that is, in the right kind of boats. The starting point would be the Union Pacific Railroad bridge over the Green River. To this crossing boats could be transported by flatcar. The next step was to procure boats and provision the outfit for an exploration of the upper Colorado.

[18] Letter, S. Garman to Gertrude Lewis, April 2, 1869. With permission of Mrs. Florence Fifer Bohrer.

7

1869 · Preparations at Green River

EACH noon the sun stood higher, each day light lingered longer. Winter had passed. Powell had ample opportunity to mull over the maps and notes which were spread upon the table in the cabin. His plans for the conquest of the mighty Colorado were completed. Again and again he reviewed the project.

The object of the expedition was to explore the upper Colorado River and solve the mysteries of its three-hundred-mile canyon. The whole region was terra incognita—so acknowledged by the federal land office. The official maps before him showed a great blank space three hundred to five hundred miles long and one hundred to two hundred miles wide. On the Gorlinski map,[1] the latest in his possession, the line of the Green River stopped at the foot of Brown's Hole and the Grand River was shown only to the boundary between Colorado and Utah. The two branches of the upper Colorado were connected by hypothetical lines to show their probable courses and their junction to form the Colorado River proper.

The Major weighed his information. Beginning with the junction of the Grand and Green, the river rushes through gorges averaging three thousand feet deep. It was said that the walls were perpendicular, that no one could descend safely, that no one could climb out. But the Major had his doubts. He could climb down the canyons which he studied along the Green, although they were only a thousand feet deep.

The canyons extended for fifteen hundred miles and in that distance not one settlement or outpost was to be found along its course. Some portions of the gorges were four, five, even six thousand feet deep. At

---

[1] A half dozen maps of equal quality were available in 1868. The Major does not mention any particular map, but E. Wright Allen, brother of Rhodes Allen, wrote as follows: "For many years I had my brother's map that he had with him in Colorado. Maj. Powell bought them for several of the students who went with him. As I recall the map was printed by . . . the U.S. Land Office and was drawn by Gurlinsky [Gorlinski]. It was a big wall map." Letter, E. Wright Allen to W. C. Darrah, May 5, 1947.

Green River Station in Wyoming the elevation of the river stands at 6,075 feet; at the Río Virgen, Arizona, seven hundred feet—the river drops a mile in this journey of nine hundred miles. (Compare the Mississippi which drops 1,670 feet in 2,560 miles—only 320 feet in its lower 1,300 miles.)

The Colorado River itself was the problem, the mystery. How did the river descend that vertical mile? There were rapids, falls, and furious eddies, which everyone agreed rendered passage if not utterly impossible, too dangerous to attempt.

No one had ever navigated the waters of the upper Colorado, although bullboats—constructed of buffalo hide stretched over willow frames— had been taken for a distance down the Green, and several daring parties had made short runs near the few known crossings of the river. There was also the story of James White and his raft.[2] But the disasters which had befallen those who ventured into the abysmal recesses and tumultuous waters discouraged any serious attempt to descend the river.

Lt. J. C. Ives had ascended the Colorado River with a party in 1857 and managed to reach Vegas Wash, above Black Canyon. He had with him Dr. John Strong Newberry, an able geologist, who wrote the first accurate account of the canyons of the Colorado. Newberry described the naked country, the deep gorges, the erosion phenomena of the region, and with rare insight suggested explanations for the remarkable features of the Colorado River canyons. Without doubt Powell's interest in and approach to the geology of the canyon country was influenced by Newberry's work. The Major acknowledged his indebtedness.[3]

Powell had familiarized himself with the topography of the Colorado country. He had obtained all available maps and survey reports published by the federal government and made copies of manuscripts and sketch maps loaned to him by Mormon missionaries. He talked with Indians, settlers, and trappers and from their varied accounts sifted such information as seemed usable.

The Major sought out James White, who, it had been reported, came through the canyons from the San Juan River to Callville on a raft in eleven days, but the fellow's simple story seemed too vague to credit.

[2] The most critical account of White's alleged journey is in Stanton, *Colorado River Controversies*. See however Dawson, *65th Cong. 1st Sess. Sen. Doc. 42.*

[3] J. C. Ives, *Report on the Colorado River of the West,* 1861. John Strong Newberry was the geologist with this party. For Powell's appreciation of Newberry's conclusions see *Exploration of the Colorado River*, pp. 197–98. There were other early government explorations of the canyoned sections of the Colorado River below Grand Wash—Gunnison in 1853 and Macomb in 1859.

Another man boasted that he, with several friends, had laid out a whole town at the junction of the San Juan, only to be driven away by hostile Indians.

From this maze of fact, fable, and fancy the Major drew several conclusions: first, there were not one but many canyons; then, that the river could be traversed in boats; finally, that there was a profound geological lesson to be learned from the canyons. Major Powell was ready to make the attempt.

In March the winter camp was abandoned and the party struck out in a northwesterly direction for Fort Bridger. They followed the trail [4] used by Powell in his reconnoitering earlier in the year, reaching the Bear (Yampa) River, a distance of forty-five miles, by an open valley after three days' travel. They crossed a short ten-mile stretch between the Bear and Elk rivers of utterly worthless country that afforded easy movement. To the north of Elk River the rolling country round about was covered with grass while the hills were timbered in oak. Beyond, and for the remaining distance to the Vermillion River, they traveled over rolling sagebrush, varied somewhat by stands of cedar on the hills. The party crossed the Vermilion and followed the north side of the Green to Brown's Hole.

Brown's Hole, a favorite rendezvous for mountaineers, was a natural park approximately twenty miles long and four miles wide. In this pleasant valley the party rested. There had been little snow, in places the grass was green, and the weather—considering the season—was delightful. The Major spread out a map and pointed out the course of the river from Green River Station, the jumping-off point for the proposed exploration. Wes and Emma walked to the hills, climbed the summit, and looked down upon the valley and the river. Once again he assured her of his determination to succeed in this project.

The journey was continued, crossing the Green at Henry's Fork and following the stream to its head forty miles above the junction. From this point to Fort Bridger the distance was only thirty miles, but the country was as desolate as can be found.

Fort Bridger [5] was situated in the fertile dissected valley of Black's Fork on the Green River. It had been established as a trading post by the most famous mountaineer of them all, Jim Bridger, in 1843. The military reservation had been established in 1859 after the "Mormon

[4] The fullest account of this trip to Fort Bridger was recorded by O. G. Howland, *Rocky Mountain News*, May 14, 1869. See also Powell's description of the route in *Geology of the Uinta Mountains*.

[5] See R. S. Ellison, *Fort Bridger, A Brief History*.

War." The post buildings consisted of barracks, commissary, and sta-bles, enclosed in a stockade.

The first citizen, Judge William A. Carter, had an immense store and warehouse and did a profitable business with emigrants, the garrison, and friendly Indians. Judge Carter, who had come to Black's Fork as a settler with Gen. Albert Sidney Johnston, built his first store in 1858. He prospered with the years, acquired a family, and enjoyed the lei-surely life of a gentleman. The Judge had a fine spacious home planted with small trees and surrounded by a board fence and a boardwalk.

Powell had come to Fort Bridger to pack his winter collections and ship them to Bloomington, but once arrived at the post Judge Carter welcomed the Major and Mrs. Powell as his guests. In his library they discussed the Major's plans for the exploration of the Colorado. During their conversations the Judge suggested that a quiet intelligent young officer in the garrison, Sergeant Major Bradley, would make a useful member of the party. Sergeant Bradley was a frequent caller at the Carter home and had made good use of the judge's library. Bradley was somewhat interested in the geology of the region and was most anxious to get out of the army.

George Young Bradley,[6] a member of Company B, Thirty-sixth In-fantry, was a native of Newbury, Massachusetts. He was a skilled boatsman and, to the Major, who nearly always made snap decisions, appeared to be a most suitable member for one of his crews. Bradley had served in the Second Massachusetts Volunteer Infantry during the war, had been wounded at Fredericksburg a few weeks after enlistment, and had been placed in the reserve. After the war had ended he tried his luck as a druggist, but he was unsuccessful and in 1867 reenlisted in the army, requesting frontier duty. Now, after two years of monotony, he said he "would gladly explore the river Styx" to be released from the service. For nearly a year his company along with most of the other por-tions of the post garrison had been escorting engineering parties engaged in the construction of the Union Pacific Railroad through western Wyoming and guarding the overland stage route. He had had enough of it.

There was a little obstacle—Bradley would have to obtain an official release or discharge, but Powell mentioned casually that he could take care of the matter.

Originally Powell had planned to construct boats in the field; in fact, tools for this specific purpose had been taken along, but greater fa-

[6] W. C. Darrah, *Utah Hist. Quart.*, Vol. 15, pp. 30–72.

miliarity with the swift waters of the White River had convinced him that no ordinary boats would ever survive the battering and punishment in the rapids of those streams. Meanwhile, after the expedition had been originally organized, the final route for the Union Pacific Railroad was selected and the main road now extended beyond Green River. Boats could be hauled to the railroad bridge across the river, making it a suitable point to which supplies could be hauled. Major Powell then requested the college authorities to purchase good boats and to freight them to Green River. The more he studied the White and the Green the more convinced he became that he would have to design his own boats. Powell thereupon drew up some sketches and decided to have boats of special construction made by a first-rate builder in Chicago.[7]

The Major and Mrs. Powell took the train at Granger and returned east to take up the next phase of the preparations. Emma left her husband at Chicago to visit her family in Detroit, where she planned to remain while the exploration was in progress.

After a brief stopover at Normal the Major proceeded to Washington where he hoped to fare a little better than last time with Congress. He sought from President Grant an endorsement to authorize army posts to issue rations for a party of twelve men. In this he was, as usual, successful, but he failed to gain any financial support from Congress although the privilege of using army supplies was confirmed by a joint resolution.[8]

Somewhat disappointed, Powell was heartened by renewed contacts with Joseph Henry and Spencer Baird of the Smithsonian Institution, and with Representative Garfield and Senator Cullom. Inability to get funds from Congress made it necessary for the Major to return to Normal and face the various organizations which had helped him in the past, and tell them of his need to raise additional money for the exploration. He again diverted his own salary and was granted five hundred dollars by the trustees of Illinois State Normal University.[9] Illinois Industrial University contributed five hundred dollars and the Chicago Academy of Sciences, through the influence of Dr. Elisha Benjamin Andrews, a similar sum. A few personal friends subscribed small

[7] No sketch or photograph of the boats used in 1869 is known; all published illustrations are of the improved type used in 1871. Powell personally supervised the construction. Chicago *Tribune,* May 8, 1869.

[8] Permission to draw rations was actually a renewal of the original order of 1868.

[9] "Permit me, through your paper, to explain the purposes for which this expedition is made, and its organization, as statements have been made in the public press that are somewhat inaccurate. The expedition is under the auspices of the Illinois Natural History Society. . . ." J. W. Powell, Chicago *Tribune,* May 29, 1869.

amounts to support the work. The Union Pacific Railroad and the Burlington Railroad again issued passes for the men and supplies, sparing Powell this very considerable item of expense.

The next few weeks were spent in placing orders for the miscellaneous items of equipment—arms and ammunition, tools and instruments, and bedding—which would be necessary to outfit the party. It now appeared that not more than ten men would make the trip, and four boats were considered sufficient to carry all of the men and materials down the river.

The Major went to Bagley, a master boatbuilder, to show him a design of his own invention. Powell explained in detail what he wanted in the construction, the quality of materials, and the specifications of workmanship. Three of the boats were to be twenty-one feet long, of well-seasoned white oak, double-ribbed with double stem and sternposts, and further strengthened by bulkheads at each end. The fourth boat, to be of identical design but smaller in size, was to be only sixteen feet long and constructed of white pine, and would, therefore, be of lighter weight. This light construction, plus a sharp cutwater, would give faster rowing, superior maneuverability, and easier handling in time of trouble. The Major intended to use it as a lead boat, which would go ahead and signal to the larger boats at points of danger. Assured that the boats would be ready in four weeks, he went about the business of procuring supplies.

On May 4th, after the four boats were secured to a flatcar and the other supplies loaded in a boxcar, Powell went to Wheaton with Emma to visit Father and Mother Powell. After bidding the family goodbye they hurried to Detroit. This was Wes's first expedition since his marriage in which Emma did not take part.

Mrs. Powell understood her husband's determination and resourcefulness. She shared, perhaps unconsciously, his confidence and, knowing of his careful preparations, was unafraid. "I shall feel no fear if I have no word from my husband for ten months," she wrote.

The Major and Walter left Chicago on May 7th and reached the town of Green River Station on May 11th. The others were already there. They had established a camp along the stream about a half mile below the town to await the arrival of their leader. How strange and motley this crew! joining forces for an adventure for which there was no pay and no reward.[10] The Major furnished food, arms, and equip-

---

[10] No one received pay for participation in the expedition. Contemporary newspapers, letters, and the *Congressional Globe* make this clear. Many years later after Major Powell's

ment—nothing more. Some of the men had spent years on the frontier as trappers or bullwhackers, and yet they were men with intellectual interests and had at least common-school educations. All but two of them were veterans of the Civil War.

First there was John Colton Sumner, twenty-nine,[11] who had become a hunter and trapper after four years of service in the Union Army, and had built himself a cabin and outfitting shack in Middle Park. Jack Sumner had accompanied the Major in the 1867 and 1868 expeditions. His knowledge of the country and his familiarity with boats gave him a key position in the organization.

Oramel G. Howland,[12] thirty-six years of age, six months older than the Major, hailed from Vermont, and had come west in 1860 to seek a fortune in Colorado. A printer and editor, he had worked on Byer's *Rocky Mountain News* and other western papers. Howland had been active in the affairs of the Typographical Union and the Methodist Church; his rough gaunt appearance belied a truly gentle character. Seneca B. Howland, twenty-six, had come west, at his elder brother's insistence, to join the expedition. He had fought in the war and had been wounded at Gettysburg.

William H. Dunn,[13] about thirty, who with O. G. Howland had served the Major both in 1867 and 1868, was the most picturesque mountaineer in the crowd. Dressed habitually in dirty buckskin, with raven hair hanging down his shoulders, he had a supreme disgust for water, scissors, and razor.

William Hawkins,[14] sometimes known as Rhodes or simply "Missouri," had proved his mettle despite the suspicion over the Gus Lanken affair in the 1868 expedition. Hawkins was a fugitive from justice, the result of a minor brush with the law which had even disrupted his service in the Union Army. Full of deviltry and always anxious for adventure, still in his mid-twenties, he was one of the dependables of the party.

death Sumner cried that he had never been paid for his services. The only possible basis for this claim is the commutation clause in the War Department order allowing Powell to draw army rations. By declining the meat ration Powell could obtain cash and hire hunters. See Chicago *Tribune*, May 29, 1869.

[11] W. C. Darrah, *Utah Hist. Quart.*, Vol. 15, pp. 109–12. Sumner in later years became embittered against Powell. The statements attributed to Jack Sumner from 1890 to 1907 must be interpreted in this light. See Stanton, *Colorado River Controversies*.

[12] *ibid.*, pp. 93–94.

[13] *ibid.*, p. 94.

[14] *ibid.*, pp. 106–7.

The youngster of the outfit was a Scotch lad of twenty, Andrew Hall.[15] Too young to join the Union Army, Andy Hall left his home in Illinois to seek his fortune. For four years he roamed the plains, engaged in a dozen Indian skirmishes, and generally raised hell wherever he found it. He was in a sense a genius, full of fun, strong and daring. With judgment far beyond his years and with a humor that never failed him, Andy was the life of the party.

George Bradley had obtained his release from the army. The Major had arranged for that with President Grant. A newcomer and somewhat aloof, Bradley kept to himself. He appeared to be wiry and not particularly strong, but the fellows liked him.

The town of Green River was a scattering of a hundred or so ugly buildings, most of them flimsy unpainted wooden structures with a few others of adobe or brick. The large red section-house on the southeast edge of town was the biggest building in the vicinity. The streets were thick with a yellow dust which was transformed into paste by showers and turned to slime in the rainy season.

Constructed early in 1868 when it had been selected as a terminal station for the railroad, Green River had mushroomed into being at the old emigrant crossing and by September had two thousand inhabitants and many substantial wood buildings. Altogether it appeared to have permanence and promise. To the chagrin of the residents Bryan, fifteen miles to the west, was chosen instead as the base for the terminal buildings, and the future of Green River collapsed overnight. Now in May 1869 there were barely a hundred people remaining in the town, most of whom were drifters staying for a few days near civilization.

The Major arrived at Green River on May 11th, one train later than the flatcars which had brought out the boats and the scientific instruments. With him was his brother, Capt. Walter Henry Powell,[16] a moody fellow who still suffered from the effects of his imprisonment during the war. Most of the men who had worked with the 1868 expedition understood Walter and overlooked his behavior. He was of strong build but his disposition did not allow him to take a fair share of the work. He was gifted with a fine bass voice and upon occasion, when he was willing, would entertain his companions with a repertoire of popular ballads, but often he was sullen, ill-tempered, and at best unpredictable. He was the least popular member of the crew.

[15] Andrew Hall was not a lad of sixteen as is usually stated. *ibid.*, Vol. 16, pp. 505–8.
[16] *ibid.*, Vol. 15, p. 89.

When the freight train arrived from the East, one car, carrying cordage, canvas, and some of the scientific instruments, was missing. Frantic telegraph messages soon revealed that it had been misdirected or intentionally diverted from its route. It was located some hours later and hurried to its destination.

Waiting the arrival of supplies was not the only worry which faced the Major. A stranger who called himself Capt. Samuel Adams [17] was waiting for him. The men were surprised one morning by this friendly and well-spoken but determined fellow who approached the camp and inquired for Major Powell. When informed that the Major had not yet arrived from the East, he introduced himself and said that he had been authorized to take command of the expedition to explore the Colorado canyons. This was news to the party, who had never before heard of Captain Adams, nor had there been the slightest intimation that anyone but Powell was to lead the expedition. Sumner spoke up and said that until Major Powell arrived they would make him welcome and see what arrangements would be made. The captain was a little short of funds and found it necessary to borrow money from the group. There was nothing unusual in this—a stranger was not able to get a check cashed out in that country.

Captain Adams did not remain at the camp but went to Bryan, returning each day and repeating his inquiry for the Major. Major Powell's poise was not easily disturbed and when confronted with the captain merely asked by what authority he spoke. Adams had on his person a number of letters which he attempted to pass off as authorization for his leadership of the exploration. The documents were nothing more than replies from persons to whom Adams had previously addressed letters seeking approval of a projected exploration of the Colorado River. Not one word in these letters could be construed as granting him any authority whatsoever, and most of them did not even come from persons in authority.

Adams was certainly outnumbered by the Powell party and the Major told him firmly where to peddle his schemes. Whether Adams was an impostor, an adventurer, or a confidence man could not be gathered from his manner or conversation, but all felt relieved when he left, apparently without any particular bitterness. As might be expected the captain in his hurried departure neglected to repay the money he had borrowed.

Major Powell found his men impatient to get moving after the long

[17] See Chapter 11, p. 183.

winter of inactivity. They had already been at Green River for three weeks and had found little else than raw whiskey and Ah Chug's apple pies to interest them. Ah Chug, the Chinese cook at the station eating house, made all the pies they could eat for 25 cents each.

The boats were removed from the flatcars, let down into the river at the railroad bridge, and rowed down to the camp on the east bank of the Green. For the first time the men realized that the Major had designed an unusual boat. The bulkheads were four feet in length, giving plenty of buoyancy which would keep the boat afloat if capsized. The oars were eighteen feet long and in each boat there was a hemp rope 130 feet in length. Powell told his men that in a few days they would begin practice in handling the boats and learn the flag signals which he would use from his position in the lead boat. The men grumbled a little among themselves because this was the first notion they had that the expedition would be in camp for some time longer, for the Major had not told anyone of the probable starting date.

The next day Major Powell explained the method by which their scientific observations were to be made. The Major himself would make observations for latitude with the sextant and longitude by the method of lunar distances. The most important work however would be to prepare a map as carefully as conditions would permit. This map would show the meandering course of the river. O. G. Howland was placed in charge of the map drawing. At each bend in the river the direction was to be determined by compass and then the distance between bends estimated. Observers in each boat were to make independent estimates of the distances and the variations in their estimates were to be averaged or corrected. Astronomic stations would be taken fifty miles apart and the intervening distances would be connected by the river measurements. Three times a day the altitude above sea level would be measured at the water's edge. Using the water's edge as an ever-falling base line, the altitudes of the canyon walls would be determined. All of the men were to take turns with the barometric work, but Dunn and Walter Powell were to be held responsible for most of it. Geological sections, measurements, and descriptions of rock strata exposed along the course of the river would be made by the Major and Bradley. Of course, Powell assured his men that although the scientific observations were the objective of their exploration, each man was expected to do his share of whatever physical work and danger would be encountered. Every man was to be a boatsman first.

Powell told his men that they would be assigned to the boats, but that he hoped they would choose their own crews. He explained that the light boat would carry no freight and as commander of the expedition he would serve as pilot and take the lead.

While everything was being made ready for the departure, the Major was approached by Frank Goodman,[18] a cheerful florid Englishman who begged to join the party for the adventure. He had been around the camp for some days and appeared to be strong and willing. He was accepted without question by all of the party. It was soon evident that his idea of adventure did not mix well with the work that was demanded of him. Goodman's rosy expectations were unappreciated by the others, but they decided that he would soon learn.

Jack Sumner and Bill Dunn, it was decided, would be the Major's two oarsmen. Walter Powell and George Bradley would take the second boat, Andy Hall and Billy Hawkins the third, and O. G. Howland, Seneca Howland, and Frank Goodman the fourth.

Powell had already named his boat the *Emma Dean* in honor of his wife, and the other men, not to be outdone, chose appropriate names for their boats. Andy Hall and Billy Hawkins promptly called theirs the *Maid-of-the-Canyon.* Bradley and Walter chose *Kitty Clyde's Sister.* The Howland brothers and Goodman were uninspired so the rest christened their boat the *No-Name.*

Before many days of practicing with the boats and signals, these colorful names were abbreviated to the *Dean,* the *Sister,* the *Maid,* and the *No-Name.*

The party was supplied with provisions considered to be sufficient for ten months [19] though Powell did not believe that the trip would take more than half that time. The food consisted of the usual army rations—flour, sugar, beans, dried apples, salt pork, coffee, and a little tea. They had also obtained a few sides of bacon and some rice. The bulky regulation army mess kit, a mighty armful, fell to Hawkins, chosen the cook, against his wishes and certainly his better judgment. Reconnaissance along the rim of the canyons had indicated that it would be difficult to haul supplies down to the river along the route. The only source of replenishment, the White River Agency, could be reached only by a two-day overland trip. The party might easily be imprisoned in the canyons if during the winter ice jammed the river. It was assumed, of course, that their larder could be augmented from time to time with game and fish and they were well equipped with tackle and with guns for this purpose.

[18] *Utah Hist. Quart.,* Vol. 15, p. 108.
[19] Chicago *Tribune,* July 5, 1869.

The rations were divided into three equal portions, one to be stored in each of the three oaken boats. The tools—axes, augers, hammers, saws, and small pieces—were divided in like manner. The light pine boat carried as little baggage as possible—only a few instruments, three guns, and one change of clothing.

The Ute Indians were known to be friendly to most white travelers, but some of the other tribes, notably the Apaches, were far more hostile, and it was decided to arm each man in the expedition so that he would be prepared for all eventualities. Each man was a veritable walking arsenal, well armed for defense or procuring game. There were two revolvers apiece, some of them Colt dragoons and other army pieces. There were four or five Winchester rifles, breechloaders carrying seventeen shots, and two or three carbines for mounting service or hunting buffalo. There were several ponderous double-barreled rifles. Each man had two hunting knives, which could be used as bayonets, and much more ammunition than there was any need for. The Major took with him some calico, tobacco, and trinkets with which he could treat with the Indians if the occasion demanded.

Among the instruments which were borrowed from the Smithsonian Institution and from the Illinois Industrial University were mercurial barometers of simple construction—long glass tubes with a bulb of mercury open at the bottom but covered with a leather flap. These barometers, though relatively accurate, were an infernal nuisance. If for any reason the mercury was tipped out or the barometer broken, the tubes had to be boiled to drive off the air to create a vacuum. It was an almost daily occurrence to damage or otherwise upset the barometers. Most of the other instruments were used for surveying and taking astronomical observations.

Finally on May 23rd everything was in readiness. The Major announced to his men that their canyon voyage would begin on the morrow. Next morning all hands were up before dawn to check the boats and pack the provisions. Their safety would depend upon both.

About noon the men rowed the boats upstream to the railroad bridge, tied them fast, and called upon Jake Field's [20] eating parlor for a lighthearted meal of ham, eggs, and apple pie—and one last drink of Jake's homemade whiskey.

---

[20] Jacob W. Field was the proprietor of a trading post and outfitting house which in the 1870's became a well-known establishment. William, *Pacific Tourist*, p. 101.

8

1869 · First Expedition Down the Colorado

ON MAY 24, 1869, at one o'clock in the afternoon, amid the cheering of the townspeople who came to see them off, the Powell party nosed their four boats into the current of Green River just below the bridge at Green River Station. Major Powell, with Jack Sumner and Bill Dunn, in the light pine *Emma Dean* led the way, and following close behind, Walter Powell and George Bradley in the *Kitty Clyde's Sister,* Andy Hall and Billy Hawkins in the *Maid-of-the-Canyon,* and O. G. Howland, Seneca Howland, and Frank Goodman in the *No-Name.* The men rowed the boats beyond sight of their friends standing on the bridge and the exploration of the "Great Unknown" was under way.[1]

The river, eighty yards wide at the railroad crossing, was in late spring a very shallow stream, scarcely five or six feet deep with a current of five miles an hour. The sloping banks, barren and rocky, glistened with alkali crusted upon them when pools trapped during

[1] The source materials for the 1869 expedition are extensive and scattered. Recently, however, the Utah State Historical Society has published the essential records with comprehensive annotation. My account is based entirely upon original sources. I have disregarded even F. S. Dellenbaugh's *Romance of the Colorado River.* There are three diaries of the expedition: in order of importance, G. Y. Bradley, J. W. Powell, and J. C. Sumner. There are letters by Major Powell, O. G. Howland, Walter Powell, and Andy Hall. Of contemporary accounts there are, besides the newspaper dispatches, the Major's "Official" 1875 report, *Exploration of the Colorado River of the West,* a similar narrative in *Scribner's Monthly,* 1875, and his preliminary account in W. A. Bell, *New Tracks in North America,* pp. 554–664. The secondary sources are generally unreliable. On one extreme is Summers, *Conquerors of the River,* which is admittedly fiction, yet no less than eminent geologists have accepted it as a true account. R. B. Stanton's *Colorado River Controversies* is in some respects worse because it purports to be a scholarly treatment on certain phases of river history. This book, hypercritical of Powell, was actually written by Chalfant and does not represent the opinions of Stanton. The facts are manhandled in a reprehensible manner. Stanton, deceased before the book was edited, deserves none of the criticism against *Colorado River Controversies.* In such books as Freeman, *The Colorado,* Corle, *Listen Bright Angel,* Waters, *The Colorado,* the accounts of Powell's exploration are based entirely upon secondary sources. Dellenbaugh wrote *Romance of the Colorado River* more than thirty years after he had participated in the second expedition of 1871–1872. He did not know of the existence of Bradley's diary nor the letters of Hall and Howland. For a critical appraisal of all known materials pertaining to the 1869 expedition the reader is referred to *Utah Hist. Quart.,* Vols. 15, 16, and 17.

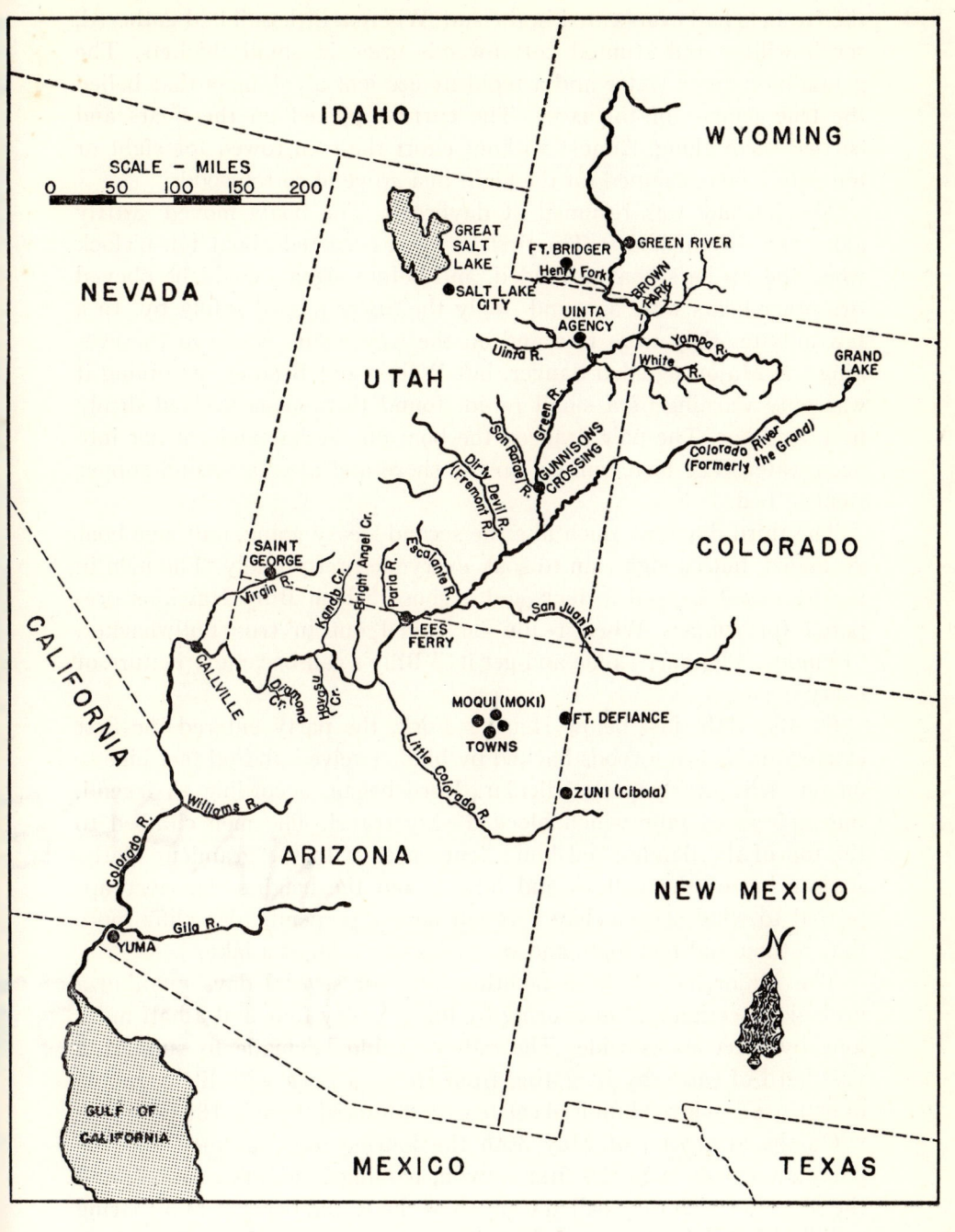

the freshets had evaporated in the sun. Where a little soil had gathered, scrub willow and stunted cottonwoods grew in small thickets. The gentle blue-green water and a tepid breeze lent a calmness that belied the true temper of the river. The current picked up the boats and carried them along. Almost without effort the men rowed for eight or ten miles and encamped for the night in a grove of cottonwoods.

The journey was resumed at daybreak. The boats moved swiftly along for several hours. The first incident occurred about ten o'clock when the Major's boat grounded, and before signals could be obeyed two other boats were aground—only the *Sister* passed safely by. In a few minutes they were free and on the way again. Early in the evening the Major signaled danger, but Walter and Bradley, assuming it was only warning of a small rapid, found themselves wedged firmly in a sand bar. The pair dragged the boat off the bar and got her into deep water. The men camped on the shore and after a second supper went to bed.

The third day was much like the second—easy going, only one boat grounded, but enough rain to soak everyone pretty badly. The men in the lead boat bagged a duck and a goose, which Billy Hawkins prepared for supper. When ready he called out in true bullwhacker, "Plunder! Plunder! Come and get it!" Billy's call became a feature of every meal.

On the 27th, just below Henry's Fork, the party entered the first canyon amid cottonwoods backed by bluffs twelve hundred feet high—on one side nearly perpendicular. Here began, according to legend, the rapids and falls which blocked easy travel. The men climbed to the top of the flaming red bluffs, entranced with the grandeur of the sculpturing of the valleys and hills. From the heights the river appeared to wind serpent-like through nearly perpendicular cliffs more than a thousand feet high, and was deep and calm as a lake.

The Major halted the expedition here for several days, making a geological section and measuring by line a valley four and a half miles long by three miles wide. The valley "could be made to support a vast herd of cattle by irrigating from Henry's Fork with little trouble or expense"—eleven hundred cattle were wintered there in 1868.

On the afternoon of May 30th the journey was resumed and the party passed through the first canyon, naming it Flaming Gorge, and the second, which they called Canyon of the Rapid because of a roaring rapid with a fall of several feet. There was plenty of water, and although the men removed shoes and coats in preparation for a ducking, everyone ran it safely. The party passed a third canyon, naming it Kingfisher Canyon.[2]

The next day was spent in passing rapids, one so bad as to require letting the boats down by ropes. Their progress had been but ten miles, and the end of the day found the party encamped at another difficult rapid which could be passed only by a let-down with ropes.

The first of June there was more of the same, but the going was faster. The first let-down was followed by a long ride at lightning speed through swirling water and tumultuous waves until another fall was encountered. After another let-down with ropes the men enjoyed another long fast ride—whooping and shouting as the boats were whipped along. Already they had become contemptuous of calm water; let a white foam show itself and their listlessness was transformed into jolly action. Near nightfall they came upon a blockade caused by a great fall of red sandstone. There was daylight enough to lift down only one boat because the cargo—two thousand pounds to each boat—had to be carried over a precarious trail around the fall. The men found the name "Ashley" painted on a large rock some height above the shore and appropriately called the place Ashley Falls. Curiously, the Major was ignorant of the identity of his predecessor. Ashley, who he thought was a trapper, was indeed Gen. William H. Ashley, who in 1825 [3] descended the canyons in bull boats from a point near the present town of Fontanelle to the Uinta River.

A short easy run of fifteen miles next day through Red Canyon brought them to a pleasant natural campsite at a spot known to all trappers as Brown's Hole. On this famous ground, the one traditional rendezvous of all mountaineers, the Powell party remained for several days examining the country and making observations.

On June 5th the men crossed the river about fifteen miles below Brown's Hole and measured a line to the bluffs—three and a half miles—which extended fifteen or twenty miles along the river. The next day was a day of labor—the river was so broad and still and the wind so contrary that the crews had to row all the way. After fifteen miles of wearisome toil the boats came to the mouth of the canyon below Brown's Hole. The almost perpendicular walls seemed to close

[2] Kingfisher Canyon was so named in 1869, not 1871 as claimed by Dellenbaugh. The Powell party, of course, named the canyons as they progressed; the second expedition named many landmarks not christened by the first party. The Major renamed various localities in later years.

[3] Gen. William H. Ashley was a famous explorer, politician, and fur trader. See H. C. Dale, *Ashley-Smith Explorations*.

in forebodingly, towering more than two thousand feet above the river bed. The next few days were spent in exploring the country on both sides of the river.

On June 8th the Major decided to continue the journey, and what had seemed to be fairly easy rapids when viewed from the bluffs above proved to be difficult and hazardous. The farther the party progressed, the wilder the river became. As the foaming waters whipped the boats they galloped and bucked through the rapids.

Andy surprised the Major with a display of learning by suggesting that the canyon be named Lodore after the waterfall in Cumberland (England) commemorated in Southey's poem. The black massive walls were ominous, but no more than the river with its spinning funnels and treacherous crosscurrents. The rush of water was accompanied by a deep rumbling caused by the bumping and banging of huge boulders being carried along the bottom of the river by the force of the rushing water.

Suddenly, shortly after noon the lead boat, running a considerable distance ahead of the others, came upon an alarming stretch; first a short fall of ten or twelve feet, which was run easily, but below it, curving around a bend and going out of sight, a long steep rapid with a trough perhaps sixty feet long filled with rocks. From below the men could hear a steady drumming roar as from other fierce rapids beyond their view. Immediately in front of them the water boiled furiously and the deafening sound, bottled in the canyon, promised a sinister situation.

As the lead boat approached the chute at the foot of the first rapid, the Major shouted to his crew. Sumner and Dunn spun the *Dean* to shore and Powell leaped to the rocks to see if a portage would be necessary, leaving Dunn to signal to the other boats to land. The *Sister* landed safely, so the Major felt no more concern for the others. He walked down the shore to examine the ground for a portage. Suddenly he heard a shout and turning around he saw the *No-Name* coming over the falls. Howland had seen the signal in time but, because the boat had shipped so much water, it was nearly unmanageable in the swift current.

The first fall was not great and the *No-Name* came down easily, but the relentless current swept it into a channel filled with dangerous rocks which broke the waves into whirlpools and beat them into foam. As the *No-Name* tumbled into the chute it was dashed upon a rock, the impact throwing the men clear.[4] All three, Howland, Seneca, and Goodman, clambered in again and retrieved two of the oars. Meanwhile the *Maid* reached shore above and the Major now hurried down the rocks. The other crews too, realizing the gravity of the situation, were coming down the shore as fast as possible.

The *No-Name* was stove in and sinking slowly. Howland apparently decided to run her as long as possible and to try to reach a sand bar in midstream, a couple of hundred yards below. The current carried the boat into another rock-filled riffle. The boat was taking a terrific thumping and was starting to break up. At the instant Goodman was washed overboard the Howland brothers leaped free. O. G. Howland reached the bar and saw his brother safe on the bar about a hundred feet farther downstream. Fifty feet above, Frank Goodman was hanging on for dear life to a boulder as big as a barrel, begging weakly for assistance. He had taken in so much water he was in danger of drowning. The Howland brothers managed to get a piece of driftwood to him, and he clung to it until his companions reached him.

During this time the men on shore were rushing down to help the crew of the *No-Name,* but by that wild ride they had been carried out of sight. The marooned trio built a small fire after drying their matches, but their plight was precarious. The river was rising rapidly. Meanwhile the rest onshore were lifting down the light *Dean.* When the instruments were dumped out Sumner, at great risk, took the *Dean* across the channel and brought back Howland, Seneca, and Goodman. "We were as glad to shake hands with them as if they had been on a voyage round the world and wrecked on a distant coast."[5] They were unhurt except for some bad bruises.

They had lost everything except shirts and drawers—the uniform they wore in passing all bad rapids. Their clothing, bedding and other personal belongings were gone. So were two thousand pounds of provisions. One-third of their larder had vanished, half of the mess kit, and three of the barometers. The men sat glumly by the campfire at the head of a rapid more than a mile long, gazing at the test which awaited them in the morning. They called the spot Disaster Falls. A disaster

[4] Howland said, on June 19, "About one o'clock the signal boat signals at the foot of a very bad rapid to go ashore . . . . but owing to not understanding the signal, the crew of the 'No Name' failed very effectually, owing in the main, to having so much water aboard as to make her nearly or quite unmanageable; otherwise, the mistake was seen by us in time to save her." *Rocky Mountain News,* July 17, 1869.

[5] J. W. Powell, July 18, 1869 (*cf.* Chicago *Tribune,* Aug. 20, 1869).

it was. Without the barometers it would be impossible to determine the altitude of the mountains through which they passed. They had come less than 150 miles, had not even reached the junction of the Uinta and the Green, and had nine hundred miles more to go. They had lost one boat and had nearly lost three of their comrades.

Half a mile down the river the after-cabin of the *No-Name* had stranded on the rocks. The barometers and other valued articles were in it, but the Major would not risk his men in trying to retrieve them. He considered going out to Salt Lake City and telegraphing to New York for new barometers. By morning he had considered many plans, concluding finally to attempt to get to the wreckage if it was still there.

When day dawned the wreckage of the *No-Name* was there; it had been carried only fifty feet lower from where it had been the night before. The water was receding, so the Major ordered the portage first. In the afternoon Jack Sumner and Andy Hall volunteered to take the *Dean* to the wreck and to try to locate the barometers. Major Powell joined in when the men onshore gave rousing cheers for their comrades when they returned successfully from the wreck. He was pleased that they were elated in saving the scientific instruments. When the *Dean* landed Andy held high a two-gallon jug of whiskey which had been stowed away against the Major's orders. This was the object of all the cheering! "I am glad they did," Powell wrote that day, "for they think it does them good—as they are drenched every day by the melting snow that runs down this river." As for the rations, Bradley mused, "We have plenty of rations left, much more than we care to carry around the rapids, especially when they are more than a mile long." [6]

Amidst a sublime setting of walls towering thousands of feet above the river and of water lashed to foam and rushing with astonishing fury, they carried down the supplies, picking their way over the boulders, and lowered the boats by rope to avoid the worst of Disaster Falls. The fun was over. Day after day for six days each test was more grueling than the last. A run of five miles in one day was considered good. There was scarcely a day that the men were not soaked with spray, and often the boats were upset or someone was pitched overboard. The supplies too were repeatedly soaked by the spray or immersion. The beans were sprouting, the dried apples swelling, and the flour moldering. To make matters worse, although mountain sheep were occasionally seen, no one had been able to kill game of any kind for

[6] G. Y. Bradley, MS, *Diary*, June 9, 1869.

more than a week. Hawkins was worried about this damage to their supplies. The Major was by no means unconcerned, but he was confident that he would be able to obtain ample replenishments from the agency.

Hawkins prepared the monotonous fare cheerfully and eating was a pleasure, regardless. As the strips of bacon sliced from a rancid side curled with crispness on long sticks over the fire, the dripping grease was caught in a tin pan. Biscuits, nicknamed gods (a blasphemous euphemism), made from flour, water, and a bit of soda were baked in gold-pans. When ready the familiar "Plunder, plunder" brought the men from their camp tasks.

The river smoothed and widened after leaving the canyon of Lodore. For hours the boats drifted along and the men let the current bear them down the river. At times the cliffs opened and great deserts reached beyond to distant mountains. Sometimes the boats moved dreamily through parklands with occasional herds of elk and deer grazing along the grassy banks. They passed grassy islands in the river. It was a very welcome relief from the toil of Lodore. Now and then their respite was interrupted when the walls closed in and short but dangerous rapids were encountered. Thus they passed through Whirlpool and Split Mountain canyons. The river cut a course due south in Wyoming, looped westward at Lodore into Colorado, and now resumed a southward course in eastern Utah. They had run through the Uinta Mountains and were now passing through the badlands of Utah.

On the evening of June 17th the party camped on a strand fifty yards wide and about a quarter of a mile in length and thickly overgrown with pine, willow, sagebrush, and grass. While the men were waiting for Andy to dish out supper a gust of wind spread the cooking fire to a few pine trees, and before anyone considered it serious another gust fanned the blaze to a sheet of flame that swept down upon the canyon. The men rushed for the boats and dropped down the river a few rods, but the flames caught up with them again. Only by running a bad rapid in twilight were they able to gain safety. One man lost his hat, another a shirt, another his pants. Walter Powell lost a part of his prized mustache. Several others were painfully scorched about the face. In the rush Hawkins snatched up the mess kit and started for a boat. In attempting to jump, he slipped and fell into ten feet of water and lost the mess kit. From then on the baling cups—one cup for two men—served coffee.[7]

The next day after a short run of five miles at lightning speed the

[7] O. G. Howland, *Rocky Mountain News*, Aug. 18, 1869.

party came upon the Yampa River which enters the Green from the east. Here the Major and his men remained for several days making a set of observations. The walls had lowered to approximately eight hundred feet. The weather had been delightful, the fishing was good, and the men were in excellent spirits. The rations were spread out to dry and one sack of spoiled rice was thrown out. Instead of the monotonous fare, Bradley enlivened the provender with a ten-pound white-fish, Andy and Howland with a string of twenty fine trout, and Bill Hawkins with a large buck fat as a beef. He had shot it on a mountain 2,800 feet high some miles from camp and carried in both hindquarters himself. Goodman brought in a forequarter. Bradley, next day, considering the scarcity of game, went out and brought in the other quarter, which had been tied to a tree out of reach of wolves. The Major and Jack Sumner took turns getting sick, and the party had to remain in camp until the pair were well enough to continue. A sick man was a double liability in the boats—he might not be able to act quickly in time of trouble and the other crewmen might not be able to take care of a helpless companion.

The final few days of June were marked by fairly easy going; each day a good run was made. On the 27th they made sixty-three miles, some of it by rowing. The greatest evil was mosquitoes so mean and numerous that the men were in anguish from literally thousands of bites. Suddenly on June 28th they came upon the junction of the Uinta River. The White River entered the Green about a mile below on the other side. The first stage of their journey had ended safely. The Major wrote letters to his wife, his mother, the *Chicago Tribune,* and to President Edwards of Normal. He then made plans to go overland to the Uinta Indian Agency to replenish the supplies of the expedition and to make some incidental observations on the Indians.[8]

Powell remained at the junction camp for several days making observations and hunting unsuccessfully for a fossil outcrop reported by Gen. B. M. Hughes when he crossed the river along the Berthoud trail near this point with twenty-two wagons in 1865. On July 2nd the Major, Bill, and Frank Goodman left for the agency, Walter Powell and Andy Hall having gone ahead with goods which could be traded. Bradley, Sumner, the Howlands, and Dunn remained in camp to fight mosquitoes and rattlesnakes.

The days during which they had not been able to communicate with

---

[8] Capt. Pardyn Dodds, the agent of the Uinta Indian Agency, was at Salt Lake City purchasing food for his commissary.

the world about and beyond the canyon walls had gathered into weeks. No word from the men had reached their homes, and it would be a week or two more before the letters dispatched by the Major at the agency could be delivered to their destinations. While Major Powell was enjoying his brief stopover at the mouth of Uinta River the *Cheyenne Leader* related a story of his death with the loss of the entire party at Brown's Hole. The accounts gave gruesome details of the disaster in a terrifying whirlpool. One John A. Risdon suddenly appeared from nowhere and passed himself as the sole survivor of the party of twenty-one men who, according to his story, having abandoned their special boats, had embarked down the river in a canoe twenty-one feet long.[9] The sympathy that Risdon received from all quarters included sufficient funds for him to return to Illinois and gain notoriety wherever he went. He even called upon the Governor of Illinois and made public appearances. At first a few newspapers like the Detroit *Press* and the Chicago *Tribune* editorially doubted Risdon's story, although the details he provided were almost convincing. Mrs. Powell and a number of other persons retaliated in print denouncing Risdon as an impostor, pointing out that no person by that name ever belonged to the Major's party and calling attention to other inaccuracies in his yarn.

Before Risdon could be disposed of another man, calling himself Jack Sumner, appeared in Wyoming and said that he, not Risdon, was the sole survivor of the disaster. Within a few more days Risdon was unmasked as an escaped convict who had cooked up the whole business to raise funds. The fraudulent "Jack Sumner" was likewise exposed. Finally, with the receipt of letters from the Major, the rumor gradually subsided, and the fact that the Major was quite alive became somewhat reluctantly accepted.

The rumor had started with the drowning of Mr. John Hook, who, two days after the Major left Green River Station, decided to make his own exploration of the canyons, but being less fortunate than the Major, met his death in rapids too difficult for his risky boat. When the intelligence of the drowning reached Fort Bridger Powell was confused with Hook, and the story blossomed into a first-class fantasy. The newspapers of the country made far more of the alleged disaster than they did of the factual information of the expedition.

Major Powell visited the Uinta Indian Agency and the Ute settle-

[9] John A. Risdon was an impostor, confidence man, and horse-thief. Omaha *Republican*, July 3, 1869, and Chicago *Tribune*, July 2–10, 1869.

ment. Among the Utes he met Tsauwiat, a chief who was reputed to be more than a hundred years old, with skin in deep folds and wrinkles on his hands and body.[10] Tsauwiat's wife, aged but much younger than he, was an intelligent, talkative, and influential woman who enjoyed the unusual privilege of sitting in the council ring. With great pride she showed the Major their carefully cultivated fields of wheat, turnips, beets, potatoes, and other vegetables. Each Indian had a third of an acre of land and the plantings were growing handsomely. The land was irrigated under the supervision of white men, but the Indians were learning aptly how to plow, sow, and water their farms. They refused, however, to build houses, attributing their unwillingness to evil spirits. Powell observed that their general filthiness would make any house uninhabitable. As the Major took leave with samples of handiwork he had purchased the red men were preparing to go to see the new railroad—a tribute to the universal curiosity of mankind.

The past year had been a very lean one for the Indians; their stores were meager and new crops had not yet matured. The shelves at the agency were almost empty. The agent had, in fact, gone to Salt Lake City for the express purpose of securing additional stores. Meanwhile very slight help could be obtained at the agency post. The Major bartered for and purchased all that could be spared.

On July 5th the land parties returned to the river camp. Bill Hawkins and Andy, with two Utes, arrived with three hundred pounds of flour for which the Major had traded off some coffee, tobacco, calico, and trinkets brought along for trading with the Indians. When the Major returned to camp several days later and rejoined the party with such trifling supplies as he could buy, the men expressed anxiety. They had had discouraging luck at fishing and hunting, and thus had been forced to rely upon reduced rations for some time. What they had been able to capture or kill did not compensate for the other deficiencies. To make matters more serious, they had just thrown away three sacks of moldy flour, two rancid hams, and some wormy beans.

There was no dissension, but it was almost certain to be difficult to make the food last unless their fortune was considerably better than heretofore. As a meager supplement to the fare, Andy dried strips of venison on a frame of green willow twigs built over a fire. They must now proceed as rapidly as convenient and terminate the trip within four months. Goodman, being discouraged and unable to raise an

---

[10] Tsauwiat (Sowiette) was a famous friend of the Mormons in 1850 and thereafter.

outfit, left the party at the agency. His departure was not regretted.

The next morning the men took to their boats and set out from the last signs of civilization for a distance, according to government maps, of nearly eight hundred miles. Just above the mouth of the White River, on an island in the Green, a garden had been planted. Fresh fruit had been mighty scarce and the temptation to steal some greens was irresistible. The Major, Andy, and Bill Dunn filled their arms with young beets, turnips, carrots, and potatoes. The men rowed a few miles down the river and paused to enjoy the stolen fruit. Of course the season was not advanced enough to yield sizable vegetables, so Andy cooked up the whole mess as greens. It was a not-quite-unpleasant stew. After eating their fill and disposing of the remainder, the men resumed the journey. They had not gone a mile before all hands except Bradley and Howland were violently nauseated. Bradley explained that the potato tops were so bitter he had not eaten any. The Major said their illness was caused by a narcotic in the potato leaves, but Hall swore that it was all his fault; in their haste he had only half-cooked the stuff. Sumner wrote in his diary, "We all learned one lesson—never to rob gardens." [11] Despite the experience the progress for the day amounted to thirty-seven miles. Next day they rowed thirty-four miles through a channel with no more current than a lazy canal.

On July 8th the Major, Bradley, and Walter went out with barometers to measure the west wall. The face was steep and difficult and in one place the Major found himself on a small ledge, unable to get up or down. His body was turned in such a manner that the stump of his arm rested against the rocks. Holding on with the fingers of his good arm to steady himself, and not daring to let go, he called for help. Bradley, comprehending the Major's predicament, picked his way to a ledge above, took off his drawers, braced himself, and let the legs down as a rope. Powell, tense, his fingers already trembling, waited a moment, released his grip on the rocks, and reached for the dangling drawers. Within a split second he had grabbed hold, whereupon Bradley pulled him up safely.[12] It was too close to think about. After measuring the summit at 1,598 feet they climbed down without further incident and returned to the boats. During the afternoon nine rapids were passed,

[11] This anecdote is related in detail in the Bradley and Sumner diaries.
[12] G. Y. Bradley, MS, *Diary*, July 8, 1869; J. W. Powell, *Exploration of the Colorado River*, p. 34 (in which he erroneously dates the incident June 18th).

all by running, but in one of them all the boats were filled with water. Near nightfall the Major called a halt at the head of a rapid which he concluded was too dangerous to run.

While making a long portage in the morning Bradley found fossil shark teeth, and the Major gathered fossil shells similar to those occurring at Fort Bridger. Before the day was over they made twenty miles, passing twenty rapids, two of them requiring let-downs. A terrible gale of hot dry air swept through the canyon—grim warning that to climb out and walk to civilization would mean almost certain death. The boats were beginning to show signs of serious wear due to the frequent battering against the jagged rocks. It was decided to stop over for a day and repair them. While the work was being done the Major and Howland measured the east side of the canyon, which, four miles back from the river, towered four thousand feet.

The men admired—but also resented a little—the Major's supreme self-assurance in running the rapids, as in doing everything else. When the Major met his match on Sunday, July 11th, the men quietly enjoyed proof that he could be upset too. In attempting to run a rapid the *Emma Dean* was swamped. Two rifles, in this remote wilderness worth far more than their three hundred dollars cost, and watches valued at eight hundred dollars were lost. The Major lost his bedding and one of the barometers. Powell was thrown clear of the boat and because he could not hold on to the side as it rolled over and over, he struck out and swam to shore. Sumner and Dunn tugged the boat onshore but lost the oars. All this happened within half a mile of the day's starting point.

The river became more difficult as they continued. On July 12th the men were forced to make twenty portages in passing ten bad rapids. The next day, running through lower canyon walls, they passed the mouth of the Little White River, a stream two rods wide and a foot deep coming in from the west. About one o'clock they came to the old Spanish Crossing where for centuries it was possible to ford the Green River—it being 250 yards wide but very shallow.

The country about was dry, useless, and destitute. Hardly a bird, in this desert of scrubby cottonwoods, broke the monotony. To this series of canyons the Major gave the names Desolation Canyon to the upper part and Coal Canyon (subsequently renamed Gray Canyon) to the lower portion.

For two or three days the air was hazed with the acrid smoke of a distant forest fire. Great fires, which often were set by Indians driving game, ravaged thousands upon thousands of acres of timber. The Major had witnessed several such fires and had traveled through vast burned-over areas in 1867 and 1868.

On July 16th as the day was drawing to a close and lengthening shadows imposed a threatening aspect upon the dark canyons, without warning, but to the delight of everyone, the Grand River broke into the Green with a strong but calm current. They landed the boats and pitched camp. For miles around there was scarcely any timber, trees, or shrubs except a few straggling hackberries. The Green was about eighty yards across, the Grand about one hundred and twenty-five. At the moment, both streams were approximately ten feet deep, but flood lines on the sides indicated that there was an annual rise of twenty-five to thirty feet at the junction.

For four days the men remained in camp taking observations, making needed repairs, going over the stores, and sleeping off heavy doses of beaver-tail soup. The flour was in very sorry condition. By careful sifting through mosquito netting, the lumps and molded portions were removed. Two hundred pounds had to be discarded. The flour bags were washed thoroughly, dried, and refilled. Only six hundred pounds of flour remained and the outlook was far from reassuring. The Major had intended to remain at the junction until August 7th to observe the solar eclipse, but because of the dwindling food supplies, it was decided to delay only long enough to measure latitude and longitude. Previously the junction of the Grand and Green had not been located within a hundred miles of this spot.

On July 21st the real work of exploration began. Rapids were encountered about two miles from the junction, and before long rough going became virtually continuous. Four portages, two of them within a hundred yards of each other, were necessary to advance eight and one-half miles. Beds that night were made by piling rocks along the edge of the water and spreading sand over them.

The next day was marked by another short run, less than two miles, but this time because the Major had called a halt so that he could examine the disarranged strata which dipped in both directions away from the river. This was the axis of a vast fold in the strata and from that point the upper rocks gradually came down with a gentle dip to the southwest. The Major wrote in his journal, "Unraveled the mystery of the rocks." [13] While the Major and Walter were making barometric readings, Bill Hawkins, yearning for better food, picked up the sextant

[13] J. W. Powell, MS, *Geological Notes*. See also *Utah Hist. Quart.*, Vol. 15, pp. 132–39.

to determine the latitude and longitude to the nearest "pie." The men found fresh moccasin tracks in the sand near the camp, but no other trace of the owner could be found. The south wall was only one thousand feet high and an Indian might descend to the river without difficulty.

On July 23rd the boats came to a long succession of rapids. Five of them were run and four portages were made within half a mile. By nightfall they had gone a little more than four miles and camped at the head of furious cataracts. From where the men stood it was evident that at least four would have to be portaged. Thirty feet above the river driftwood wedged between the rocks stood as mute testimony to the high water which in some seasons lashed through the canyons.

July 24th was spent letting the boats down over the four rapids, progressing only three-quarters of a mile in ten hours of hard labor. The Major sat on a boulder along the shore studying the waves, which, had it not been for the canyon walls, would look more like a gale at sea. The ridges of the waves stacked and piled at all angles to the river with swells, cones, and even crests of foam, which fell back upon the parent wave.

Four days of rough going took a toll of the boats. Both of the heavy oaken ones were leaking badly. The men were impatient to continue, but reluctant to postpone necessary repairs. On the 26th the Major, finding a lateral canyon, landed, and with Walter, Bradley, Seneca, and Andy, began climbing, hoping to get enough pitch to calk the boats. The heat was so oppressive that everyone backed out except the Major. He was lucky enough to reach the summit and gather two pounds of pitch, which he filled into his empty shirt sleeve. Caught in a bad storm and downpour, Powell made a descent as hastily as mud and the rugged country permitted. He crossed a mountain torrent rushing down a dry stream bed, mixing up a thick spattering red paste as it moved ahead. The Major managed to get to the camp ten minutes before the creek did, where, to his surprise, it had rained but little.

The next day was memorable, not because of the portages, although they did pass seven rapids, but because two mountain sheep were killed. With the reduced state of provisions this godsend was hailed as the greatest event of the trip. Sour bread and rotten bacon were poor fare for hard work. Even the Major, who usually disregarded discomforts as trifles, had written this masterpiece of understatement in his diary, "Supper poor."

For twelve days the men had toiled and worked their way through Cataract Canyon, stopping only once to measure the altitude of the walls. On the evening of the 28th the boats came to a creek entering the river from the west. The stream was not given on any of the maps. Sumner described the water "about as filthy as the washing from the sewers of some large, dirty city, but stinks more than cologne ever did." The Major named it Dirty Devil Creek.

The next afternoon, high on a terrace, the men sighted the ruins of Pueblo cliff dwellers. The entire party climbed up to explore the uninhabited buildings. Most of the walls had fallen down but the architectural features were plainly evident. The dwelling consisted of four rooms, 13 x 16, 13 x 18, 13 x 16, and 13 x 28 feet in dimension, arranged as an L, two rooms in each direction. The rafters had rotted completely and the mortar had crumbled away. The men found many specimens of curiously marked fragments of pottery scattered about the site. The Major estimated that the ruins were at least two centuries old, but likely much more ancient.

The men had been anxiously anticipating their arrival at the San Juan River for several days. A Mormon map in their possession gave the distance from the junction—by land of course—as fifty miles, but by the official federal map, "probably" a hundred miles. On the last day of July they had to row twenty miles against a strong head wind and enroute found granite boulders for the first time since leaving Green River Station—an ominous warning of trouble ahead. About two o'clock in the afternoon they reached the San Juan, another dirty stream, which at the moment was thirty yards wide and fifteen inches deep. So this was the place where some big liar said he had laid out an entire city! The measured distance between the Grand River junction and the San Juan was 116 miles, which to the Powell party meant eighteen portages, forty-five rapids run, and eleven days of discouraging and wearisome labor.

For two days the Major, supremely indifferent to the diminishing supplies—the larder was now short of everything but flour and coffee— and growing anxiety of his comrades, ordered a halt for several days to make observations. Bradley recorded the sentiments of all of the men in his diary:

August 2nd . . . doomed to be here another day, perhaps more than that for Major has been taking observations ever since we came here and seems no nearer done now than when he began. He ought to get the latitude and longitude of every mouth of a river not known before and we are willing to face starvation if necessary to do it but further than that he should not ask us to wait, and he must go on soon or the consequences will be different from what he anticipates.

If we could get game or fish we should be all right, but we have not caught a single mess of fish since we left the junction.

The next day the Major agreed to move on, and spirits were buoyed by finding two mountain sheep in a little valley opening to the south. Jack Sumner killed one, and although they chased the other for nearly an hour, they were unable to bag it.

For two or three days the going was easy. On August 3rd they advanced thirty-three miles and the party camped at the Crossing of the Fathers. Next day they reached the Paria River, thirty-five miles below. Rapids had, however, reappeared. All hands had learned to prefer rapids to still water, but some of the men, grown weary, wanted their rapids very mild.

On the 5th two furious rapids were passed, the first by running and the second by two difficult portages. In the latter the river fell fifteen feet in twenty-five yards. While lifting the *Maid-of-the-Canyon* over the rocks the bottom was stove in. The *Maid* had to be repaired before the voyage could be resumed, so the men were forced to camp on a sand bar in a heavy wind and downpour of rain.

The next morning the men and boats were ready to get under way and head into the rapids—one per mile. The men were suffering more each day from exposure and hunger. The constant wetting, perspiring, and insufficient food, were beginning to tell on everyone, but least of all on the Major. Actually, his infirmity, which prevented him from doing some of the difficult physical labor, preserved his resistance. Each portage exhausted the men a little more and sapped morale as well as strength.

An eclipse predicted for August 7th gave the men a needed respite. The boats too were aging sadly. Bradley had to make four new ribs for his and the other boats needed calking. Meanwhile the Major and Walter climbed to the summit of the mountains to make observations on the eclipse, but clouds obscured the view.[14]

On August 8th there was terrible work. Driftwood was so scarce that it took all hands to find enough to bake bread and boil coffee. On August 9th it was worse with four long portages and twenty-seven bad rapids run in thirteen miles. There were never so many portages in one day before, but then, never so little to carry. The walls of the canyon now averaged three thousand feet. While the Major admired the "scenery on a grand scale," and "walked a mile on marble pave-

[14] The eclipse was the subject of wide public interest, newspapers in many cities publishing full-page stories of the celestial event.

ment polished smooth in many places, in others embossed in a thousand fantastic patterns," the men looked instead at their ragged clothing and were "interested now only in how we shall get through the canyon and once more to civilization though we are more than ever sanguine of success." Continuing this musing Bradley wrote:

Fortunately we are a happy-go-lucky set of fellows and look more to our present comfort than our future danger and as the cook has a fine lot of beans cooking with every prospect that his sweating and swearing will issue in an ample breakfast in the morning, we shall make our beds tonight and no doubt sleep as soundly as if surrounded by all the comforts of home.

In mid-afternoon on August 10th the party came upon the Little Colorado River, "a loathesome little stream . . . as disgusting as there is on the continent; 3 rods wide and about 3 feet deep, half of its volume and 2/3 of its weight is mud and salt." [15] The canyon walls were nearly four thousand feet high and practically inaccessible. The Major called for a stopover for two or three days to determine latitude and longitude. If James White had gone through the canyons from this point to Callville on a raft, the men figured that they had little to fear from waterfalls below. They derived little comfort from the report. The truth was that the men were discontented, uneasy, and anxious to move on. Bradley wrote in his diary under August 11th:

If Major does not do something soon I fear the consequences, but he is contented and seems to think that biscuit made of sour and musty flour and a few dried apples is ample to sustain a laboring man. If he can only study geology he will be happy without food or shelter, but the rest of us are not afflicted with it to an alarming extent.[16]

For three chilling days, more like November than August, it had rained in torrents. They were slowly starving. At the moment rain had extinguished the fire and they huddled in the shelter of their boats. When on half-rations they had been mirthful, on quarter-rations, grimly humorous; now, with almost no rations, they were no longer amused. The shredded canvas was too rotten and tattered to shed water and there were but four blankets for the eight men. Their

[15] J. C. Sumner, MS, *Diary;* also G. Y. Bradley, MS, *Diary,* Aug. 10. The Little Colorado brings down a burden of red mud at certain periods of the year when there is water in the upper river. The greater the flow of water, the greater the erosion and corrasion—hence, greater transportation of sediment. At other periods, when the water is low and its velocity diminished, it is perfectly clear at its junction with the Colorado. Seasonal precipitation and spring thaws determine the amount of sediment carried by the tributary streams. Intense local storms influence the type of sediment the stream carries from time to time.

[16] G. Y. Bradley, MS, *Diary,* August 11, 1869.

stomachs were empty. With forced humor they recounted the earlier days of comfort and plenty with rubber ponchos and beans and bacon. Rain or not, they resumed travel. It was better to starve on the move than to die in a warmthless camp. Suddenly the sun came out and within half an hour the temperature climbed from extreme cold to stifling heat—the thermometer registered 125 degrees—and the men cursed their lot for the first time.

On the 13th the party encountered almost innumerable rapids. After several portages camp that night was made at the head of the longest rapid yet seen—more than a mile long, with a fall estimated to be fifty feet and filled with rocks. The men took turns ridiculing the story of Mr. White and his raft. Assuredly he had not gone through this place. The river proved to be a hell of foam and water, and the wildest by far. The men portaged half the distance and then rode the remainder of the rapid, one boat at a time. Though frightened, when it was safely passed they could still laugh at the scrape. Before nightfall they met another rapid which, however, could not be run by any boat at the present stage of water level. The portage was half completed when darkness closed in. After a supper of bread and coffee the men perched like cliff swallows on the bare rocks wherever the ledges afforded space enough for a man to sleep.

In the morning the little boat was lowered with great difficulty, and in letting her down the bottom was nearly stove in. Bradley volunteered to attempt to shoot the rapid in his boat. After due deliberation on all of the risks the rations, or what was left of them, were put on board. Bradley and Walter got in and the rest shoved the boat into the current. Away it went, swept with terrible force by the riotous waves, into the whirlpools below. Round and round the boat whirled until thrown toward the edge, when the men could gain control and row into the eddy. Safely there, they rested on the oars to have the fun of watching Billy Hawkins duplicate the feat. Hawkins planned his strategy, waited a few minutes, then let her go. Although the *Maid* had shipped but little water, the *Sister* was nearly swamped, and Hawkins, in failing to keep far enough from shore, had an oar splintered in the rocks. The shock numbed his arm clear up to the shoulder.

The men, rejoicing at their safe passage, continued for eight miles, running twelve more bad rapids, and paused for dinner. In the afternoon Howland had the misfortune to lose his notes and the sketch map of the river from the Little Colorado to the last portage. It would have been useless to try to find them so the men agreed to camp at the first opportunity. After a short run of three and a half miles they came to a landing shaded by a large willow. A few rods below, a sparkling creek—cool, swift, and clear as crystal—entered from the north. Some of the fellows walked up the creek with the Major to hunt oar timber and returned with reports not only of abundant driftwood, but also of trout. With the assurance of benevolent shade against the sultry heat and fish to eat, the weary men stretched their worn bodies on the sand and rested the remainder of the day. The Major named the stream Silver Creek, but later, on the lecture platform, changed it to the more romantic Bright Angel to compensate for the Dirty Devil above.[17]

The poor condition of the boats was the main reason for remaining at Silver Creek a second day. With the unsatisfactory tools available it was difficult to shape a twelve-foot oar. The little boat had its cut-water broken, and though not leaking, was much weakened. Each boat was repaired and strengthened as well as possible. While repairs were in progress the cook spread out the rations to dry, but in so doing lost the baking soda when a boat rope caught the box and drew it into the water. From this point on theirs was unleavened bread.

The trip was resumed on August 17th with almost continuous rapids and two grueling portages. In one let-down the *Maid* struck a rock, loosening her head block. The boats had deteriorated too much to withstand much more battering. After the damage was repaired the men examined several old Pueblo ruins and collected fragments of pottery.

The rations were now barely sufficient to sustain life, the diet being reduced to heavy bread and coffee—reason enough for sinking morale. But the treacherous river, demanding hard work with disappointing forward progress to show for it, helped not one bit—only nineteen miles passed in three days. Even with a fair run of eight miles on the 20th, and better than twenty next day, the dashing wildness of the river and the gnawing hunger reminded them that such progress was not enough. The canyon walls stood more than four thousand feet high and the labyrinth of lateral canyons, some almost as large as the main canyon, cast a shadow of dread over the minds of the miserable men on the river below.

On the 23rd, for the first time, some of the party showed signs of losing heart. Below the camp spread a rapid which Bradley regarded as easy and safe. The Major was noncommittal, but most of the men preferred to make a portage rather than to risk a run.

[17] The name Bright Angel was first used by the Major on the lecture platform in December 1869.

Next morning the majority did not feel any more willing to attempt it, so the day began with a long haul. Twenty-two miles were accomplished on the 24th and thirty-five miles on the 25th. According to the Mormon estimate the distance to Grand Wash from the Little Colorado was seventy to eighty miles. Yet they had already run more than 120 miles; how much more remained they had no idea. That day the last sack of flour was opened, with somber ceremony, at a cheerless supper.

Another thirty-five miles was made on August 26th by passing thirty-one rapids with but one let-down, and that one, more by choice than necessity. The men spied an Indian garden on the shore, the first they had seen in many weeks. Despite the previous unhappy experience with stolen fruit, they pilfered a dozen squashes, which served only to increase their appetites for fresh food.

After a moderate run of twelve miles on the morning of the 27th, the men were discouraged by coming again to the dreaded granite at noon. Bradley wrote in his diary, "the worst rapid yet seen." They were sick at heart. Bradley continued:

The water dashes against the left bank and then is thrown furiously back against the right. The billows are huge and I fear our boats could not ride them if we could keep them off the rocks. The spectacle is appalling to us. We have only subsistence for about five days and have been trying half a day to get around this one rapid while there are three others in sight below. What they are we cannot tell, only that they are huge ones. If we could let our boats down to that point and then have a foothold all the rest of the way but we have tried all the P.M. without success. Shall keep trying tomorrow and I hope by going farther back in the mountains and then coming down opposite we may succeed. Think Major has now gone to try it. There is discontent in camp tonight and I fear some of the party will take to the mountains but hope not. This is decidedly the darkest day of the trip but I don't despair yet. I shall be one to try to run it rather than take to the mountains.[18]

After supper the elder Howland asked the Major to have a talk with him. Together they walked a short distance beyond the hearing of the others, and Howland urged that they abandon the river here. Howland, his brother Seneca, and Bill Dunn, had determined to go no farther in the boats. Naturally the Major objected. Howland returned to the camp and everyone but the Major went to sleep; for Powell there could be no sleep. The safety of his men, the attainment of their goal, were dependent upon his decision.

He pondered their predicament. Beyond these walls was a desert of rock and sand, but a freedom they had not known for three months.

[18] G. Y. Bradley, ms, *Diary*, August 27, 1869.

Directly ahead of them was an unknown terror, but rapids perhaps no worse than others they had run. Their provisions were nearly gone and the men were utterly disheartened. The Major decided to calculate by dead reckoning where they were.

It was a clear night with bright stars pinned against a thin ribbon of inky sky visible from the canyon floor. With the sextant he measured the latitude and figured that they were only forty-five miles air line from the mouth of the Río Virgen. By the circuitous channel of the river it might be twice that, perhaps ninety or a hundred miles. A hundred miles—two or three days, perhaps four, to the end. Four days and they would reach food and safety. The Major walked over and awakened Howland to tell him where they were. But Howland was not impressed and returned to sleep.

All night long the Major paced up and down a little sand beach which stretched for a few yards along the river. He decided then to wake Walter and tell him of Howland's determination to leave. Walter promised to remain with the boats. Then he called, one by one, Hawkins, Sumner, Bradley, and Hall, and they all agreed to go on. Daylight at last came. Not a word about the incident was mentioned, but breakfast was like a funeral. Each man must have known the gravity of the fateful decisions which had to be taken. The Howland brothers and Dunn still refused to go farther. Billy took all the flour, baked it into biscuits, and at the Major's command divided them into two equal portions. Each of the trio took a gun, ammunition, and a share of the biscuits. Each group thought that the other was taking the greater risk. Bradley wrote, "They left us with good feelings though we deeply regret their loss for they are as fine fellows as I ever had the good fortune to meet." [19]

The remaining six men decided to leave the *Dean,* the weakest of the boats, because there were too few hands to manage them all.

[19] *ibid.,* August 28, 1869. No more bitter controversy reflects upon Powell's leadership of the expedition than the affair at Separation Rapids. Yet the simple fact is they were afraid to go farther and deserted—with consent, however; they were free to go. Andy Hall, in a letter to his brother, Sept. 10, 1869, minced no words: "Just before we came out of the canyon three of the men left us on the head of rapids. They were afraid to run it so they left us in a bad place. We were then short of hands and we had to abandon the Major's boat." The accusation that Powell had ordered the men to leave and in so doing sent them to their deaths was circulated by Sumner and Hawkins. With the years Sumner in particular had grown bitter, and as misfortunes heaped upon him, the bitterness increased. Keplinger urged Stanton to discount Sumner's remarks. The Major was by this time gone, and it was not easy to refute the charges. See Wallace Stegner, *Colorado Magazine,* Vol. 24, pp. 61–68. It is extremely unlikely that there were no antagonisms or differences among the members of the party. Hotheads like Walter Powell and Jack Sumner undoubtedly had "words" if not blows.

Barometers, pottery, minerals, fossils, all their too meager scientific collections, were cached should they return another year. They boarded the *Maid* and the *Sister* and dashed out into the tumultuous river with all the courage they could muster. Rowing with strained muscles into the greatest billows, they were carried helplessly into the waves. By good fortune both boats came out at the bottom right side up, though well filled with water.

> The three boys stood on the cliff looking at us and having waved them adieu we dashed through the next rapid and then into an eddy where we stopped to catch our breath and bail out the water from our nearly sunken boats. We never had such a rapid before, but we have run a worse one this afternoon.[20]

Indeed, for Bradley it was a worse one. In attempting to let his boat down he remained in it to keep her off the rocks while the others took the rope, 130 feet long, up the cliff. The men climbed higher and the current carried the boat farther until the rope was stretched taut. Bradley's shout of alarm could not be heard over the roar of the water. Fearing that the boat would be dashed to pieces and he perish, Bradley took his knife, waved goodbye to the Major, and cut the rope. The cut end snapped thirty feet into the air as the boat lunged into the cataract. By steering with a single oar—first on one side and then on the other—he guided her safely through to an eddy, stood up, and waved his hat to the rest on the cliff.[21] The Major, Jack Sumner, and Walter came to see if Bradley was safe, whereupon Bill and Andy got into the other boat and brought her through without mishap.

The 29th was Sunday. The rapids grew less formidable; the country began to open. Suddenly the rolling brown desert with greasewood and creosote bush spread before them and the men knew that the dangers were over—if they could reach food before their slim provender was completely exhausted. "All we regret now is that the three boys who took to the mountains are not here to share our joy and triumph." [22] Forty-two miles they had made that day. Powell's sternness melted. As commander he had to be strict, uncompromising, seemingly indifferent. Without discipline or without respect for authority, the venture would have failed. Now he was exuberant:

> Ever before us has been an unknown danger, heavier than immediate peril. Every waking hour passed in the Grand Canyon has been one of toil. We have

[20] *ibid.*

[21] *ibid.*; J. C. Sumner, MS, *Diary;* J. W. Powell, MS, *Diary.* Bradley wrote, "It stands A No. 1 of the trip," a verdict in which Powell concurred.

[22] G. Y. Bradley, MS, *Diary,* August 29, 1869.

watched with deep solicitude the steady disappearance of our scant supply of rations, and from time to time have seen the river snatch a portion of the little left, while we were ahungered. And danger and toil were endured in those gloomy depths, where ofttimes the clouds hid the sky by day, and but a narrow zone of stars could be seen at night. Only during the few hours of deep sleep, consequent on hard labor, has the roar of the waters been hushed. Now the danger is over; now the toil has ceased; now the gloom has disappeared; now the firmament is bounded only by the horizon; and what a vast expanse of constellations can be seen.

The river rolls by us in silent majesty; the quiet of the camp is sweet; our joy is almost ecstasy. We sit till long after midnight, talking of the Grand Canyon, talking of home, but chiefly talking of the three men who left us. Are they wandering in those depths, unable to find a way out? Are they searching over the desert lands above for water, or are they nearing the settlements? [23]

The men took to the boats at sunrise, and expecting a long hard pull, rowed until a little past noon, making twenty-six miles. All the while the country was improving. They were again in a world of smells and fresh dry air. Birds were singing. They saw nothing but smooth water and rolling desert until mid-morning when they passed a Paiute Indian and his squaw wallowing in the hot sand in front of their hut. After dinner—if it could have been called such—the men rowed seven miles more and unexpectedly came to the mouth of the Río Virgen, a wide muddy stream along which it was known the Mormons had several settlements. In the middle of the river stood three men and a boy—not hostile Indians, but Mormons fishing with a net.

The Major explained who he was and introduced his companions, but no introduction was needed. Brigham Young had instructed his people to be on the alert for any signs of survivors of the expedition. The Mormons immediately took the men, now overjoyed with their deliverance, to their cabins, and cooked a banquet of fish, squash, and biscuits, augmented with melons. The famished explorers ate as much as they could, went to sleep, and awoke still hungry.

The last great exploration into unknown and unmapped country in the United States had been completed. The Grand Canyon of the Colorado had been conquered, its mystery dissipated.

[23] J. W. Powell, *Explorations of the Colorado River*, p. 103.

9

1869-1870 · Among the Cliff Dwellers

MAJOR POWELL and his comrades rested at the cabin of Brother Joseph Asey while waiting for an Indian runner to return from St. Thomas. The messenger arrived in the early afternoon of August 31st bearing a letter from Bishop Leithead. The Bishop and two or three other Mormons were coming down immediately with a wagon and supplies. The party arrived at sundown bringing flour, melons, and mail. These were the first letters any of the Powell party had received since they left Green River Station three and a half months before. When the men helped to unload the melons they found a chest of luxuries—cheese, bread, and butter, which they had not tasted for months!

Next morning the expedition was officially disbanded. From here down to the Gulf of California the river was well known. The men shook hands—Jack Sumner, the skillful; Bradley, the fearless, who saved the Major's life; Andy, the humorous; Billy, the strong. No commander ever had a more faithful crew. The Major and Walter Powell decided to go to Salt Lake City and return east. The other men took the boats, packed a few supplies, and heartily resumed the voyage down the Colorado. Jack Sumner and George Bradley left the river at Fort Yuma, but Andy Hall and Billy Hawkins went to tidewater. Powell and his men had scattered, never to meet as a group again.

The Major and his brother returned with Bishop Leithead to St. Thomas and from there took the trail to St. George. Powell was anxious about the Howland brothers and Dunn. He went northeastward to St. George hoping to learn whether the trio had reached the settlement safely. He made inquiries of Erastus Snow, president of the Southern Conference, and J. E. Johnson without avail.[1] Failing in this search, he continued on to Salt Lake City.

---

[1] J. E. Johnson to W. N. Byers, Nov. 11, 1869. "Major Powell arrived here in seven or eight days after the three left him, all safe, and was anxious about the others." *Rocky Mountain News*, Nov. 25, 1869.

Oramel Howland, Seneca Howland, and Bill Dunn had taken the greater risk. On September 7th at 5:15 p.m., two days after Major Powell had left St. George, the following telegram was received by the operator there:

Powell's three men killed by three She-bits, (5 days ago, one Indian's day's journey from Washington) Indian report that they were found in an exhausted state, fed by the She-bits, and put on the trail leading to Washington, after which they saw a squaw gathering seed and shot her. Whereupon the She-bits followed up and killed all three. Two of the She-bits who killed the men are in the Washington camp with two of the guns. Indian George has gone to secure what papers and property there is left.[2]

When the Major arrived in Salt Lake City on September 15th and was informed of the death of the three men, he did not consider it "at all certain" that they were his men and "utterly discredits the report that they killed a squaw, as, he says, they were honorable men and gentlemen." Powell said, "I have known O. G. Howland personally for many years and I have no hesitation in pronouncing this part of the story as a libel. It was not in the man's faithful, genial nature to do such a thing." [3]

The story could not be true. His men would have harmed no one, except in self-defense. More puzzling, the Shewits, accused of the killings, were a peaceful tribe, the least likely in the whole region to commit such an atrocity. It was too late now for the Major to retrace his steps and investigate the murders.

Major Powell returned to the States a national hero. The notoriety stirred up by Risdon's story had focused widespread interest in the outcome of the canyon expedition. Powell's conquest of the Colorado River had captured the public fancy, and the newspapers from coast to coast had reported the meager details of the expedition that were available.

Apparently Major Powell was not the only contender for the honor of exploring the Colorado River. The Omaha *Republican* on September 16th carried an interview with Capt. Samuel Adams in which he did his best to discredit Major Powell:

This river [the Colorado] and the almost unknown country through which it winds its way from the Rocky Mountains to the Gulf of California, has been so much misrepresented by professional letter writers and a more recent explorer, who has expended nothing individually and incurred none of the hardships inseparably connected with the development of the west. The public, in consequence, have been much deceived, and very great injustice has been done

[2] Telegram to Pres. E. Snow, Sept. 7, 1869, *Bleak's Annals.*
[3] Chicago *Tribune,* Sept. 28, 1869; also, Cheyenne *Leader,* Sept. 18, 1869.

to the mineral and agricultural resources of a neglected section of territory which must soon attract the attention of the government. . . .

Soon as the public will know and appreciate these facts, and the press of the East will no longer be led astray by a recent explorer in this, the eleventh hour, whose vision was so remarkably acute, that at the distance of three hundred miles from Green River, he could see the cañons of the Colorado in all their length and depth, and whose letters stated that he was the first to ascend Long's Peak, when it is a matter of public notoriety, that women and men had gone before him for the past ten years, the date of whose ascent was marked upon the place of his triumph.

Captain Adams had nursed his grudge. As soon as he learned the Major had safely passed through the canyons he chose to strike out blindly with lies and vituperation. Of his own explorations Captain Adams said, "Through all of the canyons I have ascended and descended several times within the past three years," which, of course, was pure fabrication.

The Major met Emma in Detroit where she had remained with her father. But if Mrs. Powell had any expectations that her husband would settle down to his professorial duties, she was to be disappointed. He had already made plans for another, this time a more extensive, exploration.

Back at Normal University the Major was enthusiastically received by the students and many friends among the faculty. His prolonged absence had, however, been resented by some of his less adventurous colleagues. Piles of unopened boxes of specimens gathered during the preceding years were stored in the museum rooms. These were unstudied material, unfinished work, but the Major apparently had little time or inclination to examine them. A few of the more spectacular pieces had been identified and duplicates distributed among the patron institutions in order to relieve their understandable pressure for the specimens promised in return for financial support. Obviously, however, until the collections were identified and investigated adequately, the distribution of specimens had to wait.

News of Powell's resignation of the post at Illinois Industrial University—a post which he had never filled—had leaked out during his absence.[4] The confidential offer and the resignation revealed quite clearly that the Major had no intention to remain long at Normal. His reputation as an explorer had risen substantially, but his esteem at the college

---

[4] Powell resigned from Illinois Industrial University on March 10, 1869, "on account of his continued detention with his expedition." At the same meeting of the trustees J. B. Turner was elected as a regent.

had skidded downward. The Major did not always play the game cautiously.

During the fall and winter Powell made a number of public appearances at Detroit, Cincinnati, Wheaton, Chicago, Hennepin, Bloomington, and at many other places. The first three of these are of more than passing interest.

The newspaper account of the Major's first public lecture is in many respects the most important fragment revealing how clearly he understood, how accurately he interpreted, the geological processes which had carved the canyons. The Major, bursting with enthusiasm, addressed the Young Men's Society in Detroit on November 9, 1869:

Major Powell said the basin of the Colorado extends over a continent equal to Iowa, Illinois, Wisconsin, Minnesota and Missouri, 750 miles in length and 500 in breadth. Snow falls on nearly all sides. In summer these snows melt into millions of cataracts, these swell into rivers, and these form the great Colorado. It should be borne in mind that these waters fall on the rim of the basin [later the Major named it the Great Basin], and pouring down, wear deeper and deeper into the solid rock. . . .

The speaker proceeded to give a geological description of the country. The dips, contractions or folds of the different formations were made plain to the audience by a number of colored diagrams. Part of the progress the party made was along dipping slopes of these upturned formations. . . . [In the Grand Canyon,] the rock still dipping in their direction, they were ascending one strata after another. The walls here were 3500 to 6000 or 7000 feet high. It was difficult to give the correct height of the rocks, the tops being broken off 3000 or 4000 feet for a mile or more back. The speaker wanted the audience to fancy a gorge a mile deep, no wider than one of our streets, and as long as from Detroit to Chicago.

The lecturer entered into a series of speculations as to the geological age of the canyons of the Colorado, and basing his deductions on the amount of alluvial deposits carried by the Mississippi yearly to the ocean, which is one inch of soil in 265 years, he placed it at 60,000,000 of years. But as the amount of rain which falls in the Mississippi valley is much greater, and consequently more wearing, than in the Colorado basin, the age of the latter might be much more than the number of years stated. . . . He dwelt at some length on the formation of lakes and streams at altitudes above timberline and the clouds; also their influence on the surface as their streams washed down century after century. . . . [He concluded] after alluding to the sensation which the sublimity of the scene inspired.[5]

On December 14th the Major lectured at Pike's Music Hall in Cincinnati for the benefit of the Union Bethel Fair.[6] The audience listened

[5] This lecture was fully reported the next day in the Detroit *Post*, Nov. 10, 1869.
[6] Cincinnati *Daily Enquirer*, Dec. 15, 1869.

to seven songs by the Yankee Kitchen Choir before the Major lectured on the "Canyons of the Colorado" for an hour and a half. In this lecture he gave particular heed to the romantic and dramatic possibilities of his story; Silver Creek, for instance, was renamed Bright Angel to pair off the Dirty Devil River. Otherwise it was essentially the same lecture that he had given in Detroit.

On Christmas evening Father, Mother, old friends, and neighbors gathered in a blowing snowstorm in the chapel of Wheaton College to hear Wes Powell describe his exploration.[7] This time he paid even greater attention to literary polish. This is not to imply that he took liberties with the truth, for it was difficult to overdramatize a feat itself so dramatic in execution and success, or exaggerate the grandeur of the Colorado canyons—a grandeur expressed better by emotion than by words.

Powell, in spite of a voice a little too weak to be adaptable to public speaking, was as much in his element on the lecture platform as in the wilderness. He enjoyed lecturing with the same lusty enthusiasm that he enjoyed nearly everything else. Besides, these engagements were a means of raising funds for further explorations.

Shortly after the Major's return to the college, he was invited to contribute a short sketch of his canyon voyage for a revised edition of Dr. William A. Bell's *New Tracks in North America*.[8] This report, brief to a fault—perhaps at the editor's insistence—is a very important document. It is a carefully prepared synopsis of the results of the exploration revealing far more than appears evident upon casual reading:

Some lateral canyons have their own lateral canyons, there a fourth series cutting the walls into sections whose towering summits though large enough to support cathedrals, seem scarcely to furnish footing for a man.

Now and then, on this and that side, the rocks were vertical from the water's edge, rising one above the other as they stretched back in a gentle slope for miles. These mounds have been cut out by the showers.

By this time the river had cut through the sandstones and reached the limestones below them at this point, and as we advanced the channel was cut into this new strata.

The river had cut its own channel. It was running before the rock formations were folded creating the mountain range. The river, then, had not

[7] There is some question whether this date is correct; it may have been October 25, 1869. The Major spent the holidays with his parents and spoke in the town during his visit.

[8] Powell had met Dr. William A. Bell and Gen. J. M. Palmer in Cheyenne. Correspondence between Powell and Bell continued for several years. "Major J. W. Powell's Report on his Explorations of the Río Colorado in 1869" appeared as an appendix in Bell, *New Tracks in North America*, pp. 559–64.

cut its way down through the mountains for thousands of feet, but had maintained the same elevation throughout the process, cutting its channel as the fold was lifted—like a saw revolving on a fixed pivot while the log, through which it cuts, is raised to it. Rains fell upon the rocks, gathered into streams, and the wash of the rains cut the formations almost as fast as they were uplifted. The mountains were not thrust up as peaks, but a great block of the earth's crust rose slowly and from this the mountains were carved by the clouds. [These words are not mine; I have paraphrased Powell, selecting a hundred words or so from a much longer description.] Powell continues:

We speak of mountains forming clouds about their tops, the clouds have formed the mountains. Lift a district of granite, or marble, into their region and they gather about it, and hurl their storms against it by beating the rocks into sands, and then they carry them out into the sea, carving out cañons, gulches, and valleys, and leaving plateaus and mountains embossed on the surface.[9]

Without the perspective of time these ideas would not appear to advance any notable scientific concept. In Powell's student days instruction in geology covered only the simplest rudiments of the science. A time scale, based on the sequence of strata, had been calculated for England, France, and eastern North America on the basis of fossil evidence, and Lyell's fundamental principle of Uniformitarianism was gaining recognition. Uniformitarianism, stripped of its unwieldy name, means only that to the everyday forces of nature—rain, wind, frost, ice, earthquake, and volcano—which today shape the face of the earth can be attributed all the great geological changes of the past. The opposing doctrine of Catastrophism, which postulated great "upheavals" in contrast with simpler processes, dominated the thinking of virtually all geologists even in the 1870's.

Nevertheless Powell, from the very beginning of his acquaintance with the canyon country, did not hesitate to accept the evidence of erosion by the Colorado River, incredible as it must have seemed. He saw with his own eyes and believed what he saw. He did not postulate some great convulsion of nature such as was done years later in the speculation over the origin of the Yosemite canyon. Thirty years later many European geologists were still unconvinced of Powell's explanation. No less a person than the great J. D. Dana of Yale was slow to accept Powell's interpretation. However, when he did Dana immediately in-

[9] J. W. Powell, *Explorations of the Colorado River*, p. 154.

vited the Major to submit to the *American Journal of Science* a paper describing his work.

Powell not only recognized the vastness of the work performed by erosion in cutting the canyon, but he reasoned from it logically. The sediment had been carried away and somewhere had been deposited, and the energy of falling water had performed both these tasks. The river—the falling water—was raised gradually by subterranean forces. What these forces were which uplifted the plateau was beyond intelligent speculation at the time, but Powell did not hesitate to accept the fact of uplift. He thus reached the trilogy of geological processes which he ever after maintained—uplift, erosion, and sedimentation. This is the concept of the cycle of topographic development which became established as the science of physiography. Powell developed the theory in detail over a period of five or six years; in essence he comprehended it in 1869.

In the Major's short account written for Dr. Bell are included a wonderfully succinct description of the "axis of a vast fold in the strata," and a striking statement of the Pueblo ruins first seen by him in the canyons:

I have mentioned the terraces of the southern bends; these have been the sites of ancient Indian villages, inhabited by a race of diminutive people now almost extinct. Their little clusters of houses, found on the south side of the river, were 800 or 1000 feet above the water. They were built on stone laid in mortar, and seem to have had reservoirs for water. Fragments of their pottery are found scattered about in great profusion, and deeply-worn foot paths leading from village to village, or down to the river, or up to the summit plain, were frequently seen. On the northern bend their dwellings were near the river. Some of the ruins seem to be centuries old, and others to have been inhabited by the present generation—the latter were found near the mouth of the Little Colorado. Other ruins and fragments of pottery were found in the canyons above, and away up in the valleys of the Uintah. Only a few villages of these interesting people now remain in the country to the south-east.[10]

For devious reasons many historians—not scientists—have belittled the scientific results of this 1869 expedition. One writer called them "nil," another "almost zero." This is not true. Besides Major Powell's incomplete and unpublished journal and the Bradley journal, four brief summaries of the work of this expedition were published before the second exploration was undertaken.

The Major was himself critical of, and unsatisfied with, the accomplishments of the 1869 trip. Parts of the notes were lost when the Howlands and Dunn abandoned the outfit, and the collections, meager

[10] Bell, *op. cit.*, p. 560.

as they were, had to be cached and left behind. Finally, they were so hurried in the closing weeks of the exploration that many points of interest had to be passed without investigation.

Even so, the accomplishments were not negligible. Astronomic stations were made approximately fifty miles apart and observations for latitude were made with the sextant and for longitude by the method of lunar distances. The meandering course of the river was determined by compass, the observations being made from point to point. The intervening distances were estimated, three different men making guesses and the consensus accepted as the final estimate. In this way, the astronomic stations were connected on a sketch map. Barometric readings for altitude were taken three times a day at the water's edge, and using this line as an ever-falling base, the altitudes of the canyon walls and the mountain peaks wherever they could be visited were measured by instrument. The results of all of these observations were used in the construction of geological sections which were made along the course of the river. A sketch map, on which the chief topographic features of the canyons were indicated, was kept by the elder Howland. Even though a part of the records kept were lost by Howland at the time the three men left the party, Powell had not only copies of his own diaries but also field notes and other records written en route.[11]

Far more important than these tangible and obviously inaccurate records were the broader observations which Powell formulated in his mind. As soon as the eye was accustomed to the grandeur and the complexity of the gorges, their uniformity, indeed monotony, began to impress upon his mind a working theory of their origin. The side canyons were nothing more than gorges cut by torrential tributary streams—no different in fundamental aspect from the meandering Mississippi system.

The Major planned a second canyon expedition, not to duplicate the work of the first, but to supplement it. Experience had taught him that the boats needed improvement, the problem of supplies and other difficulties had to be overcome. The proposed second exploration was to cover two years, with at least eight months on the water. During the first trip frequent immersions resulted in spoilage of the food. It would not be possible to carry supplies safely for periods longer than two months and the only practical way in which a second expedition of the canyons could be supplied would be to find a means of transporting provisions down to the river at conveniently located bases.

During March of 1870 Powell made the rounds again to obtain finan-

[11] The method of work for the expedition is described in *43rd Cong. 1st Sess. H.R. 612.*

cial support for his expedition. On the ninth he appeared before the annual meeting of the board of regents of Illinois Industrial University, but as would be expected, this time he failed.

In Washington he visited Joseph Henry and Spencer Baird of the Smithsonian Institution, called upon Salmon P. Chase, whom he had not seen since childhood days in Ohio, and sought out Representative Garfield. Garfield was ever ready to aid the cause of education or science and was by all odds the most persuasive orator in the House. Chase was chairman of the board of regents of the Smithsonian Institution, and like Garfield, another of the regents, rarely missed the board meetings. Largely through their influence, and especially Garfield's, Congress appropriated $10,000 for explorations to be undertaken during the fiscal year ending June 30, 1871. With this encouragement, and with assurances that, unless unforeseen circumstances interfered, a similar sum would be appropriated the following year, Powell went ahead with his preparations.[12]

In this manner Powell's work received federal endorsement. His exploration became a quasi-official survey in a field in which there were already three distinct government surveys: two, headed by Clarence King and Lt. George W. Wheeler, were under the jurisdiction of the War Department; the third, directed by Dr. Ferdinand Vandiveer Hayden, was under the authority of the Federal Land Office in the Department of the Interior. Powell was placed under the jurisdiction of the Department of the Interior. (He was in no sense a government employee, still retaining his professorship and curatorship at Illinois State Normal University. He took no salary for himself from these appropriations.) There had been some rivalry among the three official surveys, and the entry into the field of a fourth under an independent and aggressive leader like the Major could only aggravate the situation.

Before starting west in August Powell engaged his brother-in-law, A. H. Thompson, Nell's husband and principal of the schools of Bloomington, as chief topographer for the field explorations. It was Thompson's job to prepare a preliminary base map and procure the various scientific instruments which would be needed for astronomic and topographic work. Powell turned over to him the notes, sketches, and rough maps made during the 1869 expedition and other published maps of the general area in which the proposed explorations would take place.

[12] The appropriation was approved by act of Congress on July 12, 1870. Powell was officially instructed by Secretary of the Interior J. D. Cox, July 18, 1870.

With this information Thompson, assisted by a draftsman, worked all winter to good advantage.

Unlike the first canyon exploration, which had been a traverse of the river, the second aimed to explore a belt of fifteen miles on both sides of the river, using the river chiefly as a base line. It should be recognized and emphasized that the appropriation was not made for the express purpose of a second descent of the canyons, nor did Major Powell request such; the appropriation was for a "Geographical and Topographical Survey of the Colorado River of the West," as Powell's survey was officially named, and Powell was charged with the exploration of the Colorado River, its tributaries, and the country adjacent to the river system. Powell himself never regarded the proposed 1871–1872 expedition as a canyon exploration.

On August 20th Major Powell arrived in Salt Lake City with F. M. Bishop and Walter Graves, topographer and assistant.[13] The Major here organized a party to explore the plateau country north of the Grand Canyon to discover routes by which rations could be carried from the Mormon settlements in Utah down to convenient points along the Colorado River. Between Gunnison's Crossing and the foot of Grand Canyon there were but two known approaches by which the river could be reached: the Crossing of the Fathers, about thirty miles north of the Arizona line; and another trail a few miles below the mouth of the Paria. But these two points were so near to each other that only one of them would be needed.

The Major had spent considerable time with the Mormons during the preceding three seasons.[14] At all times he had found them friendly and helpful, extending to him, a stranger, every cooperation when he visited their country. There is something characteristic of the Major in his observations of these Mormons. Instead of discussing, as did nearly every other traveler, their practice of polygamy, hierarchy, or their religious beliefs—in all of which he was interested—he described their bounteous agriculture, their surprising lack of medical information, and their efficient methods of settlement.

The Major called upon Pres. Brigham Young to pay his respects to the head of the Mormon people and to ask for the services of a guide

[13] Walter H. Graves, assistant topographer, was a resident of Bloomington. He was a first cousin of O. G. Howland; his father, Thomas Graves, was a brother of Howland's mother, Elvira Graves Howland.

[14] J. W. Powell, MS, *Journal No. 8, 1870*, land trip; F. M. Bishop, MS, *Journal*, Aug. 15, 1870, to Sept. 19, 1870. See also *Scribner's Monthly*, Vol. 11, Dec. 1875, pp. 194–96.

and interpreter who understood the Indian character. Young recommended Jacob Hamblin, a missionary who had devoted his life to the establishment of peace among the Indians and the whites in the western territories.

Jacob Hamblin,[15] the buckskin apostle, was a spare giant of a man who appeared a good deal taller than his six feet two inches. He had been born in 1819 at Salem, Ohio, and had gone to Utah with the original band of Mormon emigrants. An angel of the Lord appeared and communicated to him that if he should never draw the blood of an Indian, no Indian would ever draw his. After this revelation Hamblin dedicated his life to securing peace between the red men and the whites. His labors had been rewarded by treaties with the Utes and Shoshones, and his visits to the Moqui villages had resulted in friendly feelings with these remnant tribes of Arizona. Despite many years of tireless effort, however, he made little headway with the Navajoes, who had resisted fiercely the encroachment of the white man. When Kit Carson directed the herding of the Navajoes into Canyon De Chelly and starved them out, their ultimate hopelessness was evident. Nevertheless they remained embittered and defiant.

With a letter of introduction in hand the Major went to see Hamblin, and explained that the previous year he had descended the Colorado River and that among his objectives for the present season was a visit to the Indians in the neighborhood of Mt. Trumbull, who, it had been rumored, killed three of his men. He hoped not only to prevent a repetition of such a calamity the next year when he resumed explorations of the Grand Canyon, but also to investigate the true reasons for the murder of the Howlands and Dunn.

This old Mormon "Leatherstockings" was respected and trusted by the Indians; he knew many Indian languages and dialects and annually visited the Moqui (Hopi) towns to the south. The Major offered liberal terms and Jacob agreed to serve as guide for the coming season. Two young Mormons, Charlie Benn and A. Nebeker, were also engaged as teamsters.

The unrest of the Indians of Utah, Wyoming, and Colorado was a constant cause of anxiety. The Utes had resisted the encroachment by the Mormon settlers. In 1865 bitterness had reached a nervously dangerous pitch, but gradually the Indians had been subdued, and by 1870 were gathered for the most part in reservations. Old Jacob had secured treaties with all of these "Lamanites." Nevertheless, frequent killings

[15] J. A. Little, *Jacob Hamblin*. See Paul Bailey, *Jacob Hamblin—Buckskin Apostle*.

of whites, and Indians for that matter, attested to the fact that passions were not fully controlled. So much misery befell the Indian when the miners, surveyors, and settlers pushed them into poorer and poorer land that the loser—always the Indian—often resorted to violence.

The Major planned to travel to the Uinkaret Mountains and determine to his own satisfaction the true causes for the slaying of his three men, which on the frontier had been but another incident not deserving of further investigation. When everything was in readiness Powell's party worked its way southward to the valley of the Sevier River, traveled up its headwaters, and reached the summit of a great watershed. There on the upper Kanab at the foot of Pink Cliffs they established a rendezvous camp by the springs, whose waters joined to form the Kanab River. Powell planned to make reconnoitering trips, radiating southward and eastward from this base, to familiarize himself with the country.

Hamblin gathered together a number of Kaibabits and their chief, Chuar,[16] who lived in the vicinity and induced them to camp with the Powell party. These Indians promised to show the Major the water pockets and springs. They warned him that it would not be possible to reach the Colorado River from this approach.

A pack train to transport supplies, bedding, and instruments was assembled, and on the ninth of September the party moved from the beautiful meadow at the head of the Kanab, crossed the line of low hills at the head of the Río Virgen, passed to the south by an enchanting little valley, and shortly before noon abruptly came to the brink of a great line of cliffs. Behind them they had left green meadows, cold springs, and forest-covered slopes; below them, stretching southward until it merged into the haze, a painted desert of rocks, cut by deep sharp gorges and studded with towering pinnacles of naked rocks, displayed in the dazzling sunlight a brilliance of red, vermilion, and brown.

That evening the Kaibabit Indians who were traveling with Powell were gathered about the campfire. Chief Chuar was speaking to his men, and upon the urging of Jacob Hamblin, related for the Major's benefit several ancient traditions of his people. Powell listened with a new understanding as Chuar described how his people came to be, how the earth was formed, why the sun keeps its course, and who the ghosts are. This little band of savages had discovered for themselves a simple explanation for the whole world as they knew it.

On September 13th, the pack train left Kanab for Mt. Trumbull. A

---

[16] Chuar was Chief Chuarruumpeak, whom Major Powell held in high esteem. See *Truth and Error*, Chapter I.

three days' journey over an obscure Indian trail was ahead of them. Near their general destination they camped at a great spring called Yellow Rock Water by the Indians and Pipe Spring by the Mormons. Pipe Spring was situated in Arizona just over the Utah line. All of the Indians except Chief Chuar and Shuts, who were to act as guides to water pockets, which were extremely scarce in this region, had been sent back to the rendezvous camp. Chuar informed the Major that they were now in the land of the Uinkarets, and before long they approached several squaws, stark naked, gathering fruits of cactus, which were growing in profusion. Nearby a few lazy braves were idling the time away doing nothing. At Powell's request the Uinkarets sent a messenger to the Shewits, who lived thirty miles to the southwest.

The following morning some twelve or fifteen Shewits came to the camp and Hamblin called a council for a peace talk. Old Jacob rose and with great deliberation began by explaining why Major Powell had come among them.[17] He tried to assure the Indians that his visit would bring no evil, that he was not hunting gold or silver. He told them also that next summer Powell wanted to go down the river again with a company of men and that the Indians must be friends and not kill any more of the men who might have to leave the river. The Indians listened to Jacob's words mutely. After Jacob had finished he sat down.

The Major then took his stand before the council ring and explained in Paiute, the only Indian tongue in which he was at the time conversant, why he had come among them. Across the big waters and beyond the deep canyon there were many white men and men of other colors, black and yellow. Each of these races had customs and habits which were interesting. In the white man's country he who knew the most was the most respected. White men wanted to know about the Indians and he had come to study and tell other white men what he learned among them. He assured the Indians, as Jacob had done, that he was not seeking gold or silver; he was coming only to make friends and to study.

Hamblin observed this energetic little man, fearless as an Indian brave and as persistent as a missionary. He had watched the Major ask the women at their domestic tasks what seeds they were using and what they were making. He had seen the Kaibabits put on a demonstration rabbit hunt just to show Powell how they drove game into a net. He must have admired the ease with which the Major gained the friendship of these shy people. Everything engaged his interest—rocks, soil, insects,

---

[17] Powell described this meeting with the Shewits (Shevwits) in *Explorations of the Colorado River*, pp. 128–31.

plants, language, and customs. Jacob was an unlettered man, but he had the breadth of understanding which could recognize Powell's zeal.

When the Major sat down, a spokesman for the Indians rose and replied that some of their neighbors across the river had told them the three white men were miners who had abused their women and had shot a squaw, that if the white men found mines in their country, great evil would come among them. He admitted freely that the three men had been directed to a spring, ambushed, and there slain with arrows.

The Indian stated further that they believed all that Jacob Hamblin had told them, and had they known the truth about Powell's men, they would not have killed them. Pointing to the Major and giving him the name Ka-pu-rats, which in Paiute means one-arm-off, the speaker assured Hamblin that Ka-pu-rats could travel and sleep in their country unmolested and that the Indians would show his men the watering places. Thus satisfied, the Major shook hands and presented gifts to the Shewits and sent them off, without revenge or malice in his heart.

One of Major Powell's objectives in his 1870 explorations was to visit the province of Tusayan. He had learned from Jacob Hamblin that seven villages in Northeastern Arizona were in nearly primitive condition, and though they had been discovered by the Spanish Jesuit priests many years before, retained their simple customs and pagan religion.

There were, in scattered places in Nevada, Utah, Colorado, New Mexico, and Arizona, ruins of many Indian Pueblo villages. The nomadic Indian inhabitants of these regions had no authentic information concerning the former tenants of the ruins, saying merely that the gods had destroyed them because they knew too much. It was with this puzzle in mind that the Major wanted to visit the Indian villages of Arizona.

After five days' overland journey through difficult country, the Major's party came to the dilapidated town of Oraibi.[18] There, on high cliffs, perched an aggregation of storied houses. Through his Indian guides he explained the purpose of his visit to the Oraibi chief and after a hospitable reception Powell was permitted to examine their habitations at his leisure. The houses were built of stone and plaster, some of two and others of three or four stories, each story being somewhat offset. The small rooms on the lower floor were not more than six or eight feet square and were used chiefly for the storage of foods. The second floor usually contained the main assembly room of the building and on the higher stories the family rooms were located. A family room might be as much as fifteen feet by twenty-five feet, and the ceiling seven feet

[18] J. W. Powell, "The Seven Moqui Villages," in *Scribner's Monthly*, Oct. 1875.

high. In one end of each family room was a stone chimney and a small fireplace. These were identical in construction with the ruins the Major had examined along the canyons. Inside of the house everything was kept with great care and cleanliness, though in the courtyard outside filth of every description littered the ground.

The precarious living which the region yielded to these people was impressive to anyone who had come from more fruitful country. The habitations were built on cliffs or promontories, where the inhabitants could seek safe refuge from the warlike nomadic Apaches and Navajoes from the country beyond. In these recesses the Indians were far removed from firewood and forest game. Thus they were dependent on a slender agricultural subsistence, planting corn, melons, and squash in the spring in soil which offered discouraging promise of adequate crops.

One after another the seven Moqui villages presented the same appearance. In all, there were not more than 2,700 inhabitants, though the size and number of the buildings was evidence that in former years a much greater population had tenanted them.

The pottery, domestic utensils, and other equipment found in these dwellings, and the construction of the buildings, were so distinctive that it was quite clear that the relics found in the ruins scattered in so many places in the West were of more or less similar design. Furthermore, the Major's studies of the language and mythology of the Tusayan people convinced him almost intuitively that they were related to the Utes, Paiutes, and Shoshones, the nomadic Indians who roamed so widely over the Rocky Mountain region.

The two months the Major remained with these simple and friendly Indians were revealing. He found an opportunity to study an unspoiled people and learned from them, without the hindrances of confusing traits and ideas absorbed from contacts with white men, the fundamental character and beliefs of their race.

It was now Hamblin's turn to ask a favor. As the final achievement in his career as a peacemaker he hoped to obtain a treaty with the Navajoes and to establish a pact of friendship between the Navajoes and the Mormon frontier towns. No Mormon had ever faced a Navajo for a peace talk. The Major suggested that now was a good time to try. Several thousand of the tribesmen were gathering at Fort Defiance for their annuity, an annuity which was a penance for the brutal subjugation of the Navajoes by the American government.

Early in November Jacob Hamblin, Major Powell, and a small party went to Fort Defiance and there, with the aid of Capt. F. F. Bennett, held a peace council. The Major was the leading spokesman. Facing Chief Barbenceta, he reminded the Navajoes of their hopeless condition and that they were at the fort to receive an annuity from the government. He then explained that the Mormons, like all white men, pay taxes, helping to provide for the Indians and their reservations. Holding up the stump of his arm as a token that he too was a warrior, he introduced Jacob Hamblin as a man of peace. The Navajoes had known for a long time of Jacob Hamblin, for a longer time indeed than they had known of the prowess of Major Powell. Their words were good. On November 5th a treaty of peace between the Navajoes and the Mormons was signed at Fort Defiance.[19] Jacob Hamblin had completed the life-work he had set out to do.

The work of the season had been completed successfully. Several promising routes by which the river party could be supplied had been located. The mystery of the killing of the Howland brothers and Bill Dunn had been resolved; apparently, it had been a mistake and his men were guiltless of any wrong. The seven towns in Tusayan had provided him with a wealth of new ideas about the Pueblo ruins and he had gained an appreciation of the character of the Indian. Jacob Hamblin had lived up to his reputation and had made it possible for the Major to accomplish many things in a short season.

In December Major Powell returned east to recruit a new party and to complete preparations for a second exploration of the Colorado country.

[19] The Treaty of Fort Defiance was signed on Nov. 5, 1870. Letter, Capt. F. F. Bennett, "To Whom It May Concern." I am indebted to Mr. Pearson H. Corbett of St. George, in whose possession is the original, for this account. See also *Utah Hist. Quart.*, Vol. 15, p. 153.

10

1871 · Second Expedition Down the Colorado

IN ILLINOIS Major Powell went about the business of organizing a second expedition to make a more thorough exploration of the Canyon country. He realized now that the efficiency of the scientific work would be as dependent upon the preparations and supplies as on the skill of his men. The project would cover the greater part of two years with at least eight months of the time to be spent on the Colorado River. Confidently he had completed field preparations before returning to the university. At least two good routes by which food could be hauled down to the river finally had been located. Experience had taught him how barren the canyon really was.

The men of the first party had been loyal, cooperative, and resourceful. Their courage and teamwork through near catastrophe, and in spite of gnawing hunger, had made his achievement possible. Nevertheless, there were two critical weaknesses in the first organization: the men lacked technical training; and a far more serious limitation was the haste forced upon them by the dwindling food supplies.

The second exploration was not, to the Major's way of thinking, an adventure. The mystery surrounding the river had been solved. Whatever more he learned would be supplementary. The Major was now ready to recruit a party. This was an easy matter. Scores of young men came in person to see Powell to beg for a place in the boats, while many others wrote for an opportunity to participate in the adventure. Some of them even offered to buy their way.

Dissension had developed during the closing weeks of August during the 1869 trip. Yet the Major was fortunate that the dissatisfaction had not appeared earlier and had not disrupted the whole project. It was not in the Major's character to demand or even expect every man in the close companionship of a daring voyage lasting so many weeks to come through without an unblemished record. He could forgive and forget.

Nevertheless, only Jack Sumner of the first expedition was asked to accompany the second.

It is somewhat surprising that the members of the 1871 expedition were hired from a close group of the Major's friends and relatives when he might have selected men of much greater experience and professional training. Considering the scientific work to be done, the personnel was far from professional: Prof. Almon H. Thompson, a brother-in-law, was the geographer; W. Clement (Clem) Powell, a twenty-year-old cousin, had no particular training and was hired as a boatman; Frank Richardson was a family friend from Chicago; Fred Dellenbaugh, son of a Buffalo physician and a distant relative of Thompson, was a gifted self-taught artist of seventeen but was hired primarily as a boatman. There were four friends from Illinois: S. V. Jones, a student of mathematics and surveying; J. F. Steward, an amateur geologist; F. M. Bishop, a surveyor and teacher; and Andrew Hattan, hired as the cook. The only real outsider was E. O. Beaman, a professional photographer from New York City and engaged in Chicago at the time. All but three, the youngsters Fred, Clem, and Frank, had seen active service with the Union armies. Steward had suffered a severe back injury in battle, but seemed to have recovered. Bishop had been shot clean through the left lung, but he too seemed to be in robust health. The rest were in top physical condition.

In February the Major went again to the Bagley Boat Yard at the north end of Clark Street bridge in Chicago and placed before the proprietor an improved design for three boats. These were modeled after the craft used on the first voyage except for an additional middle bulkhead, making three instead of two. These craft were square-sterned and smooth, twenty-two feet long with a twenty-foot keel and capable of drawing twenty-two inches. There were heavy stern rowlocks to hold an eighteen-foot steering oar. The added bulkhead would provide greater buoyancy, permit less shipping of water, and in general increase the protection of the men and supplies. When the Major came again at the end of March to see the boats he was accompanied by Fred Dellenbaugh, Beaman, and Clem Powell. The boats, which rested on Bagley's wharf, had a porpoiselike appearance. The waves were running high on Lake Michigan, and with the aid of a few men from the yard to round out the crews, and with a couple of newspaper men, the boats were taken out for a test run—with cigars and champagne for provisions. After the trial the Major was satisfied that these craft would ride on any water.

The members of the expedition were to gather at Green River Station about May 1st. As the time approached, the party began to assemble, and the first contingent left for the official starting point. On April 20th the Major and Emma went to Bram's home in Aurora where Reverend Powell had been visiting. Fred Dellenbaugh had joined the Major in Chicago. The next day Clem arrived from Naperville. The group took the train to St. Louis. Bram went along as far as Topeka to visit Martha and her family, and Reverend Powell, with a fellow clergyman, Reverend Jesse Smith, was en route for Denver. Meanwhile, Harry and Nell Thompson had left on the twenty-fourth for St. Louis.[1]

The enthusiasm and excitement of the members of the second expedition were in marked contrast to the casual and matter-of-fact attitude of the mountaineers who had made up the first party. In Wyoming, as the train crossed the mountains at 8,200 feet, the men passed over an iron bridge where it was possible to look down a precipice of more than two thousand feet. At Summit Station all the passengers alighted and amused themselves by snowballing each other. The party coming from the East reached Green River Station at six o'clock in the morning of April 28th and had a hearty breakfast with Jake Field.

The preceding two years had been hard on Green River Station. Of the hundred or so flimsy buildings which had constituted the town in 1869 only thirteen habitable buildings remained and some of these were merely tents with board sides. All that remained of the noisy boom days were crumbling adobe walls. The population consisted of a few whites, a number of Chinese railway maintenance laborers, and a few stragglers, mostly mountaineers in town for business. Ah Chug, the cook at the station eating house, who still sold his apple pies at twenty-five cents, was there, and grinned gratefully when the Major recognized him.

The flatcar with the boats was resting on a siding near the station, and after breakfast the car was pushed to the east end of the bridge

---

[1] The source materials for the second Colorado River expedition are remarkably complete. Virtually every member of the party kept a journal and most of them earned a little on the side by sending dispatches to home-town newspapers. Thompson's diaries were published in 1940 in *Utah Hist. Quart.*, Vol. 7. The society has recently collected the important journals and documents in a heroic volume of the Quarterly (Vols. 16–17).

It is a curious fact that Major Powell looked upon the work of the 1871–1872 exploration as routine surveying and mapping. Accordingly, I have treated the expedition in this light; to do otherwise would exaggerate its significance. For a rich narrative of the expedition, charmingly and enthusiastically written, see F. S. Dellenbaugh, *A Canyon Voyage*. There are many minor inaccuracies, but these do not detract from the story.

Of the individual diaries and journals, the following, in approximate order of value, are of particular interest: A. H. Thompson, J. W. Powell, S. V. Jones, W. Clement Powell, F. M. Bishop, and J. F. Steward. The last two named suffer because they are late transcriptions of shorthand field notes and show considerable editing.

spanning the Green. The boys lowered the boats into the river, took a short ride downstream, and then came back to ferry the baggage to their first camp site. The boats were steered down a few hundred yards to a little cove on the left bank. Here the boats were dragged up on the beach and put into operating condition; their bottoms were calked, they were repainted, and canvas nailed to the fronts of the cabins. A clearing was cut among the willow thickets and tents were pitched. Mr. Field, who owned an outfitting house in the village, loaned them a table and benches, so they lived in relative luxury. The men still wore their city clothes, even to white shirts and flowing ties, but before camp was broken exploring costumes of heavy cotton overalls, pullover shirts buttoned part way, woolen underwear, sturdy hobnail shoes, and felt hats were donned with jocular ceremony. The underwear, in two sections, had proved to be a most useful item of equipment during the first trip.

Mrs. Powell and Mrs. Thompson came to Green River with the party and remained for several days, helping to prepare the supplies for the descent. Nell Thompson had sewn silk American flags for each of the boats. When time grew burdensome—there being almost nothing in camp for the ladies to do—they left on May 3rd for Salt Lake City, where they planned to remain for the summer. The Major and Professor Thompson escorted their wives to the city, and until their return two weeks later, there was very little for the rest to do, although the ex-soldiers in the outfit had not forgotten how to idle about camp. One eastbound train and one westbound train each day provided the only excitement. Fred had painted a great cloth banner, "Powell's Colorado Exploring Expedition," and the passengers waved handkerchiefs to the men as they passed over the Green River bridge. No doubt they had been informed of the Powell party by the trainmen. There was, besides a little fishing, some target practice and a little tippling at Jake Fields. About the only pastime left was eating, and even in this there were limits.

When the Major and Professor Thompson returned from Salt Lake City they were accompanied by Jack Hillers, who was to take Jack Sumner's place. Sumner, by all means the most dependable of the 1869 party, had been signed up for the second trip, but deep snows in the mountains prevented him from leaving his retreat and joining the expedition. The Major had with him Sumner's diary of that first voyage, and though it was written on a few pages of foolscap in the most casual manner, the journal was a thrilling and honest record of the trials ahead.

No one knew better than Powell how much better the second expedition was equipped than was its predecessor. Not only were the boats superior, but the supplies were immeasurably better. Each man had a life preserver. Fresh provisions would be brought in to the expedition at four points: the mouth of the Uinta; the mouth of the Dirty Devil; the Crossing of the Fathers; and at the mouth of the Paria. Then too, there would be much better protection for the supplies taken along. Everything was placed in rubber sacks except the bacon, which, being greasy, would damage the rubber. These sacks were practically water-tight when closed. The rubber sacks in turn were encased in cotton bags and then put in gunny bags for added protection. Each man was allowed one hundred pounds of personal luggage, including blankets, and a rubber bag for them. There were eleven hundred pounds of flour distributed in twenty-two sacks of fifty pounds each.

The Major named his boat the *Emma Dean* and had as his crew S. V. Jones, Jack Hillers, and Fred Dellenbaugh. Professor Thompson named his the *Nellie Powell* in honor of his wife. J. F. Steward, F. M. Bishop, and Frank Richardson made up the crew of the *Nellie*. The third boat, the *Cañonita*, was manned by E. O. Beaman, Andrew Hattan, and Clem Powell.

On May 22, 1871, the men turned out early, carried the last odds and ends to the boats, and then at seven o'clock went over to Jake Field's for breakfast. It was a gay and bursting meal which lasted more than two hours, and they toasted the trip with a couple of bottles of wine. At ten o'clock they pushed the boats into the stream while all of the inhabitants of the town lined the shore to wave them off. One young deaf and dumb fellow made vigorous gestures signifying a terrible smashup for the voyagers, but disregarding this warning the members of the second Colorado expedition began their journey lightheartedly. The boats were admirably suited for the river work, the prospect for provisions was bright, the crews were congenial, and the stage of water was low. The low water portended considerable labor in portaging but meant minimum danger in running the rapids. Major Powell had obtained from Mr. Field a sturdy armchair, which was lashed to the middle bulkhead of the *Emma Dean*. This perch served as a lookout from which the chief could look ahead and signal to the other crews in time of danger or trouble. Although this arrangement made the *Dean* somewhat top-heavy, it was not considered a hazard.[2]

[2] The decision to use the lookout chair had been a casual one. Several photographs of the *Dean* show the arrangement and the ever-ready life preserver. Powell found the chair thoroughly practical.

The first day's run covered eight miles and camp for the night was made on the right bank along an outcrop of coal. The next morning about daylight rain began and for a while turned to snow. The air was miserably cold and the men remained in camp, huddled about a fire, until nearly one o'clock. They rowed for six miles that day and camped in a grove of cottonwoods where there was plenty of firewood. They had run through one small rapid, too modest to cause any anxiety. The fellows caught a mess of trout and had a first-rate fish fry to celebrate the day.

During the run Thompson and the Major had made observations for latitude and time at ten stations and established the procedure which would be used throughout the trip. The course of the river was to be charted during the descent. Thompson and Jones would sight ahead at each bend of the river with a prismatic compass and make an estimate of the length of each sight. Measurements of the walls, the width of the stream, and the velocity of the water were also to be made. Geological notes were to be kept by the Major, Professor Thompson, and Steward. Fred was to sketch interesting formations at Powell's or Thompson's request. Beaman was to photograph features considered to be of significance or special beauty.

Beaman's job was a particularly tedious one. The art of photography had not reached a high degree of perfection by 1871. The equipment necessary for the photographic department weighed more than a ton. The camera, in a strong box, had to be lugged by one man while the chemical and plate-holder box and the dark-box had to be carried by two other men. It was necessary when a photograph was taken to make a wet plate by placing a plain glass slide in a bath of gelatin and silver solution, then expose the plate, still wet, in the camera. The time and the lighting were determined by experience and rule of thumb. After exposure the plate had to be developed immediately in the dark-box before the equipment could be moved. As many as three or four exposures were made during an afternoon.

The first fifty miles of the voyage ran through undulating sagebrush country so poor as to offer little temptation to a settler. Game was plentiful, surprising the eye at every bend of the river. On some of the islands deer, antelope, otter, and beaver were numerous. On the 24th the men landed to climb a wide canyon. Beaman took two photographs while the geographers measured the height of Needle and Boston Loaf buttes. On the 29th the first real rapids were reached and it proved to be an exciting experience. The men had been anxious to see how the boats would ride the waves, but such fears proved to be needless. This first time though, because of the inexperience of the crews, all of the boats shipped water as they rolled from side to side.

The Major, remembering the mishaps and misjudgments of the first trip, demanded absolute caution and obedience. Upon approaching a rapid the boats were invariably landed at the head and plans were made to avoid as much as possible points of danger in taking the fall. On June 2nd they reached a point where the river narrowed suddenly and plunged off into rapid after rapid. They did not seem to be too serious and all three boats struck out for the main current. The Major waved energetically to order the boats to shore, but his signals were misunderstood and too late to bring the boats around. The craft were unmanageable and were swept onto the rocks in an extreme current, careening from boulder to boulder. Thompson's boat filled and rolled over, but the crew sprang onto the rocks just as she filled and, holding to the ropes, held her fast. Aside from a good ducking and lost oars, which were subsequently recovered, the only damage was to a compass and kettle. Early in the afternoon of June 5th the roar of Ashley Falls in the distance warned of danger ahead. The Major, taking no chances on this short but fierce tumble, ordered the men to approach cautiously. The boats were emptied and the *Dean* and the *Cañonita* were lined down while the supplies were portaged over the rocks.

Beaman took several views of the falls from below while Fred sketched in his notebook "Ashley 1825," recording correctly the inscription on a great boulder which Powell had not yet fully appreciated. In the darkness of night "Prof." read *Hiawatha* by the flames of a campfire with the thunderous music of the water of Ashley Falls as a background. In the morning the cabins of the boats were packed like trunks, the blankets rolled and placed in their rubber bags, all of the food packed in rubber sacks, tied securely, and stowed away. Only the instruments needed for the day's work were kept out. Guns, scientific instruments, life preservers, and a kettle for bailing were the only articles kept free. The hatches were battened down, the canvas covers drawn over the decks. Nothing less than a smashup could damage the supplies. For five days the crews worked cautiously and exhaustingly and then rested for the next two days doing scientific and repair work.

Richardson could not keep out of minor trouble. He had a faculty for getting bruised and scraped. To top his achievements, while eating he sat on a hot coal, ignited his pants, yelled "fire," and jumped into the river. He was pulled out swearing uproariously. He not only had blistered his bottom, but had burned out the seat and one leg of his trousers. The other leg had to be cut off and used to patch the damage. For this he earned the name "Little Breeches" in derision of the trousers he was obliged to wear.

The river became almost placid, and to idle the time, the boats were lashed together and allowed to drift with the current while the Major on his perch read *Lady of the Lake*. It was June 8th when the men reached Brown's Park and dropped down the river to Christ Hillman's cabin, where the Major had camped twice before, once when Emma was with him. The place was now occupied by a number of Texan herders with twenty-two hundred head of cattle. A Mr. Harrell and Mr. Bacon from California had wintered there with eighty-five hundred Texan cattle, eighty ponies, and ten Mexican herders. Powell's men were welcomed, and the stopover was a pleasant interruption. They swapped a bag of flour and a side of bacon for two quarters of fresh beef. The boys wrote letters home and left them, with some parcels of specimens, with Harrell, who offered to take them to the post office at Green River Station. "Little Breeches" resigned from the company and went home. He simply was not cut out to be an explorer and the Major had asked him to leave before he became a victim of a more serious mishap. Steward had offered to trade his revolver for Richardson's flute and the deal would have been consummated but for Bishop. Bishop wanted to do some target practice with the revolver, and on his second shot the barrel burst and the trade was off. Henceforth the only music would come from Fred's mouth organ.

Although it was not evident to the men, Thompson realized that the Major was champing at the bit. Powell could not hurry the river work and still record the observations which were needed; but, all of this he had experienced before. Events moved on quietly until June 17th when the drumming roar of bad rapids ahead warned them of the approach of Lodore. Life preservers were inflated, the men alerted, and they entered the canyon. That afternoon they stopped early and camped at the head of a stretch of wicked rapids. The next morning about ten they broke camp and passed Disaster Falls without mishap. For three days they had rough going. On the twentieth they toiled over a long portage, stopping halfway through to rest. Lower Disaster Falls was passed the following day. The second party had a taste now of the work ahead. The 1869 party had learned by grim experience, almost too late, that there were two kinds of portages. The second party, with the practice of only a few dozen rapids behind them, had become proficient at both. A genuine portage was accomplished by unloading all of the baggage—twenty-two hundred pounds to each boat—and lugging it over the rocks. If necessary, the boats were dragged over the rocks and let down as gently as possible by ropes. The other kind was a lining or kicking portage which was less work but much more dangerous. While two or three men held the sides of the boat and kept kicking and pushing her over the rocks, two or more of the other men would manage or guide the boat by ropes, letting her down a few yards at a time. In either case it was tiresome work.

For two days, June 22nd and 23rd, they camped at the head of Triplet Falls. They found remains of the *No-Name*, which had been wrecked there two years before, a grim reminder of some of the misfortunes that had plagued the first exploring party. A particularly dangerous part of the rough going, a long wild chute which Sumner had called "Hell's Half Mile," was passed with only slight mishap although the men agreed that the name was appropriate. On Sunday, June 25th, they emerged from Lodore and pitched camp just above the mouth of the Yampa. The declivity had been 420 feet in 20¾ miles and thus far they had dropped 975 feet in 153 miles. Powell remained at this camp for a week. He ascended the Yampa Canyon while the other men made scientific observations in the vicinity. To add a little excitement to camp life, Clem and Steward decided to cross the river on a cedar log. Everything went well until they met an eddy at mid-stream which pulled the log under. Steward, realizing that their combined weight was too much to be sustained, let go and was drawn under. Three times he rose to the surface and finally managed to swim free. Meanwhile Clem hung on until he was rescued. Thereafter the men stuck to the boats for ferrying.

The diaries became a ritual. Each evening the men wrote up the events of the day and passed their journals around. Occasionally the toil of the portage was too exhausting and the diary-keeping was skipped for a day or so. The boys were mindful that there would be ample records of their adventure for posterity. Even the scientific notes, which were kept on rough paper, were recopied neatly in a more permanent manner each evening.[3]

The boys were awakened on the "Glorious Fourth" by Fred shooting his gun in honor of the day and the "Prof." and Bishop soon joined in. By way of celebration the day was spent in complete idleness—unusual

---

[3] A fine series of the daily temporary notes recorded by S. V. Jones are in the possession of the New York Public Library. Each day measurements were made at consecutively numbered stations. The data included height of walls, width of river, altitude, distance between stations, course of the river, and structural features of the rocks and river.

indeed—and at the festive dinner, consisting of ham and canned peaches in addition to the regular fare, Fred brought out a surprise package of candy which he had purchased at Gunther's in Chicago.

On July 7th at Island Park the Major went ahead with the *Dean* and, without stops, hurried to the mouth of the Uinta where a wagon trail led from the river to the Uinta Indian Agency. Here he had planned to pick up mail and haul in the first load of supplies to replenish their stores and obtain materials to repair the boats. On reaching the agency, however, he learned that Emma had been ill and he proceeded immediately to Salt Lake City, leaving instructions for Thompson to work on the map and await his return. With the supervision of the river party and the technical work in the able hands of Thompson, the Major was free to move wherever he wished. He had lost a good deal of his interest in the river proper and was casting his eye upon some of the larger geological features of the plateau country. He made several excursions to the Indian villages and searched everywhere for remains of the Pueblos.

Mrs. Powell was in Salt Lake City awaiting the arrival of her first child. She had been ill for a good deal of the time and the Major went to see her on several occasions during the summer. As side trips to these visits to Salt Lake City, the Major investigated the Henry Mountains and some of the topographic features of the arid regions. Meanwhile the party on the river was making slow progress, much of the time being consumed with picture-taking, and by now the men hated the whole photographic department as an infernal nuisance. The camera, in its strongbox, was a heavy load to carry up and down precipitous cliffs. The chemical and plate-holder box was worse, but even this, in the words of Dellenbaugh, was "a feather-weight compared to the imitation hand organ which served as a dark room." [4] The photographic equipment was a burden, but it was also their prized possession. Only a photographic record of the canyon country could do justice to the natural wonders found there.

When the river party arrived at the Uinta and went into camp, Thompson, with Beaman as a companion, walked the thirty miles to the Indian agency. A large supply of rations had been stored there the previous fall, and arrangements for hauling the goods down to the river had to be

---

[4] Dellenbaugh, *op. cit.*, p. 58. The photographic technique at this time was hardly conducive to wilderness art. The wet-plate method required a gelatin or albumin bath, silvering, developing, and storage with extremely unwieldy equipment. The work of such frontier photographers as W. H. Jackson, E. O. Beaman, C. R. Savage, and J. K. Hillers is truly remarkable.

made. At the agency Thompson was met by Jones and Bishop, who told him that the Major had gone on to Salt Lake City. A message from Jacob Hamblin was also at the agency telling Powell and Thompson that it would not be possible to take supplies down to the mouth of the Dirty Devil River. Exploration of the proposed route had revealed that the stream, for the greater part of its course, flows through a very narrow canyon with water filling the entire channel. It would be utterly impossible to gain a footing along the more precipitous walls or to descend along the shore. This was discouraging news and Thompson, unfamiliar with Hamblin's trustworthiness, even suspected that Hamblin had made only a half-hearted attempt to locate a trail. The necessary adjustments in their scheduled program would mean that the provisions from the agency would be just sufficient to carry them through, and might not last if they were delayed at any point along the river. Thompson spent a little time at the Indian reservation and found its administration to be inefficient and deteriorated. He shared none of the Major's optimism over the future welfare of the Indian.[5]

The Major returned to camp on the evening of July 26th. He had discovered that the river which Hamblin had considered to be the Dirty Devil was actually the San Rafael, and its descent would be indeed an undertaking. Now, Powell determined to try to locate a route down the Dirty Devil and put the second supply train on the correct trail. He remained with his men only two days, planning the work with them and directing Thompson to continue down the river to Gunnison's Crossing, where Powell would rejoin them September 3rd. This would mean that the river party would have time to kill through Desolation Canyon, the most miserable stretch of the river, or waste it in boredom at some desolate spot such as Gunnison's Crossing. "Prof.," in deference to his men managed to do some of both. The boats passed nine rapids in less than seven miles and found drift of the *No-Name* two hundred miles from the place where it had been wrecked two years before. Along the entire course they encountered exceedingly low water, on August 17th scraping bottom as they went but having to pass eight rapids in five miles. By going at a snail's pace, to the disgust of the crews, they had taken almost three weeks to get through Desolation Canyon, a distance of only ninety-seven miles. Because of the low water, on only one occasion did they have a chance to make a good run in the boats. On August 25th the party

---

[5] A. H. Thompson, MS, *Diary*, July 28, 1871: "My impressions of the Indians, the Agency, are unchanged. The Agency as at present conducted is a cheat, a swindle. The Indians do not make good agriculturalists. The attempt to raise grains, etc., fails."

reached the Gunnison and had to wait four long days for the Major. Powell, after repeated attempts to find a means of getting down to the Dirty Devil, had failed as badly as Hamblin.[6] However, to provide some food for the river party, he had managed to purchase limited supplies, of flour, sugar, and jerked beef, which could be spared by isolated Mormon villages. Everyone including the Major hoped fervently that this makeshift would tide them over until they could run down to the next food supply at the Crossing of the Fathers.

Powell made his way to the foot of Gray Canyon where Thompson and the boat party awaited him. Thompson had brought the boats through safely, but because of the stage of water—more than forty feet below high-water mark—it had been arduous labor.[7] They had been forced to make more than one hundred portages along the course of two canyons in which the first party had made only three. The men, even Thompson, did not appreciate the difficulties and disappointments which Hamblin and the Major had experienced in their search for the Dirty Devil. In private they grumbled and criticized their leader. The food supplies which the Major was able to obtain—only three hundred pounds—would be scarcely enough to see them through. However, they did appreciate the overalls and shoes which the Major had bought for each man. They always needed shoes. No pair made could stand the repeated soaking and scuffing encountered in the day's work. Back at the Uinta agency the boys had hired an Indian to make moccasins, which they wore in the boats in order to save regular shoes for shore duty.[8] Bare feet were unendurable because of the blistering heat and the alkali sands on the small islands and the sharp rocks both in and out of the water.

The Major was accompanied by Jacob Hamblin and two of his sons, who turned out to be jolly fellows and good singers. It did not take Clem and Fred long to learn from them how to roll cigarettes. After supper the Major and the Hamblins entertained the boys with Indian songs.

[6] Thompson was angry at this failure; bitterly he wrote (*Diary*, August 29, 1871), "I cannot learn that the Major made any serious effort to get in and do not believe he did. Mr. Hamblin probably made slight effort to rush the Dirty Devil or some attempt." Thompson was wrong; both Hamblin and Powell had made persistent attempts.

[7] The stage of water of the Colorado River is extremely variable, rising rapidly concommitantly with heavy rains over tributary basins. From year to year and season to season the stage varies and of course determines the character of the river. Comparison of the experiences of the two Powell expeditions, Stanton, Kolb brothers, Freeman, Stone, and Kelly will show how important the stage is. Failure to understand this fundamental factor caused the various parties to question and criticize the measurements, descriptions, and veracity of the others.

[8] J. F. Steward, MS, *Diary;* also Dellenbaugh, *op. cit.*

Old Jacob did not look the part of the Mormon buckskin apostle, the most fearless and famous of all Mormon missionaries. Jacob was treated to a short boat ride down to camp, but that mode of travel was not to his liking. He much preferred the hazards of the trail to the uncertainty of the water of the Colorado. Again the men could scarcely believe that this quiet mild-mannered man was the far-famed missionary. Hamblin remained in camp for several days while the scientific notes and personal letters were prepared for mailing.

Two weeks of easy boating took the party safely through the swift and unbroken waters of Labyrinth and Stillwater Canyons. On September 14th they paused long enough to explore the Indian ruins which the Major had visited in 1869. The next day they reached the junction of the Grand and Green. The provisions were going fast and a conference was held to appraise the situation. It was decided to place every man on strict rations consisting of three thin strips of bacon, a chunk of bread the size of a fist, and coffee for each meal. It was a grim coincidence that on this slim fare they would have to work their passage through Cataract Canyon, which, according to Jack Sumner's diary, would be punishing work. On the 19th the men pushed off in good spirits. On the last day of September they emerged from Narrow Canyon, reached the mouth of the Dirty Devil, and camped upon the exact spot on which the 1869 party had rested. The remnant ashes of the old campfire and a rusty pocketknife marked the site. It would be nip and tuck to reach the Crossing of the Fathers before the food gave out. In order to plan for the completion of scientific observations next season, the *Cañonita* was cached at the Dirty Devil. This would permit a small party to take the boat, survey Gray Canyon, and rejoin the main party.

On October 9th the Major left for Salt Lake City. He had been so impatient to go that he had not intended to remain long enough for the men to write letters to their families. Thompson rather testily urged him to consider their feelings and he finally consented to wait overnight.[9]

There was a good deal of discontent among the members of the expedition, engendered no doubt by idleness, short rations, and incompatibility. The prolonged absence of the Major, misinterpreted as disinterest on his part, served to aggravate the situation.[10] In a sense the Major was to blame. If he had come right out and explained the pur-

[9] The Major's impatience and thoughtlessness was a cause of considerable irritation.
[10] Major Powell's notebooks show that he was exploring and making observations on the geology and archeology of the regions. During the summer the Major made two trips to Salt Lake City to visit Emma.

poses of his independent work, the men would have been satisfied. Instead, Powell, always in the character of the commander, chose to be secretive, going here and there according to his own plan but taking no one, not even Thompson, into his confidence. If the Major had been killed by Indians or met with an accident, his party, waiting indefinitely, would have faced disaster. Undoubtedly this possibility had not occurred to Powell. He rarely allowed such thoughts to interfere with his activities. Clem Powell and Fred Dellenbaugh grew to dislike each other soon after the expedition got under way. It was a case of petty jealousy. Clem at first had been granted many favors from the Major, who was his elder cousin. Gradually Fred became a favorite not only of the Major but especially of "Prof." Thompson. His sense of humor, lively conversation, and unquestioned ability were attractive. Thus the antagonism nourished. As a consequence of this foolishness, many years later Dellenbaugh, writing his account of the second canyon voyage, was denied use of Clem's five journals.[11]

Some of the men, like Steward and Beaman, could raise an oath upon very slight provocation and were accordingly viewed as coarse fellows by their more pious companions. There is downright abhorrence in one diary: "Perhaps I miss the dear privileges of the Christian Church, thrown as I am among so many who if not infidels, full-grown, are embryotic and I fear are germs of vigorous growth." "There is such a makeup in the present party as is not suited for culture or refinement." [12] In all, there was a gradual disintegration of the comradeship which made the earlier days on the river so enjoyable. Had the Major remained in actual command of the river party, he would have kept personal differences from smouldering by keeping all hands busy, but Thompson was helpless. He was forced to idle in doldrums waiting for his chief, or to hurry past interesting problems because of short rations. The reason always to be remembered was the Major's attitude toward the river work; it was purely routine observing and mapping.

While the Major had gone to see his wife the men were establishing winter headquarters at Kanab.[13] Shortly after their arrival Brigham

---

[11] Mrs. W. C. Powell denied use of the journals chiefly because of Clem's unkind remarks about Dellenbaugh and other companions. Clem's misery and discouragement are reflected in the diaries. His failure to "make the grade" in the photographic department was a bitter disappointment.

[12] F. M. Bishop, *Diary,* July 30 and August 20, 1871.

[13] It was necessary to establish a base camp to prepare a topographic map. During the winter and spring of 1871–1872 the men surveyed the Kaibab and Kanab plateaus, the area between the Paria and Virgin Rivers, etc. For example, Powell wrote, *Geology of the Uinta Mountains,* p. 52, "The section which I shall give of these three groups [White Cliff,

Young, the Mormon leader, came on his annual visit to the settlement. On this occasion President Young was accompanied by only one of his wives, Bishop Snow with his favorite Bishopess, and George A. Smith with one wife. The official party was escorted by five men. Brigham Young expressed a great interest in the work of the expedition and offered the men free use of the telegraph to Salt Lake City. The next day the distinguished party left for St. George, a distance of eighty miles.

Kanab, a Mormon settlement, had been laid out the year before. The old fort—an open square stockaded on one side—still housed a few families but most of them, about a hundred in all, had built substantial dwellings on the city lots. Irrigation ditches on both sides of the broad streets made it possible to water any of the lots. Kanab was a thriving village.[14] The farms produced good crops of potatoes and corn. Grape vines, apple, pear, and cherry trees had been planted but were not yet old enough to bear fruit. It was an ideal location for a base camp. A blacksmith, tinsmith, and other tradesmen worked in the village, the women would sew clothing, and ample food and other provisions were readily available. Moreover the geology of the region could be examined conveniently from this situation.

The Powell party erected tents and floored them as protection against dampness, constructed rough furniture, and in one of the tents set up a large table for drafting. Here the survey measurements were transcribed and plotted. Thompson did most of the actual map drawing, but F. M. Bishop and Fred Dellenbaugh assisted in the detailing.

Early in December the camp was transformed by the influx of feminine citizens. A hospital train of five wagons came in from Salt Lake City not only with Mrs. Powell and Mrs. Thompson, but also with the baby, Mary, not yet three months old, and a very attractive young Mormon nurse.[15] The unmarried men in the party were charmed by her presence. Nell had brought with her Fuzz, a little dog of uncertain ancestry which had been shipped from Normal to cheer her a bit. The Powell family occupied a large army tent. The most conspicuous article of furniture was a sturdy table on which reposed a clothes basket serving

Vermilion Cliff, and Shinarump formations] was made along the course of the Kanab in the winter of 1871."

[14] I have a photograph of the fort taken by Beaman in 1871; also an extensive file of recollections of the Powell party by old-timers interviewed by Mrs. Blanche H. Mace of Kanab.

[15] Mary Dean Powell, born September 8, 1871 in Salt Lake City, was the only child of John Wesley and Emma Dean Powell.

as a cradle for the baby. Both Nell and Emma possessed fine voices and Nell, as all the Powell brothers and sisters, had a great repertoire of ballads. The wives entertained the company with a delightful variety of tunes. Nearly every evening the entire party gathered in the firelight for community singing.

By day work on the maps continued, and the men not assigned to that task made observations on the topography of the country round about. However, snow and cold soon limited these activities and forced the men to spend a good deal of time idling, especially because the days were so short. Christmas came upon the party without any special preparations. Nell and Emma conjured up a holiday feast and at the call to supper everyone except Beaman gathered in the eating tent for the occasion. Spread before them was an array of ham, sardines, bread, butter, plum pudding, milk, and coffee. After supper they joined in singing Christmas carols and tunes of home. Jack Hillers and Jack Steward brought out a couple of bottles of wine and the boys sat by the warming fire in the big tent and joined the rounds as the bottles were passed. Mrs. Hamblin had sent an apple for each member of the Powell party and the Mormon families nearby had invited some of the fellows for dinner and eggnog. Only Beaman accepted, the others preferring to remain together for the holiday.

The new year came in like a roaring lion, stormy and bitter cold, but a ball was held on New Year's Eve and both the storm and cold were forgotten in the excitement. When the festivities were at their height the Major made his appearance, but took no part in the dancing or jollity. The Major had just returned from a trip down to Kanab Wash and had taken quite a beating in the rough weather. The following week the Mormons staged a gay leap-year ball and all of the men of the expedition were invited to attend. However, they were not permitted to join in any of the dancing and merely sat on the sidelines, enjoying the fun nonetheless.

The Major took advantage of the nearness of a band of Ute Indians; he held council with them and gained permission to record their history and mythology. The Indians sang and danced, played games, performed their domestic skills, related their myths, and explained their vocabulary while Emma took notes and made sketches.

Unknown to the Major, on December 28th Father Powell died at the home of Lida at Cedar Point, Kansas.[16] Reverend Powell had taken a

---

[16] Joseph Powell and his wife, Mary Dean Powell, are buried in Wheaton, Illinois. Mrs. Powell had died at Wheaton on March 12, 1870.

few days from his work at the Belleville Mission in southern Illinois to visit his children and their families over the holidays. Wes had long since been forgiven for devoting his life to science; he had been a considerate and respectful son.

Three of the men wanted to be released from the expedition. Bishop, who had been shot through the lung during the war, was badly run down, and not being as strong as the others, was anxious to part from the group. Steward was also played out; he had lost interest. Beaman, on the contrary, with an eye to business, wanted to strike out on his own and do a little fancy photography in the country to the south. Of the others, Jones was suffering from rheumatism and had to move about on crutches; Hattan was ill, but he and the "Deacon," as Jones was called, preferred to stick to the party. Inadequate diet was the underlying cause of the misery.[17]

During January the Major and his family prepared to return east. The Major planned to go to Washington to appeal to Congress for a substantial appropriation to continue field work. Presumably the mapping of the river would be completed this year, but the Rocky Mountain country remained a vast little-known region. New villages and posts were springing up. These were joined by trails which maintained during most of the year the threads of communication and commerce. Railroads and the telegraph contributed to the expansion of population and the development of the territories. Nevertheless, a real knowledge of the country was lacking.

[17] This deterioration of health is recorded by Dellenbaugh, *op. cit.*, pp. 145–46. The recurrence of old army injuries, nervous disorders, and lameness which incapacitated several of the men were typical symptoms of the beriberi and scurvy.

11

1872 · Seeking Federal Support

IT WAS not easy to sit down and write a brief summary of the scientific results of the year's work such as Congress expected. The observations of five years in the field combined to suggest problems enough for a lifetime. The area which Powell had been exploring since 1867 was scientifically almost unknown.

In no other part of the world is so vast an area denuded and laid bare by the combined force of uplift and erosion. The rocks of this great plateau country dip gently to the north in such manner that along a line extending from the southern bend of the Grand Canyon northward to the region in which the Dirty Devil (Frémont) River rises, more than 25,000 feet of strata are exposed in sequence. The upturned edges of five miles of strata, the pages of earth history, are open for inspection.[1] Powell first recognized this marvelous succession when he traveled westward from the White River camp to Fort Bridger in 1868. In fact he had named many of its individual members. But this was only the setting.

The plateau, much of it desert and utterly bare of vegetation, was dissected by an intricate ramifying system of canyons, which revealed the deep anatomy of the crust of the earth. Three processes had carved the bizarre and gigantic features of the country—disturbance of the level of the geological formations, which resulted in folds and faults, eruptive agencies, and erosion. Each process had its part, but erosion produced the labyrinth of gorges that made the country so nearly inaccessible. The work of 1871, instead of solving the geology of the Colorado River, suggested greater problems. Ten years of exploration would not be enough to describe even the chief features of this wonderful region.

[1] Major Powell, in the first three paragraphs of his *Geology of the Uinta Mountains*, introduces his interpretation of the geology of the Colorado River region. These concise statements, in identical or similar phraseology, were used by Powell in some of his lectures in 1869.

The more Powell weighed his data, the more he determined to do the job right. Government aid to the extent of twelve thousand dollars had made possible a much more thorough survey than would have been possible on his personal resources. Suppose the federal government could be persuaded to finance the entire program?

One morning when all of the boys were busy at their tasks, the Major asked Thompson to saddle his horse and ride out with him for a little discussion. As they rode along Powell talked about their useful work and their many unfinished problems. He explained that he planned to go to Washington to appeal for an additional appropriation, this time either for a survey of the valleys of the Sevier and Río Virgen Rivers, or for the publication of their results. He was not yet sure which. Gradually working to the point, the Major asked Harry directly, "If I fail, will you work without salary next year to complete this work?"

"Yes," Thompson replied, "but I must have enough to live on."

"Of course," was Powell's answer.

"Then," said Thompson, "I am perfectly willing to work until we get this job finished, be it one or two years." [To which Thompson added in his diary], "The Major will get the appropriation, without a doubt." [2]

There is a genuine zeal for knowledge in the forthright and assured way in which both Thompson and Powell made up their minds to stick to the unfinished work. No other motive than the pursuit of knowledge, the love of science, could have lured them into this task. Neither had an interest in wealth, and neither entertained any desire to take up residence in the country to try to "strike it rich."

Most of the men in the party were eager to continue the work in 1872. The Major had funds sufficient for wages to last until early summer. Certain reorganizations in the party were necessary even though the main personnel remained the same. The three who wanted to be released —Steward, who was badly run down, Bishop, who was also exhausted, and Beaman, who wanted to strike out on his own—were paid and permitted to resign.

Whatever else the West may have meant to other men, to Powell it was an exciting field for exploration and research. With a passion for investigation, but with a greater passion for action, the Major had found an occupation to consume his curiosity and energy. Geology was but a fraction of it.

The plains had led to the mountains, the mountains to the parks, the

[2] A. H. Thompson, MS, *Diary,* Dec. 12, 1871.

parks to the canyons. The little-known arid region which spread beyond the Rockies was a revelation. And then the Indians, so much a product of their environment, their customs, language, and mythology, presented other problems.

Powell did, indeed, take an active interest in everything. While watching over his little family and carrying out field work, the Major was moved by the plight of the destitute Utes of southern Utah, who were camped near his winter headquarters. It had been a severe winter, and the summer before, pestilential grasshoppers had stripped the foliage, and the Indians were in a nearly starved condition being unable to gather seeds or fruits.

The Major sent Jacob Hamblin with a letter of appeal to Maj. Charles F. Powell, a U.S. Special Indian Agent, pleading for help for four tribes —the Unkar, Kanigats, Kaibabits, and the Shewits (the same tribe that had murdered the Howland brothers and Bill Dunn):

All of these bands are in a destitute condition. . . . The Indians are begging from the Whites, who are themselves poor by reason of the grasshoppers. The Kaibabits are encamped about three miles from me and I have visited them often and I find them in a truly suffering condition. They have exchanged their ornaments and clothing for food and do not have enough. Can you do something for them? It will be an act of humanity. . . .[3]

Charles Powell replied, "I can do nothing until funds are sent me for their relief." This agent, of a very different breed of Powells, was about to be relieved of his position for good reasons. He was an example of the incompetency and dishonesty which had corroded their way into the Bureau of Indian Affairs. This was not the first instance that the Major had solicited aid for the Utes, and it shows the warmth of his sympathy.

Powell's interest in the Indians extended beyond the study of their habits. They were creatures in their native habitat. There was the problem—the land and its occupance. It presented a boundless field for study. Powell wanted to persuade the federal government to finance this program too.

In the winter camp at Kanab in 1872 Powell made two decisions which marked the turning point in his career. Taking leave of his men the Major, with Mrs. Powell and the baby, went to Salt Lake City without so much as mentioning what was on his mind. Perhaps it would be premature. The Major kept his own counsel. He had only casually dis-

[3] J. W. Powell to Charles F. Powell, Jan. 16, 1872.

cussed his plans with Emma. Not even a hint had been given to Harry Thompson.

The Powells went straight to Washington. If he could secure an appropriation for 1873, the Major would resign immediately from the university and take up legal residence in Washington. There he could use his influence to obtain annual appropriations for the support of his field work.

Up to this time Powell had drawn no salary for his exploring activities, yet he determined to remain in the public service even though he should fail, for the time being, in obtaining an official appointment. The salary from the professorship at Illinois State University at Normal had satisfied his needs—in fact he had saved some money and had a clear title to property in Normal.[4] Now that he intended to resign from the university this would mean that he would have no certain income from any source. As usual he could fall back upon his resourcefulness.

There was a great deal more than was printed in the newspapers to the annual scurry for appropriations for scientific work and exploration. With the Major's very first success at gaining an annual guaranty, he was drawn into the stream of politics. He had learned, however, that most of the deals and the petty politics had to be done quietly.

Early in 1871, having gained the support of his old army acquaintance, General—now Senator—Logan, and through the offices of A. C. Osborne, a railroad promoter from Brooklyn, the support of several other Congressmen, Powell found himself obliged to do a little canvassing on behalf of the Great Southern Railroad.[5] Major Powell received an unblushing request from Osborne to persuade Logan to support a bill in favor of the building of the Great Southern. He was even instructed to confer "frequently and freely" with the Senator and with Colonel Alberger. Mr. Osborne promised that whatever aid Powell could render would not be forgotten or unrewarded.

How much the Major accomplished, or tried to accomplish, is not recorded. He was nonetheless obliged to take a part in a number of such machinations because they were indispensable to activate the Col-

---

[4] The U.S. Census for 1870 (data taken August 9th) values Powell's real estate at $4,000 and personal property at $800. The Major owned a house and several lots in Normal. Incidentally Emma Powell, while her husband indulged his wanderlust, operated a boarding school for young girls. Some writers have considered Powell to be impecunious, one observing "young Powell's future seemed headed for obscurity and poverty." No child of Joseph and Mary Powell was headed for poverty, least of all Wes. Reverend Powell bequeathed an estate of more than $13,000 divided equally among his surviving eight children —each of whom knew the parable of the talents.

[5] A. C. Osborn to J. W. Powell, Feb. 21, 1871.

orado expeditions. It was unpleasant business but he had no choice. He had accepted favors from the railroads, not the least of which were free passes for all of his men and supplies on each of the expeditions from 1867 to 1872. Inasmuch as the larger railroads were usually on friendly terms with one another, in a very unofficial manner of course, Powell found himself solicited by the Kansas Pacific Railroad and by others.

Before many months passed Powell was either advised by wiser heads or had learned through painful experience that the less he had to do with such business, the better off he would be in the long run. He knew that whenever he could not escape deals there should be as little correspondence as possible.

The chief uncertainty was the annual appropriation which had to be persuaded from Congress—not that Congress was unwilling; the federal government at the moment was supporting, in addition to Powell's, three other independent surveys in the western territories.[6] A survey of the fortieth parallel had been established in 1867 under the jurisdiction of the War Department. Clarence King was in charge of this survey. In the same year a geological and geographical survey of the territories under the leadership of Dr. Ferdinand V. Hayden was established under the jurisdiction of the Department of the Interior. Two years later the War Department put still another party in the field, a military and topographical survey west of the hundredth meridian under Lt. George M. Wheeler.

The problem was to obtain some semblance of permanence, some assurance of continuing support. Powell had been in the field since 1867 but had not received any financial support from Congress until 1870. In the earlier years the expenses were met out of the Major's own pocket, augmented by small sums contributed by educational institutions and the cooperation of fellow explorers who were willing to pay their own way. Powell had been granted authority to draw rations at government rates, which represented a substantial saving, especially at the high prices encountered in the western settlements. Even in 1870, when the survey of the Colorado River region under Major Powell received official recognition, the financial support was very limited. For the fiscal year of 1870–1871 the appropriation was

[6] These four independent federal surveys reflect official and nationwide interest in the public domain. The construction of transcontinental railways, exploitation of natural resources, expanding population, and postwar restlessness contributed to the excitement. These surveys, which became competitive and hostile to one another, figure in succeeding chapters.

only ten thousand dollars and for the past year twelve thousand. Powell had hoped to obtain twenty thousand dollars for the year 1872–1873, but of this he had no assurance.

Powell drew no salary as leader of the expedition and little of the appropriations was used for his personal needs. Whenever he required money, which was frequently, he scheduled a lecture tour or wrote an article for some popular magazine. After Beaman quit the party the Major realized that the photographic section of his expedition also could provide a sizeable income both for himself and for the photographer. The original negatives were considered to be the property of the expedition but duplicate negatives and prints were sold through dealers in the stereoscopic views. The royalties received from these sales were divided among the Major, Thompson, and the photographer.[7] In these side ventures Powell did moderately well and in addition managed to keep before the public in most of the large cities from New York to Milwaukee.

Money may have been the chief uncertainty in administration, but the greatest obstacle was to avoid collision with a party of a rival survey. The areas assigned to each of these surveys overlapped considerably and there was unavoidable duplication of effort. Petty rivalries engendered antagonism and jealousy and the makings for a very unhealthy situation were apparent. Wheeler was no scientist, Powell was no educated scholar, King was too cautious, Hayden too superficial; and so it went, each party and its adherents criticizing the qualifications of the others.

Powell's reputation as the first explorer of the Grand Canyon had helped him in many ways to gain recognition for his survey. Not long after returning to Washington, however, there were others who, with loud fanfare, challenged this priority. The friends of James White who went through a portion of the Grand Canyon on a raft in 1867 claimed that Powell deliberately ignored White's feat. No serious support was given to Mr. White's claim, however. A much more spec-

---

[7] On February 1, 1872, a disagreement between Major Powell and Beaman erupted and the upshot of the argument was Beaman's decision to resign. Powell bought out his interest in the photographs and negatives (stereoscopic or double plates). The sale of the views was a profitable venture. It is not possible to recapitulate the income from this source but in the first six months of 1874 the Major received $4,100 from the sale of stereoscopic views. This was shared with Hillers and Thompson on the basis of 40%–30%–30%, Hillers however, only on prints of his own negatives. Powell, owning the Beaman and Fennemore negatives, took a double share for these views. The late A. C. Lane told me that members of the Geological Survey in the late eighties joked that "stereo" views had paid off the mortgage on the Powell home.

tacular challenge came in 1872 when the self-styled captain, Samuel Adams, publicly announced that he had explored the Colorado River during 1864, 1865, 1866, and 1867 and through friends petitioned Congress for twenty thousand dollars as token reimbursement for his labor and effort.[8] Twenty thousand dollars was the budget that the Major had asked for a year's work. When questioned as to why he had not divulged his discoveries of the Colorado when they were made, Captain Adams replied, with inconsistent modesty, that so novel were his discoveries that he had been afraid his reports would be disbelieved and his story ridiculed.

It developed that the resolution on behalf of Adams had been quietly introduced in Congress by Rep. George W. Julian in 1870 after Major Powell had returned safely from his exploration. This resolution had been lost in committee for two years. Naturally the Major was questioned about Samuel Adams's claims. R. M. McCormick, a Representative from Arizona, asked Powell to give his appraisal of Adams's work.[9] The bitter denunciation which Powell wrote tore his story to shreds sentence by sentence. In support of Adams's claim ten letters published in 1870 were submitted to Congress, but none of them could be authenticated even for date and the inaccuracies and looseness of the story were self-evident. The very parts of the territory which Adams claimed to have explored in 1864 for the first time had been carefully surveyed by Lt. Joseph C. Ives in 1857, and other portions of the country described in detail by Adams were pure imagery and bore no relation to facts or figures. Not the least remarkable of Captain Adams's claims was the alleged discovery of vast fields of wild grain— oats, barley, and wheat—waist high and capable of supporting herds of cattle. Powell sarcastically remarked that this statement would surely astonish Dr. Vasey, the botanist who had been a member of the 1868 expedition.

Major Powell did not speak unknowingly of Mr. Adams. In 1869 awaiting him at Green River Station was this very same man who brazenly informed him that he, not Powell, had been authorized to lead the expedition down the canyons.

Even though these claimants, White and Adams, have been discredited, the shadow of doubt, the ever-present question, remains in

[8] *42nd Cong. 1st Sess. H.R. Misc. Doc. 37,* introduced December 19, 1870.

[9] R. M. McCormick to J. W. Powell, April 20, 1872; Powell to McCormick; MS journal of Capt. Sam Adams, Huntington Library. Adams has all the earmarks of a fraud. The "diary," of which I have seen only a photostat copy, seems to be written at one or best, two times.

documented history. The underdogs have had their defenders even against uncontested truth and fact.

Not all of Powell's activity in Washington in 1872 was political. His personal plans were rapidly materializing. On the first of June the Major and Mrs. Powell purchased from James W. Drane a three-story house in the 900 block on "M" Street Northwest at an agreed price of fourteen thousand dollars.[10] On June 15th they obtained a mortgage with Charles Bradley of Detroit for $7,880. This instrument of mortgage was notarized in Wayne County, Michigan, and called for the repayment of the sum over a period of four years. The deed and trust were recorded in Washington on July 5, 1872.

Major Powell's decision to resign from his professorship was entirely his. Although the board of education was jolted, there must have been a measure of relief to the university authorities when the following note was received by the secretary of the board just in time for their regular spring meeting:

Normal, June 26, 1872.

To the Honorable Board of Education of the State of Illinois.

Gentlemen:

I hereby tender my resignation of the office of curator of the museum. I sincerely thank you for the honor you have conferred in committing that trust to me.

I am, with great respect, your obedient servant,

J. W. Powell.[11]

There were no embellishments and no pleasantries. The only reason underlying this resignation was that the Major had found field work more interesting and much more exciting. He had a penchant for organization and he was casting his eyes on greener pastures. The board debated heatedly on the question of Powell's resignation and at length accepted it. Any other action would have done them no good. The Major would have walked out regardless. College equilibrium is easily upset by rugged and independent individualists. To have expected the Major to conform to academic rules and regulations is pretty nearly unthinkable. His colleagues should have known better.

It was an open secret that some of Powell's teaching colleagues had complained about his prolonged absences from the university. Per-

[10] This was 910 "M" street. Deed and trust recorded in District of Columbia Liber 683, 1872, p. 365. The mortgage was covered by notes: (1) $3,000 payable in two years at 10%, (2) $2,000 in three years at 8% and (3) $2,880 in four years at 8%. Powell repaid the indebtedness within the contractual period.

[11] Proc. Bd. Ed., 1872, p. 3.

haps there was in this resentment a tinge of envy and dissatisfaction. The Major's ability and reputation were willingly acknowledged, but it was obvious that pressure and obligations arising from his exploring activities forced Powell to neglect routine college duties. True enough, the board of education had consented to his leaves of absence and contributed financial support with the view of increasing the scientific collections of the state museum. They were aware of his prestige value. However, the collections, which were accumulating, were neither catalogued nor identified and the optimistic estimates of their quantity and value, as calculated by the Major, did not agree with those of Dr. George Vasey or Prof. S. A. Forbes, who had in turn taken over the curatorship.[12] Harry Thompson had been acting curator in 1869, but when he joined the Major in the second Colorado expedition, Vasey succeeded him. By necessity their services were temporary and superficial in the expectancy of the Major's permanent return to his college post.[13]

A little unfinished business remained at Normal after Major Powell first resigned his post and made arrangements for disposing of his house. From time to time Powell had culled from the collections stored in museums various materials for examination and study. Some of these were his own property, but in others ownership was not established. A committee headed by Jesse Fell [14] was appointed to look into the matter but their efforts were not very successful. The ownership of specimens were exceedingly confused. Powell possessed extensive private collections assembled over many years before accepting a position at the Normal University. He had donated some of these to the museum, but just which ones had not been accurately recorded. The ownership of the collections made in the western territories was no clearer. In 1867 and 1868, although they were sponsored by Illinois institutions, the expeditions were in large part paid for with Powell's own money. The expedition in 1869, because of the hardships which were encountered, had sent back no substantial collections, indeed the collections were exceedingly meager. Beginning with 1870, when the Major received federal appropriations for his work, and was therefore

[12] See Cook and McHugh, *A History of the Illinois State Normal University*, 1882, for the sequence of events attending the curatorship.

[13] One of the difficulties stemmed from Powell's unwillingness to distribute specimens to those institutions which had supported his 1868 and 1869 expeditions. When, if ever, the specimens would be identified was a justifiable question. Yet Thompson, in the capacity of acting curator, urged Powell to delay the distribution of specimens no matter how insistent the clamor. A. H. Thompson to J. W. Powell, Feb. 14, 1871.

[14] This committee was composed of Jesse W. Fell, C. F. Noettling, and E. A. Gastman.

in government employ, the ownership was subject to legitimate contest.

No doubt each of these complications was investigated by the committee. Nevertheless Mr. Fell wrote to Joseph Henry, secretary of the Smithsonian Institution, that all of Powell's materials must be returned to Illinois and that Normal University was laying claim to them.[15] The claim was ignored and later disallowed on the premise that the specimens were gathered while the Major was in the employ of the federal government. Whatever may have been the outward merits of the case, it is certainly true that Powell had taken some of his own collections from the museum at Normal. Whether they had ever been officially given to the college can never be determined. It was a sore point with the college authorities and the incident was remembered for a good many years after the Major had left his professorship.

This little personal contest established a far-reaching precedent. There were numerous exploring parties of a semiofficial nature which were financed in entirety or in part by federal grants. In the majority of cases no provisions were made for determining ownership of the materials. The fact that the Smithsonian Institution was in charge of the U.S. National Museum and that the National Museum was to obtain the official collections made the Powell case legalistically, at least, fairly simple. Other expeditions were carried out at great expense with rich rewards but the materials remained in the private ownership of the personnel who were engaged in the exploration. It was not until many years later that the strict requirement that all materials collected on government-sponsored parties remain in the title of the government was passed by Congress. In the case of Major Powell's collections it is more than likely that the decision would not have been rendered in favor of the Smithsonian Institution had Powell not actually wanted the materials in Washington.

The Major had gathered together a very comprehensive library of scientific and literary books heavily weighted on the scientific side. Like his collections they were stored in boxes and crude shelves because he used them only during those short periods when he was home for the winter. The library filled one room of his home, and when he came to sell his house in preparation for the move to Washington it was im-

---

[15] Fell, Noettling, and Gastman to Joseph Henry, Dec. 3, 1872: "this Committee was instructed . . . to procure a speedy return of the specimens . . . as all of said specimens *belong to this institution and are claimed* by it." A penciled note on the letter reads, "knows nothing of specimens belonging to the State of Illinois. Major Powell sent certain collections made by him while in the service of the U.S. and as U.S. employee sent by him in pursuance of law by Congress. When Powell comes back will refer to him. /S/A.M."

possible to move the books until the dwelling which he had purchased was available. He had learned one lesson—he could not mix "mine and thine" without encountering trouble and questions as to ownership.

Returning from Washington, Major Powell made a brief stopover at Normal to put the house up for sale and to make arrangements for the storage of his personal library and laboratory equipment. A part of the furniture was given to neighbors, a few good pieces were sold, and the remainder shipped to Washington. The Major and Mrs. Powell attended commencement exercises at Wesleyan and said good-by to many of their friends in Bloomington.[16]

The house at Normal found a ready buyer. Mr. S. G. Reeder on August 9th contracted for the place for $2,600, one thousand dollars in cash and the balance on March 1, 1873.[17] Mr. Reeder found it possible to pay the sum in full, closing the deal with Bram Powell, who had been given power of attorney during his brother's absence, for $2,450. Powell's library was still in the house and it was promptly insured for one thousand dollars against loss or damage. Powell had uprooted himself from Illinois.

Harvey C. DeMotte, professor of mathematics at Wesleyan, and Mrs. DeMotte had accepted the Major's invitation to join his field party for the summer. DeMotte was to serve as an assistant topographer, engaging in some of the land work needed to plot the course of the river more accurately. Emma and the baby went to Detroit and the Major and the DeMottes returned to join the expedition.

During this time, Thompson, to whom the Major had entrusted "entire charge of the geographic work," had not been idle. For many weeks "Prof." had been working on the map. Bishop was doing most of the drawing while Fred copied their bearings and made rough sketches for him.

The photographic department had been a headache. When Beaman left the party Clem Powell was assigned to take his place but Clem was unable to get good pictures with the chemicals Beaman left. Thompson was so incensed that he stopped payment on Beaman's salary check on the supposition that he had deliberately ruined the solutions. Thompson could print good pictures with fresh solutions but had only failures with those left by Beaman. Clem, however, did not have the knack to do the work well.[18] James Fennemore, a professional photographer

[16] *Illinois Wesleyan Alumni Journal,* V. 1, p. 167.

[17] S. G. Reeder to J. W. Powell, Aug. 9, 1872; Oct. 2, 1872.

[18] A. H. Thompson, MS, *Diary.* Clem's disappointments and Thompson's patient criticisms are mentioned in W. Clement Powell, MS, *Diary.*

working in the establishment of Charles R. Savage in Salt Lake City, was hired for the season. Fennemore had ability but he did not like to climb canyon walls. Clem continued for a while as an assistant, but when Jack Hillers proved to be more suitable Clem was transferred to other work. When Fennemore voluntarily left the party Hillers took full charge of all of the photography. Jack's work is among the best done by the pioneer photographers of the West.[19]

On March 21st Thompson broke camp at Pipe Spring for a trip to Mount Trumbull, the most prominent peak in the Uinkaret Mountains. The trail had started out straight and easy but soon became rough. First wagons, and then horses were left behind. On the 25th the party climbed the mountain leaving Fred Dellenbaugh and Jones on the summit to take observations and Hillers and Fennemore to take views of the surrounding country.

Another section of the party skirted the rim of the canyon to find trails down to the river. Snowstorms in the Uinkaret Mountains forced Thompson to restrict his work to lower altitudes. He moved his party to the region of St. George, Washington, and Fort Pierce. In this way the men were busy until May 8th when they returned to Kanab.

Thompson made another difficult overland trip through unknown country from Kanab to the mouth of the Dirty Devil River. Starting on May 29th, by June 3rd the party reached a large stream, unnamed, which they could not ford. They followed the stream for several days, observed how it "canyoned," and realized that this was the stream Jacob Hamblin's men had mistaken for the Dirty Devil the year before. "It is utterly impossible to think of crossing. . . . Cannot pack down it. . . . We are stopped," "Prof." wrote in his diary. This stream was named Escalante. Thompson led his men back to the head of the canyon, finally made a crossing, proceeded to the Dirty Devil, and picked a trail down to the Colorado River. They pitched camp at the mouth of the Dirty Devil on June 22nd.

Here the party was divided as had been planned. Hillers, Dellenbaugh, Fennemore, and Johnson were to put the *Cañonita*, which had been cached since the previous September, in condition and finish the river work from the Dirty Devil to the mouth of the Paria while Thompson and the others were to obtain supplies and wait for the

[19] Only a few of Hillers' negatives, which numbered several thousand, have been published. A few have been described in Steward's "Notes on Hillers' Photographs of the Paiute and Ute Indians," *Smith. Misc. Coll.*, V. 98, No. 18.

Major. Then the entire outfit would pass through the Grand Canyon by boat.

The Major said he expected to arrive about the first of July and tentatively scheduled resumption of the river work for July 15th. By July 30th Thompson began to get a little irritated. He had received no mail from Powell for some weeks. He was more peeved when that day the *Deseret News* which arrived with the mail—still no letters from the Major—reported that he had arrived in Salt Lake City on July 17th with DeMotte.[20]

On the morning of August 2nd Professor DeMotte and Captain Bishop arrived at the camp and at four in the afternoon the Major appeared, as free as ever. Bishop had returned to work with the land party for the season in the capacity of an assistant topographer.

Major Powell had spent a week in Salt Lake City making arrangements to check the telegraph and devising a system of time signals to be used to determine the longitude of Kanab and for other triangulations. Even with good chronometers for precision work, the time pieces had to be checked accurately. Now the Major was ready to begin work.

The Major, DeMotte, Thompson, and a small party of Indians passed along the south edge of the Kaibab Plateau and established a series of stations, which were to be used to locate the meandering line of the Colorado River. When this topographic work was completed the party continued along the east brink of the plateau, crossed House Rock Valley, and picked its way to the mouth of the Paria.

On August 13th they found the river party, which was waiting for them at the junction of the Paria and the Colorado. The fellows, who had been in the field for a long winter and an even longer summer, had languished in idleness awaiting the return of Major Powell, who had been expected ever since the 2nd of August.

A few preliminaries delayed resumption of the survey of the river, but on August 17th everything was ready to complete the river work. The *Nellie* was abandoned as unseaworthy, and with two boats they pushed into the Colorado and ran into Marble Canyon. The party ran down about eleven miles from the mouth of the Paria to a point where the walls stood a thousand feet high and where Powell observed the "cañon could be crossed by a suspension bridge."

In 1871 the stage of water had been very low, much lower than the

[20] A. H. Thompson, MS, *Diary*. See also DeMotte, *Illinois Wesleyan Alumni Journal*, V. 1, pp. 233–39.

first party had encountered two years before. Now the level was extremely high and judging from high-water marks and recent driftwood had been so for some months. Melting of the heavy snows of the preceding severe winter augmented by torrential rains had swelled the river to an abnormal stage.[21]

On the 18th Thompson entered in his diary, "camped just below a huge rapid that made a most infernal roaring all night." Two days later the party ran into a dry side gulch above which two springs poured out of the cliff. A few plants grew on the wall around the springs. Wrote Thompson, "The Major thinks that the place is called 'Vasey's Paradise' but if it is, it is a Hell of a Paradise." [22]

Going was rough all the way to the mouth of the Little Colorado five days away. They had lowered, according to their measurements, 585 feet in the sixty-five miles through Marble Canyon, running sixty-three rapids with portaging of four and lining of three others. At one place the boats were hurled along at a tremendous speed when, suddenly, ahead of them, in such a position that it could not be avoided, loomed a fearful commotion of waters indicating large rocks jutting to the surface of the river. The Major stood on the middle deck with his life preserver in place, and gripping the arm of his deck chair to prevent being thrown off balance by the lurching of the boat, gazed at the maelstrom.

It looked to him like the end for us and he exclaimed calmly: "By God, boys, we're gone." With terrific impetus we speeded into the seething boiling turmoil, expecting to feel a crush and to have the *Dean* crumble beneath us, but instead of that unfortunate result she shot through smoothly without a scratch, the rocks being deeper than appeared by the commotion on the surface.[23]

The river was narrow, in many places not more than seventy-five feet and hardly ever exceeding two hundred feet. They had encountered whirlpools strong enough to turn the boat all the way through Marble Canyon. In this same stretch of river in 1869 Powell had walked over the water-smoothed multicolored marble for mile after mile.

On the 24th of August the men entered the Grand Canyon proper in

[21] The higher the stage of water the fewer portages but the more treacherous the water. The extreme observed differences between the high and low stages were as much as sixty to one hundred feet. A. H. Thompson, MS, *Diary*, Aug. 30, 1872, wrote, "It must rise fearfully fast in these narrow canyons. We have found driftwood at least one hundred feet above the present level of the water."

[22] A. H. Thompson, MS, *Diary*, Aug. 20, 1872.

[23] F. S. Dellenbaugh, MS, *Diary*, Aug. 22, 1872; quotation also given in *A Canyon Voyage*, p. 221.

great spirits. It was more of the same and in four days they had passed over six rapids, including one by making a footage over half of it and running the other part. This rapid had the largest fall which they had yet tackled. They estimated the descent to be forty feet in one-half of a mile. Next day they ran the Sockdologer, a 130 foot drop in three-quarters of a mile as Thompson measured it.

At the mouth of Kanab Creek supplies were waiting, and the land party had become anxious, almost pessimistic, because the boats and their crews were long overdue. The descent in this seventy miles was 890 feet. The Major rested his men from their exhausting work and pondered his future course. The water was continually rising and had become treacherous, swift, and at times frightening.

The earth shook with the rush of water. The boats were taking heavy pounding and the men were forced to lay up for repairs. The *Dean* was leaking badly and her seams could not be made tight. Heavy rains continued and in one night the river rose fifteen feet. That afternoon Powell had ordered the men to take the boats up on the rocks for greater safety but during the evening they had to lift the boats still higher. Powell wrote, "Anxious night." Their anxiety was relieved when, at about midnight, the river ceased to rise.

Ever since they had passed the Sockdologer on August 28th the hazards had multiplied. Jones had a close call on the first of September. The *Dean* was having a rough time and he was thrown out. Shipmates pulled him in. September 3rd got off to a bad start and the mishaps augured no good. The fierce current whipped the boats along. The *Dean,* as usual in the lead, plunged into a small rapid, gained momentum, and bore down upon a larger one. It was impossible to make a landing. The Major stood up to get a better view of the declivity. Just as the boat shot through, a giant wave struck the *Dean* and instantly capsized her. Fred and Jones were not wearing life preservers, although the Major and Jack were—and fortunately so. The Major and Hillers were pulled down head first but a moment later were thrown into the air. Fred and Jones managed to reach the upturned boat. After resting at the side to regain breath the quartet righted her. The men joked with the Major "about his zeal in going to examine the geology at the bottom of the river." [24] Later the same day Fred was thrown out by a wild lurch of the boat and the Major and Jones had to jump in to help him.

[24] F. S. Dellenbaugh, MS, *Diary; A Canyon Voyage,* p. 237.

Powell, disregarding the personal accidents (nothing less than the loss of a boat was a mishap), entered in his diary appropriate comments on the river:

Started about 2:30 and had an awe-inspiring ride through two rapids one setting toward the cliff on the right. The current set the boats against the broken waters along the foot of the cliff with great force so that she seemed to strike against a rock. But, passing that in a wild mad current through a narrow gorge that was frightful. On the river sped! bearing us so swift a rate that no landing could be made.[25]

The river was full of white pools—worse than they had ever seen it before. Time after time it was utterly impossible to land and an upset would have meant almost certain disaster. In some places the increase in volume of the water was a decided advantage; the rocks were covered so that the men were spared the labor of many portages but, at the same time, in the very narrow portions of the canyon the river became so swift that it was extremely perilous. In these narrow passages driftwood lodged high on the walls showed that the difference between high- and low-water mark was ninety to one hundred feet. Powell wrote in the journal, "It is difficult to describe the raging of the water through such places." Thompson observed, "It must rise fearfully fast in these narrow canyons."

The Major studied the river cautiously. The map of the lower portion of the Grand Canyon made in 1869 was preserved and Thompson had already made use of the 1869 notes in preparing a preliminary plat for the present expedition. Although he had hoped to make a more thorough geological examination of some of the parts, there was no justification for exposing the party to any unnecessary dangers. Accurate mapping sufficient for their needs could be made from the rim of the plateau.

On Sunday, September 8th, Thompson approached Powell and suggested that it would be advisable to send one boat to Mt. Trumbull and call a halt to the trip, but after deliberation that night the two decided to quit where they were. In the morning the Major at breakfast said, "Well, boys, our voyage is done." Thompson continued in his diary, "All are very pleased. The fact is that each one is impressed with the impossibility of continuing down the river."[26]

The second expedition therefore did not make a complete traverse

[25] J. W. Powell, MS, *Diary*, Sept. 23, 1872.
[26] A. H. Thompson, MS, *Diary*, Sept. 9, 1872. In fact Thompson had written on Sept. 7th, "It is nonsense to think of trying the 'lower land' with this water."

of the Colorado River and the technical information which Powell had concerning the lower portions of the Grand Canyon of the Colorado was actually gathered by him in 1869. Despite the loss of most of the field notes during the first trip, the creditable portion which was preserved spared the second party from making what would have otherwise been a hazardous, if not foolhardy, attempt to duplicate the work.

The river work was finished, plans for continuing the mapping were arranged, and the Major outlined to Thompson his plans for the next two years, dependent of course on federal appropriations for the work.

12

1873 · A Special Commission Among the Utes

THE plains Indians that Major Powell chanced to meet along the wagon route and trails in 1867 were, for the most part, degenerate and dirty tribesmen who clustered parasitically about the outposts and villages. The more unspoiled Indians were feared and avoided. Powell's plan to cross the Bad Lands on his first trip west had been rejected by General Sherman because of the danger of depredation. Even the Indians in the parks of Colorado had long been in contact with trappers, prospectors, and settlers. In the give and take of association the Indian had given up much of the best in his nature.

The Major crisscrossed the arid regions of Utah, Arizona, and Nevada scores of times in the ensuing five years, meeting during his travels scattered bands of Utes, Paiutes, Shoshones, and other Indians. They were without exception wretched and poverty stricken but, unlike all other tribes, relatively unspoiled. Most of them practiced no agriculture, and as they were forced from their favorite valleys and the game, upon which they were dependent, was exterminated, these proud nomadic people were driven deeper and deeper into unfavorable country. The traditional seed gathering, augmented occasionally by a woefully feeble attempt at agriculture, could not nourish the population.

The Utes had been subdued and after bitter resistance against Mormon encroachment had been herded into reservations, which hardly deserved the name. The years of 1870 and 1871 were plagued with hordes of grasshoppers, and their condition had deteriorated badly.

Aside from the sympathy which Powell felt keenly, he recognized that the dispossession of the Indian was inevitable. For the time being, at least, the Major was working against time, recording their vocabularies and mythology and making collections of their handiwork. He was, as a scientist, interested in their primitive condition because within a few more years their native culture would be, if not lost, badly contaminated.

Powell had no fear—absolutely no fear—in traveling among the Indians. Alone and unarmed, not even with a revolver, the Major wandered far beyond the boundaries of white settlements into regions in which even men of God did not travel without protection. He testified:

I have worked in that country since 1867, and I have had no military escort with me. I can get along with the Indians by peaceable methods much better than by military methods. If I should go into that country with a body of troops, I would thus take a hostile attitude, and would be compelled to fight my way among them, but in all that country I can go alone or with one or two men, or I can send out one or two men and they can travel anywhere without trouble. I have been studying Indian languages and Indian habits and customs, having been specially instructed by Professor Henry to do so, and it would have been impossible for me to carry on those studies if I had had troops with me. . . .

When Lt. Wheeler's . . . parties were in Nevada, I was in eastern Utah two hundred or three hundred miles away. One night, while in camp, I found that signal fires were flashing from mountain top to mountain top, across the country, and that the Indians were excited about something,—they would not tell me what. Some time after that a party of Indians came to me and explained that when Lt. Wheeler's party was passing down into southern Nevada the soldiers whom he had with him had killed one Indian and had shot another in the face so as to cause blindness. The news of that was telegraphed, from mountain to mountain, not only over Nevada but over Utah, Arizona, and New Mexico. . . . I knew the fact that there was trouble shortly after it occurred, although I was two hundred or three hundred miles away. Of course I did not know the circumstances, but I knew that there was trouble.

The subsequent year, when Lt. Wheeler passed through that country, as soon as his party took the field, delegations came to me from Panamit Mountain near the California line, from Nevada, and from Utah, asking me whether the Government had sent out an expedition to kill the Indians. Some of them came three hundred miles, and for three months or more the Indians throughout the country were on the *qui vive.* . . .

The other Indians (except the Sioux and those of the southern plains) are thoroughly subdued. They fully appreciate the utter hopelessness of contending against the Government of the United States, and they are everywhere asking for means and opportunity to become agriculturists. . . .

During these explorations . . . I have had from 2 to 20 or even 30 Indians employed, and I have had from 100 to 400 Indians encamped about me, and during that time I have no knowledge of their having stolen one cent from me.[1]

The Major had achieved a reputation for dealing with the Indian. The Mormons generally had a great respect for Powell and the Indians spoke highly of "Kapurats." It is little cause for surprise then that when G. W. Ingalls was appointed as the new Ute agent to replace the

[1] *43rd Cong. 1st Sess. H.R. Doc. 612,* p. 52.

incompetent Major Charles F. Powell he turned to Major John Wesley Powell for help.

George W. Ingalls of Springfield, Illinois, was appointed as agent for the Paiute Indians of southeastern Nevada with his office at Pioche. Upon arrival at his new post Ingalls found himself in a situation that threatened bloodshed. His predecessor had deliberately cut the props out from under him by telling the Indians that the new agent "would at once visit them with supplies and at the same time endeavor to secure any deprived rights"—promises which obviously could not be fulfilled.[2]

It was this same C. F. Powell who had misappropriated funds, wasted money, and generally neglected his responsibilities. He had made his job a soft one but had determined to make it a difficult position to his successor. In addition, C. F. Powell refused to turn over his books and papers until good and ready to do so.[3]

Ingalls found his Indians destitute. All were in poverty and required immediate assistance to survive the coming fall and winter. Moreover, fifteen hundred of his charges had crossed the Colorado River into California, and the residents considered the invasion a threat to their lives and property. To say the least, Ingalls had his hands full. He wanted to provide temporary help and he was determined to rehabilitate the Utes by a long-range systematic effort.

As soon as the quarterly budget became available—the credit of the agency under his predecessor being too bad to contract for supplies in advance—Ingalls distributed food to his people. Ingalls rode over most of the region which comprised his district, a considerable part of it in company with the Major.

The chiefs of many of the bands were called to a great council near Kanab during the first week in October 1872. The Major addressed them in their native tongue "setting forth the advantages derived by the Indians if they would generally adopt . . . agricultural and mechanical pursuits."[4]

---

[2] Charles F. Powell was appointed as "Special Agent for the Pi-Ute Indians of S. E. Nevada" on August 3, 1871. C. F. Powell's attempt to compromise G. W. Ingalls before he arrived is described sarcastically by Ingalls in a letter of August 27, 1872, to F. A. Walker, Commissioner of Indian Affairs. Ingalls received his appointment on August 6, 1872.

[3] A considerable correspondence passed between Ingalls and Walker in the years 1872–1874. Many of these letters give detailed complaints against the brazen irregularities which typified the administration of the majority of Indian agencies. The tragic condition of the Indians of this period is described in Sarah Winnemucca Hopkins, *Life Among the Pi-Utes.*

[4] G. W. Ingalls to F. A. Walker, Nov. 1, 1872.

Ingalls wrote to Commissioner F. A. Walker respectfully suggesting that as much land as necessary be set off for the exclusive use of his agency and reporting how much assistance the Major had given him as interpreter and adviser. A few days later Ingalls wired to Walker for permission to come to Washington to discuss the present and future of his agency in confidence.

Early in February 1873, Ingalls sent an inquiry to Powell asking about the condition of the Paiutes of southern Nevada and Utah, his own acquaintance with these Indians being as yet limited. The Major penned a reply on February 13th:

> The Pai-Utes are now divided into a number of small bands, each having its own chief, but these all acknowledging allegiance to Tagon or "Cave Creek John" who is also the immediate chief of a smaller band that is usually found somewhere in the vicinity of Cedar City in Utah Territory.
>
> Within the last two years I have met the chiefs of almost every one of these bands and have held many conversations with them concerning the propriety of their nomadic habits and adopting civilized life.[5]

Powell went on to explain that the Paiutes desired to cultivate the soil but wanted to settle down near their present locations. The chief difficulty was that the whites had already settled in all of the good valleys in the territory. However, there were several sites which would make suitable reservations such as "Grass Valley lying east of the Sevier and north from Glenwood in Utah" and the Uinta Valley, "a fine site" for all the Utes and Paiutes "if the latter could be induced to unite with the former." Powell referred to a hereditary enmity between these two tribes. The letter closed with a suggestion that the chiefs be escorted on a tour of the great eastern cities including Washington. "Perhaps this would be instrumental in collecting all the Pai-Utes on a reservation, somewhere."

Ingalls wanted something more than information. The pair had talked over all of these points at the agency and in Washington. This was the beginning of a three-way correspondence to have Powell appointed a special commissioner to study the Paiute problem.

A few weeks later Ingalls followed up with a formal suggestion already tentatively approved by E. P. Smith, the new Indian commissioner, that Powell be commissioned to accompany Ingalls to visit the Indians of Utah and eastern Nevada for the purpose of locating them upon reservations. Commissioner Smith wanted to include the Shoshones in the investigation, which complicated matters somewhat be-

[5] J. W. Powell to G. W. Ingalls, Feb. 13, 1873.

cause it was almost impossible to find anyone with sufficient influence over the Shoshones to prevail upon them to meet the commission in the Uinta Valley. Said the Major, "I know of no man to whom that work could be trusted." [6] The alternative, to visit the Shoshones, would require more time and more money than would be available.

The groundwork had been completed by April 15th, coincident of course with the annual appropriation by Congress, so that Ingalls could write to Smith:

Having been personally advised by Indians, Mormons, and others of Major Powell's influence with the Indians of Colorado and Utah, and knowing that he can address them correctly in their own tongue, I am led to believe it would greatly serve the interest of the government and do much toward securing permanent peace and prosperity among the Indians if he be invited to visit them with the writer for the purpose indicated in this and accompanying communications.[7]

A week later the commission was approved by C. Delano, Secretary of the Interior, in which department the Indian bureau then was organized.

Powell accepted this commission—indeed he sought it—because it afforded an opportunity to study many of the small bands of Indians and again travel over the territory, as well as to give him a chance to do something in the way of securing decency and justice for these people. Naturally, the emphasis on the field work would be in ethnology, but there would be many occasions to investigate the geology of the regions through which he passed.

On May 6th Powell and Ingalls arrived in Salt Lake City, ready for work, only to find frenzied excitement over the Modoc war—a three months' skirmish between three companies of soldiers and two hundred Modocs, including women and children, who had attempted to reoccupy land they had ceded to the government. The small band of Modocs had managed to hold out against overwhelming odds in the steadfasts of broken lava beds.

The commissioners were greeted on their arrival not with deputations from the Indians, but by delegations from the white population demanding complete removal of all Indians to a safe distance. These delegations claimed to have indisputable evidence that the Indians were preparing to wage a war of extermination against the whites. The Governor of Utah had received petitions demanding adequate military protection; the citizens were in mortal peril.

[6] J. W. Powell to G. W. Ingalls, April 13, 1873.
[7] G. W. Ingalls to E. P. Smith, Commissioner of Indian Affairs, April 15, 1873.

Under these circumstances Ingalls and Powell altered their plans and proceeded at once to investigate the basis for the alarm. Just as they suspected, the Indians were far more terrified than the whites, and the absurd anxiety of the settlers was groundless. After visiting the Indian communities in Sanpete Valley, Deep Creek, and the adjoining country they were convinced that the alarm would quickly subside. It was the Indians who had to be reassured that no punitive measures were in preparation.

Meanwhile polite invitations to the numerous Indian chiefs were dispatched, requesting that tribal delegations meet with the special commission for conversations. A camp was established outside the limits of Salt Lake City, and Powell and Ingalls awaited the arrival of the delegations. All but a few of the tribes sent representatives and took part in the discussions.

The most persistent charge brought out during these preliminary meetings was the dishonesty of many of the government agents. The Indians had legitimate grievances on this score. The more serious result was, naturally, lack of trust in the government. Ingalls wired to the commissioner of Indian affairs urging that Major Powell come to Washington to present their preliminary joint report in person. This was advisable because some of the agents and agency employees had strong political connections in the Capitol. One of Powell's recommendations called for the immediate removal of two officials because of disgusting immorality and gross misappropriation of funds, and for the thorough investigation of two others. All four suspects were subsequently dismissed as a result of the charges made by the Indians and confirmed by Powell and Ingalls.

The Major and Ingalls knew well enough that correspondence would achieve nothing but delay. If the cooperation of the Indians was to be secured, an honest effort on their behalf had to be made at once. Ingalls, without the support of an outsider like Powell, would have been helpless in his attempts to clean house. It was Powell's prestige, and not any fundamental change for the better in bureau policy, that forced early action on the part of responsible officials.

Powell returned to Salt Lake City as soon as he had been assured of sanction for the tentative recommendations of the special commissioners, and proceeded with the work of the commission. A minor benefit from this visit to Washington was an allowance of eight dollars per day as compensation for his services while employed by the Indian office.

Throughout the period from July to October and during part of November, Powell and Ingalls visited all of the bands of Indians known to live in the area, making a careful census of their numbers and condition. After a short period together, while meeting with several delegations of Shoshones, the two commissioners separated. Powell, in company with the physician from the agency, moved southward to Skull Valley and Deep Creek while Ingalls went north to Fort Hall. About the first of August the two rejoined and together proceeded south through Utah into Arizona to ask Agent Critchlow of the Uinta reservation to help persuade the Utes to settle there.

Critchlow was of little assistance. He had fears for his family, and instead of wanting more Indians he wanted the army to establish a military post on his reservation. Critchlow was another of the incompetent and dishonest agents. Every one of the diaries kept by members of Powell's 1871 Colorado River expedition recorded their disgust at the way things were run at the Uinta agency. Ingalls notified the Washington headquarters, "Major Powell will advise you concerning Agent Critchlow and his relations with the Indians." [8]

By mid-November the work was considered completed, though in part it was hurried, and the commissioners returned to Washington, arriving there on December 1st. The report which Powell submitted on the day of the arrival was thought out and written during the long train ride east. The opinions clearly embody some of the plans voiced earlier by Ingalls and certainly some of the pet ideas of the Major. The literary composition is Powell's.

The report embodied four sections: an estimate of the number of Indians in each tribe; the conditions of each tribe; specific recommendations for placing these wandering bands on reservations; and an eloquent plea for discontinuing military measures against the Indians.[9]

Probably the most remarkable result of the commission was the census which showed that there were only 5,500 Indians in the whole territory visited—Utah, parts of Arizona, Nevada, eastern Idaho, and southeastern California. There were forty-four tribes of "Utes"—Paiutes (31), Utes (7), Gosiutes (5), and Pahvants (1)—and thirty-eight tribes

---

[8] G. W. Ingalls to E. P. Smith, May 14, 1873. The secrecy with which Major Powell performed his duties as a special commissioner and kept his own counsel is evident from an entry in A. H. Thompson, MS, *Diary*, June 14, 1873: "Major is going to Washington ostensibly on Indian Affairs, really to draw money to run things." On June 3rd, however, Ingalls had telegraphed E. P. Smith, "It is deemed best that Powell come to Washington to advise with Department" (concerning dishonest Indian agents). On June 4th Commissioner Smith authorized the Major's return to Washington.

[9] *Rep. Spec. Comm. J. W. Powell and G. W. Ingalls*, Dec. 18, 1873. Printed also in *Ann. Rep. Comm. Ind. Affairs for 1873*, 1874, pp. 41–46, 47–74.

of Shoshones. More than three thousand of the Indians lived in Nevada, about fifteen hundred in Utah. The largest bands had only two hundred people. Even admitting the probability of inaccuracies, the small total was astonishing.

The hunting grounds of these Indians had been spoiled and their favorite valleys had been occupied by whites. To obtain the barest subsistence the tribes had to split into smaller bands and scatter over wide areas. The older men in the tribes knew that they could no longer exist by hunting, fishing, and seed gathering. They understood too that settlement of the country by whites was inevitable. The delegations had pleaded with Powell and Ingalls for land of their own and for assistance in becoming farmers and stock raisers.

Powell put it this way, "Nothing then remains but to remove them from the country or let them stay in their present condition, to be finally extinguished by want, loathsome disease, and the disasters consequent upon the incessant conflict with white men." [10]

As Powell had warned, the Paiutes refused to live with the Utes, claiming that the Utes, whom they outnumbered three to one, had been their enemies for generations, having killed their grandfathers, their fathers, brothers, and sons. And the Utes, they said, were skilled in sorcery.

Ingalls and the Major had examined several potential reservation sites for soil, water, game, timber, and other resources, and after comparisons recommended three specific locations: the Utes, Gosiutes, and Pahvants to be placed on the Uinta reservation; the Shoshones to be gathered at Fort Hall; and the Paiutes to be settled in the Moapa Valley. The primary consideration was whether the land could be used by the Indian in supporting himself adequately with reasonable industry.

The gathering of these scattered little bands of Indians into reservations was in itself not enough. The whole issue was vastly more complex: What should be done after getting them settled?

Both Powell and Ingalls were aware of the indifference with which their report would be received. They had no grandiose illusions. The Indian bureau was administered by a group of men who owed their positions to political friendships. A few of the administrators had a sincere interest in the Indians, but most of them did not. Moreover any important decision would have to be confirmed or authorized by Congress. There was the impasse. Western Congressmen, virtually without exception, wanted to get rid of the Indian, and the eastern Congressmen considered the Indian a purely sectional problem.

[10] *ibid.*

A few excerpts from the report of the special commissioners indicate the kind of policy which they urged upon the Department of the Interior:

The time has passed when it was necessary to buy peace.

If they are not to be collected on reservations they should no longer receive aid from the General Government, for every dollar given them in their present condition is an injury.

The Indian in his relations with the white man rarely associates with the better class, but finds his companions with the lowest and vilest of society— men whose object is to corrupt and plunder. He thus learns from the superior race everything that is bad, nothing that is good.

The commission does not consider that a reservation should be looked upon in the light of a pen where a horde of savages are to be fed with flour and beef, to be supplied with blankets from the Government bounty, and to be furnished with paint and gew-gaws by the greed of traders, but that a reservation should be a school of industry and a home for these unfortunate people.

No able-bodied Indian should be either fed or clothed except in payment for labor, even though such labor is expended in providing for his own future wants.

They should not be provided with ready-made clothing. Substantial fabrics should be given them from which they can manufacture their own garments (fabrics, thread, needles, buttons; instruction by patient and intelligent women).

The Indians should not be furnished with tents.

Each Indian family should be supplied with a cow, to enable them to start in the accumulation of property. The Indians now understand the value of domestic cattle . . . it is interesting to notice that, as soon as an Indian acquires property, he more thoroughly appreciates the rights of property and becomes an advocate of law and order.

On each reservation there should be a blacksmith, carpenter, and a saddle and harness maker, and each . . . should employ several Indian apprentices.

An efficient medical department should be organized on each reservation. . . . The magician or "medicine man" wields much influence, and such influence is always bad; but in the presence of an intelligent physician it is soon lost.

It is unnecessary to mention the power which schools would have over the rising generation of Indians. Next to teaching them to work, the most important thing is to teach them the English language. Into their own language is woven so much mythology and sorcery that a new one is needed in order to aid them in advancing beyond their baneful superstitions; and the ideas and thoughts of civilized life cannot be communicated to them in their own tongues. . . .

Relation of the Army to these Indians

Your commission cannot refrain from expressing its opinion concerning the effect of the presence of soldiers among the Indians where they are no longer needed to keep them under subjugation. They regard the presence of a soldier as a standing menace and to them the very name of soldier is synonymous with all that is offensive and evil. To the soldier they attribute their social demoralization and the unmentionable diseases with which they are infested.

The Indians object to going on reservations for two main reasons: "We do not wish to desert the graves of our fathers," and "We do not wish to give our women to the embrace of the soldiers."

Some hungry Indian steals a beef, some tired Indian steals a horse, a vicious Indian commits a depredation and flies to the mountains. No effort is made to punish the real offender, but the first Indian met is shot at sight. Then, perhaps, the Indians retaliate and the news is spread through the country that war has broken out with the Indians. Troops are sent into the district and wander around the mountains and return. Perhaps a few Indians are killed, and perhaps a few white men. . . . His methods of warfare are such that we cannot cope with him without resorting to means which are repugnant to civilized people; and after spending thousands, or even millions of dollars, on an affair which was but a petty larceny, we make peace with the Indians, and enter into an agreement to secure him lands, which we cannot fulfill, and give to him annuities, the expense of which are a burden on the public Treasury.

Permit the remark here, that the expense and civil methods stand in very glaring contrast. Within the territory which has heretofore been described it is probable that about two million dollars will be expended in support of troops during the present fiscal year, and much less than two hundred thousand dollars through the Indian Department for feeding, clothing, and civilizing the Indians.

The Indian has no knowledge of legal methods, and avenges his own wrongs by ways which are traditional with him, while the prejudices against savages which have grown through centuries of treacherous and bloody warfare, and the prejudices of race, which are always greatly exaggerated among the lower class of people, with whom the Indian is most liable to associate, are such that the Indian cannot secure justice through the intervention of the local authorities. [11]

The mechanical recommendations of the special commissioners, such as setting aside several sites for reservations and gathering the more willing bands, were carried out with but slight delay.

A year later Ingalls could make an optimistic report on the affairs of the Moapa reservation: Six bands of the Paiutes were moved to that place and each given a tract of land which was plowed for them because the Indians had no plows or animals. The land was planted in wheat, barley, corn, melons, and squashes, and yielded crops valued at seven thousand dollars. It was the pride of the Indians that their farms, managed as by white men, had afforded them a far better and easier livelihood. Ingalls reminded his superiors that had the small appropriation he requested been granted he would have been able to buy mules, harness, plows, and seed wheat, barley, and corn. The ancestors of the Paiutes,

[11] *ibid*. The section "Relation of the Army" appears on pp. 65–66.

even some of the elders, had been agricultural, but they were destitute when brought to the reservation.

Despite this encouraging example, which doubtless owed its success to the earnestness of Ingalls, the fundamental recommendations by Powell and Ingalls, their appeal for greater justice to the Indians, went unheeded. It was not their failure; it was the failure of generations.

Major Powell's attitude toward the Indian is best stated in his own words:

> He who sees only their crimes, and studies the history of their barbarities as it has been recorded for the past three or four centuries, can see in the Indian race only hordes of demons who stand in the way of the progress of civilization, and who must, and ought to be destroyed. He who has a more intimate knowledge of Indian character and life sometimes forgets their baser traits, and sees only their virtues, their truth, their fidelity to a trust, their simple and innocent sports, and wonders that a morally degenerate, but powerful civilization, should destroy that primitive life. Social problems are so complex that few are willing, or able, to comprehend all the factors, and so the people are divided into two great parties, one crying for blood, and demanding the destruction of the Indians, the other begging that he may be left in his aboriginal condition, and that the progress of civilization may be stayed. Vain is the clamor of either party; the march of humanity cannot be stayed; fields must be made, and gardens planted in the little valleys among the mountains of that Western land, as they have been in the broader valleys and plains of the East, and the mountains must yield their treasure of ore to the miner, and, whether we desire it or not, the ancient inhabitants of the country must be lost; and we may comfort ourselves with the reflection that they are not destroyed, but are gradually absorbed, and become a part of more civilized communities.[12]

Powell used the opportunity to visit these many scattered bands of Indians to fullest measure. He was enabled to complete his series of vocabularies of all of the Shoshone and Ute tribes. He was the only person to do so firsthand. He made a study of their mythologies and social institutions, recording these in elaborate detail. He collected a great quantity of handicraft to illustrate their dress, mode of life, food, art of war, and religious ceremony. So many specimens were accumulated that in addition to the extraordinary collection deposited in the Smithsonian Institution, duplicate series were sent to Illinois Wesleyan and Normal University, while smaller assortments were exchanged with other museums.

Powell had become something more than a geologist—he was now an ethnologist.

[12] *Scribner's Monthly*, Vol. 10, p. 677.

13

1873-1876 · A New Concept of the Canyon Country

WASHINGTON in 1873 had not yet acquired the charm and dignity becoming to the capital of a great country. It was still an oversized town with growing pains. When the Powells came to Washington to take up residence—a permanent residence they hoped—the streets, excepting a few main thoroughfares, were unpaved and ill-kept. Even the sewers were inadequate for their functions. A veritable tornado of cleanup, patch-up, and fix-up had turned the city on end. Gangs of laborers were grading the streets and the sidewalks were being planted with feeble-looking plane and maple seedlings. Parking areas were laid out on one side of many of the broad avenues. Sidewalks of wood or brick were appearing along the residential streets. It seemed that work was in progress simultaneously in every part of the city as contracts for construction were tossed about extravagantly.

Major Powell's professional activities resembled somewhat this municipal extravaganza. Officially he was the director of the "Geological and Geographical Survey of the Colorado River of the West and its Tributaries," but at the same time he was pursuing energetically investigations of the Indians, arid lands, federal land policies, and a half-dozen branches of geology. The Major might be riding off in all directions but he had one main objective in sight, to establish his headquarters in Washington, which was fast becoming the chief center of scientific work in North America.

Major Powell's survey was under the supervision of the Smithsonian Institution, although at first it had been placed under the Department of the Interior. Just how this change came about no one seemed to know. The Major never discussed the matter. He had a tiny room in the Smithsonian building and he consulted frequently with Professor Henry and Dr. Spencer Baird, but usually he worked at home.

There were quiet residential neighborhoods even close to the great government buildings, but one had to search around to find a vacant dwelling. The Powells had been fortunate to obtain with little effort a house in a good neighborhood. The family was installed comfortably at 910 "M" Street, N.W., a house which stood in a row of three-story brick structures with very small courtyards guarded with low wrought-iron picket fences. Number 910 was distinguished from the others in the block by a low round arched roof which overhung the doorway. An iron hitching post, mounted with a grinning head of a horse, and two struggling maple saplings decorated the sidewalk, which had recently been laid with brick.[1]

The Major's study was on the rear of the second floor. It was furnished with a drawing table, a large walnut desk, a chair, and a bookcase. Often Emma pulled in a small rocker and did her darning or sewing while her husband was working. Like as not she would soon begin talking but Wes could open or shut his ears as his mood or activity demanded. Even when he paid not the slightest attention Wes enjoyed her presence.

Powell lived a little more than a mile from the Smithsonian Institution. He rarely used the street car, preferring to walk. Almost invariably he would go down to the corner, turn onto Ninth Street, walk briskly past the Interior building to Pennsylvania Avenue, cut diagonally to Seventh, cross the mall, and stride over the grass to the bizarre red-towered Smithsonian building. The Major with his reddish beard, which he called russet, and his stump arm became a familiar figure as he strode along, humming as he went.

On Sundays the Major took his toddling daughter to the great equestrian statue of General Scott on Sixteenth Street, pausing on the way at the Fourteenth-Street circle to rest on one of the rustic benches and watch the fountain or, in season, to admire the beds of tulips, iris, and geraniums planted there. When Mary was a little older the walks were longer; sometimes to the equestrian statue of Jackson near the White House, sometimes along the mall to the Smithsonian building. The Major delighted in showing his child the specimens of birds, wolverine, and Indian crafts he had collected and sent to the museum.

The Major's simple pleasures and his unassuming frankness seemed a paradox when compared with his energy and industry. His friends and

---

[1] The house is still standing but the neighborhood has deteriorated. I examined the house in 1947 and Mrs. Lillian Menelly made a floor plan of the interior in 1945. Several photographs taken between 1885 and 1900 gave additional data.

associates marveled at his many sides. He could be aggressive, stubborn, or compliant; he could work and play. He found leisure whenever he wished. Powell's chief diversion was whist, although he was usually too busy to indulge in it; most of his friends would not stop with a few games. He was a good bowler but limited himself to two or three strings. He was known among the scientific men of Washington as one of the best bowlers and billiard players in the District.[2] Despite all of these activities the Major gained weight rapidly, approaching 170 pounds. Powell purchased a double team of good horses [3] and frequently went riding on horseback far out into the country, beyond the east branch of the Potomac, through the small truck farms which in season provided Washington with much of its produce. This neighborhood had the nearest semblance to the prairie of Illinois and he reveled in the smells of farms.

Major Powell had campaigned persistently but unobtrusively since 1872 for a sensible consolidation of the geological surveys of the western territories. The needless duplication of work and expense, to say nothing of the petty jealousies and rivalries which had been engendered, were well known. During the 1873 field season one of Hayden's parties collided with Wheeler's in Colorado and the War Department demanded an inquiry. Finally Congress took official notice of this situation and on April 15, 1874, the House of Representatives passed a resolution requesting from President Grant information respecting "the surveys operating in the same or contiguous areas of the territories west of the Mississippi." Specifically, Congress wanted to know whether it would be practicable to consolidate the surveys under one department or, failing in this, to define accurately the geographic regions which were to be surveyed by each.[4]

A few weeks after the resolution by Congress the Major received a request for a statement of his personal opinion on the value of consolidation of the surveys. Identical inquiries were sent to Hayden, to the Secretary of War, and to the chief of army engineers. Quite naturally each chief urged complete and final unification, advancing arguments as to why the combined survey should be placed under his own control. Powell chose a different course.

In a carefully worded reply Major Powell explained how accurately

[2] Major Powell's billiard mace, with which he "could make draw shots as well as caroms," is affixed to the wall of the taproom of the Cosmos Club.

[3] This bay team is mentioned in several contemporary letters. Powell rode horseback for diversion until he became enfeebled in late life.

[4] *43rd Cong. 1st Sess. H.R. Rep. 612.*

he was able to perform his topographic work at a very modest cost and at the same time make observations on the forests, mineral resources, water supply for irrigation, and ethnology of the Indians. So far as the real issue, the controversy, was concerned, Powell limited his arguments not as to who should head a unified survey, but whether control should be vested in a military or a civilian department. This side of the argument had not as yet been considered. He urged that the administration of the survey be vested in a civilian authority. Clarence King's survey of the fortieth parallel had been under the jurisdiction of the War Department but its work was finished, and King sought no funds for further exploration. King was therefore out of the competition. However, the survey of the hundredth meridian was not. This survey, also under the War Department, was directed by Lieutenant Wheeler, who had become Hayden's—and Powell's—most unrelenting antagonist.

The several replies were sent to President Grant by the end of April and Grant, as requested by Congress, on May 2nd transmitted his message, together with the various statements of officers of the War Department and the Department of the Interior and of Dr. Hayden and Major Powell. Grant's opinion was that it made no difference which department controlled surveying work; the decision should be based on which could do the work best and most economically. He did, however, recommend that the War Department be given the control, assuming that in that department the special skills required were readily available.

Congressional hearings were held to consider the various documents which were submitted to try to reach some satisfactory decision in the face of widely divergent views. The committee called Wheeler, Hayden, and Powell to testify before the committee on public lands. Wheeler appeared first and upon interrogation pleaded with the committee not to involve him in any geological questions, "Because," he said, "I am not a geologist and I have no special attainments in that line." He explained that his party was composed of twenty-five persons not counting a military escort of sixty men. When asked about his budget he replied that $90,000 had been allocated for his work during 1873.

Wheeler turned out to be a testy and an unwilling witness. In justice to the lieutenant it must be recognized that he was considerably hampered by his rank in the maze of army etiquette and discipline. Repeatedly he was obliged to remind the members of the committee that he was not permitted to make any statement questioning the policies of the War Department.

Dr. Hayden appeared to testify armed with records, documents, and petitions to lend weight to his side of the controversy. Opening his case Hayden remarked, "I desire to have placed on record the fact that the civilian side of the controversy before you has not been its author. We have all the time stood on the defensive." [5]

Hayden accused Wheeler of coming to Colorado deliberately to precipitate a conflict, although this ignored the fact that Wheeler had been ordered to do so. He then submitted to the committee memorials in favor of a civilian rather than a military authority over a consolidated survey. He had composed the preamble himself and had solicited the cooperation of the scientific faculties of Yale, Harvard, and the Massachusetts Institute of Technology. Many of the greatest names in American science were affixed to the petitions. In addition letters to the same effect were obtained from Asa Gray, W. B. Rogers, J. D. Dana, Arnold Guyot, Wolcott Gibbs, and many others. Hayden had seized upon this phase of the issue, first advanced by Major Powell, recognizing that if consolidation would come at this time, at the least, the War Department would take over. Unification would work to the greatest disadvantage to Hayden.

After discussing various arguments in favor of placing a combined survey under the Department of the Interior, Hayden pleaded earnestly, "I think more mature reflection will show that this is an erroneous idea. . . . There should be a continuance of the special surveys."

Major Powell was called before the committee on May 18th. The first question directed to him was, "How long have you been a student of geology?" He replied, "About nineteen years. I should say, however, that I was in the Army nearly four years of that time and my geological studies were very much interrupted." [6]

After various preliminary questions Mr. Townsend, chairman of the committee, asked, "How did it occur that your explorations were under the Smithsonian and not under the Interior Department?" This was a question a lot of people wondered about because the Major's first federal appropriation specifically placed him under the jurisdiction of the Secretary of the Interior. That was in 1870. Major Powell replied:

I don't know I have the right to explain committee matters. A question was asked in the committee room on appropriations concerning my collections. A member of that committee asked me what was done with the collections. I told him that they went to the Smithsonian Institution, and I said that if there was any question about it, it might be inserted in the law. He said he would have that

[5] *ibid.*, p. 30. Hayden, in testimony presented May 13, 1874.
[6] Powell thus says he was a geologist since 1856. This places his interest two years earlier than his trip to the Iron Mountain region of Missouri, his first purely geological field trip.

attended to and he made a memorandum of it. It seems that afterwards, seeing this memorandum, that the collections were to go to the Smithsonian Institution, he accidentally sent my whole work there.[7]

So it had been an accident that placed Powell under the jurisdiction of the Secretary of the Smithsonian. No wonder the mistake had not been corrected; it was a perfect arrangement. The Smithsonian's only interest was scientific knowledge with no meddling in politics. Besides, Professor Henry had the highest regard for Powell's ability and diversified program.

Major Powell suggested to the public lands committee that his survey should be transferred to the Department of the Interior. When asked if he would consent to work with Dr. Hayden he replied that he "would be perfectly willing to work under anybody," and he was "sure that such arrangements would be agreeable."

Mr. Townsend, chairman of the committee on public lands, then requested Powell to explain his method of mapping and the general objectives of his surveys. The Major unrolled a large map prepared by the War Department. Pointing to a prominent blank space not penetrated by the army surveys, he said that this was the region he had been authorized to explore—and the work was finished. He then passed around sketches and maps to show that Wheeler, one, two, and even three years later, followed him and reexplored 26,000 square miles of country. This was a flagrant waste of time and money. Powell called for a blackboard and by diagrams and charts described his methods of triangulation and surveying. To close his arguments and to emphasize the low cost of his work, Powell reminded the committee he never wanted, or needed, military escorts.

The comprehensive surveying which the Major had in mind was fundamentally different from that practiced by Hayden, Wheeler, and King. Powell had ever in mind the future of the public domain. He stated:

It is of the most immediate and pressing importance that a general survey should be made for the purpose of determining the several areas which can be redeemed by irrigation. But I will not further discuss the importance of a survey for economic and scientific purposes, but will simply say that a survey which meets all these demands must be thorough and accurate, and if it fails in any of these particulars . . . will necessitate a resurvey of the country, involving the General Government in greatly-increased expense.[8]

[7] *ibid.*, p. 54. Testimony given on May 20, 1874.
[8] *ibid.*, p. 10. Statement read to the committee on public lands.

1. John Wesley Powell, 1859.

2. Emma Dean Powell, ca. 1869.

3. Major John Wesley Powell, 1865.

4. Start of the second Colorado expedition at Green River Station, Wyoming, May 1871. From left to right: in the *Cañonita*, Andrew Hattan, W. C. Powell, E. O. Beaman; in the *Emma Dean*, S. V. Jones, Jack Hillers, Major Powell, Fred Dellenbaugh; in the *Nellie Powell*, A. H. Thompson, J. F. Steward, F. M. Bishop, Frank Richardson.

5. Lodore Canyon. Jones, Hillers, and Dellenbaugh in the *Emma Dean*.

6. The Colorado River near the upper end of the Grand Canyon.

7. Repairing boats at First Granite Gorge, Grand Canyon.

8. Lava Falls, Grand Canyon.

9. The Sockdologer Rapid, Grand Canyon.

10. Glen Canyon, Utah.

11. Marble Canyon, Arizona. A. H. Thompson in foreground.

12. Another view of Marble Canyon, Arizona. In the foreground is the *Emma Dean* showing the armchair in which Major Powell sat.

13. Hillers, Dellenbaugh, and Johnson repairing the *Cañonita*.

14. Major Powell and a Paiute Indian, 1873.

15. A family of Uinta Utes, ca. 1873.

16. Across the house tops at Zuni, 1879.

17. John Wesley Powell, 1898.

Each of the principals, Hayden, Wheeler, and Powell, was recalled for rebuttal. The acrimonious charges and unkind insinuations between Hayden and Wheeler gave the committee plenty to think about. Intense bitterness existed between the various surveys as is evident in the sworn statements of Dr. H. C. Yarrow and Dr. F. Kampf, submitted on behalf of Lt. Wheeler's survey. Yarrow accused Hayden of saying to him, "You can tell Wheeler that if he stirs a finger or attempts to interfere with me or my survey in any way, I will utterly crush him—as I have enough Congressional influence to do so, and will bring it all to bear." [9]

And according to Kampf, Hayden had told him "that if Lt. Wheeler was only out of the field it would be an easy matter for him [Hayden] to absorb all western explorations and surveys."

Some of the exchanges were even more shocking. The committee rebuked Dr. Hayden and Lt. Wheeler "for their ill-judged and hasty expressions which good taste would have withheld."

Throughout this whole controversy Major Powell behaved with dignity. The committee was impressed with his earnestness and his seeming indifference to the outcome of deliberations. The members of the committee knew, just the same, that Major Powell in the beginning had worked behind the scenes to initiate the congressional investigation.

The upshot of this congressional flurry was to temporize in the face of incompatible opinions; there was no adequate information on which an intelligent compromise could be reached. Powell's survey was however made the "Second Division of the Survey of the Western Territories." Even though they had been on the same side, Hayden became suspicious of Powell's motives—not for bringing the issue to the front but rather for pursuing it in the manner he did.

Gradually Major Powell surrounded himself by a small group of competent young scientists. In July 1873, G. K. Gilbert,[10] who was the most capable of Lieutenant Wheeler's men, wrote a letter to Powell asking for technical advice concerning the geology of the region around Fort Wingate. In the same letter he suggested that Powell examine the Zuni Indians of Arizona because he would find them an interesting people. Gilbert and Powell had met in Washington a year earlier and their mutual respect led to the immediate determination of Gilbert to

[9] This and the two following statements are printed on pages 62 and 63 of the cited report.
[10] Grove Karl Gilbert, who figures prominently in subsequent chapters.

leave Wheeler and join Powell's staff. Lieutenant Wheeler regarded this as piracy and never forgave the Major for it. As a convenience in his own field work Powell had engaged the services of John C. Pilling,[11] who was something of a geologist but who served primarily as an amanuensis. Beginning in 1873 he accompanied the Major in all his explorations in the West, taking care of correspondence, correcting manuscripts, and otherwise assisting in the routine work of the survey. Jack Hillers,[12] who had saved the Major's life when the *Dean* was upset in the Colorado, continued as the official photographer for all of Powell's surveys. Hillers' buoyant spirit and, at times, ribald sense of humor endeared him to the Major. He was the one man who could be breezy and flippant with his chief. Hillers alone dared write to the Major, "Love to Mrs. Powell and kisses for the girls," or that he was "tired of photographing churches, schoolhouses and fence rails" when he was sent to take pictures of the Cherokees.

Major Powell continued his investigations of the Uinta Mountains. In 1874 he outfitted a pack train at Jake Field's post at Green River Station. The pack train followed Little Bitter Creek across the Quien Hornet Mountains and through Red Creek Canyon into Brown's Park. From the Park, Powell proceeded southward to the junction of the Snake and Yampa Rivers, across the Yampa Plateau, and from there to the Uinta Valley, crossing the Uinta Mountains to the head of Sheep's Creek and returning to Green River Station. In 1875 Powell returned again to Green River Station and this time started eastward to Rock Springs and Salt Wells, then south to the Vermilion and to the eastern foot of Dry Mountains, then westward through Brown's Park, past Flaming Gorge to the head of Sheep Creek, and finally through the Cameo Mountains to Green River Station.

During both years the pack train moved slowly and the Major made many side trips to examine the effects of the geological processes which sculptured the region. Meanwhile an able party under Thompson's supervision mapped the lands of southern Utah and adjacent Arizona, using Kanab as a base of operations.

The financial arrangements for the several geological surveys continued to be a source of apprehension. Congress, upon request and after due annual deliberation, appropriated money for field work. As soon as funds were assured, each survey assembled its party, packed its gear, and took to the region to which it had been assigned. Since the funds

---

[11] John C. Pilling served with Powell until his death in 1895.
[12] John K. Hillers served with Powell until 1900.

were expendable within a given fiscal year, as soon as the snows of late autumn drove the parties from the mountains, most of the men were obliged to return to their homes and wait anxiously for favorable action by Congress while the chiefs pulled strings in Washington. Considering that there were four distinct surveys working in the same general region, the waste of money as well as the waste of effort involved in such duplication is obvious. Powell managed to reserve for himself an annual salary of $3,000 out of the appropriation. The difficulty was to keep aside a sufficient sum for traveling and other work which might take him away from Washington during the winter months. In the field the director had to hire temporary help as he needed it and to disburse his budget in such a way as to have enough left to pay himself. Major Powell took his salary during this entire period only when he actually needed it. He spent all he could spare on Harry Thompson and the other topographers. Until Powell's financial condition was secure and the title to his house clear, he augmented his income by lyceum lectures, articles for popular magazines, and especially by the sale of stereoscopic views. In fact, despite these various sources of income, the Major was more frequently broke than not. The borrowing "to tide him over" was a family joke: Major from Bram, Bram from Thompson, Thompson from the Major, Bram from the Major, and so it went in a spirit of fraternal cooperation.[13]

During the late winter of 1874 the Major, accompanied by Jack Hillers, made a month-long lecture tour through Illinois and Wisconsin, opening at Chicago on February 15th and closing with appearances in his old home town of Wheaton on March 8th and at Aurora on March 9th.[14] There were only three lectures—"Canyons of the Colorado," "The Ancient Moqui Towns," and "Indian Life Beyond the Rocky Mountains"—but these were combined in several ways and under various titles. In some cities Powell gave but a single lecture and in others two or all three of them. After paying Jack for his services as an assistant in charge of the stereopticon, the Major cleared more than six hundred dollars.

On April 7th the Major returned to Washington and found that Harry Thompson had preceded him. Harry had engaged for Nell and himself a room at 915 New York Avenue, only a short distance from the Powell home. Harry and the Major discussed how and where the

---

[13] A. H. Thompson, MS, *Diary*, Dec. 1873–Mar. 1874.

[14] Contemporary newspapers reported these lectures in varying detail. The lectures in Milwaukee, Chicago, Jacksonville (Illinois), and Adrian (Michigan) were fully covered by the press. On several occasions the Major appeared before a poor house.

detailed mapping should be completed. The Major said that it was no one else's business to know what the map looked like and the drawing-board work could be done in his study. There Thompson worked on the "Great Map" until June 7th, when the 1874 field party again took leave of Washington for another season in Utah.

To the outsider, Powell's first years in Washington seemed to be taken up with the preparation of data and the writing of reports on his explorations. Whereas Hayden's survey had already published a dozen book-length reports with many technical articles by distinguished scientists like E. D. Cope, a paleontologist, A. C. Peale, a geologist, and Leo Lesquereaux, a paleobotanist, the Powell survey had issued nothing but a few brief preliminary reports of little permanent scientific value. Representative Garfield and Spencer Baird urged the Major to complete the writing of an adequate report on the canyon explorations. Sooner or later the supporters, as well as the opponents, of Powell's survey would demand proof of accomplishments, and appropriation bills facing the annual fiscal skirmish might well depend on such documents.

Powell had four principal projects in mind. The most urgent of these was a report of the Colorado River explorations. Then, his study of the geology of the Uinta Mountains was nearly completed. The two other investigations, a description of the arid lands of the West and an introduction to the study of Indian languages, were slowly taking form, but they might have to wait for several years.

Every summer since 1867 the Major had resumed field investigations in the plateau country. Thompson continued as the chief geographer of the Powell surveys, and with able assistant geologists like G. K. Gilbert, C. E. Dutton, and C. A. White, the parties had explored the arid lands of the whole Great Basin province. In all of this work the Major had allocated to each of his assistants a degree of freedom and independence not to be found in any other government project. He not only encouraged independent thinking in his subordinates, but he gave them liberty to choose their own problems and to move about from place to place in pursuit of their own ideas. This was not indulgence without a purpose. Powell could not confine himself to the limits of any one problem and he did not require others to be so limited. The Major rarely remained with his field parties; he left the actual administration in Thompson's hands and thus felt free to do as he pleased. Gilbert and Dutton had joined Powell's party because of the opportunity to gain professional standing. Lieutenant Wheeler, for instance, had not permitted Gilbert to publish his own findings, insisting that "in due time" reports would be issued by the War Department.

On June 16, 1874, Powell personally delivered the manuscript describing his exploration of the Colorado River to Secretary Henry. The full title of the monograph, *Exploration of the Colorado River of the West and Its Tributaries Explored in 1869, 1870, 1871 and 1872 Under the Direction of the Secretary of the Smithsonian Institution*,[15] contains a deliberate misstatement. The 1869 expedition was, in Major Powell's own words when the party was about to undertake the venture, "under the sponsorship of the Illinois Natural History Society." The contents include a journal of the exploration of the Green and Colorado in 1869, Powell's land explorations of 1870, and a report by A. H. Thompson of his trip to the mouth of the Dirty Devil River.

The second part of the book includes several chapters containing Powell's geological descriptions and discussions. The journal of the canyon voyage is one of the most exciting accounts of an exploration ever written. To prepare this story five years after the breathless undertaking, Powell used his own diary, beginning with July 2, 1869, at the mouth of the Uinta River, and Jack Sumner's from the same date. For the first lap—that is, from May 24th at Green River Station to July 1st—he had six letters, dated June 2nd, 6th, 7th, 18th, 20th, and 23rd, written to and published by the Chicago *Tribune*. Long sections from these letters were copied verbatim for the narrative. Nevertheless, the account was amplified by drawing upon information gathered by the second expedition—without crediting it. No mention of the second expedition as such is to be found in the entire text. Generous credit is given to Thompson in the preface, but the other loyal men who accompanied the Major on his 1871–1872 trip were disregarded by their chief.[16]

The publication of Major Powell's first great monograph served him well. Several thousand copies of the book were distributed by members of Congress and the remainder were sold quickly through the Government Printing Office. Powell's scientific reputation had been firmly established. Up to this time he had published but a few short technical contributions to the *American Journal of Science* and similar periodicals, some of these short notes being nothing more than discussions later

[15] For a critical appraisal of Powell's official report of the 1869 expedition, see W. C. Darrah, *Utah Hist. Quart.*, Vol. 15, pp. 16–17.

[16] The Major's indifference or neglect of his 1871 party is almost inexplicable. The underlying reason is that Powell regarded only the pioneer trip as an adventure; the subsequent work was routine. This cannot be overemphasized.

given in his full report. The map which accompanies the monograph was drawn by Thompson and detailed by John Steward and Fred Dellenbaugh. This base map was used in the preparation of a more detailed structural map for Powell's *Geology of the Uinta Mountains*.

As soon as the first monograph was printed and distributed, Powell began the final revision of the *Geology of the Uinta Mountains*,[17] incorporating the information gathered during his field trips of 1874 and 1875. The map, which was redrawn from that in the 1875 report, was beautifully done and the Major was proud of it. Thompson, DeMotte, and Bishop received generous credit for their participation in the mapping.

Major Powell's interpretation of the surface geology of the region and his penetrating concept of the interrelationships of geological processes show how far he had advanced beyond his earlier views. A new science was in the making. He wrote:

The region of country embraced in the map . . . is one of great geological interest. Three great categories of facts are here represented on a grand scale, viz: facts relating to displacement, facts relating to degradation, and facts relating to sedimentation. The displacements are of great magnitude, and because the beds involved are sedimentary strata but rarely altered, the characteristics of these displacements are plainly revealed, so that in our studies of them we have been able to arrive at conclusions, both quantitative and qualitative, with some degree of certainty.

While displacement has been great, degradation has also been great, yet the country has not been planed down to a general base-level, but stands in mountain cliffs and escarped hills, where the strata are plainly revealed.

The formations which we are able to study here have an aggregate thickness of 50,000 feet, and embrace groups of Paleozoic, Mesozoic, and Cenozoic Ages. Throughout nearly the entire region there is a condition of surface which renders the study of the geology comparatively easy. By reason of great altitude and extreme aridity the rocks are rarely masked by subaerial gravels, soil, or vegetation. . . .

The whole region has been flexed and faulted on a vast scale; the flexures are truncated by erosion, and the faults are crossed by cañons and lines of cliffs; and thus by a combination of circumstances the whole region is an open book to the geologist, revealing a wonderfully complicated structure and a grand succession of formations. . . .

I have many times witnessed the action of a storm in an arid region where the disintegrated rocks were unprotected by forests, shrubbery, or turf, and as often have I been impressed with the wonderful power of the infrequent storm in the prairie or forest of a land more richly clad. The same contrast may be ob-

[17] J. W. Powell, *Report on the Geology . . . of the Uinta Mountains*, Washington, D.C., Gov. Print. Off., 1876.

served in a region brought under the dominion of man by cultivation where the surface of a plowed field is swept away by a storm, and the furrows are the channels for floods of mud, while the meadow receives the rain with outstretched arms of verdure, which bear it gently to the earth, where it is gathered into quiet rills, which feed a stream of mud flowing from the field from which the plowman was driven by the storm.

We may now conclude that the higher the mountain, the more rapid its degradation; that high mountains cannot live much longer than low mountains, and that mountains cannot remain long as mountains; they are ephemeral topographic forms. Geologically all existing mountains may be old or young as compared with other existing mountains.[18]

The two monographs reveal Powell's interest in mountains, plateaus, and rivers; in uplift and erosion; in the ever-changing surface of the earth. Some streams were older than others. The Green River was older than the Uinta Mountains. It was a novel concept: the river cutting its way unrelentingly through thousands of feet of strata—cutting precipitous canyons and grinding great falls to rapids or mere riffles.

A few geologists in Europe, notably Hutton and Lyell, had propounded theories of earth processes akin to those observed every day about us, but such ideas were not widely accepted. King had postulated sudden upheavals thrusting mountains five to eight miles high; Powell believed that the mountains and plateaus were never much higher than they are today, the rivers cutting their channels as the mountains were gradually elevated.

In the depths of the Grand Canyon Powell traced the courses of ancient limestones and ocean floors, and beneath them he found the twisted and metamorphosed roots of still more ancient mountains—the schists (Powell called the rock "granite") worn with time to a level plain. Some of the peaks of that venerable system were islands, and their tops penetrated into the Cambrian strata above. A poor diagram of this was given in the *Exploration of the Colorado River,* but a very good sketch was included in the *Geology of the Uinta Mountains*. With penetrating vision Powell saw that the mighty earth processes are slow, progressive, and inevitable.

Powell thus had a clear concept of erosion, both natural and man made. Erosion continues under natural circumstances until entire mountain ranges are destroyed. The canyon country represents the slow processes of natural erosion, erosion at a minimum rate. On the other hand, land under tillage and human development suffers from accelerated

[18] *ibid.,* first three quoted paragraphs from "Preface," p. iii, then in order quoted from pages 37, 188, and 196.

erosion, man-made by destroying the soil's protective cover. The process is inevitable; only the rate is controllable.

Geology, to the popular mind, and at that time to most professional geologists, was a scientific ally of mining. Major Powell never looked upon geology as a study of minerals, rocks, and fossils or as an adjunct of mining, but rather as the means to study the land. With his early experience as a farmer and his sympathy for the people, Powell paid little heed to special mining or industrial interests.

Slowly the Major was formulating a pioneer, indeed unique, concept of this vast portion of the earth's surface shaped and sculptured on a grand scale by geological processes. Circumstances had made most of this region the public domain, that is, lands under government ownership. He recognized that so different was this land from the humid East that, unless its limitations were adequately considered, settlement and development would be catastrophic. Thus even in a purely technical monograph, Powell was hammering away for an intelligent understanding of the western territories.

The Major now found time to take a greater part in the scientific affairs of Washington. The city had become the permanent home of a considerable number of scientists and, although duties took many of them away from the city during the summer months, the long winter season provided an unusual opportunity for association among men with kindred interests. Most of the scientists were members of those few federal bureaus which were devoted, at least in part, to research. Among the more distinguished members of this group were Joseph Henry, Simon Newcomb, Spencer Baird, Julius Hilgard, and of course the geologists of the surveys like Hayden, Gilbert, and Meek. The men of science who held government positions were not often victims of the turnover attendant upon political allegiance. Tenure of office under normal circumstances was more or less secure for an indefinitely long period.

The chief gathering place for the scientists of Washington and vicinity was the Philosophical Society.[19] Meetings were held in the old Ford Theater on Tenth Street between "E" and "F," which since the assassination of Lincoln had never again opened its doors to gaiety. The building had been seized by the government and converted into the

---

[19] The proceedings of the Philosophical Society of Washington were published in occasional bulletins. They are more generally available reprinted in the *Smith. Misc. Coll.* (Bulls. Vols. I, II, III, 1871–1880, in *Smith. Misc. Coll.*, Vol. 20, 1881.)

Army Medical Library, an adjunct to the surgeon general's office. Here the society met fortnightly, flanked by long rows of shelves from floor to ceiling crowded with musty books on the ailments and scourges of man. A few multicolored charts of human anatomy broke the monotony of black buckram and tan muslin. The programs of the society were devoted to the presentation of short formal papers followed by open discussion. There were no facilities for serving refreshments in the library so most of the fellows, ignoring age and position, adjourned to a saloon on Tenth Street near "G" for beer and pretzels, where the conversations doubtless became more philosophical.

The Major first attended meetings of the Philosophical Society as a guest on March 9, 1872, when he accepted the invitation of Joseph Henry to present a paper on the structural geology of the valley of the Colorado. Although he was an occasional visitor, the Major did not become a regular member until January 17, 1874. Thereafter he contributed two papers a year and took lively part in the discussion at virtually every meeting he attended.

The Major also had been a member of the American Association for the Advancement of Science since 1872 and, in recognition of the publication of his monograph, he had been elected to fellowship in 1875.

In 1874 Powell had made his first public appearance in the political arena in Washington. A year later, publication of his first great monograph brought the Major deserved professional recognition. Neither of these incidents was spectacular, but Congressmen and newsmen, as well as scientists, were aware of the presence of a cagey fighter and a most capable man.

Donn Piatt, whose barbed pen had pricked many public figures of the day, ridiculed Powell in the *Gazette* for December 19, 1875:

Major Powell, if it would do anybody, himself included, any good, has but a superficial knowledge of geology. He picks up a bone here and there and gets some terminologist to put a name on it when he gets back to Washington. That is paleontology. He enriches the Smithsonian Institute with a few pieces of shattered earthenware of which there is already a supererogation, which is archeology. He makes an annual report with an express view to another appropriation, and that is art. There is no exaggeration in this. At the hands of the educated ninny-hammers of Congress he gets an annual $25,000 to $50,000 with a roving commission to go anywhere he pleases, employ whom he pleases, do as he pleases and write and publish what he pleases with no official accounting to anybody. This is high art. This is nothing against Powell. He is an industrial.

There is another of the same sort, F. V. Hayden, calls himself U.S. Geologist.

He is in some way not explained, an appendix to the Interior Department as Powell is to the Smithsonian. He gets twice as much money annually as Powell and goes geologizing, paleontologizing, herpetologizing and archeologizing miscellaneously around and through the region bounded by the Hundredth Meridian.

Piatt revealed his sympathies in this political contest by lauding the work of Lieutenant Wheeler and the bogus Captain Adams.

Hayden, who had been satirized by Piatt on several previous occasions, became enraged and vindictive. The Major, however, waited a week, then with the aid of friends met Piatt socially. During a pleasant conversation Powell remarked dryly that he was surprised that his modest efforts on behalf of the Smithsonian had been noticed by the press. He was never molested by Piatt again.[20]

Another paper, the *Illustrated Washington Chronicle,* discounting journalistic gush, held a somewhat better opinion of Major Powell, placing him in the "very front rank" of men of science.

His abilities are considered by the most eminent scientists in this country, and his studies of the aboriginal races of America will one day win for him golden fame. He is an enthusiastic worker in the field, and a careful writer and compiler of his researches. His marked powers will one day cause him to be as well known to the general public as he now is to the distinguished scientific men of the United States.

Major Powell, the distinguished geologist, was in Washington to stay.

[20] G. K. Gilbert, recollection given before Cosmos Club, *Procs., 25th Anniv. Mtg.,* 1904, pp. 39–42.

14

1877-1878 · A Proposal for Reform
of the Land Acts

NEARLY thirty times between 1867 and 1877 Major Powell traveled across the plains to the Rocky Mountains and the Great Basin beyond. Within ten years the western territories had changed from wilderness and frontier to settlement and development. The United States had changed from pioneer economic individualism to corporate trade—a transformation long in the making but sudden in its completion. Powell was at first merely an interested spectator. What he saw led him into the arena of politics not as a politician but as a crusader for the protection of the public domain.

In 1867, when Powell crossed the plains by wagon train from Council Bluffs, the region was substantially uninhabited, with a stage stable, an eating place, or a farm placed at about five-mile intervals. Bands of Indians and herds of buffalo roamed over much of the country. A few villages and isolated farms had taken root. In 1868 the railroads penetrated the plains and a year later the Union Pacific spanned the continent. Two weeks after its completion Powell and his party had gone by train to Green River Station. Settlers followed close behind. Millions of acres of land from the public domain were opened to homesteading and preemption, and in the very areas of limited rainfall the population swelled with the high tide of optimism and enthusiasm.

In ignorance of the true character of the lands beyond the old Northwest Territory, it was assumed that the public domain—all the way to the Pacific—was more or less uniform. In the agitation for a definite federal land policy in the 1830's, the opposing Whigs and Jacksonian Democrats accepted this view without question. The Preemption Act of 1841, which gave a settler the right to take up lands prior to survey and to purchase subsequently the claim at a minimum price, encouraged migration to the unknown lands beyond.

Later, disturbing accounts by travelers and traders, supported by scientists and surveyors, cast a grave doubt over the character of the far-western territories. The "Great American Desert," as it was called on the maps, became greater and greater. A forbidding barrier, it was believed, spread across the face of the West. But the Great American Desert was a myth. Arid regions there were, but in the popular mind, as so often happens, with the puncture of this inflated myth the real desert was ignored. Why worry?—"Rain follows the plow." [1]

No more insidious belief ever lured men beyond the limits of common sense. Somehow the notion got started and before long acquired the dignity of a scientific theory. Hayden and his associates insisted that cultivation of the plains would bring about a permanent increase in annual rainfall. Even the construction of railroads would in some mysterious way increase precipitation.

Alarmed by the inexcusable irresponsibility of the proponents of such ideas, and angered by the unconcealed pillage of the natural wealth of the public domain, Powell, a self-appointed crusader, went to work. On April 24, 1874, when Congress took under consideration a proposal to merge the various geographical surveys, Powell submitted his views on consolidation and included the following statement: [2]

About two-fifths of the entire area of the United States has a climate so arid that agriculture cannot be pursued without irrigation. When all of the waters running in the streams found in this region are conducted on the land, there will be but a small portion of the country redeemed, varying in the different territories perhaps from one to three per cent. Already the greater number of smaller streams such as can be controlled by individuals who wish to gain a livelihood by agriculture, are used for this purpose, the largest streams which will irrigate greater areas can only be managed by cooperative organization, great capitalists, or by the General or State Governments.

It is of the most pressing importance that a general survey be made for the purpose of determining the several areas which can thus be redeemed by irrigation. . . .

Speaking from personal observation, he proposed in essence that a scientific examination or assessment of the public domain be made to determine how it should be utilized.

The Major was the first to recognize the real boundary between East and West, between humid and arid, a boundary as clearly fixed by Na-

[1] For an excellent review of these concepts, "Great American Desert" and the antithetic "Rain Follows the Plow," see H. N. Smith, *Hunt. Lib. Quart.*, Vol. 10, pp. 169–93.

[2] *43rd Cong. 1st Sess. H.R. Rep. 612*, April 10, 1874, p. 10. Powell repeated this same statement with slight modifications on a dozen occasions.

ture as though man himself had drawn it. This line coincided approximately with the hundredth meridian, or to state it otherwise, through the Dakotas, Nebraska, Kansas, Oklahoma, and Texas. The farther west toward the Rockies, the drier the plains, the scantier the grass. Beyond the Rockies, in the Great Basin, the high plateaus were in part true deserts.

There was water locked in the snows of winter to be gathered for use when needed—provided that an understanding government would protect the homesteader and the land. With no more than five years' experience in the arid regions, the Major had grasped the opportunity and the limitations of the western territories. Thus, as a by-product of the survey of the southern Utah and adjacent plateau country, Powell began a study on the arid lands of the United States.

It is curious how scattered experience and random observation combine to form patterns in the mind. In Wisconsin almost thirty years before, Powell as a lad had felled great trees to clear the virgin forest and to lay bare a few acres of land to sunshine. In Illinois he had broken the prairie with steel plowshare and oxen, tearing the sod that took centuries to develop. During the war years, along the Mississippi the Major had sloughed his way through bottomlands, flooded in spring, quagmires in summer. Eroded from lands a thousand miles upstream, the silt and muck were carried down to choke the channels below.

In the East that Powell knew, the natural vegetation owed its existence to the moisture which nature lavished upon the land. Moisture was dependable—dependable as the equinoxes. In unusual years rains might fail. They might not come in the proper season or in a suitable amount. The fall might be scanty and dwarf the crops or delay too long the harvest; or they might be excessive and delay growth, induce the blight, and rot the crops. But only one year in very many took a heavy toll. To the west of the hundredth meridian this was not so; moisture was not dependable, farming was an ever-present gamble. Good years there might be, but tragic years would follow.

From the mountain peaks the Major had seen the expanses below and understood the relation between the water and the land. In the mountains there was always water—the dense forests which covered the flanks of the hills were proof of the fact. Myriads of small lakes dotted the intermontane valleys. The heavy snows of winter accumulated in great fields to melt with the return of spring, pour into the dried-up stream beds, and scour them with mighty torrents rushing toward the level of the seas. In summer the rains beat against the mountains, but the clouds, now dry, gained the summit and rolled eastward, warming as they went, parching the surface of the land until the crust glistened with alkali. Between the humid forest in the mountains and the desert below were broad grasslands, which provided a natural pasturage for grazing—but depended just as certainly on the economy of water.

Were it not for human problems involved in this pattern of land and water, the Major might have limited his observations to the geography and geology of the regions he traversed. But he had witnessed hordes of homesteaders crossing beyond the meridian of dependable moisture to take up farms held in perpetual mortgage by Nature.

There were three antagonistic, or at least competitive, interests in the western territories: farming, grazing, and mining. There was a fundamental antagonism between the homesteader, who grew crops, and the cattleman, who raised beef. So long as these competitive enterprises took up different types of land and did not conflict over water, their differences were not serious.

Shortly after the close of the Civil War the cattle business so expanded that thousands of herds appeared suddenly in every state and territory from Texas to California and north to Utah. When powerful cattle interests maintained enormous herds of cattle that foraged over millions of acres of unfenced land—most of it in the public domain—protection of the grass became a necessity. Water holes and sources of water were taken up, sometimes legally, more often through subterfuge. The monopolistic control of water grew in many localities.

With homesteaders, a comparable situation had developed. The first settlers filing on lands bordering streams had the distinct advantage of a relatively permanent source of water close at hand. As late-comers took up less desirable lands farther removed from water, a dependable water supply became an uncertain problem. These homesteaders generally lacked the capital and power to hold the sources of water and before long found themselves at the mercy of larger and wealthier competitors, often in the guise of water companies.

Between the cattle raisers and the homesteaders were the mining companies, which had comparatively little interest in land as such but which did require water for processing ores. For the most part mining communities were in mountainous regions, where water was plentiful, but it was in their power to divert or pollute streams which would be useful to agricultural interests.

Major Powell had watched all three of these factions grow in importance, and with their growth, the inevitable friction. His sympathies were with the farmer, although for a short time in 1872 he had seriously considered entering a partnership with Pardyn Dodds in a grazing venture in Utah,[3] but backed out when he realized that such an affair would interfere with his scientific work.

In 1866 the Mineral Land Act opened the public domain to exploration and development. It was this rebirth of interest in the West that led to the creation of the numerous scientific—as opposed to purely exploratory—surveys beginning with that of Clarence King. The Homestead Act, passed in 1862 and signed by Abraham Lincoln, though supplementing the Preemption Act, which remained in operation, was perhaps the outstanding piece of legislation dealing with the public domain. Under the terms of this law a settler could take up a quarter section of 160 acres of land, and if he constructed a building on it, lived in it, and made certain improvements, all fees were written off and the land could be obtained without cost. A quarter section became known as "a poor man's farm" on the assumption that any ambitious man could obtain for himself and for his family a good parcel of land and earn for himself permanent prosperity.

Instead of working to the benefit of settlement, the Homestead Act, by its interpretation, was open to all kinds of fraud.[4] In some cases miniature houses twelve inches by sixteen inches were placed on the land, and sworn statements were submitted to the land office that buildings had been erected on the claim. A still more brazen trick was to place a wooden packing case at the point where four quarter sections adjoined and then file claim to all four under false names. Another abuse, with the deliberate collusion of the surveyors, was in the defining of the boundaries. The law stated that the sections had to be marked clearly on the four corners by stakes charred at one end. A common practice was for the surveyor to stand on the corner, strike a match, allow it to burn itself out, and then throw it away. Sworn statements were submitted that the claimant wished to file on a given section and that the lands were marked in the manner required by law; then the homesteader would take up the land and place the boundaries wherever he liked. These and countless other malpractices suggest the extent to which lands

[3] Whether the financial panic of 1873 forced Powell to abandon the scheme, or the probability of permanent federal support for his scientific work made a money-making venture unnecessary, is impossible to determine. The most definite record of the proposed partnership is a letter from Pardyn Dodds to J. W. Powell, Sept. 15, 1872. From 1868–1872 the cattle trade had reached its greatest expansion. Already in 1872 a decline was evident.

[4] For an appraisal of the operation of the Homestead Act see W. P. Webb, *The Great Plains*, Chap. IX, and B. H. Hibbard, *A History of Public Land Policies*.

were obtained fraudulently from the federal domain. So long as such claims passed in the hands of individual settlers, no great harm would come from the evil. The problem was that corporations, companies, and monopolies chose variations of these devices to obtain lands bearing minerals or valuable timber, and then exploited them for private profit. Corporate monopolies filed claims in the names of employees and paid confederates. Even purely fictitious names were used to obtain millions of acres of public land.

Assuming that the disposal of the public lands had been honest, it would still have been impossible to distribute lands wisely. Mineral lands were not recognized as such, or regulated by law, until 1866, timberlands until 1873, and desert lands until 1877. No wonder then that when robber barons plundered the public domain of millions upon millions of dollars, they were protected by inept laws and, when necessary, by controlled political machines. Reform was a Herculean contest.

At the spring meeting of the National Academy of Sciences in the latter part of April 1877 Major Powell delivered a speech which lasted little more than thirty minutes. The title was simply, "The Public Domain." Although he was not at this time a member of the academy, he had been invited to present a paper on some subject of his own choosing. The newspapers, after reporting a few trivialities about an academic tiff between Professor Hayden, Professor Cope, and Professor Marsh, mentioned:

A matter of graver and more general interests was brought up in Major Powell's description of our public lands. If it be true that there is scarcely any good land left fit for a poor man's homestead farm, the sooner the fact is announced the better.[5]

The first clear statement demanding a change in the federal land system was voiced on this occasion by Major Powell. His argument was neatly summed up in the New York *Tribune* for April 28, 1877:

The present land system of the country, whether as to the purchase, preemption, or homestead plans, is not at all suitable for the area of the arid region. If it offers, for instance, title to timber lands on the homestead plan, the result is that as nobody can make a homestead on such lands, the timber is simply stolen, except in instances where it was worth while to dig a mine. In the whole region, land as mere land is of no value; what is really valuable is the water privilege. Rich men and stock companies have appropriated all the streams, and they charge for the use of the water. Government sections of 160 acres that do not contain water are practically, or at all events comparatively worthless. All the

[5] New York *Tribune*, April 28, 1877.

good public lands fit for settlement are sold. There is not left unsold in the whole United States, of land which a poor man could turn into a farm, enough to make one average county in Wisconsin. . . . The homestead plan can only be applied in the pasturage area after being so modified as to include very much larger space than now to a homestead, and to provide for the abutment of some portion, in each instance, upon a stream where flocks can be watered. The owner of such a tract may expect to pasture from 10,000 to 20,000 head of cattle; the grass is thin and poor, and no man can make a living by pasturing a few cattle upon a tract of one or two hundred acres.

A lively discussion followed the speaker. Prof. L. H. Morgan made a plea for considering the Indian claims to certain portions of the areas of the public domain. It would be an excellent opportunity, he said, to alleviate some of the injustices done to the Indians at the same time a general revision of the land laws were attempted. Joseph Henry commented that he had long been convinced of the unfitness of the public land distribution because it was based on the misconception that there was more or less uniformity in the characteristics of the entire country.

Powell was not alone, of course, in his anxiety over the future of the public domain, but he was the first to take the stump and demand specific reforms in the federal land policy. In 1873 the American Association for the Advancement of Science memorialized Congress urging the creation of forest reserves and calling attention to the necessity for planting trees, protecting forests, and educating the people about forestry. Congress was unwilling to adopt any such sweeping program with respect to one of the most lucrative—to private exploiters, of course—resources of the public lands and merely created in the Department of the Interior an office to gather statistics on the production of timber in the United States. When Carl Schurz became Secretary of the Interior in the Hayes cabinet and appointed John A. Williamson as commissioner of the General Land Office, he won the enmity of the vested interests almost as soon as he took his oath. Williamson began energetically to enforce the long abused laws pertaining to timber, mineral, and homestead claims. Congress had no liking for this effort. In the ensuing legislative battles Rep. John Taylor Morgan of Alabama went so far as to deny that Schurz had the legal authority to protect the national domain.

Powell's explorations were intimately concerned with this region, and while directing scientific surveys, he witnessed the gradual establishment of permanent settlements in the more inhabitable portions. The area of the central great plains, sometimes called the high plains of western United States, was a land of contrast, a vast treeless region, nearly level, in which there is insufficient rainfall for the type of agriculture practiced in the eastern part of the country. To the easterner who traveled over its expanses it appeared forbidding and uninhabitable. The techniques of pioneering, which had moved the frontier beyond the Appalachians and beyond the Mississippi, were not suited to development or occupation of this kind of country.

In the East, the log cabin was the beginning of civilization; in the West, the miner's camp. In the East, agriculture began with the settler's clearing; in the West, with the exploitation of wealthy men.

In the log-cabin years a poor man in Ohio might clear an acre of land at a time and extend his potato-patch, his cornfield, and his meadow, from year to year, and do all with his own hands and energy, and thus hew his way from poverty to plenty. At the same time his wife could plant hollyhocks, sweet williams, marigolds, and roses in boxed beds of earth around the cabin door. So field and garden were all within the compass of a poor man's love of industry and his wife's love of beauty.[6]

Originally, Powell had intended to write a technical description of the public domain describing the character of all the lands which still belonged to the federal government. Such a task, to describe the coastal swamps of the southern Atlantic states, the everglades of Florida, the flood plains of the Mississippi, and the country of the upper Great Lakes, in all of which the critical problem was drainage, would take half a lifetime. The monograph was, therefore, limited to the arid regions of the West, where the critical problem was irrigation.

Powell had been slowly revising his manuscript on the *Lands of the Arid Region* [7] and, believing he had dallied long enough, determined to complete the job as quickly as possible after the close of the 1876 season. On April 1, 1878, it was submitted to J. A. Williamson, chief of the General Land Office, who in turn transmitted it to Carl Schurz. A few days later the House committee on appropriations ordered that the monograph be printed. The first edition was only eighteen hundred copies and was exhausted in a few months. Within twelve months a second edition of five thousand copies was issued and this too was exhausted in a very short time.

It might appear strange that, with so many copies of the report distributed free, there was little acclaim for Powell's views. It was a brave and revolutionary book. Certain natural phenomena tended to obscure the arguments which he advanced. G. K. Gilbert, who had been assigned to investigate the features of Great Salt Lake, discovered that the level

---

[6] *Century Magazine*, Vol. 40, p. 111.

[7] The full title is *Report on the Lands of the Arid Region of the United States with a More Detailed Account of the Lands of Utah*, 1st ed. 1877; 2nd ed. 1879.

of the lake was rising and that the country in general was enjoying a period of increased rainfall. That there had been a favorable rainfall for some years was indeed well known. The army posts in Kansas and neighboring states had reported an increase of sixteen to twenty per cent in annual rainfall over a period of twenty years. With the optimism born of enthusiasm, settlers believed that rain followed the plow and that, as new lands were developed, in some manner rainfall was permanently increased. This foolish opinion reflected wishful thinking, nothing more. In his report the Major ridiculed any effects that man-made works might have on precipitation, explaining that at best they could exert a trifling influence.

. . . if it be true that increase of the water supply is due to increase in precipitation, as many have supposed, the fact is not cheering to the agriculturist of the arid region. . . . Usually such changes go in cycles, and the opposite or compensating change may reasonably be anticipated . . . we shall have to expect a speedy return to extreme aridity, in which case a large portion of the agricultural industries of these now growing up would be destroyed.[8]

Therefore he preferred to consider the problem *not increased rainfall, rather, increased erosion.* This was an ugly thought because it implied that instead of a change for the better it was, if not a change for the worse, simply an abnormal cycle. Those who were reaping the benefits of profitable agriculture paid no attention to his words.

The report on the arid region proposed a fivefold classification of the western public lands: mineral, coal, irrigable, pasturage, and timber lands. The mineral lands were not considered and the abundance of lignite coals was but briefly mentioned, being regarded as "inexhaustible by any population which the country can support for any length of time that human pre-vision can contemplate." [9] It was recommended, however, that a geological survey be made to determine their extent. The purpose of the report, aside from the technical description of the other three types of lands, was to suggest ways by which these lands could be utilized and protected. He recognized that a revolution in administration would be needed to develop the arid country.

It is difficult to understand how little correct knowledge of the arid parts of the United States was available to the General Land Office and even to business interests. The regions of the West were explored in a haphazard fashion and no comprehensive classification of the land had ever been attempted.

[8] *ibid.*, p. 91.
[9] *ibid.*, p. 45.

The people as well as the government were greasing the skids for a disaster to the homesteaders in the arid and semiarid regions. Enthusiastic settlers moved into areas of insecure rainfall and established farms, through inexperience and optimism failing to recognize the limitations of the land. The government made no effort to acquaint them with the difficulties ahead. Even in the regions of grass—the pasture lands—conflicting interests were at work. Cattle interests had taken up water holes to protect their grass and livestock. The Major denied that they had the moral right to sources of water needed for agricultural purposes. In certain areas in which farms had been developed, the cheapest and most dependable source of water was available from "water companies" organized to sell water at a profit. Again there was nothing illegal in this, but the Major saw in such companies the danger of an evil monopoly which would charge an exorbitant price and force the homesteaders to pay a heavy tribute.

Practically all of the vast expanses of land over which the Major worked were in the possession of the federal government. Lands were being alienated from the public domain rapidly but little or no heed was paid to their character, it being assumed that land was land. Nothing could have been more fallacious. There was an urgent need for a classification of the lands of the arid regions and Powell determined not only to provide a method of classification but also to propose certain specific legislative measures for utilizing and protecting such lands. If necessary he would overthrow the whole federal land system insofar as it operated in the western territories.

The audacity of Powell's approach to the problem of the federal land policy is the more remarkable when it is realized that he had no authorization to undertake a classification of lands of the arid regions; land classification was out of his jurisdiction. The General Land Office, supposedly responsible for that work, was, in the Major's words, "a gigantic illustration of the evils of badly directed scientific work." [10]

Powell recognized the interrelated factors which made the land problem so complex. Arid land was but the most obvious feature. The water supply was the great limiting factor. Fertility of the soil, grasslands, and forests were also important. Thus, independent of legal or political factors or conditions of human settlement, there were difficulties of tremendous importance. The knowledge necessary to understand the land problem was woefully inadequate.

Excluding possibly Arizona, Utah was the most consistently arid of all

[10] J. W. Powell, *Report on the Methods of Surveying the Public Domain*, p. 6.

these territories then virtually unsettled by white men. When in 1847 the Mormons diverted City Creek through a rude ditch to water the ground for Utah's first farm, they demonstrated the fundamental attribute of the arid region—the soil was fertile; only moisture was lacking. Although the devout saints believed that knowledge of irrigation was a divine revelation to their people, it is more probable that Indians had acquainted them with the rudiments of irrigation. By diligent toil the Mormons wrested from an unpromising land bounteous crops. The problem was to bring water to the land.

There are two simple methods for storing water: reservoirs can be constructed near the sources of the streams, the waters being impounded in the upper valleys; the water can be run into canals and diverted into ponds from which ditches carry it to the farms that are being irrigated. The first of these methods involves skillful engineering at great initial expense. The second method, ponding, though much less costly, is much less efficient. Ponding is wasteful because of the rapid evaporation which occurs in shallow bodies of water. "The greater storage of water must come from the construction of great reservoirs in the high lands where lateral valleys may be dammed up and the main streams conducted into them by canals." [11]

Powell recognized another aspect of the problem of conserving water —the destruction of forests by fire. Though he was a friend of the Indian, the Major realized that the Indians could no longer be allowed to roam at will over the public domain and set fire to the forests for the purpose of driving fur-bearing game. After the Indians had learned the luxuries of white men and measured their own wealth in furs, they hunted no longer for food but for profit. Many of the white settlers misinterpreted the purpose of these incendiary fires and regarded the Indians' behavior as wantonness and intent to destroy everything of value to the settler. The mountaineers were aware of the real motive behind these fires; the Indian was impoverished and he sought the easiest way to obtain a quick return for his efforts.

In 1868 the Major had witnessed a fire in Colorado which destroyed more timber than all that used by the citizens of the territory from the time of its earliest settlement. Within the next few years he had seen a second fire of equal extent in Colorado and at least three in Utah, each of which destroyed more timber than had been taken by the people since the occupation of the territory. Every one of the government surveying parties that had traversed the western lands had met fires in progress

[11] *ibid.*, p. 13.

or the charred remnants attesting to the former presence of this great destroyer. The younger forests were everywhere growing over fallen timber which had been burned during seasons of drought through the agency of the Indian. In every season of great drought the mountaineer saw the sky filled with clouds of smoke rising from great areas in the path of devastation.

Powell believed that with management and protection the forests would last forever, and although he appreciated the importance of forest culture and reforestation, it was the importance of woodland to water rather than the forest itself that held his interest. The snows of winter are secured by the roots of trees and shaded by the branches so that melting and run-off are retarded. These relationships were not clearly understood by anyone in 1877, but the general notions of the economy of water were gradually taking form.

What then were the reasons for the hopeless confusion and bungling?

It will be remembered that the Homestead Act of 1862 made it possible for a person to settle on a quarter section of land of 160 acres at no greater cost than a small registration fee, and then, after building at least a shack and cultivating the land for five years, to receive full title. There were, to be sure, deceptions and frauds upon the government, but the lure of free lands brought millions of honest settlers to the West. The best lands were taken first and as the flocks of eager homesteaders arrived, they spread over the lands in utter disregard of the natural limitations of the country.

As drier and less favorable portions of public lands were disposed of in this manner, it was not possible for the homesteader to gain a livelihood from 160 acres of this type of land. In many areas the grass was so scanty that a much larger tract was needed to support even a small herd. A quarter section in such regions was of no value; the pasturage afforded was entirely inadequate for a herd that even the poorest man might own. After examining many areas in the Great Basin the Major reached the conclusion that four square miles or four sections must be considered as the minimum amount necessary for a pasturage farm and that still greater amounts would be necessary in the larger part of the lands just opened to settlement. Pasturage lands, in other words, to have any practical value, must be at least 2,560 acres in extent and in many districts, larger. When the Major proposed this definite figure as a conservative minimum limit he disappointed many of the cattle raisers with whom he was acquainted and whose ranches he had examined. They believed that the estimate was too low and that the fair figure should be at least twice as much.

The Desert Land Act of 1877 was actually a hindrance to the future development of the western territories although it had been intended as an aid to settlement. The law permitted a desert land entry of 640 acres, but the settler was not allowed to homestead it. Moreover he had to pay twenty-five cents down for each acre and an additional dollar within three years. There were other requirements which had to be met to hold the land, such as that he had to irrigate at least a part of it within the three years. The nonsensical feature of the bill becomes evident when it is realized that most of the lands in this region could either not be irrigated at all, or at a most prohibitive cost. In other words, the homesteader could get good agricultural land for nothing in parcels of 160 acres whereas irrigable lands had to be purchased in blocks of 640 acres. The crowning bit of bungling was that the 640 desert acres could not be considered equivalent in any way to 160 humid acres.

Powell put the needs of the land and the homesteader in this way:

> The grasses of the pasturage lands are scant and the lands are of value only in large quantities. The farm unit should not be less than 2560 acres. Pasturage lands need small tracts of irrigable lands, hence the small streams of the general drainage system and the lone springs and streams should be preserved for such pasturage farms. The pasturage lands will not usually be fenced and hence, herds must roam in common. All of the pasturage lands should have water fronts and irrigable tracts and as the residents should be grouped and as the lands cannot be economically fenced and must be kept in common, local communal regulations or cooperation is necessary.[12]

Words such as these coming from a professor turned explorer did not convert any great number of politicians to the cause for which he fought. In the East, where a farm of one hundred acres was considered ample property capable of producing a guaranteed income, such a notion as 2,560 acres was ridiculous. Then, to parcel land according to topography instead of surveyor's lines was equally preposterous.

Powell knew that due to unfamiliarity with the West a gross misconception of the arid regions still permeated every aspect of official thinking. Men who had the knowledge could turn it to their personal advantage, and many did, deliberately preventing the spread of truth to secure their plunder. The members of Congress who represented the western territories were outnumbered by those of other regions who could not

[12] J. W. Powell, *Lands of the Arid Region*, p. 24.

have their interests at heart. It was a logical consequence that politicians voted in blocs.

Among other specific proposals were two deserving close examination. The land unit in the irrigation district was not to exceed eighty acres while the land unit in the pasturage district should be at least 2,560 acres. This is the very essence of the two opposing economic interests working to develop and exploit the West—the one, monopoly of water; the other, monopoly of land. The organization of such irrigation districts held Powell's attention for many years.

After surveying thousands of square miles of the arid region, the Major had four proposals to submit to a disinterested Congress: (1) all lands for which water is accessible for as much as 320 acres shall be classed as irrigable land; (2) the amount of land allotted to each person shall not exceed eighty acres; (3) nine or more persons qualified for homestead entry shall form an irrigation district and make such bylaws for their own government as do not interfere with the general laws of the country; and (4), the most important and far-reaching, the right to the water shall inhere in the land and in conveyance shall pass with the title of the land. Failure to use water shall after a period of five years cause the right to the water to lapse.

The last three proposals represent the crux to the whole problem: "Monopoly of the land is not to be feared. The question for legislators is to solve some practical means by which water rights may be distributed among individual farmers and water monopolies prevented." [13] The familiar laws which grew up under the Anglo-Saxon legal system and developed for the humid country do not and dare not apply to the arid region.

There was another complication. By act of Congress on July 26, 1866, and an amendment approved July 9, 1870, the government surrendered any right of public ownership over nonnavigable streams, and thus all patents granted or homesteads allowed became subject to any vested or accrued water rights which were recognized and acknowledged by local customs, laws, and decisions of the courts. Thus water rights were tacitly separated from land rights. At the same time all irrigation work was done under state laws even though the title to the land was still in federal hands.

The Major resented the growth of irrigation companies which obtained the vested rights in the waters controlled by them. Such rights

[13] *ibid.*, p. 41.

did not belong to any particular tracts of land. Here again the water rights, under existing laws, were being separated from land rights.

The right to use water should inhere in the land to be irrigated and water rights should go with land titles. . . . Monopolies will be secured, and the whole agriculture of the country will be tributary thereto—a condition of affairs which an American citizen having in view the interests of the largest number of people cannot contemplate with favor.[14]

Powell discussed these conditions and problems in his book. He stated again in simple terms the two great advantages of irrigation: first that farms so cultivated are not subject to the vicissitudes of rainfall; and second that the water for irrigation comes down from the mountains and plateaus charged with fertilizing materials gathered from the decaying vegetation matter in the soil from the higher regions, and reiterated that the limit of successful agriculture without irrigation is an average of twenty inches of annual rainfall. But at twenty inches farming will not be uniformly successful from West to East: *"Many droughts will occur and many seasons in long series will be utter failures."* [15]—how frequent and how serious they were no one could tell. Powell did not have sufficient historical information to hazard a guess but he knew that such droughts would occur. Furthermore, a broad belt separates the arid region of the West from the humid region of the East. This extends roughly from the hundredth meridian eastward to the ninety-seventh meridian, that is, the line of twenty-eight inches of rainfall. Even this belt will be subject to more or less disastrous droughts, the frequency of which will diminish from West to East. Emigrants were pouring into this vulnerable region—North Dakota, South Dakota, Nebraska, Kansas, Oklahoma, and a portion of Texas—in anticipation of unbounded prosperity. Powell called this belt the "semiarid" region in his manuscript, but upon the advice of friends who were sensitive to the political attitudes of the day, changed it to "semihumid" because it would be less offensive. To a considerable extent the whole area from the semihumid belt to the foothills of the Rockies, with the exception of isolated regions scattered here and there, is covered by grass, tall grasses nearer the East and the short grasses to the West. In the driest portions the grass is limited to bunches separated from one another in some cases by many feet of bare soil.

[14] *ibid.*, pp. 41–43.
[15] *ibid.*, p. 3; repeated also with slight changes on many occasions.

The growth and prosperity will depend largely upon a land system which will comply with the requirements of these conditions and facts. . . . The homestead and methods of acquiring title are inadequate to meet these conditions.

Then as a bold crusade, Powell proposed two definite reform laws with unmistakable purpose: "a bill to authorize the organization of irrigation districts by homestead settlements upon the public lands requiring irrigation for agricultural purposes"; and "a bill to authorize the organization of pasturage districts by homestead settlements on the public lands which are of value for pasturage purposes only." In each he wrote a provision, an earnest plea, "the right to the water necessary to irrigate the land shall inhere in the land from the date of organization of the district." [16]

In the two measures, it was presupposed that the lands had been, prior to their opening, authoritatively classified as to usability and value. Powell stated that the work of determining the areas which should be relegated to the "irrigable," "timber," and "pasturage" classifications would be comparatively inexpensive, although the work of designating and setting apart coal and mineral lands as national reserves would require a thorough geological survey.

The specific legislation which Major Powell suggested would have gone a long way toward correcting the misconceived and inadequate laws affecting the development of the western territories. His proposals were soon lost in the slow-moving machinery of government. Even Powell's immediate superiors and the men of the General Land Office passed the proposals to each next higher office with casual comments that the suggested legislation might be important but that they had not had opportunities to study the proposals in detail. The bills died in the public lands committee. The people themselves were not yet concerned with such an issue. Was not moisture "following the plow?"

[16] *ibid.*, p. 40.

15

1878-1879 . Consolidation of the Surveys

THE rivalry between the several geographical and geological surveys in the western territories grew more bitter as the years passed. Clarence King's survey of the fortieth parallel had been completed in 1872, but Wheeler's survey of the hundredth meridian, Hayden's survey of the Rocky Mountain region, and Powell's, known officially as the second division of the survey of the Rocky Mountain region, continued, all in the same general area. Whatever the official designation, it was generally conceded that Major Powell's group was an independent one. In addition to these three scientific surveys, two of which were under the Department of the Interior, there were also a land-parceling survey and the General Land Office in the Department of the Interior, and the Coast and Geodetic Survey under the jurisdiction of the Department of the Treasury.

The first important step toward consolidation of the scientific surveys was the result of an incident in the upper Arkansas River basin when Dr. Hayden's party trespassed in the region assigned to Lieutenant Wheeler. Congress was requested to define the areas to be mapped by each organization.[1] Hearings were held before the committee on public lands, during which Powell advocated complete reorganization and unification. At the same time the Major interjected into the issue the need for an accurate classification of the lands in the public domain. Powell alone among the heads of the surveys recognized the conflicting interests in the development of the West.

Each year, when the various surveys appealed for necessary appropriations and presented competitive claims and charges, the members of Congress were reminded of the underlying inefficiency and waste in such a situation. None of the proponents of consolidation had ceased to canvass for this view during the intervening years. The War Department had tried several times to induce Congress to combine the several sur-

[1] *43rd Cong. 1st Sess. H.R. Rep. 612.*

veys under its jurisdiction, but scientists in general were outspoken in objecting to military domination of the government scientific surveys. But the underlying reason for inaction was the opposition of the western bloc in Congress, especially the committee on public lands, to any government interference in the development of the West.

Far-reaching reforms in federal land policy were long overdue. Intelligent citizens, aware of the true state of affairs, were waiting for the opportunity to rationalize the system.

The western bloc viewed with alarm Powell's radical monograph, *Lands of the Arid Region.* Should the proposals advanced therein be enacted into law, the character of western development would be suddenly altered. At every move on behalf of unification of the surveys, Powell was there to repeat his contentions that two-fifths of the area of the United States is too arid to permit agriculture without irrigation, and that new institutions were needed to protect the water supplies of the arid regions. These were dangerous ideas. Powell's role in the movement for consolidation was well known, but his attitude concerning these arid regions—and that means the West—was even better known.

The proponents of unification of the several scientific surveys sought merely administrative reform. In the political background, however, was a struggle over the future of the public domain. This issue, one of the most critical in American politics following the Civil War, was whether the incalculably rich public domain should be developed in the interest of the public or be exploited by a favored few in complete disregard of the economic and social consequences.

Development of the West had been by exploitation. With full knowledge of the notoriously corrupt General Land Office, fraudulent homestead entries were filed on timber and mineral lands. Large cattle companies controlled vast acreages of the public domain through monopoly of the water supply. Independent homesteaders found themselves at the mercy of powerful corporations controlled in many instances by distant financial interests.

The General Land Office was partner to this corruption, especially in the offices of the sixteen surveyors-general. The system of awarding the land-parceling surveys to private contractors was a perverted practice. Vested interests were unalterably opposed to any reform which would change the private method of land parceling or require an accurate classification of lands and thus prevent illegal grabbing of mineral or other rights.

In 1877 the graft-ridden Grant administration went out of office and a housecleaning of the federal departments at last was possible. President Hayes brought Carl Schurz, an avowed liberal, into the cabinet as Secretary of the Interior. The Department of the Interior had been brazen in its patronage, dishonesty, and graft. The Secretary, Columbus Delano, had been forced to resign in 1875 because of the gross misconduct of the Bureau of Indian Affairs. Othniel C. Marsh, a paleontologist at Yale, while collecting fossils in the West, observed such dishonesty that, by publicizing abuses at the Red Cloud Agency, he was able to expose the ineptness of the whole department.[2]

There was, nevertheless, the greater issue, an issue in which the Department of the Interior was but a small part: the rape of the public domain. Major Powell had grasped the problem of the West and conceived a policy for its development in the interest of all the people. The struggle against landed interests and big money interests was the background in which the consolidation controversy must be understood.

The financial depression of 1877 and 1878 had put most of the members of Congress in a mood for economizing, and there was no better place to make a display of intent than to cut the appropriations for the three competitive and overlapping surveys of the territories. Indeed, Major Powell had experienced considerable anxiety in 1877. So uncertain was the future of his survey that he called upon Dr. John Strong Newberry to lend his influence to secure the appropriation. The Major had sought Newberry's help on several previous occasions, each time finding him an able and willing ally. Powell's appeal to Newberry shows plainly the anxiety and the forces at work:

Dr. J. S. Newberry   January 13, 1877
New York
MY DEAR SIR:
    Your letter with accompanying copies of letters to Mr. Hewitt and Mr. Garfield duly received. I fear that it will be a tight squeeze for us this year but hope to get through all right. While I know the Appropriation Committee and especially the Chairman will attempt to cut off Western Work, I think that the greater body of Congressmen are in favor of my work. Especially is this true with a few of the most influential men, such as Mr. Seelye, Mr. Garfield, Mr. Randall, and Mr. Hewitt. Though I have had no conversation with any of these gentlemen myself concerning the matter,

---

[2] C. Schuchert and C. M. Le Vene, *O. C. Marsh, Pioneer in Paleontology,* Chap. VI; *42nd Cong. 3rd Sess. H.R. Rep. 98; 43rd Cong. 1st Sess. H.R. Rep. 778.* The sordid history of the Department of the Interior under the Grant administration has been pictured by numerous historians, the most incisive, Allan Nevins, *Hamilton Fish: The Inner History of the Grant Administration.*

yet I hear from reliable sources that they intend to appropriate some of my work. At the other end of the Capitol, the Senators are, I believe, unanimously in favor of increasing my appropriation. But the real difficulty lies in the fact that Congress is chiefly employed over impending national issues, and the appropriation will be largely controlled by the House Committee, and while I have some very warm friends in that committee, still there are others equally in earnest to reduce expenditures, by stopping our appropriations, and I fear that their action will be accomplished by the house without challenge, from the very necessities of the case. You have so kindly interposed your influence on my behalf that I feel that it is due to you to fully explain the condition of affairs here and if I find my appropriation is really imperilled, I hope you will not consider that I am importunate and presuming should I call on you for further assistance. . . .

I am, with great respect,
J. W. POWELL [3]

Newberry replied a week later informing him that he had sent identical letters to James A. Garfield and Abram S. Hewitt. The ramifications of the smoldering feud are evident from this letter:

Hon. J. A. Garfield   January 20, 1877
MY DEAR SIR:

I know you are terribly busy and very much engrossed in the settlement of the exciting Presidential question; but I venture to ask you to turn from that for a moment and listen to a few words in behalf of science.

I learn that the matter of appropriations for Western explorations and surveys is soon to come before Congress, and it is reported that there will be some retrenchment in the expenditure for this purpose.

Now while sharing the conviction which I know you entertain that the condition of the country requires the most rigid economy on the part of both people and government, and fully approving the spirit that prompts such retrenchment, it seems to me important that retrenchment if resolved upon, may be wise and discriminating and may not be so applied as to cripple good men, and useful enterprizes, and leave the less worthy to flourish.

You know there are two civilian parties now engaged in Western Explorations, those of F. Hayden and Major Powell; and as I am intimately acquainted with these men, and the work of each, I take the liberty of reporting to you my judgment of their respective merits.

Briefly, for I know brevity will please you best, Hayden has come to be so much of a fraud that he has lost the sympathy and respect of the scientific men of the country and it may well be questioned whether he and his enterprizes should be generously assisted as they have been. In former times he was an energetic and successful explorer, and although his individual work had little scientific value, he has been the means of causing much good work to be done by others. Of late years, however, he has come

---

[3] U.S. Geol. and Geog. Survey Rocky Mt. Region, *Letters Sent,* National Archives.

to be simply the political manager of his expeditions, has spent most of his time in Washington where he has in some way accumulated a handsome property. His influence in Congress has been maintained by the hearts of the lobbyist, such as giving employment to the relatives of those by whose influence he was assisted, making large expenditure for photographs, which were distributed with an eye to political effect. For years a son and brother-in-law of Sen. Logan were connected with his parties and he thereby gained an efficient friend in the Senate. Mr. Holman was propitiated by the same means, and I could give you other similar cases. At the same time his work has deteriorated. By the death of Marvine, and the withdrawal of Gardner; whom you know, he lost his best men and has not one who can do in geology and topography what they did. The most important contributions lately made to science through his agency are papers on Paleontology prepared by experts from materials obtained through his collectors. These, however, interesting to scientists, seem hardly to belong to the category of *necessities* for which the expenditures of government should be chiefly made in these hard times.

Major Powell, however, belongs to quite a different class. He and his assistant, Mr. G. K. Gilbert, are men of first rate ability and are inspired by true scientific enthusiasm. Their work has been mainly done in the field by themselves and is chiefly geologic and topographic. In quality it ranks with the best done anywhere. It is also cheaply and honestly done. Major Powell, instead of being enriched by his connections with the government, has spent quite a large supply of his fortune. In these circumstances it seems to me that if entrenchment must come, it should fall on Hayden rather than Powell and my own judgment is that it would be wiser to increase rather than diminish Major Powell's appropriation.

I need hardly say to you that I have no relations with either of the gentlemen whose names I have mentioned which could modify my opinion of their merit; unless indeed in F. Hayden's favor. He was formerly a student of mine, and I have been his sincere and efficient friend through many years. Still I now feel compelled to speak of him as I do.

With Major Powell my relations are only those of scientific friends and the good words I say of him and Mr. Gilbert are truthful expression of my estimate of their merits.

If your judgment in this matter should coincide with mine, you will perhaps say a kind word for these gentlemen as you may have opportunity.

Yours very truly,[4]
J. S. NEWBERRY

For several years, possibly as early as 1873 or 1874, the Major had realized that the future of his survey would depend ultimately upon pub-

---

[4] Newberry sent Powell a copy of his "personal" letter to Hewitt and Garfield. It is quoted in full not because of Newberry's support but for his appraisal of Hayden's scientific work. Newberry was an honorable man and indeed a competent geologist to judge contemporary work in the territories. Professor Newberry disliked some of Powell's personal traits (J. S. Newberry to G. K. Gilbert, Sept. 22, 1877) but he did not let these feelings color his judgment of the Major's ability.

lic support, not upon Congressional interest, and that unless the work was closely allied with industry, mining, and agriculture, all the government geological surveys would be discontinued. Powell made this clear to each of his scientists when, contrary to his usual policy, he took them off their regular work.

During these years a shift in popular interest in western explorations had been in full swing. The glamor of discovery had worn off and the more prosaic investigations evoked little concern. The region had been made known, the Indians had been subdued, and the population of the territories west of the Mississippi had swelled from 3,600,000 in 1865 to more than 13,000,000 in 1877. The West was an integral part of the country. Thus, purely exploratory surveys were no longer required. This Powell appreciated and, one after another, he transferred his men from the more scientific pursuits to classification of lands in the public domain. Gilbert, Thompson, and Dutton were by 1877 engaged in the study of the arid regions and their utilization. Yet, aside from the monograph on the *Lands of the Arid Region,* Powell's interests apparently were with the Indians. His administration of a "geological" survey was, accordingly, criticized.

The War Department had been the earliest government agency in the exploring work, and through its chief officers had argued that the surveys under the chief of army engineers had priority over other land surveys, and because adequate defensive measures against the Indians and outlawry were still required, whatever surveys in the western territories were authorized should be under military jurisdiction. The need for extensive military measures against the Indians had long passed. Garrisons in isolated places were, of course, necessary, but only in a restricted sense. Powell, in 1873, mincing no words, had expressed his opinions regarding the relation between the army and the Indians.

Hayden's case was very different. Despite great personal charm— when in good humor—he was suspicious, conniving, and vindictive. His survey, which had accomplished considerable excellent work, had flourished by a combination of publicity, patronage, and persistence. Many delegates were tired of Hayden's methods of influencing Congress.

In the spring of 1878 Powell appeared in person before the appropriations committee seeking funds for the continuation of his field work. He explained the importance of accurate mapping and displayed a large map which showed the extensive and inexcusable overlapping of the various surveys.

From a purely technical standpoint the mapping, which after all was the tangible product of the surveying, was open to serious criticism. Here again Wheeler was in for the worst and Hayden, little better. The United States geographical surveys west of the hundredth meridian directed by Wheeler were begun in 1869. Their function at first was primarily mapping for geographical and military purposes and the maps were drawn on a scale of eight miles to the inch. This scale was too small for permanent or detailed geological purposes. The topography, being indicated only by hachures, was almost worthless. The Hayden surveys in the earlier years were likewise primarily for reconnaissance, and it was not until 1878 that the contour system and a large scale—four miles to the inch—were adopted for the mapping. Hayden had refused to make improvements in the topographic work, even when suggested by his own men. The King survey, organized purely for geological work, indicated topographic features on its maps by contour lines and used a four mile to the inch scale from the very beginning in 1867. The Powell surveys, organized for geographical and geological purposes, prepared large-scale maps with contour lines and accessory hachures. The four mile to the inch scale was adopted from the start.

In spite of the the unpleasant circumstances surrounding these surveys, Congress had been lavish to all of them. Since 1867 nearly $1,900,-000 had been expended for surveying and mapping the West. Of this total Hayden had received $690,000, Wheeler, $550,000, King, $387,000, and Powell, $259,000. Without any doubt, a quarter of this was wasted in duplicated effort, to say nothing of sums used unwisely. The time had come to reorganize to avoid this unnecessary expense.[5]

In the committee on appropriations, A. S. Hewitt proposed that the National Academy of Sciences review the whole subject of unification of the surveys and make specific recommendations to Congress.[6] The committee accepted his views, and when the Sundry Civil Bill was reported out for debate Hewitt's proposal was in it. The clause was accepted readily, but not without protests that the issue was political or administrative rather than scientific or technical. The National Academy of Sciences, which had been established in 1863 during the duress of war to investigate and advise upon any technical question when called upon to do so by any agency of the federal government, was requested to investigate and make recommendations for the consolidation of the various surveys of the western territories.[7] Hayden and Wheeler were dis-

[5] J. W. Powell, *Report on the Methods of Surveying the Public Domain*, p. 11.
[6] June 20, 1878.
[7] June 30, 1878.

appointed and angry at the move because it was well known that a small influential group of geologists were members of the academy, and their opinions would carry great weight in whatever recommendations were formulated. Powell was not a member of the academy, but many of his friends were.

Joseph Henry, who had been president of the academy, died only a month before Congress made its request, and since no election of officers had taken place, O. C. Marsh, the vice-president, became acting president. Marsh was visiting Europe at the time but hurried home as soon as news of the developments in Washington reached him. After consulting the various members of the council of the academy, Marsh appointed a special committee of experts to consider the congressional request. Marsh then sent letters to the Secretary of War, the Secretary of the Interior, Hayden, and Powell informing them of the appointment and function of the committee, and inviting replies giving any information or plans they wished to lay before the committee. The membership of the committee was rather interesting: James D. Dana, William B. Rogers, J. S. Newberry, W. P. Trowbridge, Simon Newcomb, and Alexander Agassiz, with Marsh holding membership ex officio. Five were geologists. The only nongeologists were Newcomb, who had been an intimate friend of Major Powell, and Trowbridge.[8]

When the committee names were made public, Brig. Gen. Andrew A. Humphreys, chief of the engineers of the War Department, protested vigorously, arguing that any properly constituted committee should include among its members officers in the government service who were engaged in surveying work. With the appointment of this committee, even though Trowbridge had graduated from West Point, there was not a single possibility that the War Department would be given authority over the federal surveys, and Hayden's chance, if there had been one, vanished at the same time. He had no friends on the committee; indeed, four members were enemies. As soon as this course of action had been made known, the struggle behind the scenes began in earnest.

Powell's reply to the committee's request for information was submitted to the academy by Carl Schurz, to whom it was addressed. This *Report on the Methods of Surveying the Public Domain* was dated November 1, 1878. Although it amounted to only sixteen printed pages, in it Powell assaulted the federal land office by name, hit Hayden's survey indirectly, and feinted a light blow against the War Depart-

---

[8] *Ann. Rep. Nat. Acad. Sci. 1878–1879*, p. 7.

ment. He charged that the General Land Office had failed to consider classification when parceling lands. There were in the archives 35,000 manuscript maps and an equal number of manuscript reports, "useless facts . . . piled up from year to year until they are buried in their own mass." "These records of the Land Office furnish a gigantic illustration of the evils of badly directed scientific work." [9]

As for the need of military surveys, the Major contrasted European and American practices:

In Europe, large standing armies are supported and the several governments stand ever prepared for war; by those nations which have or are executing the most elaborate surveys, the object is to prepare detailed charts of every possible battle-field within their dominion. . . . The relation of the United States to adjacent nations is such that . . . we need not construct maps on a scale so elaborate as we are compelled to consider the whole area of the country as a succession of battle-fields, but general charts, sufficiently elaborate for economic and scientific purposes.[10]

Powell then argued that natural history surveys—botanical and zoological—were not a proper function of the government except when specific problems "may suddenly acquire the importance of questions affecting intimately the national welfare, like the ravages of locusts and the cotton-worm, or subjects relating to the growth and production of forests." [11] All of the surveys made botanical and zoological collections, but only Hayden's placed emphasis on natural history. On the other hand, the Major pleaded for Congress to authorize a program for the investigation of Indian ethnology.

The purpose of the report was to advocate a unified federal survey capable of making accurate topographic maps and authorized to carry out a thorough geological survey and classification of land. The importance of irrigation and the need of a wise policy of utilization of the arid regions were repeated along the lines he had agitated for in 1874 and 1877.

On November 6th the National Academy of Sciences held a special meeting in New York City to discuss fully the recommendations of its committee. After a three-hour session the report was adopted, thirty seven to one, with the single dissenting vote cast by E. D. Cope.[12] Acting President Marsh then transmitted the approved report to the president

[9] *Report on the Methods of Surveying the Public Domain,* p. 6. I have previously alluded to this remark.

[10] *ibid.,* p. 13.

[11] *ibid.,* p. 14.

[12] *Ann. Rep. Nat. Acad. Sci. 1878–1879,* Appendix D, pp. 19–22.

of the Senate and a copy to the speaker of the House of Representatives. The formal recommendations, which ran to two thousand words, made three specific proposals: the organization of (1) a Coast and Geodetic Survey; (2) a United States Geological Survey; and (3) a Land Office. All three of these organizations were to be under the jurisdiction of the Department of the Interior.

Marsh succeeded also in writing into the proposal a requirement that all collections made by the federal survey be deposited in the National Museum. This was designed to prohibit two procedures adopted by Hayden: circulating collections made by his surveys among scholars, who could retain at least a part of the specimens in return for identifying and investigating interesting material; the practice of permitting scientists to accompany the expeditions at their own expense to collect scientific objects for their private use. Both of these restrictions were directed against Cope.

Hayden and Cope were bitterly disappointed. Cope considered the wording of the measure as a personal affront and resented the principals who had worked for consolidation of the surveys. Cope and Marsh had been feuding ever since 1871 and the new turn of events added salt to old wounds.[13]

The report of the National Academy was made public a few days later and Powell began immediately to build up sentiment in favor of it. It was referred to the committee on public lands, where it was in danger of being suppressed in the same manner as previous land-reform bills. The measure was adroitly transferred to the appropriations committee, of which Atkins was chairman and Hewitt a member.

Hayden had lost the fight in 1874 but he was too stubborn to realize it. He was the only man to seek openly the directorship of the combined survey. Hayden's feud with Lieutenant Wheeler had antagonized the entire War Department because of his unbridled criticisms of the scientific ability of army engineers. In the earlier attempt at consolidation, Major Powell had supported Hayden in two ways: he had argued for a civilian authority for the service; and expressed a willingness to work under him. When it appeared that consolidation was assured and the main question concerned the directorship of the combined survey, Hayden's suspicions and anxieties knew no bounds. He wrote letters to his loyal subordinates stationed in Washington asking them to keep their ears open at the Department of the Interior to keep him informed of developments. A. S. Packard of the entomological commission and

[13] H. F. Osborn, *Cope: Master Naturalist*, pp. 177–83; C. Schuchert and C. M. Le Vene, *O. C. Marsh, Pioneer in Paleontology*, Chap. x.

F. W. Pearson of Hayden's survey obediently made it their business to find out what Powell was up to. Their replies were ludicrous: [14]

Powell is still in town. Don't know when he will go out. I see him frequently, driving up and down the street industriously. He is not much around the Department, at least I do not see him. Everything is quiet over there. (Pearson, July 30, 1878.)

I have been up and around Powell's office quite frequently, and he appears to have a pretty good force of men at work. He is still in town, driving his double team. There is hardly a day that I don't see him. He may be doing something in the quiet. I can see or hear nothing. (Pearson, Aug. 17, 1878.)

You need not feel anxious, I think, about Powell's becoming Director of the Consolidated U. S. Geological Survey. In his last report of the past season he says nothing of his geological work but about his distribution of land and indian relics—not that I have anything against Powell but he does not rank high as a specialist in any department. (Packard, Dec. 8, 1878.)

I imagine your strongest opponent will be King but you are in the field and possession is nine points of the law. I tell Cope it is no use now to criticise the National Academy. (Packard, Jan. 1, 1879.)

Your note was read and destroyed. I approve of the consolidation but if your survey is tipped out it would be an outrage. How much will opposition of the War Department amount to? The pot is boiling. (Packard, Jan. 14, 1879.)

The vigor with which the Major pursued his determination to establish a consolidated geological survey earned for him considerable attention among the scientific men of Washington. It was generally assumed that he was determined to get the directorship of the survey. There was little doubt that congressional action would be favorable. Powell's many connections in the National Academy of Science and among men in public life were well known. His actions were interpreted in relation to the impending reorganization of the surveys.

On November 16, 1878, a group of friends, Garrick Mallery, Clarence Dutton, Henry Adams, Fred Endlich, Jerome Kidder, and a number of others gathered in Major Powell's parlor and organized a club to supersede the old "Saturday nights" and to provide an opportunity for social intercourse among men of science and letters in Washington. The object was the advancement of its members in science, literature, and art. It was decided to have a large membership of three hundred and to rent club rooms in the Corcoran building. There were several proposals for a suitable name, Mallery happily suggesting "Cosmos," although several purists wanted to spell it with a "K." Major Powell was elected president; William Harkness, vice-president; E. S. Holden, secretary;

[14] F. V. Hayden, *Personal Letters Received,* National Archives.

John S. Billings, treasurer; and Garrick Mallery, Clarence Dutton, and Dr. J. C. Welling, trustees.[15]

As soon as word of the foundling organization reached the ears of older members of the Philosophical Society, to which Hayden, Wheeler, and Powell belonged, the intentions of the founders of the Cosmos Club were suspected. It looked like a deliberate attempt to compete with the Philosophical Society. Major Powell had figured so prominently in the agitation for unification of the geological surveys and had a finger in so many government enterprises that the political implications of such a formal organization were feared. Although the inadequacy of the old Saturday Night Club was admitted, the need for a new social organization of the proportion of the Cosmos Club was disputed. A quarrel was avoided by extending a blanket invitation to all interested members of the Philosophical Society to join the Cosmos Club, and the new organization got off to a successful start.

Powell was "up to something," but not what Hayden suspected. He had been lobbying in the Senate, wherever he could gain influence, for a consolidated survey under the Department of the Interior with Clarence King as the director. Hayden's political strength was in the Senate and that is where the opposition had to be buttressed. Powell, probably mindful of the bitterness engendered by his part in the controversy, had no aspirations for the office. He had concluded to leave geology and devote his energies to the study of the Indians—in fact, plans were well advanced to obtain an appropriation to complete his works on the American Indian, perhaps even organize a Bureau of Ethnology with the Major as its first director, the whole enterprise to be a subdivision of the Smithsonian. How Hayden could have been ignorant of these plans remains a mystery. While Hayden was spying on Powell, the friends of Clarence King, a reluctant candidate for the office, were engineering his appointment through Congress.

Only those who saw the daily struggle knew how the Major toiled for consolidation. For six months he and those who decided to stand by the ship worked without compensation, taking a chance on ultimate payment through an appropriation from Congress. Stanley-Brown recorded how he had accompanied the Major "to newspaper offices to secure wide distribution of propaganda literature, and to the Capitol to importune members and Senators to support the measure, as well as

---

[15] The Cosmos Club of Washington, D.C., *Procs., 25th Anniv. Mtg.*, 1904, especially addresses by C. E. Dutton, G. K. Gilbert, and W. H. Holmes. The Cosmos Club graciously loaned me its copy of the proceedings.

to discussions of the measure in Congressional Committee rooms." [16]

A vivid picture of the Major in action has been preserved in manuscript by Stanley-Brown:

Members and Senators had been repeatedly interviewed. Many articles had been carefully prepared for the press. The strongest and best of the scientific element had been committed to the cause and it came up for its final hearing before the House Committee. All the interested parties had been bidden to be present. . . . Lt. Wheeler was dignified and indifferent. Clarence King being friendly did not put in an appearance. Dr. Hayden spoke in impassioned and bitter words and at considerable length. The Major showed no annoyance but clasping behind his back with his left hand what remained of his right arm, he walked thoughtfully back and forth at the end of the Committee Room. When Dr. Hayden finished there was absolute silence, save the voice of the Chairman informing the Major it was his turn to speak. Both the Chairman and audience expected an outbreak on the part of the speaker, but utterly ignoring his opponents he plunged at once into his subject and in a few minutes the Committee had forgotten all about what the others had said, as he laid before them in an impersonal calm and lucid manner the details of his scheme. It was plain to be seen that the day was won.[17]

The House committee on appropriations incorporated the whole plan proposed by the National Academy in a bill (HR 6140) which was duly reported out to Congress in February 1879. It was supported by A. S. Hewitt of New York, Peter D. Wigginton of California, James A. Garfield of Ohio, and John D. C. Atkins of Tennessee, each of whom debated ably for adoption. The opposition and the support were drawn along regional boundaries; party lines were disregarded.

Powell's role in the program was recognized by both sides. Hewitt openly attributed the National Academy's recommendations to the Major. Patterson of Colorado called the scheme "the work of one man," "this revolutionist . . . this charlatan of science and intermeddler in affairs of which he has no conception." Patterson charged, "he appeared four and two years ago . . . before the Committee on Public Lands and sought to influence it." Not sparing the gullible members of the academy, Patterson ridiculed them as "theorists who knew nothing about the practical problems of the public lands." [18]

The western bloc was, of course, trying to prevent any interference with the traditional practices of land disposal. The only important re-

[16] Joseph Stanley-Brown, MS, "An Eventful Career," p. 9. For the privilege of quoting from this and the MS notes in the following, I am indebted to Dr. Margaret Stanley-Brown.

[17] Joseph Stanley-Brown, MS, "John Wesley Powell," read before the Wash. Lit. Soc., Dec. 13, 1902, p. 4.

[18] *Cong. Rec. 45th Cong. 3rd Sess. Pt. 3.* Abundant similar testimony appears in Pt. 2.

form recommended by the academy was the establishment of a unified geological survey, among the various duties of which would be the accurate classification of federal lands. Hayden allied himself with the western bloc and resisted the academy's proposal at every turn. He and his friends assumed that Powell was making a strong bid for the directorship of the consolidated survey.

During prolonged debate all of the old arguments concerning the advantages of civilian, as opposed to military, authority, the relative merits of the different surveys, and the personalities involved were aired again. Finally Congress accepted only that portion of the plan which called for the establishment of a unified geological survey under the Department of the Interior.

For the salary of the Director of the Geological Survey, which office is hereby established under the Interior Department, who shall be appointed by the President, by and with the advice and consent of the Senate, six thousand dollars: Provided, That this officer shall have the direction of the Geological Survey, and the classification of the public lands, and examination of the geological structure, mineral resources, and products of the national domain. And that the Director and members of the Geological Survey shall have no personal or private interests in the lands or mineral wealth of the region under survey, and shall execute no surveys or examinations for private parties or corporations; and the Geological and Geographical Survey of the Territories, and the Geographical and Geological Survey of the Rocky Mountain Region, under the Department of the Interior, and the Geographical Surveys west of the one hundredth meridian, under the War Department, are hereby discontinued, to take effect on the thirtieth day of June, eighteen hundred and seventy-nine. And all collections of rocks, minerals, soils, fossils, and objects of natural history, archaeology, and ethnology, made by the Coast and Interior Survey, the Geological Survey, or by any other parties for the Government of the United States, when no longer needed for investigations in progress, shall be deposited in the National Museum.[19]

Thus, with the adoption of the report, the existing geological surveys were abolished—Wheeler's, Hayden's, and Powell's. King's survey of the fortieth parallel had already completed its work. Lieutenant Wheeler's hopes evaporated when the principle of civil control was agreed upon, but despite earlier hostility, he endorsed Powell's plan wholeheartedly.

Dr. F. V. Hayden had been engaged the longest in the exploring service, and by many was considered the logical candidate for director.

19 *ibid.*, p. 2361. The wording of the act is important. Note the limitations as well as the scope of the responsibilities.

But Columbus Delano had been an ardent friend of Hayden; Carl Schurz held that against him and recommended King. It remained for the President to name a director for the new survey. As soon as the bill authorizing consolidation was passed, Powell wrote on March 4, 1879, to Atkins asking him to approach President Hayes and Secretary of the Interior Schurz to prevent Hayden's nomination: "If Dr. Hayden is appointed all hope of further reform in the system of land surveys is at an end or indefinitely postponed." Atkins called on the President on March 10th and urged the appointment of King. Meanwhile Powell wrote to Garfield denouncing Hayden in no uncertain terms. Hewitt and Marsh wrote personal letters to Schurz and William H. Brewer of Yale approached Hayes to secure King's appointment.[20]

Hayden's friends were straining their resources too. Cope, in a letter to Schurz, accused King of being improperly involved in private mining enterprises and that he had accepted fees while in the employ of the government. Finally, Hayes offered the nomination to Clarence King.[21]

It was with considerable reluctance that King abandoned his private pursuits in mining geology to accept an administrative post for which, despite charm and talent, he did not have the temperament. King's chief characteristics were tact, organizing ability, and a thorough knowledge of the West, but his dislikes for routine and politics were handicaps. He was fortunate, however, in the opportunity of organizing a new department which did not owe commitments to other bureaus, and the organization which he constructed was of his own making. He established in Washington a small central office with a clerk and a few assistants, and stationed in strategic points throughout the territories five regional officers who were charged with the responsibility of carrying on the scientific work of the department.

It was no secret that Clarence King had little desire to remain in office for any length of time. He accepted on the assumption that he should remain only until the new bureau was firmly organized and operating efficiently.

[20] The press copies of *Letters Sent* and *Letters Received,* Survey of the Rocky Mountain Region, National Archives, preserve a comprehensive record of the pressure being exerted from all sides. H. N. Smith has given an excellent summary of the consolidation in *Miss. Vall. Hist. Rev.,* Vol. 34, pp. 37–58.

[21] Clarence King, an intriguing figure, is quite misunderstood. He is generally overrated as a geologist, and owing to his close friendship with Henry Adams, he has been given undeserved credit for influencing consolidation. King had many worthy qualities and, as will be shown later, wisely organized the infant Geological Survey. King deserves a biography.

Marsh wrote to the Major on April 6th, "Now that the battle is won we can go back to pure science again." Perhaps Marsh could, but Powell had another mission.

At the same time that the Geological Survey was authorized, Congress passed an act providing for a commission to codify and revise the public land laws of the United States. The commission was to be composed of the commissioner of the General Land Office, the director of the Geological Survey, and three civilians to be appointed by the Secretary of the Interior. On July 1, 1879, President Hayes and Carl Schurz, Secretary of the Interior, approved commissions for Alexander T. Britton of Washington, D.C., Thomas Donaldson of Philadelphia, and Major Powell. J. A. Williamson, commissioner of the General Land Office, and Clarence King served ex officio.[22]

A meeting of the commission was held on July 8th at which Williamson was elected president and Britton, temporary secretary. Little more was done at this meeting except to decide upon an approach to the problem. Two weeks later, on July 22nd, Capt. Clarence E. Dutton, who had served with Powell for several years in the western territories, was elected permanent secretary and disbursing officer of the commission.

The Major remembered the young man "who had worked for him nights, days and Sundays and helped to distribute 'Consolidation Literature' to newspaper offices on certain wintry nights." This was Joseph Stanley-Brown, who was rewarded with appointment as field secretary to the commission, and in that capacity accompanied his chief on an eventful junket to the West.[23]

The public lands commission spent the last five months of 1879 traveling throughout the West, making several thousand miles of their itinerary by stagecoach. Leadville, Colorado, was seventy-five miles from a railroad; the trip from Beaver Canyon, Utah, just north of Ogden, to Butte and Helena, Montana, took three days of continuous riding. On that leg of the journey the commission rode over unsuspected millions of dollars' worth of mineral deposits, which subsequently made Butte famous. From Salt Lake City the party went by train to Reno and across the high Sierras, pausing to observe the huge placer mines, which scarred the earth in all directions. The commission spent two days at

---

[22] This temporary executive commission signed by President Rutherford B. Hayes and the Secretary of the Interior states, ". . . that reposing special trust and confidence in the integrity, diligence, and discretion of John W. Powell of Bloomington, Illinois, I do appoint him, a member of the Commission to Codify Land Laws. . . ."

[23] Joseph Stanley-Brown, MS, "An Eventful Career."

Marysville to observe the destruction of rich agricultural bottom lands by the washings of sand and gravel from the placer mines. From Marysville the party made a side trip to Kern County, where California was experimenting with irrigation. Many types of land use and many complex situations were examined to determine what could be done to regulate the conflicting group interests.

The special commission sifted the information, and by the end of the year compiled its report. It included a chronological summary of all the laws pertaining to the public domain beginning with the purchase of the western territories in 1785. In the hundred years that had elapsed since the United States had come into being, state and territorial laws had interfered with and even superseded those of the national government. The incongruities of the situation were recognized but the recommendations were not unanimous. On many questions Powell found himself a minority of one. Two commissioners wanted to compromise existing laws in such a way that settlement in the West could be accelerated, that the lands in large territories should be classified as quickly as possible and only those of actual desert and those with known mineral wealth be held in the title of the national government. Powell refused to agree to this and his minority report restated the same opinions he had advanced in his report of 1877.

The other two commissioners, who did not want to change radically existing laws, admitted through their discussions that a thorough revision of the laws was sorely needed but that the settlement and commercialization of the West had progressed too far to allow the adoption of better land laws. As usual, little could be done in Congress. It is doubtful that much would have been done even if the report of the commissioners had been unanimous. The appointment of the commission to codify the public lands had pleased no one. The western bloc saw in it a deceleration of homesteading in their states and territories. The eastern Congressmen saw no need for more laws where laws were already in existence, and the large financial interests, with a surplus of capital for investment, did not wish government interference in the development and exploitation of the immense riches in the western lands.

The report was accepted by Congress and the authority was issued for its printing. Nothing more was done to bring about the recommended changes in disbursing public lands or to reserve resources for the public. In short, another attempt to rationalize the land policy failed completely.

The propagandizing had suited the Major's personality. The Major was not disillusioned. He knew how long it took to educate the public to gain popular support for his side. He was disappointed that his report on the arid regions came to naught, but he intended to bide his time and approach the problem in another manner. For the present, however, Major Powell had another commission. In the Sundry Civil Appropriation Bill of March 3, 1879, the same bill that authorized the Geological Survey, the following item was included:

For completing and preparing for publication the contributions to North American ethnology, under the Smithsonian Institution, twenty thousand dollars: *Provided,* that all of the archives, records, and material relating to the Indians of North America, collected by the geographical and geological survey of the Rocky Mountains, shall be turned over to the Institution, that the work may be completed and prepared for publication under its direction. . . .

In this item, Congress created the Bureau of Ethnology, as well as the Geological Survey. But the real founder of both was Major Powell.

16

1879-1881 · The Bureau of Ethnology

PROBABLY when Major Powell took up his duties as first director of the newly founded Bureau of Ethnology he believed he had abandoned geology for good. Whatever limitations Congress may have intended to impose upon the foundling agency, the Major recognized but one— the twenty thousand dollar budget. On that slim sum he set out "to organize anthropologic research in America." He did not find this authority or consent in the act, which merely allocated money to complete the work in progress and prepare reports for publication. The object of the new bureau was his own idea.

The sciences of ethnology and anthropology had rather precise definitions, but the Major on this matter too had his opinions. With characteristic energy and versatility, ethnology in his hands expanded to include studies of institutions, languages, arts, and philosophies, in addition to the traditional branches of the subject.

Powell, in his report to the Secretary of the Interior in November 1878, made an eloquent plea for the federal government to endow comprehensive investigations relating to the North American Indians, and gave practical as well as academic reasons why such a program or agency would serve the people.

Briefly, this is what the Major considered the problem of the American Indian to be:

The work is of great magnitude; more than four hundred languages belonging to about sixty different stocks having been found within the territory of the United States. Little of value can be accomplished in making investigations in other branches in the field without a thorough knowledge of the languages. Their sociology, mythology, arts, etc. are not properly known until the people themselves are understood, with their own conceptions, opinions, and motives. . . . The field of research is speedily narrowing because of the rapid change in the Indian population now in progress; all habits, customs, and opinions are fading away; even languages are disappearing; and in a very few years it will be impossible to study our North American Indians in their primitive condition, except from recorded history. For this reason ethnologic studies in America should be pushed with the utmost vigor.

But there are other cogent reasons leading to the same conclusion. In the whole area of the United States, not including Alaska, there is not an important valley unoccupied by white men. The rapid spread of civilization since 1849 had placed the white man and the Indian in direct conflict throughout the whole area, and the "Indian problem" is thus thrust upon us and it *must* be solved, wisely or unwisely. Many of the difficulties are inherent and cannot be avoided, but an equal number are unnecessary and are caused by the lack of our knowledge relating to the Indians themselves. Savagery is not inchoate civilization; it is a distinct status of society with its own institutions, customs, philosophy, and religion; and all these must necessarily be overthrown before new institutions, customs, philosophy and religion can be introduced. The failure to recognize this fact has wrought inconceivable mischief in our management of the Indians. . . .

Among all the North American Indians, when in primitive condition, personal property was almost unknown, ornaments and clothing only were recognized as the property of the individual, and these only to a limited extent. The right to the soil as landed property, the rights to the products of the chase, etc. was inherent in the gens, or clan, a body of consanguinii, a group of relatives, in some cases on the male side, in others on the female. Inheritance was never to the children of the deceased but always to the gens. No other crime was so great, no other vice so abhorrent, as the attempt of an individual to use for himself that which belonged to his gens in common; hence the personal rights to property recognized in civilization are intensely obnoxious to the Indian. He looks upon our whole system of property rights as an enormous evil and an unpardonable sin, for which the gods will eventually punish the wicked and blasphemous white man.

. . . In this matter, and many others of a similar character relating to their customs and belief, we must either deal with the Indian as he is, looking to the slow but irresistible influence of civilization . . . to effect a change, or we must reduce him to abject slavery. The attempt to transform a savage into a civilized man by a law, a policy, an administration, or a great conversion . . . in a few months or in a few years, is an impossibility clearly appreciated by scientific ethnologists who understand the institution and social conditions of the Indians.

Again, we have usually attempted to treat with the tribes through their chiefs, as if they wielded absolute power; but an Indian tribe is a pure democracy; their chieftaincy is not hereditary, and the chief is but the representative, the speaker of the tribe, and can do no act by which his tribe is bound without being instructed thus to act in due and established form. The blunders we have made and the wrongs we have inflicted upon the Indians because of a failure to recognize this fact have been cruel and inexcusable, except on the ground of our ignorance.[1]

---

[1] J. W. Powell, *Report on the Methods of Surveying the Public Domain*, pp. 15–16. The founding of the Bureau of Ethnology was the immediate result of this earnest appeal. The first two annual reports give a comprehensive introduction to Powell's ambitious program.

Viewed from this standpoint, the new bureau was not primarily an academic department devoted to pure science but an agency for investigating every phase of the life of the Indian, past and present, to better understand the Indian and to preserve the Indian languages, myths, handicrafts, and arts, which were disappearing. In this way the bureau could be of service to many other agencies of the government. However, Powell did not minimize the scientific aspects of ethnology.

That the bureau had to organize the subject of ethnology and adopt a program of work no one could deny. The study of ethnology in America was chaotic in 1879. Indian relics—graves, mounds, and flints—had for many years stimulated the curiosity of persons throughout the country. Many specimens, often worthless because they were not accompanied by proper information, found their way into private collections, or museums appended like so many little mausoleums to the colleges.

Professor Joseph Henry, the first secretary of the Smithsonian, had foreseen the need for organized action to develop a serious interest in Indian lore, and while awaiting the discovery of some talented person to undertake the project, made an effort to gather useful data for the institution. Professor Henry had circularized teachers, missionaries, engineers, army men, and local learned societies, sending them questionnaires concerning local antiquities and urging them to make prompt archaeological excavations to preserve evidence, which was nearly everywhere being rapidly destroyed by the plow. He issued directions for collecting vocabularies and other linguistic information to missionaries, government officials, factors of trading posts, in fact, everyone he could think of. A very remarkable series of returns had been harvested from this random broadcast.[2]

Of course, all the exploring surveys of the western territories had devoted considerable attention to the collection of various objects illustrating natural history and ethnology, but only the Powell surveys had made ethnology the second most important phase of the work, next to geology. During the Major's earliest expeditions to Colorado in 1867 and 1868, he had gathered examples of Indian handicrafts—mostly garments, weapons, and pottery—and had distributed the specimens among museums in Illinois. During succeeding visits to the Indians of the Great Basin region, Powell understood that whatever success might be attained in preserving these Indian crafts—or the

[2] For example, "Circular relating to Collections in Archaeology and Ethnology," *Smith. Misc. Coll.*, Vol. 8, No. 205, Jan. 15, 1867.

Indians themselves from extermination—nothing could save their languages and mythologies, and that in a very short time the primitive linguistic stocks would be so badly corrupted that it would be impossible to study them scientifically. Thus, Powell's diaries for 1869 and 1870 include vocabularies and lists of words which he had gathered among the Ute tribes. During the second canyon expedition the Major, Thompson, Jones, and Dellenbaugh made similar lists.[3]

If Powell had to throw off the mantle of traditional geology in his early researches in the western territories and give a fresh interpretation to the phenomena he observed, he had no such prejudices to overcome in the field of ethnology. Not a single university in America offered regular instruction in ethnology or anthropology. The terms "anthropology," "ethnology," and "archaeology" are somewhat confusing. Anthropology, the study of man, his physical makeup, origin, history, and development, is the inclusive science. The subject is understood by most scientists to include the other two: ethnology, the study of peoples and races; and archaeology, the study of antiquities. None of these branches of the study of man was really established in the United States in 1879. A few men like Schoolcraft, Gallatin, and Catlin had made beginnings, but nothing more. Powell's contemporaries, Brinton, Morgan, Putnam, and Mason, entertained no broad views such as his.

Archaeology was, for most of the individuals who pursued it, an avocation. Collecting trips were pleasant excursions on which one might find some striking curiosity or great rarity. Rivalries to turn up spectacular finds were believed to encourage the search. With such competition, cooperative ventures were rare and unimportant. All this might have been good fun but it was poor science. The concepts of antiquity, of chronology and kinship, were alien ideas even among serious investigators. Many collections were rendered worthless because no accurate information concerning the specimens was preserved. Powell, who was observant by nature and methodical by training, in devising new techniques as he worked, did not consider it necessary to take full field notes or write complete data on the labels accompanying the specimens he gathered. Nor did he have any penetrating idea as to the chronology of the successive Indian cultures over many centuries.

[3] Powell made a list of seven hundred Ute words in 1868–1869. Word lists are scattered throughout his journals of 1869–1873. A similar vocabulary compiled by Jones is in the Bureau of Ethnology.

There were good reasons why Joseph Henry, and after his death, Spencer Baird, urged Congress to support work in ethnology. While the various federal departments and American universities neglected to preserve or investigate the American Indians, many foreign governments were outfitting well-trained expeditions or sending competent agents to the United States and Central America to collect or purchase archaeological remains. The French government in particular had made a vast collection of relics in Latin America, and at that time had parties exploring in California, New Mexico, and Oregon. Many tons of the choicest objects had been removed to Paris.

In other words, the people of the United States were the last to recognize the interest in prehistoric American races and the contemporary Indians. Baird argued that whatever regret the American people might have at seeing these specimens leave the country—destined for Paris, Berlin, Stockholm, London, and so on—there could be no means of replacing them. The only alternative was to prevent such losses in the future by placing our own adequately equipped and financed expeditions into the field.

Powell's serious interest in the American Indian was the direct outgrowth of Professor Henry's suggestion in 1868 that he record Indian vocabularies while traveling through the Colorado River area. When Powell found the various Ute tribes virtually unspoiled by contacts with white men, he realized that this primitive and pure culture was almost the last of its kind on the continent, and he worked with the purpose to obtain as complete a record of these peoples as possible. His interest multiplied when, during the first trip through the canyons, he discovered the existence of abandoned pueblos high on the canyon walls. The very next year in company with Jacob Hamblin the Major visited the Hopi (Moqui) villages and lived among these Indians, observing their customs. He had gathered during the second expedition fragments of pottery and other works, and correctly correlated the builders of these ruins with the pueblo peoples still living in Arizona. At the same time he recognized that linguistically the Hopis were related to the nomadic Shoshones.[4]

In ensuing years the Major carried on ethnologic studies simultaneously with his geological explorations. In 1873 he had accepted a temporary commission to visit the Ute, Paiute, and Shoshone Indians

---

[4] Powell seems to have recognized the relationship intuitively. "Vocabularies were made of the Shoshone language, the Navajo, the Oraiby, the Uinta Ute and Pah-Ute. Materials were collected for a grammar and dictionary of the last-mentioned language." *42nd Cong. 2nd Sess. H.R. Misc. Doc. 173*, p. 11.

so that he would have a better opportunity to record the vocabularies and mythologies of these tribes. Powell was not content to deal with Indians through interpreters. He learned their languages, spoke to them in their own tongues, and thereby won their confidence and respect.

The centennial exposition in Philadelphia in 1876 gave a great impetus to popular, and indirectly to serious, interest in handicrafts of the American Indians. Colorful displays of costumes, headdresses, weapons, and jewelry, gathered at the expense of the Bureau of Indian Affairs, illustrated the native American cultures. The Smithsonian Institution took charge of the arrangements, the details of the Indian exhibits being supervised by Otis T. Mason, Charles Rau, Edward Foreman, and Frank H. Cushing. These men prepared the specimens and installed the exhibits, and were on hand much of the time to answer the questions of the visitors. Major Powell contributed a series of objects illustrating the handicrafts of the Utes and Paiutes. When the great exposition was over the collections were returned to Washington, and Rau, Foreman, and Cushing were appointed permanent members of the Smithsonian section on ethnology.

On October 2, 1876, Major Powell, after several conversations with Joseph Henry, wrote to him for permission to examine and publish the 670 Indian vocabularies preserved in the Smithsonian collections.[5] Many of these had not been recorded with discrimination. The Major had gathered an extensive supplementary series from the canyon country and understood the magnitude of the venture. Trumbull had previously examined the records in the Smithsonian at the request of Professor Henry but he had declined to undertake their investigation because of the enormous effort involved. Powell was authorized to study the vocabularies, and the materials were accordingly turned over to him.

Within a year, the first edition of the *Introduction to the Study of Indian Languages* appeared as one of the reports of the survey of the Rocky Mountain region.[6] The book was written as a guide to those who were interested in recording the languages still used by the tribes in the sparsely settled West. The words were grouped by subject, and instructions were given for recording, spelling, and classifying vocabularies. This work, though containing little that was new, showed a remarkable breadth of vision and established Powell as a professional

[5] J. W. Powell to Joseph Henry, Oct. 2, 1876.
[6] There were two printings of this work: first edition, 1877, second revised edition, 1880.

ethnologist of first-rate ability. It was on the basis of this monograph and the promise it held that Secretary Baird sponsored Powell for the directorship of the new bureau.

Powell's philosophy of ethnology was no less the essence of a long familiarity with the Indian than the long tradition behind his philosophy of the land. George Crookham had acquainted him with the mound builders of Ohio. Wes as a child had dug his fingers into the earthworks at Chillicothe and Jackson, and treasured the flints and artifacts he found there. In Wisconsin he had watched the pitiable Winnebagoes encamped upon his family's land and, when a little older, collected specimens in the prehistoric earthworks at Delavan a few miles from the farm. There were Indian mounds too at Decatur. Still later, as a student at Oberlin, he listened to the pleas for missionaries to work in Michigan and Oregon to teach the Indians to grow vegetables and to read the Bible. During the dull army days before the battle of Shiloh, Powell opened Indian graves and stone cists on the bluffs above the Tennessee River. These numerous amateur experiences had made an impression upon Powell deep enough to encourage him to offer a course on prehistoric man at Illinois Wesleyan University.[7] After meeting the undefiled Indian in his native environment, the Major was no longer interested in collecting stone implements or potsherds; he wanted to understand the Indian, his ancestry, customs, and beliefs. He wrote:

> After all the years I have spent among the Indians in their mountain villages, I am not certain that I have sufficiently divorced myself from the thoughts and ways of civilisation to properly appreciate their childish beliefs.[8]

The Major realized, as few before him, that the point of view of the Indian was different from that of the white man; his world was smaller, his philosophy simpler. This difference was complicated. The Indians' music cannot be recorded in the notes of civilized music; his language cannot be written in the English alphabet; his grammar transcends the structure of Aryan grammar; even his philosophy and social organization follow lines unknown to the European. Thus, in matters of government, justice, and religion the Indian was totally distinct:

> I have heard the venerable and impassioned orator on the camp meeting stand rehearse the story of the crucifixion, and seen the thousands there weep in

[7] Illinois Wesleyan University, *Cat.*, 1866, 1867.
[8] See *Jour. Am. Geog. Soc. N.Y.*, Vol. 8, pp. 251–68. Powell read his address before the society on Dec. 29, 1876. Also quoted in Bu. Ethnol., *1st Ann. Rep.*, p. 23.

contemplation of the story of divine suffering, and heard their shouts roll down the forest aisles as they gave vent to their joy at the contemplation of redemption. But the scene was not a whit more dramatic than I have witnessed in an evergreen forest of the Rocky Mountain Region, where a tribe was gathered under the great pines, and the temple of light from the blazing fire was walled by the darkness of midnight, and in the midst of the temple stood the wise old man telling, in simple savage language, the story of Ta-wats, when he conquered the sun and established the seasons and the days.[9]

Powell's personal humanist philosophy dominated not only his own researches but permeated most of the activities of the Bureau of Ethnology.

Perhaps the greatest influence on Powell's early ethnologic studies came from Lewis H. Morgan of Rochester, one of the most unappreciated original thinkers of his time.[10] Morgan had been engaged for many years in a study of Indian organization and had contributed in a variety of ways to an understanding of these disappearing peoples. Morgan had made a study of ancient civilizations and, accepting the notion of evolution, had interpreted man's social organization in the light of Darwin's theories. The Major made several trips to Rochester to supplement his correspondence with Morgan. Powell had provided him with information about Hopi kinship and inheritance customs which Morgan used in his *Ancient Society*.[11] In their conversations Powell sensed the vast field of ideas which were opened to him and came away more determined than ever to devote his scientific career to the study of the Indian.

In December 1876, the Major had been invited to lecture before the American Geographical Society in Chickering Hall, New York, and chose as his subject, "Outlines of the Philosophy of the North American Indian." He explained that "savagery is ethnic childhood" or, to state it in another way, that the growth of civilization passed through many stages which may be compared with the life of an individual; civilization was likened to adulthood. Powell was obviously influenced by L. H. Morgan.

Many opportunities to lecture came to Major Powell. At first these opportunities were arranged for him through regular lyceum agencies, but later his reputation increased until invitations were extended directly to him. Then Powell declined lyceum series "unless," as he wrote

[9] Bu. Ethnol., *1st Ann. Rep.*, p. 40.

[10] See B. J. Stern, *Lewis Henry Morgan: Social Evolutionist.*

[11] L. H. Morgan, *Ancient Society* (Kerr ed.), p. 546. A fine series of letters from Powell to Morgan is preserved in the Rush-Rhees Library of the University of Rochester. Morgan's letters to Powell are in the National Archives.

to one agent, "there is considerable in it." [12] Apparently the pay was not "considerable" enough because this particular bid was refused. Gradually Powell forsook popular lecturing and, no longer needing the extra income, turned to speaking before professional societies—usually, but not always, without fee. The Major spoke on the Indians to several societies, his warm sympathy and enthusiasm winning great favor. Illinois Wesleyan University watched John Wesley Powell grow in prominence, and in 1877 awarded the degrees of master of arts and doctor of philosophy to her illustrious former professor of geology.

The meetings of the American Association for the Advancement of Science in 1878 were held in St. Louis.[13] The Major attended with the expectation of receiving the vice-presidency of the anthropological section. It turned out that there was considerable opposition to his nomination, but friends carried him through successfully. The Major and his fellow night owls, Putnam, Bandelier, Englemann, and Broadhead, chatted about their investigations and experiences. At the convention Powell met a self-educated young geologist of striking appearance, W J McGee, [14] who had attempted to unravel the complicated history of the glacial drifts of Iowa. The Major, remembering his own difficulties in interpreting the glacial gravels of Illinois, and his own haphazard education, took the time to give McGee deserved and needed words of encouragement. Following the conclusion of the meetings, excursions to Colorado and to the Pilot Knob-Iron Mountain region of Missouri were arranged for the members of the association. The Major led the party to Colorado but Lester Ward, who had come to St. Louis with him, took the shorter trip to Pilot Knob.

The next year, when the meetings of the American Association for the Advancement of Science were held at Saratoga Springs, it was the Major's obligation to deliver an address as retiring vice-president of section "B." Speaking on "Mythologic Philosophy," Powell gave his views on the origin of philosophy.[15]

Powell's eminence as a scientist was enhanced by his participation in

[12] J. W. Powell to Am. Lit. Bu., Chicago, Feb. 15, 1876. To another agent, J. S. Bliss, Northwestern Lyceum Bureau, Janesville, Wis., he said bluntly, "I do not know when I shall be able to take the lecture field again, not soon, unless tempted by good pay" (April 7, 1877).

[13] Bandelier recorded his impressions of these meetings in several letters. See L. A. White, ed., *Pioneers of American Anthropology*, pp. 88 ff.; Lester Ward, *Glimpses of the Cosmos*.

[14] See E. R. McGee, *Life of W J McGee*, an unsatisfactory biography by his sister. Other data may be found in G. Pinchot, *Breaking New Ground*; N. H. Darton, *Ann. Assn. Am. Geog.*, Vol. 3, pp. 103–10.

[15] A.A.A.S., *Proc. 28th Mtg.*, 1880, pp. 251–78; reprinted in *Popular Science Monthly*, Vol. 15, pp. 795–808; Vol. 16, pp. 55–66.

the professional organizations which mushroomed in Washington. In 1879 a small group including Ward, Gilbert, Dutton, and the Major organized the Anthropological Society, of which Powell became first president, a position to which he was reelected for several years.[16] The Biological Society, founded in 1880 by the same group of men, elected the Major to the council for many years. The senior Philosophical Society continued its activities and in this too Powell held the presidency for several terms. It was not the mere holding of office which advanced his stature. The Major used the meetings as a testing board for his views, not only in the presentation of formal addresses—of which there were many—but by spontaneous comments as well. "The Major," Gilbert wrote, "never fails to add a spritely comment, oft times worth more than the speaker's effort." [17]

Lester Ward presented before the Anthropological Society on March 15, 1881, "Politico-Social Functions," perhaps his clearest statement of the "schism which exists . . . between the theories of political economists and the policies of states." It was a criticism of laissez-faire and a plea for government to regulate industry, business, and agriculture "because the unrestrained operation of natural laws in social phenomena invariably result in unjustifiable inequalities in the distribution of wealth . . . enormous waste of created products due to ruinous excesses in competition . . . artificially increased prices, due to oversupply . . . and dangerous monopolies, whether industrial or financial, which threaten to enslave labor and dictate commerce." [18]

When Ward finished, Powell, who presided at the meeting, remarked:

The prevailing theories of political economy became popular at a time when governments were unpopular, which is not now the case because they have become more representative in form. Former attempts at government regulation were impractical because they sought to control opinion. The form of control now exercised is of a very different kind, and is practicable and effective. The natural evolution of industry was legitimate and harmless so long as it was confined, as it must necessarily be at first, to simple differentiation, but when the differentiated parts commenced to become integrated, there arose grave social evils. I am not hostile to corporations, they are the instruments through which nearly all the operations of society will eventually be performed. But they require regulation. The principal work of legislation will ultimately be the adjustment of the relations of corporations to the public and to each other. Government has developed from its primary condition—the family. Feudalism was

[16] The organization of these various local scientific societies is a facet of the growing influence of science in federal government bureaus.

[17] G. K. Gilbert to J. S. Newberry, Nov. 19, 1882.

[18] Ward's paper was published in *Penn Monthly*, Vol. 12, pp. 321–36.

the transition stage from kinship government to property government. Modern civilized society is based on property—the unit being the individual. The social unit will eventually be a business corporation, and there will be a hierarchy of corporations, the highest of which will embrace all the rest and constitute the government. The basis of society will then cease to be property, and will become industry.[19]

The statement must not, however, be misinterpreted. Powell was not speaking of business corporations but something far more inclusive. One must search for an adequate definition, but this, taken from a formal address before the Anthropological Society on February 7, 1882, will suffice:

Men are organized into societies for religious, charitable, educational, industrial, and other ends, and such societies will here be called corporations. These organizations . . . do not constitute a part of government, but they form a part of the state and must necessarily be considered in the plan of the state.[20]

Powell believed not only that all activities in a civilized state are organized but that eventually greater and greater control would be concentrated in government: in other words, inevitable socialism—call it what one will.

Such were the attitudes, tools, and experiences which Major Powell brought with him to his position as head of the Bureau of Ethnology. He prepared a brief outline of his plans for the first three years of the new department and submitted it to Spencer Baird for consideration. The following morning Baird assured the Major that he would have a free hand.

Powell began investigations in the four great departments of human activity—"arts, institutions, languages, and opinions"—because "the facts in each field of research throw such light upon each other that one cannot be neglected without injury to the others." He believed that collections of curiosities, vocabularies, and mythologies were in themselves of trifling value unless their true meaning and interrelations were interpreted. As the first aid to researchers, the Major planned to issue manuals of instructions.

The Major's passion for organization and system manifested itself immediately in his work on linguistics. He set out to discover which of the Indian languages were sufficiently similar to make their origin certain and which of the languages were shrouded in doubt or obscurity. J. C.

[19] Anthrop. Soc. Wash., *Trans.*, Vol. 1, pp. 42–43; also in *Smith. Misc. Coll.*, Vol. 25.
[20] *ibid.*, 108–9.

Pilling, who had been the Major's amanuensis in the field, was sent to the important libraries—the Boston Public, the Boston Athenaeum, Harvard College, American Antiquarian Society at Worcester, the John Carter Brown, and many others—to begin the compilation of an elaborate "Bibliography of North American Philology," while Powell devoted as much time as he could spare to linguistics. Inasmuch as a knowledge of language was fundamental to nearly every other type of ethnologic work except the actual excavation of archaeological remains, this line of investigation was pursued first.

Considerable work in Indian languages had been done before; Powell was not the pioneer. Gallatin, that versatile adopted American and statesman, banker, and ethnologist, had published a linguistic map of North America in 1836, but this was inaccurate, very incomplete, and long obsolete. A much larger body of knowledge had been gathered since the time of Gallatin's investigations, so that preparation of a new map based upon more recent information was begun by the Bureau of Ethnology. An innovation in method, however, was adopted at the outset. Similarities of single words rather than similarities in grammar, such as tenses and genders, were used to establish relationships among the many different vocabularies. It proved to be an ambitious project and thirteen years elapsed before the map, with accompanying text, was published. The map, which excluded Mexico, was even then not considered to be final or complete, but only a summary of available information. Powell's classification of linguistic stocks, which was published in the seventh annual report of the Bureau of Ethnology, has stood the test of time and is recognized as one of the milestones in the study of the American Indian.

Powell instituted a system of employing specialists to investigate particular problems rather than creating a large permanent staff in his bureau. A budget of twenty thousand dollars would not permit the hiring of more than a few persons, but by paying part-time salaries or field expenses, a much larger number of collaborators could be attracted to the work. Such a system made possible a more diverse program and reaped the benefits of the collaboration of many specialists. Two or three instances will show how handsomely this system succeeded. One of the remarkably versatile men on the staff in the surgeon general's office was Dr. Henry C. Yarrow, who during his work with the army had become interested in the mortuary customs of the Indians. This was certainly a problem in which a medical knowledge would be essential. Powell had urged Dr. Yarrow to complete his investigations and had offered to publish them as a contribution to the survey of the Rocky Mountains region. When the Bureau of Ethnology was established Powell defrayed the expenses of numerous illustrations, and Yarrow's study was included in the first annual report issued by the bureau.

A very different type of collaboration was with Mrs. Erminnie A. Smith of Jersey City, New Jersey. Shortly after the founding of the bureau, the Major heard about her folklore soirees, which attracted a large number of amateurs from New York, Newark, and even from Camden and Philadelphia. Powell attended one of these occasions, and was so attracted by Mrs. Smith's enthusiastic interest that he engaged her to study Iroquoian languages.[21] She had grown up in western New York and was familiar with the Iroquoian tribes living there. In this work she was assisted by a young interpreter, J. N. B. Hewitt, who was himself part Iroquois (Tuscarora). Mrs. Smith died suddenly in 1886 long before her work had been completed. Hewitt was then placed in the regular employ of the bureau where he continued the task for almost forty years.

Col. Garrick Mallery contributed his *Introduction to the Study of the Sign Language,* and Lewis H. Morgan, to whom Powell owed so much, contributed *Homebuilding Among the Indians,* as other early monographs published by the Bureau of Ethnology. Thus, besides a regular staff of clerks, assistants, and a few professionals like Otis Mason and Frank Cushing, there were many collaborators, Yarrow, Morgan, Thomas, and the Mindeleff brothers, to mention but a few.

There was another task of magnitude which Powell had carved out as one of the early objectives of the bureau. This was to be the *Handbook of American Indians,* which would provide data for the government services, businessmen, and scholars. It began merely as a dictionary of all the names which had been used to designate Indian languages or Indian tribes, but it grew over a period of twenty years into a prodigious compilation in two volumes; it is an indispensable reference work for anyone working with the American Indian.

The Bureau of Ethnology, as the Major predicted, was called upon to assist other government bureaus. It was consulted on various questions concerning treaties and boundaries contracted with the Indians. It seems incongruous that such requests were directed to the Major because the Bureau of Indian Affairs would have been the logical depository for such information. The truth was that, with the gross inefficiency

[21] See Erminnie Adelle Platt Smith, D.A.B. Her "Myths of the Iroquois," Bu. Ethnol., *2nd. Ann. Rep.,* is a classic.

and ineptness of that agency, records of many treaties made with the Indians had not been preserved. Although obviously it was not Powell's responsibility to do so, he immediately set out to compile an index of all treaties made with the Indians and, without any authorization whatsoever, placed C. C. Royce, who had been working independently, in charge of the project. This monumental check list, issued eighteen years later in 1899, remains to this day the only comprehensive and authentic source for the many agreements made with the Indians from 1606 to 1885. Each treaty is described briefly, the terms listed, and the subsequent operation of the treaty cross-indexed. Powell's entry into this activity displeased the Bureau of Indian Affairs and some of the members of Congress. Yet there was an underlying academic need for the compilation. The uprooting and resettlement of tribes, far from their original homes, destroyed primitive customs, languages, and racial purity. A knowledge of the progressive dispossession of the Indian might aid in interpreting confused cultures.

The publications of the Bureau of Ethnology during the Major's directorship indicate a high rate of productivity. Nineteen comprehensive annual reports, containing nearly one hundred scientific papers, four quarto monographs, and twenty-five bulletins, were distributed liberally throughout the academic world.

Major Powell served the cause of the Indian and the Bureau of Ethnology in three ways: as a scientific investigator; as an administrator creating opportunities for others to work; and as a promoter. The Major agitated, educated, persuaded, and cajoled, varying his technique as circumstances required. But his trump card was always a willing cooperation, and with this he could beat strong opposition. Seldom did he wait for opportunities in which he could be of service; he sought them.

Many of Powell's colleagues, even Spencer Baird, failed to appreciate just how a classification of Indian languages could be put to practical use, though they readily admitted the scientific importance of the project. The Major showed them. When Brig. Gen. Francis A. Walker was preparing the groundwork for the tenth census of 1880, he consulted the Major about the confusion arising from differences among Indian languages and asked for suggestions which might improve the method of counting and classifying the Indians. Powell's linguistic classifications had been in tentative outline for several years and could easily have been given to General Walker. Rather than oblige in such an impromptu manner, Powell asked for, and received, a temporary appointment without pay *requesting* him to prepare "a classification of the Indians by their linguistic affinities." By this device the Major obtained tacit official approval and recognition, both of which are important considerations.

The first annual report of the director of the Bureau of Ethnology was not a dry compilation of statistics; it was a dazzling introduction to a new science of man. Powell mapped out an ambitious program not only for the bureau but also for himself. His personal projects included "The Evolution of Languages," "Mythology of the North American Indians," "Wyandot Government," "Stone Graves or Cists," "Origin of Man," and "Limitations to the Use of Some Anthropologic Data." On one side Powell was pursuing his investigations in the traditional phases of anthropology; on another side he was allowing his thoughts free rein to follow the devious mythologies of the savage. "Mythology is the history of ghosts," he wrote, and "many venerable ghosts stalk through our philosophies." In the Elysium of philosophy the Major found his greatest intellectual pleasures.

The Major perceived a still deeper meaning in a study of the American Indians. In the first annual report he wrote:

North America presents a wide and interesting field to the investigator [in sociology], for it has within its extent many distinct governments, and these governments, so far as investigations have been carried, are found to belong to a type more primitive than any of the feudalities from which the civilised nations of the earth sprang, as shown by concurrently recorded history.

So important are these discoveries that all human history has to be rewritten, the whole philosophy of history reconstructed. Government does not begin in the ascendency of chieftains through prowess in war, but in the slow specialisation of executive functions from communal associations based on kinship. Deliberative assemblies do not start in councils gathered by chieftains, but councils precede chieftains. Law does not begin in contract, but in the development of custom. Land tenure does not begin in grants from the monarch or the feudal lord, but a system of tenure in common by gentes or tribes is developed into a system of tenure in severalty. Evolution in society has not been from militancy to industrialism, but from organisation based on kinship to organisation based on property, and alongside of the specialisations of the industries of peace the arts of war have been specialised.

So one by one, the theories of metaphysical writers on sociology are overthrown, and the facts of history are taking their place, and the philosophy of history is being erected out of materials accumulating by objective studies of mankind.[22]

The bureau had indeed an ambitious program and its director dreamed with the enthusiasm of perpetual youth.

[22] Bu. Ethnol., *1st Ann. Rep.*, p. 83.

17

1881-1884 · Double Duty

BARELY had the Major begun his work as the director of the Bureau of Ethnology, when he was drawn back into the affairs of the Geological Survey. The men working for the Geological Survey had endured anxious weeks during the fall and winter of 1880. The survey was still young, its growth limited, but its reputation well established. An unfriendly administration could spell the doom of the bureau quietly. The periodic shifting of political fortunes contingent upon the national elections had been settled when James A. Garfield was elected to the presidency. Garfield was a friend of the survey but it was rumored that Carl Schurz would decline reappointment as Secretary of the Interior. Adding to the uncertainty, King, who should have been in Washington working for an appropriation for the Geological Survey, was in parts unknown.[1] He had been an intimate friend of the Schurz family for many years and it was feared that he would resign at the same time.

General Garfield and Powell had discussed it too. By now they were on intimate terms, their friendship cemented by a little "deal." In 1876 the Major had engaged a young man, Joseph Stanley-Brown, as a temporary secretary when John C. Pilling was obliged to go to England to secure a family inheritance. Stanley-Brown, a friend of Frank H. Cushing and Pilling, proved to be no ordinary secretary, having taught himself shorthand and typing and a smattering of science.[2] The young man, only seventeen at the time, had an opportunity to witness the planning and organizing genius of his chief. Garfield already had tried in 1878 to persuade the Major to allow Stanley-Brown to become his secretary. The Major would not consent but offered to loan his man on Sundays and holidays to take care of Garfield's correspondence—in return for continued support on behalf of consolidation. When the political cam-

---

[1] See for instance Ward Thoron, ed., *Letters of Mrs. Henry Adams,* Mrs. Adams to her father, Jan. 23, 1881.
[2] See Joseph Stanley-Brown, MS, "An Eventful Career."

paign of 1880 slid into high gear and General Garfield received the presidential nomination, the Major no longer objected. Stanley-Brown, who understood the delicacy of Washington politics, became Garfield's private secretary. "Without my knowledge, the General had again arranged matters with the Major," recorded Stanley-Brown. He continued in this capacity when Garfield assumed the presidency of the United States.

During the early part of February 1881 Clarence King, long overdue, returned to Washington. Upon learning that Schurz planned to leave the public service when the Hayes cabinet went out of office, he tried immediately to resign from the directorship of the Geological Survey. However, President Hayes persuaded King to wait until Garfield took office a few weeks later. Meanwhile Hewitt, Powell, Spencer Baird, and King informed each other of the impending move. King did not delay any longer than he had to, submitting his resignation to the new President on March 6th. It was accepted "reluctantly" on March 12th but not before King suggested the name of a successor, Major Powell. Garfield called Spencer Baird for advice and he too sponsored the Major.

One March morning in 1881 Joseph Stanley-Brown arranged an interview with the President of the United States, the director of the Geological Survey, and the Major—King was officially resigning his directorship. Stanley-Brown, who alone besides the Major knew all the details of the affair, wrote:

By agreement with Major Powell, the creator of the United States Geological Survey, Clarence King had been made its first director. In the course of a year he grew very weary of administrative work and resigned. It was my great pleasure to see to it that the Major's nomination as Director was promptly sent to the Senate for confirmation.[3]

The confirmation came on March 18th.

The shift was accomplished so quietly that Hayden, who would have moved mountains to prevent Powell's appointment, knew nothing of the business until after the Major's appointment had been approved.

When King assumed the directorship of the Geological Survey, he was charged with two responsibilities: the classification of the public land, and the examination of the mineral resources of the national domain. In attempting to carry out the provisions of the law upon which the survey was based, he found himself faced with two disturbing ambiguities in the wording of the legislation: what was meant by classification of the public lands?; what was meant by the national domain?

[3] *ibid.*, p. 18. Quoted with permission of Dr. Margaret Stanley-Brown.

Was this classification to be on a basis upon which the government should dispose of its public lands or was it to be a scientific classification of lands into arable, irrigable, desert, timber, and mineral lands? Was the public domain the entire United States or simply the region of public lands to which the federal government still held title? [4]

Major Powell brought to office a complex interpretation of "land" which wrought a sudden fundamental modification of the relation between government and the public domain and gradually changed the direction of federal administration. This change cannot be overestimated nor can the influence of the man behind it. Powell had no desire to accumulate wealth and denied the right of individuals to accumulate wealth from the public domain—that is, lands held in the title of the federal government. All natural resources including water occurring in the public lands belonged to all the people. It was this sense of possession, protection, and stewardship which made the United States Geological Survey—as Major Powell organized it—the first significant venture of the government as a "welfare state."

Some of the originators of the bill creating the Geological Survey supposed that the enabling act gave authority to survey the entire territory of the United States, but there were others who did not interpret the bill in this sense. There already existed a land office whose chief responsibility was to survey, classify, and sell public lands to homesteaders, and it possessed ample machinery to carry on all the functions ascribed to it by law. In fact, at the very time the Geological Survey was founded, the public land commission had carefully considered the whole question of the disposition of the public lands and judged that it would be impractical for the Geological Survey or any other branch of the Department of the Interior to classify in advance of sale any land without impeding the rapid settlement of the unoccupied territories.

King was spared the necessity of formulating a policy with respect to these limiting questions. His budget was barely $105,000 so that the establishment of a small organization was all that he could accomplish. King, cautious and conservative by nature, decided to confine his operations to those regions of the public land where there could be no question as to his legal authority, and therefore, any future uncertainties arising from the language of the law could not undermine the organization or upset the functions of the federal survey.

[4] C. King, U.S.G.S., *1st Ann. Rep.*, p. 5. For an appraisal of the significance of the philosophy of the founding fathers of the Geological Survey, see R. H. Gabriel, *The Course of American Democratic Thought*, pp. 168–72, 174.

Whereas King had been cautious, the Major was aggressive and ambitious: aggressive in methods, ambitious for the cause of science. Moreover, having had an important part in the agitation leading up to the consolidation of the several surveys, and understanding full well the heated arguments which preceded the founding of a unified bureau, he took office with determination and began to knock at the doors of Congressmen in search of appropriations sufficient to extend the survey to the entire United States.

King had estimated in his first annual report that if the survey were established on a permanent basis, $500,000 would be sufficient to provide for a bureau staffed with competent scientists to undertake a thorough survey of all of the mineral resources and geological structures of the country. King did not expect to gain this figure; rather, he considered it a suggestion of the scope of the work ahead. On the other hand, the Major regarded it as the minimum with which the bureau could carry on its activities effectively. Within two years the survey appropriation came close to the half-million-dollar mark.

The first task confronting Major Powell was not to seek money but to prepare an annual report for the fiscal year 1880–1881. It mattered little because office routine did not bother him and he could delegate responsibility with exactitude. This report, of which more will be said later, included a summary of map-drawing practices which, though hastily compiled, adopted a standard for future work in the topographic section of the bureau.

Powell did not relinquish his post as chief of the Bureau of Ethnology although he no longer drew a salary for it. The directorship of the survey carried an annual salary of $6,000 whereas that of the Bureau of Ethnology paid but $4,000. The Major began immediately to transact all business from one office. One of his first actions was to merge the clerical forces. Thus, the disbursement of funds for the Bureau of Ethnology was controlled by the disbursing clerk of the Geological Survey. Similarly, all of the correspondence and other administrative routine was conducted by the regular clerical force of the survey. By this device, the very limited budget of the Bureau of Ethnology could be spared some expense. There was, however, a virtual necessity for the merging; both departments were small and there were no provisions for assistant chiefs.

The policies of the survey were not as yet clearly defined. King had cautioned the Major about the ambiguities in the authority granted to the survey, saying that he had been reluctant to request a clarification lest a broad interpretation be denied. Whatever the decision, the whole matter of methods and organization of the survey would be involved.

The United States Geological Survey had been established, in the words of its founding act, to place "the work of national development and the elements of future prosperity upon the firm and enduring basis of truth and knowledge."

King, in sympathy with this purpose, had laid sound foundations for a department which would serve the people of the country chiefly as an advisory bureau providing technical information for the public needs. King was a scientist of ability but was not interested in the patronage and alliances which must be a part of the unofficial buttress of a federal bureau. No director of any important agency of the government could expect adequate appropriations unless he had "a friend at court." This had been true at least from the days of President Grant and at best the situation had improved very slightly. King ignored all this. Perhaps he had not planned to remain as director of the survey for a long period. Many of his friends said upon his resignation that from the very beginning he had intended to remain in office but one or two years. Thus, the early foundations of the survey were utterly free from any of the weaknesses arising from a political setup. He had established four regional offices in the territories—Salt Lake City, Denver, Colorado City, and San Diego—and maintained a small administrative force in Washington. Among his plans was a program for publishing serious technical works in a rather elaborate form. None of these proposed reports, however, had been completed at the time of his resignation.

As soon as Major Powell came to office he reorganized the whole system. The regional offices were maintained temporarily until a large bureau with adequate physical accommodations was developed in Washington. Here his men would have the advantages of collaboration with one another and their work would be observed by scientists in other federal bureaus. It was not the Major's intent to let the importance of the survey go unnoticed by competitors as well as colleagues. The reorganization was not intended to undo what King had accomplished; rather it was to take a more aggressive approach to the problem of the national domain.

There was a fundamental and far-reaching difference between the administrations of King and Powell. King's experience had been that of a mining geologist. He looked upon the Geological Survey as an ally of the mining industries, providing accurate scientific information which would serve the economic interests and at the same time foster the intelligent use of the great mineral resources of the country. The profligate exploitation of ore deposits disturbed few persons except scientists. King and his subordinate, S. F. Emmons, were appalled by the waste and inefficiency to be observed everywhere. In sharp contrast, Powell had but casual interest in mining or mining geology. He was not interested in wealth or industry. His professional experience was in the arid regions. The Major considered the Geological Survey to be an ally of the agricultural industries, including animal husbandry, and correlated this with a broad national policy for land use. Yet despite the wide divergence between their approaches, these two men envisioned a bureau maintained at the highest professional quality and dedicated to the advancement of knowledge and to the protection of natural wealth for all the people. Rarely have governmental agencies been guided, especially in their formative years, by more altruistic motives or maintained with more trustworthy stewardship.

Powell looked upon the Geological Survey as a great fact-finding bureau organized along purely scientific lines. Unlike King he had no intention to accept limitations in the scope of its investigations. The survey would provide information not on request but in anticipation of need. He would mold opinion, educate Congress, educate the nation. What made this attitude so strikingly different is what the Major considered the science of geology to be: nothing less than the earth and all its attributes—rocks, minerals, and fossils, to be sure, but also rivers, deserts, forest cover, irrigation, flood control, and a good deal more. As one Senator angrily put it, "Major Powell has the most ambitious scheme of geology ever conceived in the mind of man." [5] Figuratively, at least, the Senator was correct.

Geology as a science was suffering growing pains. Mineralogy, stratigraphy, and paleontology were well established but the newer approaches to the earth sciences—geophysics and geochemistry—had yet to prove their worth. Unobtrusively King had organized a small chemical laboratory at Denver to study the properties of certain types of ore bodies on the recommendation of the geologist in charge there. In 1883 Powell established a central chemical laboratory in Washington though full consolidation of the chemical research of the survey was not completed until some years later. Simultaneously he issued public statements on the potential importance of this new section of the survey.

Rather typical of the Major's manner of thought was his desire to adopt a system of nomenclature and diagrams which could be accepted

[5] Hilary Herbert of Alabama, *Cong. Rec. 52nd Cong. 1st Sess., Pt. 5,* p. 4390.

as standard among all American geologists. This desire to standardize and systematize was one of his most obvious traits. An international congress of geologists was scheduled to meet during September 1881 at Bologna, Italy, to consider the very same subject, but to establish a standard practice to be used on geological charts and atlases throughout the world. Most American scientists (except those who had completed their educations in European universities) in their provincialism paid little regard to the opinions of their foreign colleagues, especially on such academic problems as vocabulary and symbols. Moreover, the desire to have an American system unrestricted by European influence or usage was a foremost consideration. It is not surprising then that a very considerable part of the first three months of Powell's directorship was devoted to a hasty though exhaustive investigation of the history of American geological maps and the adoption of uniform nomenclature and conventional characters for diagrams on all government charts and atlases. In due time these American standards were submitted to the international congress, which was meeting in Italy. This system, which Powell compiled and announced in his first annual report, written when he had been in office for only three months, has remained the American standard with but few important changes for almost seventy years. The geologists of foreign countries had to compromise their systems because Powell's was published first and the American government had been so lavish with the disposition of its geological publications. Needless to say this project, executed with distressing temerity, caused bitter resentment among many American geologists, and especially among delegates at the convention held at Bologna.[6]

Of his many projects Powell's pet was the preparation of a detailed geological map of the United States because such a map was fundamental to a sound land classification and, in a very real sense, to a land-use policy. To further this plan he asked Congress in 1882 to grant authority "to complete a geological map of the United States."[7] By this simple device authorization for extending the work of the Geological Survey over the entire territory of the United States was obtained quietly. Congress granted the appropriation despite heated debate in both the House and Senate.

The enormity of the task of preparing a complete topographical atlas

[6] I have avoided a technical comparison of the proposals submitted to the international geological congress and discussion of the furor caused among American, as well as European, geologists by this independent *fait accompli*. The Major ignored the controversy completely.

[7] Powell announced this act triumphantly in U.S.G.S., *4th. Ann. Rep.* The insertion of the words "United States" was a sly maneuver, as will be evident later.

of the United States was as usual underestimated—even by the Major. The completed portions are published from time to time as quadrangle maps. Each quadrangle is bounded by parallels and meridians and is printed on a sheet sixteen and one-half by twenty inches. Most of the maps depict an area of thirty minutes in each direction with a scale of approximately two miles to the inch. Some areas of industrial importance are drawn to a scale of about one mile to the inch, or a quadrangle of fifteen minutes. Still larger scales are used to depict mining, irrigation, and drainage districts. On the other hand, maps to a scale of four miles to the inch, that is, one degree, are used for certain desert, and other sparsely settled, areas. These topographic maps show not only lakes, rivers, and relief, but also such cultural features as roads, towns, and bridges. Obviously the engineer, settler, farmer, and traveler, as well as the geologist, have found these maps useful.

More than a little thought went into the development of those earliest quadrangle maps, the pattern of which became the American standard. Powell planned the map taking into consideration sense perceptions and optical illusions. He explained:

In topographic maps, relief is represented usually by light and shade in hachures, but in the best maps relief is represented by lines which follow the contour at equal intervals of altitude. Such maps cannot be read by the inexperienced man, but he can develop the power so that a contour map will seem to be a picture of mountains and valleys and of hills and dales. Experience has taught me that this power is more easily gained and greatly assisted by representing relief in one color and drainage in another, as in blue. . . .[8]

The work of mapping progressed very slowly. The mechanical detail and the intricate field work would not allow hurrying. Within a few years after the initial grant of money Congress demanded more rapid results. Powell assured the committee charged with reporting on the topographic activities of the survey that he could complete the work in twenty years at a cost of $18,000,000. His critics challenged him and said that at the rate he was going it would be in one hundred years at $100,000,000.[9] His critics were wrong. Today, more than sixty years later, less than fifty per cent of the work has been completed—about 4,000 quadrangles at a cost approaching $100,000,000. Nevertheless, this project, born and nursed by Powell's aggressive ambition, is one

[8] J. W. Powell, *Truth and Error*, p. 342. Although this quotation is of a much later date, Powell had on many occasions explained the function of the symbolism and color scheme of the survey maps. The late Bailey Willis told me that these illusory aids had been devised between 1882 and 1884 after extensive experimentation.

[9] See Testimony before Cong. Jt. Comm. Investigating Fed. Sci. Bus. The mapping problem is discussed in *49th Cong., 1st Sess., Sen. Misc. Doc. 82*, pp. 1–49, especially 41–43.

of his most useful contributions to the American people. More than 20,000,000 of these topographic quadrangle maps have been sold through the Geological Survey.

As soon as the preparation of a geological map had been authorized and the scope of the topographic work extended to include the entire area of the United States, Powell reorganized the topographic division of the survey into four regional offices, northeast, southeast, central, and western. He established also a division of mining statistics and technology to investigate the mineral resources of the United States.

Although the literary and cartographic output of the Geological Survey was at first modest, publications began to appear in an ever-increasing quantity. In 1884 a division of publication had to be set up. Pilling was officially designated the editor although he had for some years past performed the editorial work of the bureau. When the editorial duties multiplied still further, W. A. Croffut, an experienced editor and journalist, was engaged. Croffut's methods caused some annoyance because scientific or scholarly style was sacrificed for what he considered appeal and publicity. Lester Ward, for instance, complained scathingly about the mutilation of one of his papers. Nevertheless the Major had his eye on publicity—not for himself but for his bureaus.[10]

Another of the new divisions which the Major created, paleontology, was a source of considerable trouble. O. C. Marsh,[11] when offered the position as chief of the division, was very reluctant to accept because of his own affluence and his comfortable situation at Yale. He enjoyed a post which was too pleasant to surrender without any particular benefit. The Major enticed Marsh by granting him special permission to conduct his own researches and those of the survey at Yale with a budget of approximately $15,000 a year; $4,000 of this was for his own salary as a division chief. With this windfall Marsh capitulated. He was thereby enabled to employ additional assistance for the corps he had already gathered together at his own expense. With preparators, technical assistants, and artists, and large allowances for freight bills, he could turn out a prodigious amount of work.

There was purpose behind this appointment. Marsh would make a powerful ally. He had influence at Yale, important friends in Congress, and numerous business connections in New York and Boston and among Yale alumni—to which of course must be added his presidency of the

---

[10] The Major's employment of a professional journalist to handle publicity caused a little consternation. Whether Powell innovated this practice in government bureaus I have been unable to determine. It is now an established practice.

[11] See C. Schuchert and C. M. LeVene, *O. C. Marsh: Pioneer in Paleontology*, Chap. XI.

National Academy of Science. Furthermore, with Marsh in the survey there could be no excuse for bringing Cope into the same organization. Cope was exerting pressure to get into the survey and it might soon become difficult to keep him out.

It was impossible within the budget allowed by Congress to engage specialists to investigate all the branches of geology, but the Major could do the next best thing; he could augment the staff with part-time employees. He had already used this method to striking advantage in the Bureau of Ethnology. By paying small sums for work actually rendered, he was able to secure the cooperation of many distinguished scholars and amateurs throughout the country. With a little common sense and with the careful selection of scientists this method could provide strong protection for the survey. Within two years the Major placed on a part-time basis sixty-five recognized scientists, the majority being college professors and state geologists and the remainder mining engineers, metallurgists, and the like. Outsiders looking in thought they saw in the survey a well-laden feast to fatten the professional friends of the Major.

The old members of the survey who were carried over at the time of consolidation were the mainstay of the department—Gilbert, Dutton, Thompson, Walcott, Hague, and Emmons. The new men who were brought in on a full-time basis maintained the high caliber established by King. Among the most remarkable were W J McGee, Bailey Willis, and Lester Ward. McGee, born on the frontier of Irish parents, and large of body, was self-taught. He had observed at his own instigation the succession of glacial deposits over Iowa, and through Powell had come to the attention of King, who recommended him for work with the tenth census to collect information on building stones of the Midwest. In 1882 Powell, who paid no heed to academic degrees, invited McGee to join the survey at $1,200 a year.[12] McGee began his service at the bottom of the ladder. Bailey Willis,[13] polished, scholarly, and well-

[12] W J McGee, a handsome man of commanding appearance, married Anita Newcomb, daughter of Simon Newcomb, the astronomer. He had met her at the Powell home and Mrs. Newcomb, regarding W J as socially inferior, blamed the Major for the romance. Professor Newcomb and the Major held each other in genuine esteem but Mrs. Newcomb was of a very different opinion. Intermarriages, friendships, and petty animosities had professional as well as personal ramifications.

[13] See the autobiographic Bailey Willis, *A Yanqui in Patagonia*. Dr. Willis in a series of eleven letters recorded reminiscences of his early associations with the survey. Unlike many of his eminence Willis cautioned me concerning his own prejudices about personalities. Now that they are gone I can disclose that these include McGee and Darton. Dr. Darton fortunately gave me many of his recollections. The opinions of both have been weighed judiciously with the assistance of other geologists of the old survey days.

educated, also had worked for the tenth census on economic metals. His specialty was topographic mapping in difficult country and the Major assigned him at once to the mapping division of the survey.

Lester Ward [14] was regarded by most of his colleagues as the least capable member of the survey, yet the Major considered him a genius of the first degree. Ward, a native of Joliet, Illinois, had become a clerk for the Department of the Treasury after service in the Civil War, and had completed his education at Columbian (George Washington) University. He studied economics although his chief interest was in botany. He had served briefly with Powell in Utah studying the prairie grasses in the semiarid region, but had no secure position at any time before his coming to the survey. The only excuse the Major had for hiring Ward was to place him in the paleobotany section, in which capacity Ward became justly famous, but at no time was paleobotany the chief interest of Lester Ward. Already in 1869 he had begun writing miscellaneous articles on sociology but had kept his activities in this field quiet until 1879 when he divulged the nature of his project to Major Powell. The real reason for Ward's appointment was to give him an opportunity to continue his sociological writings, which the Major thought would not be completed in any other way. Since sociology bears little intimate or obvious relation to geology, this indulgence was an annoyance to the other members of the survey. If at any time the Major had a favorite, it was Lester Ward.[15] In 1881 Ward completed the manuscript of his *Dynamic Sociology*, but in his attempt to find a publisher obtained nothing but refusals. Major Powell interceded and induced Appleton's in New York, who were at the time issuing the more important semi-popular scientific works of the country, to include Ward's book in their series.

There is a very curious relationship between the philosophy of Lester Ward and Powell. It is impossible to determine to what extent Powell and Ward influenced each other. Ward, according to his diaries, began his manuscript in 1869 and implies that not until 1879 did the Major begin to help him finish the work. The Major, on the other hand, had published various papers on ethnology and philosophy in 1875, but had expressed some views as early as 1869. The approach by Ward and

[14] No adequate biography of Lester Ward has yet appeared. The excessively laudatory *Lester Ward, The American Aristotle* by Samuel Chugarman makes scant mention of Ward's scientific work.

[15] This favoritism has been mentioned by three sources: N. H. Darton, David White, and A. C. Lane. In 1933, long before I had begun research on the Major, David White showed me the portrait of Powell in the Cosmos Club and discussed the relation of Lester Ward and Frank H. Knowlton, paleobotanists in the old survey organization.

Powell to the same problems is strikingly similar, with, however, one fundamental difference in emphasis—Ward was fundamentally a sociologist, Powell an ethnologist. It is to be remembered too that Ward spent a summer with Powell in Utah in 1875 and that his diaries for these critical years were destroyed by the second Mrs. Ward.[16] Happily neither Ward nor Powell fretted about it if indeed they did recognize the kinship of ideas. In all probability their ideas were products of the same stream of thought; each influenced the other's opinions.

The Major always adopted a liberal attitude toward the time and facilities afforded by government bureaus. For his own part he felt no hesitation in doing any kind of work on government time and he permitted all of his subordinates to do likewise. In return for this liberty he expected the willing cooperation of his men in giving up evenings, Saturdays, Sundays, or holidays if an emergency or deadline had to be met. Powell never demanded that his men work by the clock. So long as regular progress was being made, they could come and go at will, but they had to reckon with the chief if there was any negligence or dereliction of duty.

The Major always knew what he wanted in directing survey work. In 1883 when the first quadrangle maps were being prepared for public distribution, he called in Bailey Willis and explained that there was needed a brief set of symbols and drawings to explain the legends on a government map. These symbols were to be so clear and elementary that they could be readily understood by a high school student, a farmer, or a traveler. Willis made eight attempts before he pleased his chief and on the eighth, the Major said, "Now, my boy, you've done it." [17]

Powell had little regard for tradition or for the conventions which had grown up around the administrative offices in the government bureaus. The door to his office was always open and his desk so placed that passers-by could be hailed into his presence. Always approachable, he preferred the company of his younger associates to the stiff courtesy calls of persons on official business. He ignored all formalities of rank and replaced with good-natured camaraderie the inaccessibility which was found in most high places.

The office was always in a state of agitation. With increased administrative duties and corresponding lessening of physical activity the Major had grown overweight. His loose long hair, brushed back but never

[16] B. J. Stern, ed., *Young Ward's Diary*, p. 320. It is probable that common gossip about Ward's private affairs colored his colleagues' estimations of his scientific reputation. "A prophet is not without honor. . . ."

[17] Bailey Willis to William Culp Darrah.

parted, and his long and tobacco stained red-brown beard, noticeably unkempt, gave the appearance of greater age than he had attained. His face was deeply wrinkled, partly because of long suffering pain and partly because of the vigorous outdoor life he had led for many years. His eyes, deep set, half closed, had a twinkle which revealed the alertness and enthusiasm with which he met every situation. He enjoyed dictation and whether his audience consisted of his secretary, Miss May Clark, or a large gathering, he spoke as if the world were hearing his words. He would sit in his swivel chair, swinging from side to side with his one hand behind his head, speaking with deliberate and carefully chosen phrases, or he would stride across the floor holding a lighted cigar until the long ash fell unnoticed.[18] He drew no fine distinctions as to what work was legitimate. For himself he dictated philosophy, ethnology, irrigation, or anything else as the spirit moved him. It was no secret that Ward had completed his great *Dynamic Sociology* during the regular hours of the Geological Survey. It would never concern the Major that such a thing, which was for the good of mankind, might be questioned. Always in the background was Powell's confident combative spirit, which spared his men a feeling of uncertainty about their positions. It was this combination of informality, leniency, and enthusiastic interest which made the survey a congenial place for men of diverse scientific interests.

Administrative efficiency was the watchword and the Major, with an eye to complete control of his bureaus, requested the Secretary of the Interior to designate him as "Special Disbursing Agent of the United States Geological Survey," which, when granted on August 24, 1882, gave him absolute and sole control of the expenditures within his gross budget. (That same day Powell read in the papers that Andy Hall,[19] riding the stage in defense of the U.S. mail, was shot by highwaymen a short distance from Globe, Arizona.)

There are tragedies as well as joys and successes in a man's life. To consider with kindly feelings the troubles of his men was always in the Major's character. The spring of 1883 was a sad one for the members of the survey stationed in Washington. Bessie, the seven-year-old daughter of G. K. Gilbert, died of diphtheria.[20] Mrs. Gilbert and her sons were

[18] Marcus Baker, "Personal Reminiscences of One of His Staff," *Open Court,* Vol. 17, p. 348. Unpublished reminiscences of F. W. Hodge, J. R. Swanton, W. H. Hobbs, and Clark Wissler have also been used in this connection.

[19] *Arizona Gazette* (Phoenix), Aug. 27 and 28, 1882. Mr. J. W. Wentworth, a resident of Globe at the time, has provided additional information.

[20] W. M. Davis, "Grove Karl Gilbert," *Biog. Mem. Nat. Acad. Sci.,* Vol. 21, No. 5, p. 140.

gravely ill and Gilbert had nursed them all until he was exhausted. Friends from the survey and their wives took turns caring for the patients. Mrs. Powell remained with little Bessie during the last days of suffering when her parents were too ill to tend her themselves.

In 1881, on July 2nd, at the railroad station, President Garfield was shot by a crazed and disappointed office seeker. After a few days it appeared that Garfield would recover, but when weeks passed and he lingered on, tortured by fever and by the unbearable Washington heat, fears for his life returned. Many offers of help and advice to make the stricken President more comfortable were sent to the White House, and Simon Newcomb and Major Powell met at the Cosmos Club on July 9th to discuss some of the more promising proposals for cooling the sickroom. Out of this meeting came a contraption for blowing air over cakes of ice which provided some comfort for the dying President.[21]

The first years in the Geological Survey had been spectacularly successful. Admiringly, Lester Ward wrote a sketch of Major Powell, which he published in the *Popular Science Monthly,* saying, "Major Powell . . . is a pattern of the American self-made man, and well illustrates in his life and achievements what may be accomplished with honest, steady adherence to a definite purpose." [22] Columbian University made him a trustee [23] and awarded him an honorary LL.D. degree, and earlier than this, in 1880, Powell had been elected to membership in the National Academy of Sciences. Honors were showered upon him as he grew in prestige and power.

Some men would have settled into a comfortable position in the government service beyond the reach of partisan political quarrels to enjoy prestige and security. But the Major did not look upon his job as a sinecure. Here was the opportunity to accomplish what he had set out to do; overhaul the federal land policy—a policy embracing the incalculable natural wealth of the country, the arid regions, irrigation and agriculture, and the Indian problem. In a broader sense he was determined to dignify the scientific work of the federal government.

Powell was well aware that such a program would run into trouble head-on. Cattle interests, mining companies, landed interests, and heavy

---

[21] Simon Newcomb, *Reminiscences of an Astronomer,* p. 357; Joseph Stanley-Brown, MS, *John Wesley Powell; an address,* p. 5. The Smithsonian, builder of the cooling device, later became involved in a fraudulent litigation over alleged violations of patent rights.

[22] *Popular Science Monthly,* Vol. 20, pp. 390–97; quote from p. 390.

[23] For an appreciation of Powell's service as trustee see *Columbian Univ. Hist. Cat. 1821–1891,* p. 21. Also, *Columbian Univ. Ann. Rep. Pres. 1901–1902,* p. 4.

investors would find objectionable features in any land policy of the general government. Nevertheless he felt a responsibility to future generations of Americans and girded for the fight.

In the brief span of ten years in government employ, a considerable part of which was only semiofficial, Powell labored for the establishment of a unified federal geological survey and a bureau for the study of the American Indian. Ever since 1874 he had argued that time was short and that the future development of the West would depend in large part on understanding the public domain. Congress created the United States Geological Survey and the Bureau of Ethnology in the year 1879. Two years later Major Powell found himself directing the activities of both. He was in a powerful position.

18

1884-1887 · The Survey and Science
in America

THE Geological Survey flourished handsomely under Powell's administration: funds had been provided for topographic surveying; a geological map of the United States was to be ready in seven or eight years;
paleontology had become an important subdivision of the organization;
a competent staff of congenial scientists had been brought together; the
publications of the survey, issued in generous editions and adequately
illustrated and printed, were liberally distributed. The United States
Geological Survey won admiration throughout the world.

Powell's first budget request was satisfied by an appropriation of
$254,940—nearly a hundred thousand dollars more than King had ob-
tained for the fiscal year ending June 30, 1881. For 1884 the Major
received $339,640 and the next year, $489,040.

Each increase in appropriations represented a new field of geological
work or a new region in which work had begun. The Major had his men
studying mineral resources, metallurgy, geography, paleontology in all
its branches, soils, ground water, rivers, flood control, irrigation, general geology in many parts of the country, and of course topographic surveying. The office in Washington was kept on modest proportions, but
the influence of the Geological Survey had reached to every state and
territory and to virtually every university in the country.

It is not strange that some members of the old independent surveys
who were left out of the combined survey envied the opportunities
afforded the Major. Hayden had, of course, been continued on the payroll of the Geological Survey at $4,000 a year as a principal geologist
to complete the preparation of his scientific monographs, but this left
Cope and others on the outside. Most irritating to Cope was the selection of his rival, Marsh, as vertebrate paleontologist of the survey.
Marsh, financially independent, was able to spend his salary of $4,000

on his researches, and from his private income paid wages for assistants in addition to those provided by the regular appropriation. By special dispensation, Marsh did his work at Yale, where he held a professorship without salary. This arrangement with Marsh, however, was not unique. Hayden was doing his work in Philadelphia "where his library was better."

Cope was not one to sit by and let matters take an unhindered course if he could do anything about it. He envied Marsh's prestige and influence not only in paleontology but also, as president of the National Academy of Sciences, in scientific affairs generally.

There were others who disliked the Major, personally because of his aggressive attitude and politically because of his growing power. On one hand there were the heads of other scientific bureaus who found themselves completely outclassed in the competition for federal funds and in the struggle for recognition; on the other there was a powerful nucleus of opposition in Congress made up of men who for various reasons found the Major a formidable obstacle. Most of these however were delegates from western states who did not want the federal government to interfere with established private mineral, grazing, or irrigation interests.

There had been lingering resentment among politicians ever since Powell succeeded King because survey expenditures were at the discretion of the director without any further accounting except the regular statutory audits. To put it simply, Congress could appropriate money for the survey but could not restrict its use in any way except by specific amendment or by the enactment of a new law. And this was easier said than done. The peculiar situation had come about originally through parliamentary procedure, the survey owing its existence to an amendment to the Sundry Civil Appropriations Bill. But Powell had gone even further; he had secured the designation as "Special Disbursing Agent" of the survey and thereby won legal recognition of this power.

An additional bone of contention began in 1883. After considerable disagreement and disapproval, the Major's friends slipped into the annual Civil Appropriations Bill a provision for funds for a map of the United States. Thus the survey obtained authority to extend its investigations over the entire area of the United States. Many members of Congress considered this extension a violation of the intent of the original bill, which authorized only a survey of the "public domain." For more than two years the Major spread his work into the eastern states almost unnoticed.

The growth of the Geological Survey was but a manifestation of the expanding influence of science in every field of human activity. Excepting the Smithsonian Institution, established in 1846, for many years only the War and Navy Departments were vitally concerned with science. The War Department was in charge of the various explorations of the western territories, and had engaged in a wide variety of projects ranging from military medicine and surgery to the testing of various types of arms and equipment. To a considerable extent the research was of a purely practical nature. The Navy Department operated the Naval Observatory, which included a considerable program of astronomic and mathematical research and publication of the *Nautical Almanac*. Prof. Simon Newcomb, a close friend of the Major's, had been the naval astronomer for some years.

After 1880 the scientific activities of the government diversified rapidly as industrial prosperity, technological progress, and growing population created new opportunities in every part of the land. It was an age it seemed of unlimited progress. In 1860 the Department of Agriculture had, in addition to a superintendent, only four employees. The Department of Agriculture entered the scientific field very gradually, partly because its early directors were unimaginative and looked upon the department as a clearinghouse for information and the accumulation of statistics, and partly because other organizations were expected to provide assistance when needed. When the crops of the states in the great plains were ravaged by insects and diseases which had not yet proved serious in the eastern states, the colleges established under the Land Grant Bill turned attention to the work in their respective regions. Yeoman service to the biological sciences was performed by the pioneering land-grant colleges.

Many years passed before the Department of Agriculture developed an extensive research system. The Geological Survey from its very inception had been organized as a scientific bureau and had never been treated by its founders as anything else. One of the chief criticisms against the survey throughout its long history has been that many of its projects have little immediate commercial application.

Before many years, agencies doing similar work grew up independently in different departments. The various surveys of the territories under the War Department and the Department of the Interior and similar surveys in the Department of the Treasury had been but the first glaring example. In some cases separate agencies within the same department competed with each other. In the Department of Agriculture for instance the section on chemical research jealously guarded its exclusive prerogatives; no suspicious apparatus could be set up in any other office without its consent.

The increasing importance of science and technology in the over-all prosperity of the nation was recognized among men of science and by a considerable number of industrialists and statesmen. Industrial establishments and individual manufacturing companies were not yet educated to, or even aware of, the desirability of employing researchers for investigating technological problems. Farmers were certainly not in a position to cope with many of the technical problems which plagued agriculture.

The nineteenth century was the age of scientific discoveries. The very name of science was respected. No wonder then that, partly as a matter of business economy and partly as a determination to improve the efficiency of the many uncoordinated scientific activities of the federal government, intelligent agitation finally moved Congress to action.

Congress in the fall of 1884 [1] launched a full-scale investigation into the work and expenditures of each of the scientific agencies. A joint committee was appointed by the President and hearings were held over a period of nearly two years. The National Academy of Sciences was called upon to render its opinion on a suitable method for reorganizing scientific work for the government. As soon as the investigation began, however, political motives displaced unbiased ones and the intent was only thinly disguised. Although the administrations and expenditures of a dozen bureaus were considered, the committee concentrated on the Geological Survey. Almost half the testimony concerned Powell, who was called before the committee for interrogation on sixteen occasions. The Major made his first appearance before the committee on December 4, 1884,[2] and after answering preliminary questions gave a summary of the map work of the survey. The interrogation was resumed the following day. Two weeks later he was recalled, this time to give his opinions concerning a system for coordinating federal scientific research.

During these hearings Powell had other troubles. He had not fully recovered from an infection, complicated by a severe cold, in both eyes

[1] The testimony presented before the joint committee is recorded in *49th Cong. 1st. Sess. Misc. Doc. 82*. This document is a veritable cross section of the scientific work of the federal departments against the backdrop of contemporary politics.

[2] The National Academy of Sciences had submitted its report on September 21. The Major, a member of the academy and a leading voice in the discussions, was aware of the recommendations.

and had been confined to a dark room for several weeks preceding the meeting of the advisory committee of the National Academy. Not wishing to lose the opportunity to express to the academy his opinion on the role government should take in fostering scientific research, the Major left his sickbed to testify, but in such discomfort that he could speak for only a few minutes. Powell had more or less recovered from the illness when he appeared before the congressional investigating committee, but was still weak and suffering from the eye infection. The committee members were considerate, and although a few of the questions seemed distorted, Powell could raise no serious objection to any of them.

At the session on December 19th the Major was quizzed on virtually the whole range of survey activities. When asked, "Have you ever found anyone who knows the distinction between iron and steel?" Powell replied, "Yes, that has been determined in the laboratory of the Geological Survey." Although this was an extravagant claim, the nomenclature of iron and steel was at the time so confused that even patent litigation was bogged down in a morass of conflicting opinions.[3] For a number of years the manufacturers of iron and steel products were involved in a controversy as to how steel could be distinguished from iron. Most of the companies engaged in production referred to themselves as "iron works," and with the issuance of patents covering "steel," complicated litigation followed. The steel question had stirred Congress and a commission had been appointed to investigate the subject. Even before the survey had been consulted for an opinion, Powell had assigned his small chemical laboratory to work on the problem. It might be expected that a clear-cut explanation based upon unbiased scientific experiment would have been widely appreciated. On the contrary, many industrialists objected to the invasion of their private technical rights by Congress and by a government bureau. Major Powell ignored these protests, knowing that in time the commotion would subside. The early metallurgical work of the Geological Survey in iron, copper, and silver paved the way for the later cooperative ventures of the Bureau of Mines.

Petroleum also came in for early consideration by the Geological Survey. McGee was requested to summarize available knowledge concerning practical uses of petroleum for the annual report of 1884. There were but two important applications for natural oil—illumination and lubrication—although its derivatives had many lesser uses, such as fuels and solvents. The production of crude oil had increased to such proportions

[3] *49th Cong. 1st Sess. Misc. Doc. 82*, p. 694. At this time in the United States there was not a single steel plant with a competent metallurgist on its payroll.

that the world market was flooded with it. McGee recorded that in Russia a naturally pure though crude oil was being used to propel steamships across the Caspian Sea, and that American chemists had been able to obtain a considerable variety of substances from Pennsylvania natural oil. Powell, in one of his statements to the investigating committee—more a prophecy than a studied opinion—said:

> The quantities of petroleum in the United States are enormous; with no possibility of exhaustion within any reasonable length but the difficulty is that a very small amount of petroleum can be used . . . they do not know how to refine many of the petroleums. . . . It may be used for a great variety of other purposes for which it ought to be refined, and new methods for treating the oil must be discovered . . . light and lubrication are the two main purposes for which it is used. When we get the art of using petroleum . . . then it will be useful to this country. . . . I expect that we can use petroleum for fuel in this country and also use the waste products of its refinement in a great variety of chemical industries.[4]

A year later he became more certain of the potential importance of petroleum. He wrote to I. C. White, "I foresee in the not distant future a whole chemical industry based upon the uses of petroleum."

These statements were made nearly twenty-five years before large-scale commercial attempts were made to crack and fractionate crude oil to recover valuable by-products from it. There were mild critics of the survey's study of petroleum just as there had been over the question of iron and steel, but this time the criticisms were based more on the uselessness of the study rather than on its conflict with private enterprise. Some years after the establishment of the Geological Survey a subdivision known as the Bureau of Mines was set up as a distinct organization, and many of the practical problems which in the early days had been investigated by the survey were more properly assigned to the Bureau of Mines.

When less than a week later on December 22nd the Major was recalled to defend his practice of employing part-time professional associates and to explain how he was able to run both the Geological Survey and the Bureau of Ethnology from one office with one clerical staff, the committee had raised a temper. Concerning the administration of the Bureau of Ethnology, Major Powell explained:

> The clerical work in my office is done by clerks of the Geological Survey. For instance the disbursing of money is done by the disbursing clerk of the Geologi-

---

[4] *ibid.*, pp. 695–96. The quotation which follows this excerpt is from a letter, J. W. Powell to I. C. White, Sept. 30, 1886.

cal Survey in addition to his other duties without any compensation. The correspondence . . . which is very great . . . is so far as clerical work is concerned, conducted by the clerical force of the Geological Survey.[5]

After a full day of obstinate questioning the hearings were adjourned until January 2nd. The Major had explained the many diverse activities of the survey and how he operated the Bureau of Ethnology and the Geological Survey from one office. But the committee was far from satisfied.

Powell had been informed previously that an anonymous report of nearly 23,000 words would be distributed surreptitiously to the members of Congress. The document charged Major Powell with incompetence, extravagance, patronage, favoritism, and political dealing. Although the instigators refused to acknowledge its authorship, the plot was known to be the work of Cope, Endlich, and Prof. Persifor Frazer, a friend of both.[6]

The admitted purpose of these charges was to topple the survey and oust the Major; then either Hayden or Endlich would take over or the survey would be abolished altogether. Powell had been informed in advance of the subterfuge when several of his loyal men—Holmes, Peale, and Gannett—turned over to him letters received from Endlich, chief engineer in Cope's silver-mining venture in New Mexico. These supposedly confidential letters requested information which could be used against Powell's directorship.

It was not possible to tell just how much of the innuendo was believed by the members of the special committee. Nevertheless, the determination of some of the members to hammer away at the method of disbursing funds and the business methods of the survey showed clearly that they were determined to find out if there was any foundation for the accusations.

While the winds blew hot and cold, the National Academy of Science attempted to keep the discussions on a high plane consistent with the purpose of the hearings: how could the scientific work of the government be coordinated? The academy submitted its own recommendations for the conduct of the federal scientific agencies. These could be reduced to a specific proposal for the establishment of a Department of Science which, through a governing board composed of scientists, would supervise and coordinate but not control all the federal scientific activities.

[5] *ibid.*, p. 192.

[6] Powell accused the perpetrators by name in 1886 and again in 1890. See New York *Herald,* Jan. 12, 1890, p. 11, in which Powell explains how Cope instigated his attack on the Powell survey. F. M. Endlich was a chemist and geologist in the employ of Cope.

The academy was beset with troubles [7] no less trying than those tormenting the Major. In August Marsh appointed as a committee Gen. M. C. Meigs, W. H. Brewer of Yale, W. P. Trowbridge, E. C. Pickering of Harvard, C. A. Young of Princeton, F. A. Walker of Massachusetts Institute of Technology, S. P. Langley of Allegheny Observatory, and Simon Newcomb and General Comstock of the U.S. Army Engineering Corps. Newcomb and General Comstock were forced to resign by order of the Navy and War Departments. The military authorities would not permit subordinate officers to deliberate for or determine the policy of their respective departments. Possibly the fact that several War and Navy Department agencies would be involved in any reorganization was an important reason for the order. At any rate the military departments opposed the entire plan.

The National Academy passed a resolution calling for the establishment of a "Department of Science" with this significant statement:

Your Committee states only the general sentiment and wish of men of science, when it says that its members believe the time is near when the country will demand the institution of a branch of the executive government devoted especially to the direction and control of all the purely scientific work of the government. In this day the pursuit of science itself is directly connected with the promotion of the general welfare. . . . Should such a department now be impracticable, should public opinion not be now ready for it, the next best measure, in the opinion of scientific men, would be to transfer all such work or bureaus to some one executive department.[8]

There were many ramifications of such a plan. Would the military scientific agencies with their own peculiar objectives be submerged under a civilian authority? Would coordination diminish the individuality of the various agencies and retard rather than encourage progress? There were no simple answers to these questions.

The recommendation of the academy was received without enthusiasm by the congressional committee on September 21st. Major Powell was requested to give his personal opinion of the academy's plan. He took advantage of the chance to present his own views in full. The heart of the problem as Powell considered it was how scientific information could be utilized:

You are to decide for the people the best method of utilizing the results of all scientific research, as they pertain to the welfare of the people of the United States; and your action, should it be confirmed by Congress, will ultimately affect the deepest interests of all the people; and the influence of your action

[7] *Misc. Doc. 82, op.cit.,* pp. 1–10.
[8] *ibid.,* pp. 9–10.

will be exercised in promoting or retarding scientific research itself, which is the chief agency of civilization, and the results of which constitute the chief elements of civilization.

In response to your oral request at the session of yesterday to present to the commission my "opinions relating to the organization of the scientific work of the government on a comprehensive plan, by which the work can be more thoroughly coordinated, more systematically prosecuted, and more economically administered, than at present," I beg leave to make the following statement:

(1) The scientific institution of the government should be placed under one general management.

(2) The several bureaus engaged in research should be left to prosecute such research in all its details, without dictation from superior authority in respect to the methods of research to be used.

The various lines of research enumerated in characterizing the scientific bureaus above are such as properly pertain to the functions of government in the common judgment of mankind. . . . The subject of the endowment of such research by government has been widely discussed by statesmen and by scholars in America and in Europe alike; and the wisdom of such endowment and the fundamental principles that should control such work, have been again and again clearly enunciated. The actual practice of the several governments engaged in this work is to a large extent harmonious, but in some important particulars there is a diversity of methods. . . .[9]

Opposition against extension of government science came from several very different quarters, away from Washington, especially from certain universities who looked down upon practical science, and from the great mining interests and their financial backers. The Geological Survey was the particular target in both cases.

Hayden and Cope, seizing the chance to attack Powell, found a spokesman in Hilary Herbert from Alabama, who personally opposed the ever-multiplying activities of the Geological Survey. Herbert had an unbroken record of votes against every bill which had as its purpose protection of the public domain. Powerful aid came too from Alexander Agassiz, the son of the renowned Louis Agassiz, whom he had succeeded as director of Harvard's museum of comparative zoology. Alexander Agassiz, though having no particular personal animosity in this case, resented the intrusion of the survey into mining regions.

Hilary Herbert obtained from Agassiz sweeping criticisms of the work of the Geological Survey. Agassiz named many complaints but he harped on three of them: the Geological Survey had no business in economic geology, citing specifically the publications on the silver district of Colorado; the survey published wastefully large editions of books hav-

[9] *ibid.*, p. 30. See also *Science* (n.s.), Vol. 5, p. 51.

ing little or no use; and paleontology was something which the government should leave to individuals who would willingly do such work merely for the prestige of associating with a university or museum.[10]

Alexander Agassiz was a very wealthy man who owed his fortune to copper, and his sister Ida had married Henry Lee Higginson, Boston banker and founder of the Boston Symphony Orchestra. Mr. Agassiz could not examine the subject of mining geology through untinted glasses. While many mining companies cooperated fully with the survey, many others deliberately thwarted its work. The larger companies, usually controlled by financial interests in the East, were the least willing to share technical information. They were not anxious to see the federal government distributing information—especially theirs.

Clarence King had envisioned a "fruitful alliance" between the mining industry and the survey, believing that in such a relationship there would develop a wise use of the great natural resources and an increasing prosperity for all. It was still an age of exploitation but he had hoped that such an alliance might come to pass. Powell knew that only by vigilance and force can selfish men be made to conform to the law. He did not think in terms of copper, or silver, or timber, or water, but of protecting the natural resources "for the future generations."

Mr. Agassiz had munificently endowed the scientific work of the museum his father had founded and, like his father, fostered at Harvard one of the two or three foremost scientific centers of America. He could see no reason why the government should undertake the development of a scientific center in Washington; it was not a proper function of government.

All this made Mr. Herbert very happy. He agreed with Agassiz. Powell had no business publishing papers on iron and steel, extraction of copper from its ores, or refining petroleum, a resource which had no other use in America than for illumination and lubrication. If this was the proper function of the Geological Survey, "why not publish on blacksmithing and everything else?"

The Major had finished his testimony to the investigating committee before Hilary Herbert read from Agassiz' letters, and a reply was needed. In a prepared statement Powell challenged each criticism, and then generalized:

---

[10] There is some evidence that Cleveland had sought Agassiz' services to coordinate the scientific bureaus. See, for instance, G. R. Agassiz, ed., *Letters and Recollections of Alexander Agassiz*, p. 219.

. . . the economic results of the Survey are by no means confined to mining industries. Agriculture and Industry also are largely benefited thereby. It is investigating the flood-plain valleys of great rivers, like that of the Mississippi for the purpose of determining the conditions under which they can be redeemed. It is investigating the conditions under which the great arid regions may be most economically fertilized by irrigation. It is also investigating the conditions under which the great coast marshes and interior swamps may be drained and utilized. . . .

. . . a hundred millionaires could not do the work in scientific research now done by the General Government; and shall the work of scientific research and the progress of American civilization wait until the contagion of [Agassiz'] example shall inspire a hundred millionaires to engage in like good works? Before that time comes, scientific research will be well endowed by the people of the United States in the exercise of their wisdom and in the confident belief that knowledge is for the welfare of all of the people. If the General Government should do the work and pay for it from the public treasury, all that results from the expenditure should be given back to the people at large, through the agencies of the public libraries which they have established. To turn over all of this material to private societies or museums for publication, would be to defraud the people of that for which their money is expended.[11]

Throughout the duration of the investigation of federal research agencies, lively discussions of the merits of a federal Department of Science reached the press. The magazine *Science* carried weekly editorials and correspondence following each shift in the political winds. Hayden too declared in favor of a coordinated Department of Science. He circulated petitions to the great universities of the East and obtained replies with impressive lists of signers from Harvard, Massachusetts Institute of Technology, Yale, Princeton, and Columbia. Letters from individuals were solicited, and all possible influence was brought to bear on Congress to unify the administration of scientific work in the government.

Perhaps Hayden, Cope, and Frazer really believed that, by stirring up trouble, they would uncover dishonesty on the Major's part. It is more likely, however, that all they expected to accomplish was to establish a shadow of doubt or cast a cloud of suspicion on his character so that his tenure of office would be an embarrassment to the Department of the Interior. In either case they failed utterly.

A searching audit by the Department of the Treasury cleared Major Powell of any malpractice or complicity in fraud. The system by which the survey accounts were kept was publicly commended for its thorough-

---

[11] *Misc. Doc. 82, op. cit.,* pp. 1070–84, quotations on pp. 1079 and 1078, in order.

ness and accuracy. As for the other charges, they carried little weight. The authors had tried to hide behind anonymity. Since they declined to come out in the open and make direct accusations, the committee took no official notice of the charges. The interrogation was no whitewash. The Coast and Geodetic Survey was criticized in strong terms and several of its chief officials tendered their resignations.

The committee hearings were completed, and the printed testimony amounted to almost eleven hundred pages, but little came from the effort. The agitation among scientists on behalf of a Department of Science was abortive.[12] Neither the Congress nor the people were ready for such a department. The only immediate result was a clean bill for the Major's direction of the survey with an increase in his appropriation to more than $600,000.

The issue served another purpose; it brought into open flame the smoldering struggle by those members of the old Hayden and Wheeler surveys—mostly of Hayden's—who were left out of the Geological Survey to oust the Major from his powerful position. Powell now knew to what lengths his enemies would go to unseat him, but he refrained from any form of retaliation—he did not even drop Hayden from the survey. Perhaps Hayden was still too powerful to warrant an attempt. As for Cope, the Major continued to ignore him.

Heartened by the vote of confidence and with the assurance of additional funds, Powell returned to work. The administrative jobs were always done promptly and the Major had time for his other interests. In 1884 he attended the Montreal meeting of the British Association for the Advancement of Science, and while there expressed the opinion that a number of the wampum belts which were exhibited were not of Indian manufacture. This *ex cathedra* pronouncement caused quite a furor and the question did not die quickly. A few months later Mrs. Erminnie Smith sent a communication to *Science* to support Powell's view, explaining that a wampum factory was in operation at Paskack on the Hackensack River in New Jersey, and the Campbell brothers, who ran the establishment, were neither familiar with genuine wampum nor knew how the Indians worked the clam shells. One geologist in the survey, upon reading the article by Mrs. Smith, asked the Major how he had known the wampum belts were not made by Indians. He replied, "The tooling was not Indian." No further evidence was needed.

<hr>

[12] The recrudescence of agitation for federal patronage and centralization of research since 1945, culminating with the creation of the National Science Foundation, were in essence strangely similar to measures advocated in 1885.

Powell was gaining wide acclaim as an administrator of scientific work. He created opportunities for many scientists to work under conditions favorable for research and distributed publications of his departments liberally throughout the world on an exchange basis with other scientific organizations, and free to libraries which requested them. Thus the scientific results of the Geological Survey and the Bureau of Ethnology were shared in the spirit of cooperation.

In 1886 the University of Heidelberg, which possessed one of the most distinguished faculties of science in the world, awarded Major Powell an honorary degree. The citation shows how much European universities appreciated the practice of international scientific good will:

. . . we have conferred the rights and privileges of a doctor of philosophy, honoris causa, upon John Wesley Powell of Illinois heretofore chief of the public institution of ethnography, now of geology in the United States of America, who laboriously and wisely studying and surveying the vast and spacious regions of his own country with others, has scientifically observed and expounded the structure, form, and origin of the earth; and who has so associated with himself and brought together into one institution a great number of most distinguished geologists of his country that they have materially advanced or solved, not less wonderfully than speedily, very difficult and profound questions in mineralogy, petrography, geology, and paleontology. They have studied under his auspices as chief thereby causing these things not only to be most skillfully brought together but also to be communicated with the greatest liberality to all students of these subjects in Europe.[13]

It was more than coincidence that Harvard saw fit to include the Major among those distinguished men who received honorary degrees at the special convocation on the occasion of its two hundred and fiftieth anniversary on November 8, 1886. Powell left Washington with a delegation of scientists who also were going to the ceremony to receive degrees. The pomp and pageantry excelled anything the Major had ever witnessed. The graduates and the invited guests, in academic robes, assembled in the Yard in front of Gore Hall about 9:30 in the morning and marched in procession to Sanders Theater. President Cleveland arrived at 10:00 in a carriage drawn by four magnificent white horses preceded by mounted lancers. In accordance with tradition the sheriff of Middlesex County, in costume, called the assembly to order. After the preliminaries, James Russell Lowell delivered a short address, Oliver Wendell Holmes read a poem which he had written for the occasion, and President Eliot of Harvard bestowed the forty-two honorary degrees.

[13] This translation differs in slight detail from that generally given, *e.g.*, *Open Court*, Vol. 16, p. 716.

John Wesley Powell, whose citation read, "director of the United States Geological Survey, soldier, geologist, administrator," was inconspicuous even among the scientists who were thus honored. He was but one of fifteen, including Spencer Baird, Othniel C. Marsh, James Hall, James D. Dana, Joseph Leidy, John S. Billings, Samuel P. Langley, Asaph Hall, and Henry L. Abbott. Indeed, the roster looked like a roll call of the leading scientists of the country who were not on Harvard's faculty or previously honored by the college. Interesting too was the presence of Lucius Quintus Cincinnatus Lamar, Secretary of the Interior, who received a doctorate of laws.[14]

For the rest of the day the Major endured the eighteen speeches at the afternoon collation, had dinner with Professor Shaler, his host, and attended a reception in the evening at the Hemenway Gymnasium. Major Powell accepted the degree for what it was, a peace offering. He had no illusions. Powell was reassured that he had friends at Harvard and that the authorities either ignored the Agassiz incident or sought to minimize it.

Everything considered, 1886 had been a successful year. The survey had been strengthened by the investigation and the air had been cleared of nebulous rumors which had veiled some of its activities. Powell put more men and time into his pet projects, topography and irrigation, and allocated additional funds to each division of the work. He was formulating an estimate for an even greater appropriation for 1887–1888.

---

[14] I have considerable data on this peace offering. Powell's stanch friends at Harvard were Nathaniel Southgate Shaler and William Morris Davis. His old student, Samuel Garman, at the time on the staff of Harvard's museum of comparative zoology ("Agassiz Museum," as it is usually called in Boston), remained aloof of the controversy. However, Garman did defend the Major against the Cope charges. The Harvard College archives include the records of the commemoration.

19

1888-1891 · The Irrigation Survey

MAJOR POWELL's long maturing plans for an irrigation survey took a new lease on life when agitation for federal support of irrigation found an unexpected champion in Congress. In 1887 "Big Bill" Stewart of Nevada, after an absence of twelve years, returned to the Senate to fight for two causes—free silver and irrigation.[1]

At last the irrigation movement was gaining momentum. The ever-increasing pressure of population encroaching into marginal lands in the semiarid region brought into clear focus the fact that no more good land not needing irrigation was available to settlement. The Major had tried to make that point ten years before. Throughout the congressional investigation into the conduct of the federal scientific departments in 1884 and 1885 Powell repeated his warnings that the reclamation of additional land could be accomplished only by the investment of huge sums by private capital or by the federal government. Most of the small streams which could be diverted at moderate cost had already been developed and to redeem new areas the larger streams had to be utilized.

Settlers meant prosperity and irrigation meant reclamation of land for homesteaders. Under Stewart's leadership a coalition of western Congressmen started action.

In March 1888, through the efforts of this small group and useful behind-the-scenes cooperation by the Major, a joint resolution was adopted calling upon the Secretary of the Interior to "make an examination of that portion of the United States where agriculture is carried on by means of irrigation, as to the natural advantages for the storage of water for irrigation purposes with the practicability of constructing reservoirs, together with the capacity of streams, and the cost of construction and the capacity of reservoirs and such other facts as bear on the question." [2]

---

[1] W. M. Stewart, *Reminiscences*. See also the excellent review by E. W. Sterling in *Miss. Vall. Hist. Rev.*, Vol. 27, pp. 421–34.

[2] Senate resolution, Feb. 13, 1888; Powell's first communication, Feb. 13, 1888.

Major Powell, because he was virtually the only authority in the government service on the scientific aspects of irrigation and because of his prominence during many years in the agitation for a federal land policy, was naturally called upon to estimate the costs of an irrigation survey.

As director of the Geological Survey he had been able to devote considerable attention, both personally and through his scientific subordinates, to the gathering of information on sources of water, water flow in streams, rainfall, and evaporation. The topographic parties had been gathering soil samples and making soil maps in addition to their regular duties. Powell's expanding concept of the complex economy of water had gone beyond his view of 1878. In 1882 the Major realized that utilization for irrigation of the Missouri and other detritus-laden streams would furnish at least a partial solution to the serious engineering problems caused by floods and silting. The use of water for irrigation involved far more than arid land.

When the call for action came the Major, well aware of the trend of events, was ready. Through William F. Vilas, Secretary of the Interior, he sought an initial appropriation of $250,000 to implement an irrigation survey.[3]

More than a little maneuvering of the familiar variety was needed to obtain funds for the recommended survey. The clique, of which Stewart was the leader, attached a rider to the Sundry Appropriations Bill over the protest of the appropriation committee and succeeded in getting it through. By this move the committee on public lands, which would legitimately have had authority, was deprived of an opportunity to study and report on the measure.

In the House of Representatives an amendment providing that "all lands made susceptible of irrigation" by the reservoirs and canals be reserved was proposed by George Symes of Colorado. This proposal was obviously intended to prevent speculation in lands which might be benefited by irrigation and especially to prevent the organization of water companies which could later reap huge profits from homesteaders. There was considerable question as to the wisdom of this amendment and Symes himself attempted unsuccessfully to withdraw it. In accordance with congressional procedure the bill next went into conference to adjust differences, and it emerged with an additional amendment which authorized the President at his discretion to open any or all lands

---

[3] On March 29 Sec. of the Int. William F. Vilas transmitted several letters from Powell to the joint committee including his proposal for an initial appropriation of $250,000.

to entry. It was believed that with this safeguard any unforeseen situation could be met without difficulty.

On October 2, 1888, the bill, carrying a $100,000 appropriation and authorizing the irrigation survey under the Geological Survey, became law; Powell meantime had selected his subordinates.[4] Captain Dutton was designated to take charge of the engineering and hydrographic work and A. H. Thompson to head the topographical section. Field work was begun without delay in New Mexico, Colorado, Nevada, and Montana. The plan was to make a general topographic survey and to investigate water resources. Actually the topographic work was but a continuation of surveys already in progress.

During the latter part of October Dutton established a training camp on the Rio Grande River at Embudo, New Mexico. Here a corps of young technically trained men were instructed in the methods of measuring the flow of rivers and other hydrographic techniques to prepare them for independent work in the next season.[5]

In March of 1889 Congress appropriated an additional $250,000 and the irrigation survey began in earnest. By June the Major was ready to certify several reservoir sites for reservation: Clear Lake in California; Bear Lake in Utah; and another on the Rio Grande not far from the camp. The certification of irrigable lands was a much more complicated and difficult problem; titles had to be checked, surveys had to be made, and in many cases the reservoir sites had to be investigated first.

The fundamental difficulties involved in any kind of federal control of sources of water were brought forcibly into the picture soon after the irrigation survey began operations. The city council of El Paso, Texas, had sought Major Powell's advice concerning the erection of a dam to impound waters of the Rio Grande in flood season. The ranches in the vicinity had been parched during the dry seasons for several years and settlers on both sides of the river, in Texas and Mexico, were abandoning their lands. Local opinion blamed the lack of water upon settlements in Colorado and New Mexico—the river ran dry before it reached the arid country around El Paso.[6]

The situation was anomalous—or was it but one example of the complex history of the arid region? The Rio Grande rises from many tribu-

[4] U.S.G.S., *10th Ann. Rep.*, pp. 4–23. The appropriation implementing the irrigation work forced a complete reorganization of the Geological Survey. Despite the lateness in the season, field work was begun at once "so that by the end of the calendar year [1888] five considerable tracts of country have been surveyed."

[5] *ibid.*, pp. 19–22.

[6] See Anson Mills, *My Story;* also Mills, *Equitable Distribution of the Waters of the Rio Grande,* Vol. 2.

taries in the high mountains of southern Colorado and northern New Mexico, where torrential rains and heavy snows build up vast ice fields in the winter. Southward, precipitation diminishes rapidly for five or six hundred miles until at the Mexican boundary at El Paso the average annual rainfall is about eight inches. From there to the Gulf of Mexico, a distance of twelve hundred miles, precipitation barely compensates for normal evaporation. The flood season, which begins in May, lasts about two months, after which the river shrinks rapidly and in some years dries until the pools are too small to sustain fish.

Powell sent Capt. Clarence Dutton to El Paso to investigate the situation and examine a dam site which had been suggested by local interests. The project involved the construction of a stone and cement dam sixty feet high which would submerge an area roughly fifteen miles long and seven miles wide, impounding nearly four billion cubic yards of water.

Major Powell requested the War Department to assign to the El Paso district Gen. Anson Mills to assist the Geological Survey in the work of reclaiming the valley of the Rio Grande. E. S. Nettleton was appointed supervising engineer and funds were made available for employing engineers and assistants. The El Paso problem had international complications. For centuries the Mexicans had used and depended upon the waters of the Rio Grande to irrigate their lands. After considerable negotiation and no little surveying the United States agreed to construct a dam about three miles above the town.

Coincidently General Mills was transferred by order of the War Department to Fort Selden. An irrigation company had secured a license to construct a canal through the reservation at Las Cruces. The charter granted the right of the water company to construct its canal through and over the community canals of the settlements and compel the farmers to pay water rent. The Mexican farmers rose with arms to prevent by force, if necessary, building of the canal. Senator John Reagan of Texas, Mr. W. H. H. Llewellyn representing the Las Cruces irrigation company, General Mills, Dutton, Nettleton, Powell, and many others testified at hearings. As a result the charter was revoked and Llewellyn's men were ordered off the reservation. A few months later Llewellyn threatened General Mills, "If there is no new ditch at Las Cruces, there will be no new dam at El Paso." [7]

No dam was constructed at El Paso. When it was made known that the federal government had agreed to divide the water with Mexico, Dr. Nathan Boyd obtained a charter from New Mexico to build a simi-

[7] Anson Mills, *My Story*, pp. 261–62.

lar dam at Elephant Butte to impound the waters of the Rio Grande, compelling the United States to supply water to Mexico through his company. Although the dam at Elephant Butte was not built until 1906, the dispute with its far-reaching political ramifications involved the irrigation survey at a time it could ill afford embarrassment.

A peculiar situation confronted the people of the United States. Who owns the water? [8] Two opposing schools of thought have grown up in the arid regions. The California doctrine holds that the government was the original owner and that when states were admitted to the Union they were given certain sovereign or political rights but not government property. Thus the federal government still owns the flowing streams. The Colorado doctrine holds simply that the government surrendered its right to the water when the state was admitted. No decision by the Supreme Court has ever been made on this issue.

The Elephant Butte controversy had its basis in the Colorado doctrine. It was further complicated by the problem of deciding who has the right to use the water and how much. The fundamental controversy continues unabated to the present day. Nearly 670,000,000 acres of land still remain in the public domain, roughly one-third of the area of the United States. There is scarcely a river system in the semiarid region which does not flow through public lands, yet the utilization of such waters is hamstrung by state and sectional interests.

Meanwhile the survey was being hurried as much as possible. By June of 1889 the Major had certified almost a hundred and fifty reservoir sites, and selected for segregation more than 30,500,000 acres of irrigable lands.[9] Twelve clerks in the land office were checking the titles to these lands to eliminate the areas which had passed from government ownership before they were certified for reservation.

Nevertheless there were grumbling and rumbling of trouble. Some Congressmen hoped for immediate token results to satisfy constituents. Practically every delegate could name at least a few localities which were reputedly capable of irrigation and to which homesteaders would flock as soon as the land titles were officially cleared.

Powell believed that these protests from the West could be quieted by certification of a small number of restricted areas which could be opened by presidential proclamation. Even this, however, was an enormous task.

---

[8] The issue is exceedingly complex. See S. C. Weil, *Water Rights in the Western States,* Vol. 1; C. S. Kinney, *Law of Irrigation,* 2nd ed., Vol. 1.

[9] U.S.G.S., *10th Ann. Rep.,* p. viii.

During the mounting clamor the Major received an invitation from Senator Stewart to accompany the Senate select committee on irrigation on an inspection tour of the arid regions.[10] The journey was to begin on August 1st, the itinerary including Minnesota, the Dakotas, Montana, Idaho, Washington, Oregon, and a return eastward through California, Nevada, Arizona, Colorado, and Kansas.

The party paused for a few days at Bismarck to attend the North Dakota constitutional convention, and on the spur of the moment the Major was asked to make a few pertinent comments. On Monday, August 5th, Major Powell stood before the convention and apologized that he had never in his life made a political speech and then proceeded to make some practical comments on irrigation. He reminded his listeners that in eastern Dakota there is sufficient rainfall for agriculture, in the western part permanent dependence on irrigation, and in the middle a region of great danger. The Major went on:

Years will come of abundance and years will come of disaster, and between the two the people will be prosperous and unprosperous, and the thing to do is look the question squarely in the face. . . .

You hug to yourselves the delusion that the climate is changing. This question is 4,000 years old. Nothing that man can do will change the climate. . . . There's almost enough rainfall for your purposes, but one year with another you need a little more than you get. . . . There are waters rolling by you which are quite ample to redeem your land and you must save these waters. . . .

You are to depend hereafter in a great measure on the running streams—in a small part on your artesian wells, and in part on the storage of storm waters.

Don't let these streams get out of the possession of the people . . . take lessons from California and Colorado. Fix it in your constitution that no corporation—no body of men—no capital can get possession of the right of your waters. Hold the waters in the hands of the people.[11]

The delegates applauded courteously, but this was not the harangue they wanted to hear.

No one knew better than Major Powell that the West as a whole had been enjoying a cycle of increased rainfall. Gilbert had determined beyond doubt that Salt Lake was increasing in size; the measured increase in annual rainfall in Kansas, for instance, averaged from three to five inches per year, amounting to a fifteen per cent gain over a period of fifteen years. But such changes come in cycles. Many persons believed that the establishment of settlements and tillage had brought about a permanent change in climate. They had been deluded into believing

[10] U.S.G.S., *Letters Received*, Nat. Archives, June 17, 1889.
[11] This is probably Powell's most famous speech. It has been reprinted many times, the most accessible being in *Reclamation Era*, Vol. 26, pp. 201–2.

that somehow rainfall moved westward with population, that "rainfall follows the plow."

Ten years before, the Major had described the shifting and mysterious boundary, approximating the ninety-seventh parallel, beyond which all efforts at settlement without irrigation would be disastrous. Thousands of copies of his monograph on arid regions generously distributed at federal expense had been read and put aside—for future reference.

Stewart and the Major did not see eye to eye on the problems of the arid regions, and the longer they traveled together the more they chafed each other. Powell estimated that 90,000,000 acres could be reclaimed by irrigation; the public lands commission estimated that only 30,000,000 could be redeemed. The Major's idea of the part government should take in withholding and regulating lands of the public domain was the last thing on earth Stewart wanted. Stewart wanted the government to give away irrigated or irrigable lands; Powell wanted the government to regulate the water. Regardless of the outcome, Stewart's constituents, the cattlemen in particular, demanded continued unrestricted use of the public domain.

Back in Washington the members of the committee were plunged into a brewing conflict over the kind of irrigation survey the Major had in progress. Trying to please diverse interests was trouble enough, but when the land office muddled the whole business, the confusion became hopeless.

By unexplainable oversight—or deliberate evasion—the General Land Office continued its business unmindful of the law. No notice of the act closing the public lands had been distributed to the hundreds of local offices until mid-August, fully ten months after its enactment. Meantime, speculators trailed the federal surveying parties and in plain view of the surveyors staked claims on prospective reservoir and canal sites. The flagrant disregard of the law around Bear Lake was so scandalous that the Idaho constitutional convention protested to the Secretary of the Interior. Their resolution brought immediate action when Secretary Vilas notified the land office to halt the practice promptly.[12]

William M. Stone, who was at the time acting commissioner of the land office, thereupon ordered the local offices to cancel all claims filed after October 2, 1888. This action aroused the ire of nearly every Congressman from the western states and they clamored for an immediate reversal of the order. As a result patents were issued again with warn-

[12] *51st Cong. 1st Sess. Sen. Rep. 1466.* See also *Land Office Rep., 1890,* p. 63. Cleveland's attitude is evident in his annual message delivered on Dec. 3, 1888.

ings to each claimant that the patent was at his own risk and might be invalidated. This was an unsatisfactory expedient and patents were closed a few weeks later. L. E. Groff took office as commissioner in September and, faced with the controversy, sought the opinion of the Attorney General.

Now the trouble really started. William Henry Taft, the Attorney General, and President Cleveland interpreted the act in the same way: all claims filed after October 2, 1888 must be invalidated. Powell had not yet designated any sites for settlement; in fact the boundaries of the arid regions were not even defined. It was apparent that Cleveland had no intention of opening any lands by presidential proclamation. The amendments to the act, originally intended to safeguard the public domain, caused a virtual repeal of all the existing land laws operating from roughly the hundredth parallel to the Pacific Ocean—embracing all or part of sixteen states and territories.

To add to the confusion the General Land Office estimated that since the date of the act 134,000 entries had been filed on 900,000 acres of land, and a large number of water and irrigation companies had been organized during the preceding two years.

In Congress the pressure was on to repeal the offending clauses. Three bills with this intent were introduced into the House and another, prepared by the committee on public lands, was reported in the Senate. Friend and foe of the irrigation survey awaited with interest the Major's first annual report of progress.

Powell, serenely disregarding the controversy, gave a synopsis of the irrigation problem as he saw it.[13] The area of the arid region was estimated to be 1,300,000 square miles; this is about one-third the total area of the United States. Of this only 150,000 square miles, barely eleven per cent, can be reclaimed, but "this is an empire one half as large as the entire cultivated area of the United States." Assuming irrigated land to be worth thirty dollars per acre—a minimum indeed—reclamation would add almost three billion dollars to the national wealth.

Pursuing this long-range view, Powell explained that, in expending the $100,000 appropriation of 1888 and the $250,000 appropriation of 1889, he had "interpreted the law, not as authorizing construction of irrigation works but only as directing a comprehensive investigation of prevailing conditions."[14] The conditions to which he referred were the whereabouts of irrigable lands most eligible for redemption and home-

[13] U.S.G.S., *10th and 11th Ann. Rep.*, especially 10th, pt. 2, pp. i–viii, 1–96.
[14] U.S.G.S., *10th Ann. Rep.*, pt. 2, pp. vi–viii, 2–8.

stead settlement, the amount of available water, the location of reservoir and canal sites, seepage, evaporation, the vested rights and how to maintain them, and generally the most economical method for bringing water to the land. "The future development of irrigation depends upon," the Major argued, "first, the utilization of large streams hitherto largely unused because of great cost; second, the construction of storage dams; third, the construction of storm water reservoirs; and, fourth, controlling the entire flow of smaller streams." He cautioned about "obstructing vested rights," and while recognizing their legality, insisted that they must not be permitted to stand in the way of permanent progress.

The western Senators were not satisfied with the progress of the Powell irrigation survey. Eighty per cent of the initial appropriation had been spent for topographic work. Some of them had begun to criticize the Major almost as soon as the work had been initiated and long before the Attorney General closed the public domain. Powell's unequivocal interpretation of the law angered them all the more. This business could continue for several years before irrigation works would benefit anybody. Yet no construction program could be launched without prior field work.

While wrangling continued in Congress, the surveys were busily engaged in five states. In the third annual report [15] for the fiscal year ending June 30, 1891, Thompson listed 147 reservoir sites which had been surveyed: forty-six in Colorado, thirty-nine in New Mexico, thirty-three in California, twenty-seven in Montana, and two in Nevada. Their combined area equaled 165,932 acres capable of irrigating "not less than 1,423,917 acres of crops." Thompson added, "it must not be supposed that all of these will be constructed or even that all of them are of sufficient value to warrant great expenditure."

Ridicule came from many quarters. Some Congressmen objected that their states were classed as arid; others from humid districts complained that no irrigation funds were being expended in their districts.

Cope said, "Powell has fastened upon the government a department of irrigation by which he proposed to dam the grand canyon of the Colorado River." [16]

Bona fide homesteaders did not protest against the irrigation survey nor even the temporary closing of the public domain. The pressure came from concerns like the Miller empire, which held a million acres of land,

[15] U.S.G.S., *12th Ann. Rep.*, pt. 2.
[16] New York *Herald*, Jan. 12, 1890, p. 10. This was said in ridicule and sarcasm, but Powell had seriously discussed the possibility, naming Black and Boulder canyons as likely sites.

much of it obtained through crafty purchasing and fraudulent filing of claims.[17]

The Senate select committee on irrigation, with Stewart making the charges, accused the Major of misappropriating the funds of the survey, arguing that all topographical work should have been paid for from regular Geological Survey funds, especially since the topographic work under Thompson was obviously a continuation of surveying already in progress before the establishment of an irrigation survey.

The select committee was split over the testimony presented to it. The majority, with of course Stewart in the front, made a bitter denunciation of the Major's administration of the survey. Dutton and Nettleton admitted to the committee that they personally had questioned the legality of their chief's use of irrigation funds for topographic work. The minority of the committee, John Reagan, A. P. Gorman, and James K. Jones, defended Powell not only on his management of funds but also on the grounds that a scientific survey, regardless of inevitable delays, was the only means of forestalling in western America landlordism of the kind known in Ireland.

Of course, the controversy was nothing more than a disagreement on whether the irrigation survey should be a detailed long-term investigation or whether it should be a practical reconnaissance to survey and certify lands which were already known to be promising.

Furthermore, Congress had no intention of sitting by while one man literally had control of both irrigation and the opening of public lands. Actually the operation of the act, according to the opinion of the Attorney General, placed Major Powell in this position, and for the next ten years, perhaps more, he would have these responsibilities. The land office would have no authority to carry out the laws after sites designated by Powell had been opened by presidential proclamation.

In the midst of the quarrel the region of the great plains, the region most concerned with the outcome, was visited with the most disastrous drought the West had known. The rains failed; under scorching heat farms and orchards withered to dust; springs, creeks, and even rivers disappeared leaving empty channels studded with stones. Ruined despairing settlers looked to the heavens and to Washington. Both failed in the moment of need.

The disaster put purpose into the irrigation movement. William E. Smythe began a series of educational articles in the *Omaha Bee,* and a

---

[17] See E. F. Treadwell, *The Cattle King;* also *51st Cong. 2nd Sess. H.R. Rep. 3767,* pp. 4–7.

few months later a state convention on irrigation gathered at Lincoln, Nebraska. Smythe was elected chairman and plans for calling a national convention were immediately formulated, whereupon he resigned from the *Bee*, launched the *Irrigation Age*, and organized the first irrigation congress at Salt Lake City.[18]

The Major emerged from all the excitement with enhanced reputation. The statements in his writings and speeches had furnished a scientific appraisal of the true character of arid America. Had he not predicted this very situation? But Powell's opinions did not concur with the hopes of practical politicians or those impractical enthusiasts who wanted to water every square mile of the dry lands.

During the committee tour of the previous summer the Major won ardent support from Senators Reagan and Gorman for his knowledge of irrigation, but at the same time he antagonized Stewart by his uncompromising attitude—and the dislike was mutual. These petty disagreements between two strong but different personalities soon grew into Stewart's open hostility. The Major did not fight back, depending upon his friends to hold the situation under control.

Stewart tried to win support by writing round-robin letters to his friends and colleagues insinuating that the Major, "ambitious to manage the whole subject of irrigation without regard to the views of others, induced the Interior Department to withdraw vast regions of the public lands preparatory to the selection of the necessary sites." [19] Stewart was thoroughly familiar with the events which led to closure of the lands and such statements were deliberate distortion of the facts.

Stewart tried for a time to get the irrigation survey transferred to the Department of Agriculture, but upon the advice of colleagues abandoned the plan. It was feared that Powell's influence was too great and such an attempt might result in a complete halt of irrigation work.

In April, in order to ignore the Major, an artesian survey was established under the direction of the Department of Agriculture rather than under the Geological Survey. There had been considerable agitation for drilling artesian wells in Kansas, Nebraska, and South Dakota and the clamor was partially satisfied by this move.

[18] W. E. Smythe is best known as the author of *The Conquest of Arid America*.

[19] W. M. Stewart, *Reminiscences,* p. 349. This is mild compared with letters to political colleagues. Even after Powell's death, Stewart vulturously picked the bones: "if it were not for President Roosevelt and his ninny friends who have hoodwinked the agricultural press and the Republicans of the North, we should eradicate the memory of Major Powell and his grandiose irrigation schemes." I am permitted to quote this excerpt but not the name of the recipient. Although this course is somewhat unfair to Stewart, the incident shows the lingering hatred of political animosities.

The creation of an artesian survey defiantly ignored the collective work of the Geological Survey. As early as 1877 the Major held artesian wells to be an unimportant source of water, at best useful in restricted areas. Later, in 1882 he assigned T. C. Chamberlin to investigate artesian waters with respect to irrigation. The results of that work were published in the fifth annual report, 1883–1884. If there had been room for doubt it should have been dispelled then.

Artesian wells do not manufacture water. They do not even bring to the surface as much water as goes down from the surface. The total rainfall of a region is not, therefore, increased by them. They merely pour out at one point that which has fallen elsewhere. If the total fall is inadequate to the agricultural wants of the total region, artesian wells cannot make it adequate. They may concentrate a sufficient supply upon a part but cannot supply the whole. The inadequacy of artesian wells under these conditions is apparent. Only very temperate hopes can be built.[20]

Two years earlier, another associate of the Geological Survey, C. A. White, had shown that irrigation by artesian wells under conditions of high aridity are of very limited value.

It was obvious that Powell had initiated irrigation studies almost as soon as he had gained control of the survey, and had pursued a varied program of investigation. Now, when the Major hauled out his artillery and trained the guns on proponents of artesian wells, he was well supplied with ammunition. But it was of no use. Farmers of the drought-stricken states were disappointed and political enemies chided the Major for his sour-grapes attitude.

During the summer of 1890, the summer of disastrous drought which crushed farmers throughout the great plains states, the first assault upon the law on which the irrigation survey was founded achieved a measure of success by an amendment to the Sundry Civil Appropriations Bill signed into law on August 30, 1890. The amended act reduced the $700,000 proposed by the House for topographic work west of the 101st meridian to $162,500. Although mapping of reservoir sites was continued, no mention of hydrography was included. By this simple trick hydrographic work became dependent upon regular Geological Survey funds. At the same time the appropriation for the land office was increased to facilitate settlement.

For all practical purposes the irrigation survey was discontinued when hydrography was eliminated and the appropriation for topography curtailed. The real work remained undone. The federal irrigation

[20] U.S.G.S., *5th Ann. Rep.*, p. 148.

survey had been but a small beginning which, though accomplishing a rapid reconnaissance, had of course constructed nothing. Now public interest had to be kept alive and the true picture of the arid regions described convincingly.

First of all the Major's boys, as he called them, had to be provided for. Most of them were transferred to divisions of the regular Geological Survey—Arthur Davis, Newell, Hill, Lippincott, and the others. Their experience would assuredly be called upon later and a trained staff must not be scattered. The men were enabled to complete their investigations, and gradually the first numbers of a long series of distinguished water-supply papers appeared as a tangible result of the Powell irrigation survey.

Nevertheless the irrigation movement grew. This time it was not Powell who put power in it; the catastrophic drought of 1890 did that. The irrigation movement mushroomed with the optimism of its loudest proponents. International irrigation congresses under the leadership of William E. Smythe of Utah and Col. R. J. Hinton of New Mexico made rapid strides toward organizing public opinion. By 1893 the international congress was ready to act upon resolutions calling for the federal government in cooperation with private capital to make "a million forty-acre farms" by irrigating lands in the public domain. On October 10th, under auspicious circumstances, several hundred delegates from more than twenty states and territories and a dozen foreign countries gathered in Los Angeles to adopt a program of action. In the enthusiasm of the moment common sense was thrown to the winds. The delegates to the congress were about to proclaim the "Republic of Irrigation" and "inscribe upon its massive arch those two synonymous terms Irrigation and Independence." [21]

The Major gasped at this outburst of unjustified optimism, coming as it did from men of intelligence. Powell, billed as the eminent director of the U.S. Geological Survey, had been invited to address the convention on "The Water Supplies of the Arid Region," but he decided on the spur of the moment not to present it and instead bring the delegates to their senses. "I shall tell you a few facts about the arid region." Before many minutes passed there was the buzz of dissatisfaction in the audience. The delegates were horrified and disappointed. The clamor increased until the speaker was interrupted from the floor.

I wish to make clear to you . . . there is not enough water to irrigate all the lands . . . there is not sufficient water to irrigate all the lands which could be

[21] Int. Irr. Cong., *Proc.*, 1893, pp. 106–7.

irrigated . . . only a small portion can be irrigated. . . . It is not right to speak about the area of the public domain in terms of acres that extend over the land, but in terms of acres that can be supplied with water. . . . Gentlemen, it may be unpleasant for me to give you these facts. I hesitated a good deal . . . but finally concluded to do so. . . . A few years ago the question arose whether all these lands could be turned over to cattlemen for cattle ranges. . . . I spoke again and again, begging that these lands might be held for irrigation, that the lands should not be turned over to individuals for cattle ranges . . . the people howled at me because I wasn't interested in the broad-horn problem. Now you are speaking for irrigation. . . . What matters it whether I am popular or unpopular? I tell you gentlemen you are piling up a heritage of conflict and litigation over water rights for there is not sufficient water to supply the land.[22]

Mr. Smythe of Utah cried out, addressing the Major, "Why do you admire our platform? We have said we have homes for a million more people—you say we have not." [23] The Mexican delegate, with evident enjoyment, characterized the proceedings by saying, "it was the only bullfight I have seen in this country."

The truth was that the people, even their leaders, still had grossly inaccurate knowledge of the semiarid regions. Major Powell had prophesied the disaster of drought just a year before it occurred, but he had merely repeated his earlier prophecy of 1878. Powell had described the mysterious boundary line of dependable rainfall, but no one listened. Now the multitude of people who had been caught in the misfortune grabbed for straws: artesian wells, a shelter belt of trees planted along the ninety-seventh meridian, setting off of explosions in the heavens, and what not.

In his attempt to present the facts, the Major wrote three articles for *Century Illustrated Monthly,* "The Irrigable Lands of the Arid Region," "The Non-irrigable Lands of the Arid Region," "Institutions for the Arid Lands," and a half dozen other broadsides for various periodicals.[24]

Major Powell could view the problem of the arid regions in 1890 with much broader implications than in 1878. He envisioned a unified federal land policy embracing eight interrelated problems:

1. The reclamation of 100,000,000 acres of land to be utilized for agriculture and grazing;

2. The formulation of laws to provide for the distribution of land among the people. The existing laws were obsolete and inadequate;

---

[22] *ibid.,* pp. 111–12.

[23] *ibid.,* p. 112.

[24] These appeared in *Century Illustrated Monthly Magazine, Public Opinion, The Independent, Western America, Harper's Weekly,* and *North American Review.*

3. The equitable division of the waters among the states. Again there were no laws to implement such a division. The laws of the various "arid" states were in conflict;

4. The distribution of water so "that each man may have the amount necessary to fertilize his farm";

5. The preservation of the forests for timber and the protection of forests from fire in order to protect the sources of water;

6. The protection and intelligent utilization of the grasslands between the irrigable lands and the forests;

7. The conservation of mineral deposits, which "must be kept ready to the hand of industry and the brain of enterprise";

8. The construction of power dams and the industrial utilization of water power.

A thousand millions of money must be used; who shall furnish it? Great and many industries are to be established; who shall control them? Millions of men are to labor; who shall employ them? This is a great nation, the Government is powerful; shall it engage in this work? . . .

This, then, is the proposition I make: that the entire arid region be organized into natural hydrographic districts, each one to be a commonwealth within itself for the purpose of controlling and using the great values which have been pointed out. . . . Each community should possess its own irrigation works; it would have to erect diverting dams, dig canals and construct reservoirs; and such works would have to be maintained from year to year. The plan is to establish local self-government by hydrographic basins.[25]

In 1893 the *Irrigation Age* printed an enlarged version of the paper Powell had intended to give at the Los Angeles meeting of the international congress. The first part, "The Water Supplies in the Arid Region," described the sources of supply and the uses of water. In this article the Major called the water gathered into streams, "run-off," and that lost by evaporation, "fly-off." Although the latter term did not meet acceptance, "run-off" has become familiar. The second article, "Ownership of Lands in the Arid Region," gave more evidence of the inconsistencies in federal policies toward the arid and semiarid regions. Remedial measures, long overdue, were apparently still a long way off.

In another article the Major blasted the hopes of those who placed faith in the unwarranted claims of promoters:

[25] *Century Illustrated Monthly*, Vol. 40, pp. 111–16. I have deliberately given an incomplete quotation following item 8 in the list. Powell added, "I say to the Government: Hand's Off! Furnish the people with institutions of justice, and let them do the work for themselves." (p. 113). The Major conceded that only government capital could accomplish the task.

There are those who would control the rains and change the clouds by boring artesian wells; there are those who would control the clouds by planting trees and preserving forests; there are those who would change the climate by building railroads, and there are those who would control the rains by bombarding the heavens with popgun balloons. When you meet with one of these men you may always know that a devilfish has seized him. Such errors often have a subtle power over the mind by reason of the modicum of truth which they contain. . . .

It has been the dream of mankind to control the clouds. Savage men dance for rain, and beat drums, and deck altars with the plumes of birds, and smoke pipes to create mimic clouds, and make offerings of meal to the wind gods, and perform long dramatic ceremonies as they pray for rain. All savage tribes thus seek to govern the clouds with terpsichorean worship. . . . Barbarians add costly offerings . . . more civilized people add confessions on belief. . . . But terpsichorean, sacrificial and fiducial agencies fail to change the desert into the garden, or transform the flood-storm into a refreshing shower. Years of drought and famine come and years of flood and famine come, and the climate is not changed with dance, libation or prayer.[26]

Powell's prophecy of recurrent catastrophic droughts in the semi-arid region remains—not entirely, but largely—unheeded.

[26] "Our Recent Floods," *North American Review*, Vol. 155, pp. 149–59, quotation from pp. 151–53. In this article Powell pleaded for extension of the U.S. Weather Bureau, particularly in forecasting flood and storm warning services, and of course for the hydrographic and topographic services of the Geological Survey.

20

1886-1891 · Life in Washington

THE irrigation conflict had uncovered to the public gaze an anomalous power in the hands of one individual. The director of the Geological Survey had the authority—the director called it an "obligation"—to produce a geological map of the United States. There was nothing wrong in that. No other nation had attempted a mapping project of such magnitude; no other nation had a greater need for an adequate map of its territory. The issue was not the project but the method. Major Powell used every conceivable device within his power. He had entered into agreements with state legislatures for cooperative mapping without the prior consent of Congress and by rubber-stamp methods gained subsequent approval for accomplished facts. He had diverted—even Dutton admitted that—a portion of the irrigation survey's appropriation for topographic surveying. Legally Powell acted within his authority, but it was dangerous. Gilbert too cautioned the Major that he was stretching political patience to a breaking point. Nevertheless, the mapping was to proceed, and what a project it was!

The area of the United States, exclusive of Alaska, is more than three million square miles. Mapping a territory of such magnitude involved technical difficulties which could not be anticipated, but even these were outweighed by other problems. The cost would be heavy. Since it would have to be paid by the federal treasury and thus by all the people the map, Powell argued, "should meet the wants of the greatest number of persons."

The map would have to show the areal geology of the country, but although this would be its prime function, it must aid in the study of river drainage systems, irrigation, artesian waters, catchment areas for the supply of water to cities, drainage of swamps, soils, classification of lands for agricultural purposes, and in the laying of highways, railroads, and canals.

The technical difficulties were overcome with surprising ingenuity.

A small astronomic and computing division determined geographic coordinates of certain primary points, a triangulation corps extended a system of triangulation over various portions of the country from measured base lines, while a topographic corps organized into twenty-seven parties scattered over the United States performed the detailed surveying and plane-table mapping. The hypsometric work was based upon the multiplicity of elevation levels determined by the numerous railroad surveys. The topographic corps were assigned to five principal divisions: north Atlantic, south Atlantic, Rocky Mountain, Great Basin, and Pacific. The vast plains region was intentionally disregarded, because it was of relatively simple topographic form.

There were two distinct mapping projects: a complete detailed topographic map of the United States—a staggering job—and a geological map of the country. Obviously the two were interrelated and a final geological map was simply visionary.

Early in the summer of 1883 Major Powell unfolded to McGee the plan for a preliminary geological map of the United States and placed the immediate responsibility for its execution on his shoulders. "Mc-Gee," he said, "I know what I want; you know what I want. Figure a way to do it before next March." [1] There were many state and regional maps, each with its own scale, symbolism, notation, and terminology. Out of this confusion McGee had to compile a preliminary map and a dictionary of geological names.

Following many conferences and informal discussions the idea congealed, and during November Powell instructed McGee to prepare a manuscript hand-colored map and have it ready in time for the annual fiscal skirmish. Professor Edward Hitchcock of Amherst was assigned to the project and drafting began. Two months later, to the pride of the chief, the map was finished.[2] Drawn to a scale of 1:7,115,000 (about 112.3 miles to the inch) and based upon unpublished as well as published maps, it was unavoidably generalized. Owing to inaccuracies in the source maps and to insufficient data and because there were still unexplored regions, many areas were left uncolored: Arizona, California, Idaho, Montana, Nevada, New Mexico, Oregon, Texas, Utah, and Washington. The canyon country, of which Powell knew more than any other man of his time—and probably since—embraced all or part

[1] Klotho McGee Lattin.

[2] The map used the color scheme devised by Powell and the classification of an earlier but unpublished map drawn by Hitchcock. The survey map was published in the *5th Ann. Rep.* Hitchcock subsequently published his map with his own color scheme.

of seven of these: an area of 245,000 square miles, equal to one-thirteenth of the area of the United States.

Powell secured the collaboration of several states to speed up the topographic mapping. In 1884 the Massachusetts legislature appropriated forty thousand dollars, available over a period of three years, to cooperate with the United States Geological Survey in mapping the state. The federal survey, the Major agreed, would allocate an equal sum.

Direct cooperation in topographic work was arranged between the Geological Survey and the states of New York, New Jersey, Pennsylvania, and Rhode Island, and close collaboration with the state surveys of North Carolina, Kentucky, and Alabama.[3] Powell had written in his annual report for 1884–1885, "The Director is doing all within his power to revive State Surveys . . . the best results can be accomplished only by the labors of many scientific men engaged for a long term of years."

The Major's procedure in all these negotiations was simple. In unofficial conversations with delegations of influential geologists of the various states, the parties explored probable costs and weighed the possibilities of political opposition. Then the Major pledged half of the estimated costs on condition that the respective legislatures would appropriate the rest. Needless to say, this practice would have been highly irregular had not Powell enjoyed complete legal control over the disbursement of the Geological Survey funds.

By the combination of these methods field work progressed at a rate of approximately 50,000 square miles per year, a figure considerably more impressive because the work covered regions of rough terrain and intricate geological structure. At the close of the fiscal year 1887–1888, a total of 306,140 square miles had been mapped at a cost of slightly more than three dollars an acre. At this rate, a complete survey of the country would take a century.[4]

The members of the topographic division of the Geological Survey were not unanimous in approving the Major's grandiose plan. Besides

[3] The "official" transactions of the various cooperative state programs are adequately reviewed in *Ann. Rep. 4th–12th* especially *9th* (Massachusetts), and *10th* (Rhode Island). The New York State Museum provided me with a complete set of transcripts of letters from Powell to Hall pertaining to the geological survey of New York. Hall's correspondence is preserved in the National Archives.

[4] As early as 1884 during the hearings of the congressional committee the rate of mapping was severely questioned (*49th Cong. 1st Sess. Sen. Doc. 82*, pp. 41–43) ; by 1892 the criticism had increased (*Cong. Rec.*, Vol. 23, pt. 5, p. 4377).

the risky agreements with state legislatures, which were understandably criticized by poor and sparsely settled states, and the questionable use of irrigation funds for topographic work, there was disagreement over the mapping and cartographic methods used by the survey.

The cartographic system (symbols, scales, colors, classifications, etc.) adopted in the survey maps had been devised by Powell and published by him in the second annual report a few months after he had succeeded King. It was this scheme which had been communicated to the international congress of geologists at Bologna in 1881. The system was used and tested during the ensuing years until 1889. Meanwhile many improvements in cartography had been made both in the United States and in Europe, and a wide divergence of opinion as to the merits of the system developed in the survey staff itself. It is no exaggeration that no two individuals in the organization held the same opinion.

Recognizing that there would be disruption if differences on fundamental concepts were not discussed in the open, Powell, on December 7, 1888, issued a circular posing thirty-one questions for discussion—questions pertaining to color schemes, notation, nomenclature, and unit of publication. Then during the last three days of February 1889 a conference of some twenty geologists thrashed out the whole business. The group adopted a revised system (a modification of Powell's earlier scheme) which was fully described and illustrated in detail in the tenth annual report, 1888–1889.

Seldom did the Major formally acknowledge the assistance of his colleagues; less often did he claim special credit for his own work. The exceptional pride with which he released the cartographic system is rather unexpected:

While this subject has been one of constant study by the Director for many years, he is indebted to his colleagues on the Survey for much careful experimentation and many valuable suggestions. He is especially indebted to Messrs. Gilbert and McGee, to whom the subject in all its parts and in all stages of investigation has been referred from time to time. Mr. Gilbert has supervised the experiments and selected the specific patterns in the several classes. Mr. McGee and Mr. Darton have collected from the cartographic literature of geology the symbols used in Europe and America and systematized the same for convenient examination. Mr. Holmes in the earlier years and Mr. Gill in the later have rendered efficient service as experts in the use of color. While drawing on all possible sources and receiving great aid from others, the Director is alone responsible for the final plan.[5]

[5] U.S.G.S., *10th Ann. Rep.*, p. 79.

The Major's control over his department was complete. Criticism and complaint he would consider and at times accept, but he was always master of the situation. The administration of his own bureaus, compared with the turmoil of politics, was tranquil. Powell's conspicuously successful handling of his bureaus, of congressional committees and state legislatures, engendered the belief that he was a powerful politician. In some respect Powell was a shrewd politician; in others an unwary one. Depending so largely upon his own judgment and resources, he was always potentially vulnerable. The affairs of the survey were inextricably enmeshed in national politics. The Major's strength centered in individuals, with whom he dealt in honesty, dignity, and good humor.

Good humor, kindness and friendliness were natural facets of Powell's character; contrarily, malice and vindiction were foreign to it. When the Major cast his bread upon the waters, it was returned buttered, usually on both sides. Sometime during 1875 Powell met Col. C. E. Hooker, a Representative from Mississippi who had lost his left arm in the battle of Vicksburg.[6] Amused that their hands were of the same size, they joked about the extravagance of buying two pairs of gloves when one would suffice. They agreed that henceforth whenever either purchased a pair of gloves he would send the unnecessary mate to the other. Hooker served in Congress over a period of thirty years with but two brief interruptions. Even during these interims the glove exchange was continued. Another instance is in the same spirit. Rep. D. B. Henderson, who had lost a leg in the war, suffered from a serious recurrent malady. Daily during his convalescence Powell drove Henderson, if the weather was clement, into the countryside.[7] Henderson, a member of the appropriations committee, later became Speaker of the House and Powell had, of course, an ally. It would be ridiculous to imply that friendships with Henderson and Hooker, especially in their freshmen years in Congress, had been cultivated with cool calculation, though it would be naive to ignore their influence.

Powell enjoyed appearing before congressional committees to present his views and to plead for his appropriations. There was something in the contest which satisfied his love of personal combat. Committee temper determined his strategy. Often it was necessary to use

---

[6] The long-standing friendships of Powell with Hooker and Henderson were public as well as intimate. Practically every survivor of the old days of the Geological Survey who I interviewed or with whom I corresponded mentioned these friendships and the advantage thereby accrued to the survey.

[7] D. B. Henderson, Wash. Acad. Sci., *Proc.*, Vol. 5, pp. 104–5.

artful persuasion, but when the votes were assured, the Major would have his restrained fun. In 1888 a solid majority of the members of the appropriations committee were behind the proposed budget for the Geological Survey, although two were emphatically opposed. One of them, to have his say, proposed a cut rather than an increase in the appropriation. Major Powell rose dramatically, nodded to the chairman, and said, "I am afraid I have not made my point clear. May I address the committee?" Then he began a lecture on the geology of the Laramie region, with tiresome quotations from Lester Ward's latest bulletin, having not the slightest bearing upon the appropriation. For nearly two hours Powell spoke with theatrical enthusiasm while the committee sat in silent boredom. Finally the chairman interrupted, saying that he was sorry time would not allow the director "to continue his interesting discourse" much longer. The Major apologized for having "taken up so much valuable time." The meeting was adjourned immediately. Gleefully Powell hurried back to the office to let the boys in on his little joke.[8]

It was necessary for the Major to court the cooperation of Congressmen in many ways without compromising himself. The most convenient—and effective—method of side bargaining was the employment of "Senators' nephews." Nearly all of these fellows were young relatives or friends of Congressmen who could be given temporary work with the summer field parties as rodmen or camp assistants. The practice was unavoidable but it caused some embarrassment. The Major could call a spade a spade. In the annual report for the fiscal year 1884–1885 he explained carefully how persons were hired for temporary work as well as how men were selected for the regular staff of the survey, adding, "if the improper persons are employed, it is wholly the Director's fault." [9]

Not one of the scientific or responsible positions however was filled by political appointment. Powell saw to that. Nepotism of another kind he could indulge with complacency. Harry Thompson, a brother-in-law, had served him faithfully since 1867 and had justifiably been brought into the survey when Powell became director in 1881. In 1882 nephew Arthur Powell Davis, fresh from Kansas State Normal University, joined the force as an assistant topographer. Soon afterward Harry's cousin, Robert Thompson, was appointed to the survey. As for the Major's loyal former associates, Jack Hillers, Lester Ward, Clarence

---

[8] Related to W. C. Darrah by Bailey Willis.
[9] U.S.G.S., *6th Ann. Rep.*, pp. xxv–xxvi.

Dutton, Joseph Stanley-Brown and John Pilling (and a dozen or so more) were placed on the staff.[10] Later experience demonstrated that each one of these men was far above average in ability and industry and their appointments were, from these fair standards, above reproach.

While Major Powell was mollifying Congressmen and, as critics challenged, building a staff "loyal to their chief," his men were trying to show that loyalty by beguiling Senators' daughters. The social amenities of Washington are such that the bureaucrats do not ordinarily mingle socially with the best families, so-called. And the younger bureaucrats did not find too many opportunities to mix with the political bigwigs. Directors' orders were, nevertheless, that no opportunity was to be turned down. The Major was proud of his boys and they were good enough to mix with the best. At every official celebration, at every bright function, the handsome blades were chatting with Senators' nieces. One old-timer of the survey estimated that he "had danced ten thousand miles with the wives and daughters of Congressmen." [11] Discounting a little—it may have only seemed that long— the effort was still magnanimous.

When the Major was in a familiar talkative mood he would discuss his ideas on sports, eating, or the management of his office. He might even lay a small wager, with positive opinion, on the outcome of a ball game. On one occasion he had gathered about him the chief geologists and began to tell them how they should administer their divisions. Describing executives, he distinguished three types. First, there was the chief who depends altogether on his own judgment and decides issues with military decision. Such a man makes many mistakes. Without mentioning names, he implied that a recent Secretary of the Interior was a horrible example of this kind. The second type is the conscientious fellow who cannot shift responsibility and who eventually kills himself by overwork. The third kind is the administrator who selects several assistants and then inquires of them, "Do you or do you not approve this" and proceeds accordingly. Powell flattered himself that he was of the third variety. Although he would frequently seek the advice of his subordinates, his usual procedure was to decide issues on

[10] Perusal of the payrolls will reveal temporary appointments and per diem employment for many relatives and friends: brother-in-law Charles A. Garlick one summer had a job as a packer and another season as barometric assistant; two nephews, Arthur P. Davis and C. D. Davis, served as topographer and assistant geologist; Carlos A. Kenaston, his old classmate at Oberlin, was sent to Europe to inspect hydrographic works; and there were many more.

[11] I am deeply indebted to the late Dr. Nelson H. Darton and to Mrs. Darton for this and many other recollections and suggestions.

his own, the first consideration always being, "Is this a 'bureau' or a 'department' question?" [12] In other words, did a decision involve policy of the Department of the Interior?

The Major did depend upon several of his trusted assistants. McGee had the happy faculty of taking a random statement by Powell and restating it in essence in words that pleased his chief. Powell appreciated McGee and recognized the extent to which he was indebted. Dutton was more cautious, probably due to his long service in the War Department. It was always Dutton who urged hesitation or delay and it was Dutton, not Powell, who worried about the expenditure of survey funds on problems not specifically approved by Congress. This is curious because Dutton had no official concern with the budget— McChesney was the disbursing clerk. From a scientific standpoint it was Gilbert who provided his chief with wise criticisms and technical assistance. Gilbert, the scholar, frequently had to challenge the Major for accepting incautious opinions not verified by facts. There were four other men in the survey who were members of this little administrative family—Pilling, McChesney, Gannett, and Ward. Pilling relieved the Major of most of the office routine and supervised the editing of many manuscripts prepared by the staff. Pilling had acquired some power by controlling the appointments in the clerical and office divisions and at times his influence with Major Powell made it possible for him to gain appointments or cause termination of some of the newer scientific members of the survey. McChesney was the assistant in all financial matters although he also was a geologist of some merit. Gannett was responsible for the close supervision of the many mapping projects. The survey was run on a personal basis, from the director to the division chiefs to the "boys." The director never lost his personal touch with the newest or oldest members of the staff.

Lester Ward, eccentric, philosophical and, in work, extremely solitary, was the only one on the whole staff who could discuss philosophic ideas with Powell on equal terms. Powell's scientific attitude was largely colored by a tendency to generalize. Being of a philosophical turn of mind he would often make extravagant claims or broad conclusions on meager data. These ideas were thrown out to the boys who could use them if they chose.

Gilbert described Powell in the role of director admiringly:

[12] This story has been told many times with slight variations. The version here is essentially that related by Mrs. M. D. Lincoln and William M. Davis.

Gathering about him the ablest men he could secure, he was yet always the intellectual leader, and few of his colleagues could withstand the influence of his master mind. Phenomenally fertile in ideas, he was absolutely free in their communication, with the result that many of his suggestions—a number which never can be known—were unconsciously appropriated by his associates and incorporated in their work.[13]

This congenial collaboration is acknowledged also by Dutton:

In daily intercourse with Powell and Gilbert and with a bond of affection and mutual confidence which made this study [of the Zuni plateau] a labor of love, this geological wonderland was the never-ending theme of discussion; all observations and experiences were common stock, and ideas were interchanged, amplified, and developed by mutual criticism and suggestion. The extent of my indebtedness I do not know. Neither do they. I only know it is enormous, and if a full liquidation were demanded it would bring me to bankruptcy.[14]

The staff of the Geological Survey was not without its own cliques. Some of the men carried over from the King and Hayden surveys criticized Powell's politics and rebelled at his paternalism. Hague and Emmons were particularly bitter. There were two main factions, the one composed of high-tone, well-to-do, college-bred men who came from the great eastern universities, and the other group the earthier, poorer, self-made men, most of them educated in backwoods colleges, who had worked over the Great Basin and the arid regions with the Major. The difference in polish between these two groups was not really very great but there was a difference.[15] The nostalgic history of the "Great Basin Mess" will clarify the point.

Upon Gilbert's return from Utah in 1881 he, Johnson, Russell, and McGee ate a frugal meal together in one of the rooms of the survey. Each week one of the men was obliged to take his turn and provide a home prepared lunch for the quartet. The service included wooden plates, cheap cutlery, and paper napkins. The fame of this "Great Basin Mess" soon drew other men to its membership, but according to W. M. Davis, "the formalities of election or rejection were brief and emphatic and effective." With growth, it is sad to relate, the luncheons became formalized. Silverware supplanted tin, china displaced wood, a professional caterer took the place of the provider, and a special room across the street from the survey office was hired for the club. Many illustrious personages were guests of the Great Basin Mess. At least

[13] Wash. Acad. Sci., *Proc.*, Vol. 5, p. 113.
[14] U.S.G.S., *6th Ann. Rep.*, p. 113.
[15] Alfred C. Lane patiently explained this factionalism to me in several interviews and subsequently corrected my notes therefrom.

one photograph of this group is preserved. The Major is at the head of the table; Gilbert, McGee, and Stanley-Brown are nearby. Unfortunately the picture was taken during the plush period of linen, china, and silver.[16]

Cleavages were deeper than cultural. Pure scientists, the academic breed, are authoritarian and inclined to captious criticism. Practical scientists are more prone to expediency and haste. Major Powell's insistence on the hurried preparation of a few topographic sheets and the completion of a preliminary geological map to impress Congressmen pitted the two factions within the survey against each other.

Gannett was ordered to supervise the preparation of several quadrangle maps and to get them done no matter how. The topographers assigned to the job were rather inexperienced and these early maps were decidedly short of perfection. The Congressmen, of course, had no way of knowing this and the engraved sheets which the Major exhibited at committee hearings satisfied his purpose. Bailey Willis objected strenuously to Gannett and Pilling about the inaccuracy, and for that criticism nearly lost his job. The Major sent Walcott to investigate and Willis, exonerated, was continued on the staff. Willis had been a member of the Great Basin Mess in good standing, but after this seeming disloyalty, or nonconformance, Pilling let him know that he had become persona non grata. Willis graciously withdrew, but not before presenting to Mr. Pilling a stein filled with skim milk, but inscribed in German with a verse glorifying beer. It is not recorded how Pilling took this subtle gesture.[17]

Administrative duties curtailed much of Powell's field work, but during the field season of 1886 the Major had decided to go to Arizona to examine some of the ancient pueblos in the general vicinity of Flagstaff. The geologists and topographers were working in the same general region and it seemed a good opportunity to resume some of the studies which he had begun years before. Victor Mindeleff had nearly completed his study of Indian architecture and additional illustrations were needed for that monograph. No photographer could set up his equipment inside these dark ruins and the Major had taken along his niece, Frances Dean Davis, as an artist to make sketches. Not many miles from their base camp was a pueblo ruin protected by a great ledge of rock overhanging a mesa below. The ascent to the

[16] Mrs. Klotho McGee Lattin loaned photographs of the Great Basin Mess and provided extensive data related by her father, W J McGee. Bailey Willis gave more personal recollections. See also W. M. Davis, *Mem. Nat. Acad. Sci.*, Vol. 21, pp. 122–23.
[17] Related to W. C. Darrah by Bailey Willis.

ledge was extremely hazardous, but Frances Davis and Nell Thompson had trustworthy horses. The party proceeded as far as possible, dismounted, and continued on foot. Then, so that a favorable position for the artist might be secured, the men climbed above, built a scaffolding just wide enough for one person, tied the artist in the contraption, and lowered her to the ruins. With a sketchbook, water-color paints, and a bottle of water, Miss Davis hung in space sketching for nearly an hour.

The Major watched the feat with satisfaction. The engineering was ingenious, the bravery of his niece and his men complete. The whole show put him in grand humor. At supper he called to his saddleboy, "Make ready my steed. We are going out to see the sun set." The party rode to the forest nearby to see the coloring through the trees. When the sun dropped behind the horizon and the golden clouds turned to pink, the Major burst into song, giving one after another the revival hymns he had known in his youth. The party returned to camp in high spirit.[18]

Major Powell paved the way for Bram Powell to come to Washington in 1885. The Major had recommended his brother when the District of Columbia was seeking a new superintendent for its public schools. With little hesitation Bram began to revise the curriculum, discard the system of grading, and require the teachers to continue a study program under the official guidance of the superintendent. None of these innovations was appreciated by the teachers or by the committee appointed by Congress to oversee the administration of the school system. Bram Powell had been assured that he would have authority to make such changes as he saw necessary, and the only thing that could be done now was to criticize.[19]

Bram felt that his brother Wes was not sufficiently known to the children of the city. Consequently, the fourth-grade reader written by Bram carried as the opening selection a story of the exploration of the Colorado canyons, which began, appropriately, with the very first sentence of Major Powell's official report of the expedition. The teachers were required to make trips to the Smithsonian, the Geological Survey, and other departments of the government to become familiar with the various sciences and with the work of the government.

[18] Mrs. L. D. Whittemore communicated this incident through her daughter, Miss Margaret Whittemore.

[19] William Bramwell Powell deserves greater recognition. See Washington *Evening Star,* June 27, 1900 and J. W. Cook, Nat. Ed. Assn. *Jour. Proc. and Addresses 43rd Ann. Mtg.*

On one occasion a group of fifty teachers met with Major Powell for a lecture and demonstration on the processes of physiography. The Major led them out to a slope which had been smoothly graded a few weeks before and pointed to innumerable small gullies which had been cut by the rain. On a miniature scale this mound illustrated the growth of streams and the erosion of land. Powell explained how on a larger scale the land obtains its features by these same simple processes, uplift, erosion, and sedimentation, comparing the features of the Grand Canyon to the diminutive channels of this insignificant mound.[20]

Bram was heading for a mess of trouble. He demanded the dismissal of a number of incompetent teachers, a goodly number of whom had political connections. He established the first commercial high school in the country but this innovation was termed a disgraceful waste of public money because students could take short business courses at a half-dozen private schools in Washington. Ever uncompromising and ever confident, Bram continued his own way while the opposition grew by accretion. Each year the system of grading the pupils was made more lax on the assumption that each child should develop in his own individuality. By now the teachers were virtually unanimous in their antagonism and outsiders who did not like to see the entire school system treated as a grand experiment joined forces. Wes and Bram laughed together over their difficulties, each assuring the other he was completely in the right.

A rare gift had come to Maud Powell, the daughter of Bram and Minnie. Before reaching the age of five she had displayed exceptional musical talent, and at nine was traveling alone every Saturday from Aurora to Chicago, a distance of forty miles, to take lessons on the violin with William Lewis and on the piano with Agnes Ingersoll. As a child prodigy Maud went on a six-week tour of Illinois, Wisconsin, and Minnesota with the Chicago Ladies Quartet. Bram and Minnie spent every cent they could spare, and more, to give her the best musical education available. In 1881 the appreciative townspeople of Aurora presented a purse to their famous thirteen-year-old fellow citizen to send her to the Leipzig Conservatory. While in Europe Maud Powell studied a year with Joachim in Berlin and developed her talent.

The Major, Emma, Mary, and Bram and Minnie with their son Will went to New York in 1884 to witness Maud's American debut. Tears streamed down their cheeks as the young lady, appearing with the New York Philharmonic Society, received resounding cheers for her rendition

[20] Related by Bailey Willis.

of Bruch's G Minor Concerto. For Minnie it was a heartening ovation. The tragedies of her own childhood had not fully healed. Minnie Bengelstrater, born of German and Hungarian parents, had come to America in 1849. Her father, mother, and five brothers and sisters died of yellow fever the same year. Minnie, a sister, and a brother were orphaned. She was adopted by William and Caroline Paul and thus was known by that family name. She herself was an amateur composer of some talent.[21]

There is in the life of an American scientist no greater honor than the presidency of the American Association for the Advancement of Science. It was customary since the founding of the association in 1848 for the retiring president to use the occasion to deliver an address of wide interest, the subject usually being close to the speaker's specialty or relative to some current national problem. In 1889 Major Powell as retiring president had that opportunity. The academic world and the press waited expectantly for the words of the man who held the highest scientific position in the federal government. He had advocated a federal department of science and at that moment was engrossed in the brewing irrigation conflict. Either would have afforded an appropriate topic.

The Major, on tour with the irrigation investigating committee in the West, was unable to attend the meetings of the association, which that year were held in Toronto. Gilbert consented to read his chief's paper. The title, "Evolution of the Symphony," astonished Powell's close friends. He was well known as a geologist and an ethnologist, even as a philosopher, but this was apparently a new interest.[22]

The central idea was that music evolved through the animal kingdom, through inventions of musical instruments, and gained complexity as it was developed by savage, barbarian, and then civilized peoples. Music showed adaptation to environment; the development of music paralleled biological evolution.

One can even now squirm with compassion for Gilbert, who had the dubious honor of presenting the paper. Gilbert, quiet, simple, unpretentious, delivering an oratorical and flowery address typical of Powell's most abstract brand! Gilbert's friends grinned with reserved amusement at his discomfort when he gave all he had to its delivery. Blushingly he

[21] Biographic sketches of Maud Powell are readily available in the standard reference compendia. I have considerable personal information, of particular interest a photograph of Maud, at the age of four, and her infant brother seated in the lap of Rev. Joseph Powell (1871).

[22] Wm. M. Davis, *Biog. Mem. Nat. Acad. Sci.*, Vol. 8, pp. 72–76. I have indulged in gentle ridicule, but within the decade 1935–1945 several physicists and biologists have advanced experimental evidence compatible with Powell's speculative argument.

resumed his chair and wiped the perspiration from his forehead. The round of hearty applause that followed was for his good sportsmanship rather than for anything that Powell had written and the undertone of laughter was all in fun. Gilbert won friends that day, but as an actor he played the character miserably. The address might have had passing interest to a musicologist but as a scientific paper it did not even reach mediocrity.

Two prominent professional societies owe in large part their origins to the Major's passionate enthusiasm for organization. In 1888 the National Geographic Society and the Geological Society of America were founded. The National Geographic Society was organized in January 1888 "for the increase and diffusion of geographic knowledge." [23] Gardiner G. Hubbard was elected president while A. H. Thompson was one of the five vice-presidents. Bram Powell, C. A. Kenaston, the old classmate from Oberlin now on the faculty of Howard University, and Marcus Baker were among the managers. There were some two hundred original members. At the first regular meeting held February 17th at Columbian University, Major Powell lectured on "Physiography of the United States." The fourth meeting, this time at the Cosmos Club, had a lively discussion on the proposed physical atlas of the United States with Gannett, Gilbert, Willis, Ward, and a half dozen others taking part. Apparently the issue was not settled because the discussion was continued at the fifth meeting with Willis, Cosmos Mindeleff, Gilbert, Thompson, Gannett, and Kenaston going at it again. Virtually all the men from the Geological Survey joined the National Geographic Society and took an active part in its affairs.

The Geological Society of America was a more exclusive learned society of recognized geologists, who met annually and occasionally more often. Through the publications of the society technical papers would find an outlet. Major Powell, W J McGee, J. J. Stevenson, and J. S. Newberry were among the founders. At the time a provisional constitution was drawn up and three councillors were elected to serve with the officers. Powell, Newberry, and C. H. Hitchcock were elected. The second year Powell and Hitchcock were reelected while Newberry became vice-president.[24]

In deference to Powell's recognized position of leadership in Ameri-

[23] The National Geographic Society, during the period of active participation of Powell, Thompson, and Gilbert, was semiprofessional with a decided emphasis on physiography. The minutes of the early meetings show that the organization functioned like the old Philosophical Society of Washington.

[24] See H. L. Fairchild, *The Geological Society of America 1888–1930.*

can science since 1883, reporters found him good copy. They called upon him seeking comments on public issues or upon spectacular items in the news. Any blast by the Major was guaranteed to carry a good charge of dynamite. Two incidents of 1889 are typical—the Brown disaster in the Colorado River and the Johnstown flood.

On May 25, 1889, Frank Mason Brown, having blind faith in the practicability of a "water-level" railroad from Grand Junction, Colorado, through the canyons to the Gulf of California, started with a party of sixteen men and six boats to survey the proposed twelve-hundred-mile route.[25] Before undertaking this trip Brown had written several letters and then visited Major Powell to discuss boats, supplies, and the like. The Major had asked Harry Thompson to join the discussion and then turned Brown over to Thompson. Brown returned a second day to ply Thompson with questions. For some reason neither the Major nor Harry could impress upon Brown the dangers of the expedition and the need for adequate boats. A portion of the Major's correspondence with Mr. Brown is worth noting.

Early in April Powell received a letter from Brown explaining his projected survey and inquiring for information about suitable boats. On April 9th Major Powell dictated a detailed reply giving the dimensions and construction of "the boats used by myself and party in the descent of the Colorado in 1871 and 1872 which were well adapted for the purpose." He declined Brown's offer to take along a member of the staff of the Geological Survey and closed with this warning:

While not wishing to discourage the promoters of the railroad project of which you write, I venture to suggest it is an undertaking fraught with difficulties, in fact it is impracticable, but upon this subject my views have not been asked.[26]

When the Brown party gathered for the trip Robert Brewster Stanton, the chief engineer, said his "heart sank within him" when he "first saw the boats"—frail, cedar, copper-bottomed boats only fifteen feet long and weighing but a hundred and fifty pounds. Not a single life preserver had been brought along. With heroic loyalty the Brown party succeeded in reaching the head of Soap Creek rapids below Lee's ferry. The next day, July 10th, Brown's boat capsized and he was drowned. Stanton now assumed the leadership and continued for three more harrowing

[25] For the present purpose the account of the Brown expedition given by F. S. Dellenbaugh, *Romance of the Colorado River,* is adequate.

[26] J. W. Powell to F. M. Brown, April 9, 1889. The original is in the Stanton collection in the New York Public Library. I am indebted to Mrs. Anne Stanton Burchard for permission to quote from this letter. A carbon copy is in Bu. Am. Ethnol. (Smith. Inst.).

days until a second boat capsized with the loss of two men, Peter Hansborough and H. C. Richards. The double calamity forced Stanton to halt the expedition.[27]

It was some days later when news of the disaster reached the settlements. On August 14th a reporter for the New York *Tribune* called upon the Major for an interview and asked him to comment on the failure of the Brown expedition. Powell said bluntly:

> They failed for the same reason other parties have failed. He underestimated the perils to be encountered. I think that Brown failed to comprehend the significant fact that nothing can get through the Colorado Canyon that cannot float.[28]

When asked if he knew Mr. Brown, the Major replied in the affirmative, saying that he had received letters from various persons who were interested in locating a railroad route down the Colorado River; that such a railroad could haul coal from the vast fields of Utah and Colorado to tidewater in the Gulf of California. Brown had visited the Major in his office, and although he seemed to be courageous, appeared to be impractical in many respects. Powell ridiculed the idea of a railroad because the whole region is a labyrinth of stupendous gorges in which the water often rises forty to sixty feet so that the rail bed would have to hang on the sides of the cliffs far above the highest point of flood. At the close of the interview the reporter asked Powell how he was able to conquer the canyons on his first attempt and the Major smiled and said, "I was lucky." [29]

Behind this front the Major concealed a righteous indignation because the proposed railroad, if authorized and constructed, would interfere with the reservation of the canyons as a potential source of irrigation waters, and the Major envisioned great storage dams in the Colorado River. Without giving true reasons, he had brushed off and belittled the Brown attempt. Powell, unsympathetic toward anyone who sought a fortune in the public domain, regarded Brown as a despoiler of the national domain, the coal fields which were to be mined being reserved public lands.

Robert Brewster Stanton was a brave man. He was determined to complete the railroad project and on November 25, 1889, returned to the Colorado River with good boats and successfully carried out the sur-

[27] F. S. Dellenbaugh, *op. cit.*, pp. 354–57.
[28] New York *Tribune,* Aug. 18, 1889.
[29] *ibid.*

vey.[30] Stanton believed sincerely that the Major had not tried to impress upon Frank Brown the hazards of the Colorado River. He carried this sense of injury and bitterness throughout his life.

The Johnstown flood was a very different kind of disaster. On May 30th and 31st there had been unprecedented rains, in some parts of Pennsylvania six inches in twenty-four hours. The Potomac River spread over lower Washington and the Baltimore and Ohio station could be reached only by boat. News dispatches received in Washington on Saturday morning, June 1st, carried wild statements of thousands dead and millions of dollars of damage in central and western Pennsylvania. By Monday the grim facts emerged from the rumor. The heavy rains had burst a large reservoir constructed many years earlier as a feeder dam for the old Pennsylvania canal. The reservoir, long abandoned for that purpose, had been purchased by a group of men as a private fishing preserve. The rains were too much for the weakened earth construction and the dam gave way, sending a wall of water initially twenty feet high thundering down the narrow valley of South Fork of the Conemaugh River. Seven villages were wiped out and Johnstown more than half demolished by the swirling water. Nearly twenty-three hundred persons lost their lives in the Johnstown flood.

The tragedy of the Conemaugh valley obscured the enormous destruction elsewhere. At Williamsport on the Susquehanna River, for instance, logs valued at four million dollars were swept away.

Powell followed the dispatches and went himself to the Library of Congress to look up details about Johnstown and the old feeder dam. His indignation mounted. He gave statements to the press and dashed off an article, "The Lesson of Conemaugh" to the *North American Review*. He wrote:

> In the construction of the dam there was a total neglect to consider the first and fundamental problem—the duty the dam was to perform. The works were not properly related to the natural conditions, and so a lake was made at Conemaugh which was for a long time a menace to the people below.

Then, decrying negligence in many engineering enterprises and the indifference of the public in such matters, the Major made this remark:

[30] F. S. Dellenbaugh, *op. cit.*, pp. 357–67. Robert Brewster Stanton was a capable and energetic civil engineer and promoter. His notebook and diaries (N.Y.P.L.) are beautifully methodical. Stanton wrote a compendious history of the Colorado River but no publisher has been willing to accept the entire manuscript. Mrs. Burchard has permitted me to examine her father's notes, manuscripts, and correspondence. In the limited space here full justice to the intrepid Stanton is impossible.

Modern industries are handling the forces of nature on a stupendous scale. The coal-fields of the world are now on fire to work for man; chemical forces as giant explosives, are used as his servants; the lightnings are harnessed and floods are tamed. Woe to the people who trust these powers to the hands of fools.[31]

Good advice for any age!

The fifth international geological congress convened in Washington in 1891. The Major was conspicuous at the meeting in all his glory. After the close of the formal meetings Powell and Gilbert led a western excursion intended to show the foreign visitors, firsthand, the natural wonders of the Colorado canyons and the arid region and to acquaint them with geological processes at work on a grand scale.

The Major guided a party to the Grand Canyon, impishly taking an unnecessarily arduous route, and entertained the guests with an unexpected downpour of rain and inadequate shelter for one night. His distinguished foreign friends were going to learn what geological field work in America meant—it was not browsing over copse and heather.

Gilbert had a sense of humor and diplomacy too. When arranging for transportation of the party to Salt Lake City, he had to assign Pullman berths for the delegates. Concerning this chore he wrote, "We shall herd the Germans at one end and the French at the other end, and interpose a dining car in the middle of the train to put them still further apart." [32]

Apparently the Major and Gilbert staged a good show. Shortly after the meetings were over the Cuvier prize, awarded by the Academy of Sciences of Paris every three years "for the most remarkable work either on the Animal Kingdom or Geology," was presented to Major Powell for "the collective work of the Geological Survey." [33]

Honors came thick and fast to the Major. Not even Emma knew how many there were. Illinois College gave him an honorary LL.D. He was elected to membership in the Societé d'Anthropologie of Paris and the Berliner Gesellschaft für Anthropologie, Ethnologie und Urgeschichte. Invitations to address conventions and college commencements were many. These were seldom refused. Never lose a chance to gain an audience for a cause; old Jonathan Turner had taught him that. In 1887 Major Powell addressed the alumni association of Pennsylvania State

[31] J. W. Powell, *North American Review*, Vol. 149, pp. 150–56, quotations from p. 154 and 156. Powell was invited to write the article, but the invitation followed a letter to the editor.

[32] W. M. Davis, *Mem. Nat. Acad. Sci.*, Vol. 21, p. 181.

[33] Powell was the third American to receive the Cuvier prize. Louis Agassiz and Joseph Leidy had previously been so honored. O. C. Marsh was awarded the Cuvier prize in 1897.

College on "The Scientific Work of the National Government." [34] That was shortly after the abortive attempt to reorganize the government scientific bureaus.

Congress had lost all interest in a federal Department of Science, but Powell continued agitation on the lecture platform and in the press. During the fall of 1891 he wrote a series of articles entitled "National Agencies for Scientific Research" for the *Chautauquan*.[35] Each of the papers discussed the organization, work, and achievements of a different government agency: the Smithsonian, the Department of Agriculture, the Weather Bureau, the Coast and Geodetic Survey, and ending with the Geological Survey. They comprised an earnest plea for undiminished support of scientific work and increased cooperation among departments. It was a faint voice in the clamor of more timely issues.

Inter-departmental cooperation was a real problem. But no bureau chief could accuse the Major of not practicing what he preached. When Oliver Ames, Oliver Wendell Holmes, and Edward Everett Hale were preparing a petition to Congress to preserve the Casa Grande pueblo ruin, the Bureau of Ethnology provided extensive data. Cooperation extended beyond the confines of federal departments. Beginning with 1884 mapping in cooperation with state geological surveys became an important aspect of the topographic work. Some of the opposition to the Major in Congress resulted from pressure by the home districts which were against the encroachment of a federal agency in the affairs of a state, even when such "encroachment" was invited.

In 1891 John Davis came to Congress to represent the fifth district of Kansas when the Agrarians swept the elections in many of the prairie states. Davis had espoused the cause of the farmer and laborer long before. In 1875, three years after moving to Kansas, he became proprietor and editor of the *Junction City Journal* and was correspondent for the organ of the Knights of Labor. During the years that followed he had written extensively on the land-grant college bill, tariff, public ownership of railroads, and other economic issues.[36]

John Davis might have been a newcomer to the House but he was no novice. During his brief period of service in the fifty-second and fifty-third Congresses he was a frequent and voluble speaker on banking and tariff reform. His witty logic and glowing oratory were often effective. Such was the case when Florida claimed $567,000 as reimbursement for

[34] *Keystone Weekly Gazette* (Bellefonte, Pa.), July 1, 1887; *Democratic Watchman* (Bellefonte), July 1, 1887.
[35] *Chautauquan*, Vol. 14, pp. 37–42, 160–65, 291–97, 422–25, 545–49, 668–73.
[36] For a sketch of John Davis see Topeka *Journal*, Aug. 2, 1901.

the services of her militia in the Seminole war from 1849 to 1857. The claim was preposterous but Davis wanted the facts. He called upon the Major. "Wes," he said, "it's a damned shame, it's a crime." Powell replied to his brother-in-law, "Crimes against the Indians are nothing new, nor raids on the Treasury. What do you need?" [37] The bill was in due time passed by the Senate and reported favorably to the House. Singlehandedly Davis turned the tide. On July 27, 1894, in an eloquent speech, he recited the long chronology, compiled under the Major's guidance, of injustices to the Seminoles and pointed out that it was Florida that in 1849 had forced the issue and asked for federal aid to defeat the Seminoles. The measure failed.

On another occasion John Davis was the sole Representative to appear before the Senate and House committee and on the floor of the House to advocate women's suffrage. Again he was one of three to favor the appointment of women to the public school commission. No doubt, colleagues suggested sarcastically that with three ardent suffragettes in the family, Nell Thompson, Mary Wheeler, and Martha Davis, he showed more discretion than valor on this issue. Mrs. Thompson and Mrs. Wheeler were national figures in the suffrage movement. Mrs. Davis took a less public stand so as not to injure her husband's political fortunes.

The political upsurgence which sent John Davis to Congress had a great deal to do with the fate of the Geological Survey, especially the so-called irrigation survey. And it had a great deal to do with what some people said about Major Powell. For a hundred years the American people had vacillated between a simple industrial system tied to agriculture and a complex capitalistic economy. The crippling of the South after the Civil War gave northern industry a dominating advantage and northern capital exploited the West. Opening of the wealth of the public domain brought with it insatiable greed and ruthless exploitation. Magnates prided themselves that prosperity was their gift to the nation and that idea was peddled to the people by every means of propaganda.

Powell wrote in 1890:

The great enterprises of mining, manufacturing, transporting, exchanging and financing in which the business kings of America are engaged challenge admiration and I rejoice at their prosperity and I am glad that blessings thus shower upon the people but the brilliancy of great industrial operations does

[37] A. P. Davis to Kirk Bryan.

not daze my vision. I love the cradle more than the bank counter and the cottage home is more beautiful than the palace.[38]

There is satire in that.

Powell's insistence on protection of the public domain, the reservation of minerals, and the conservation of renewable resources and waters stood in opposition to the ever-growing and centralizing capitalism which was gaining ascendancy. The great mining interests, the lumbermen, and the cattlemen were virtually unanimous in their opposition to his policies. In 1890 the issue on the single gold standard was approaching a crisis, and the majority of the people, fortified by the great newspaper interests, declared once and for all in favor of the capitalistic system. The battle for conservation was not over. Major Powell understood as none before him that success in protecting the natural wealth was endangered by the rapid concentration of natural wealth in the hands of monopolies.

The irrigation survey failed to gain support for many reasons. Strangely, the political considerations, which were the immediate cause of failure, were not the underlying reasons. The droughts had demanded immediate succor and politicians seized the opportunity to disparage the irrigation survey. But in the last analysis it was the irreconcilable opposition of two tendencies: greater concentration of capitalism against increasing statism. The Major's uncompromising character placed him in the middle of a most uncompromising struggle.

[38] *Century Magazine*, Vol. 40, p. 116.

21

1890-1894 · The Survey Under Fire

THE controversy stirred up over the irrigation issue revealed a vulnerability which Major Powell did not like to admit. He had weathered the storm but had lost a good part of his program. He had had a chance with an irrigation survey but it was a short one. Even in those states in which irrigation was not an important issue the people were aware of this great national problem. The Major had been forced on the defensive throughout the controversy. There were three or four strong leaders in Congress who were waiting for an opportunity to strike at him again. The most dangerous of these were Hilary Herbert, the self-styled watchdog of the treasury, Wolcott of Colorado, and "Big Bill" Stewart. Senator Stewart considered Powell a pernicious lobbyist and said so emphatically and profanely. Powell regarded Stewart as an unprincipled politician and an enemy of the public welfare. Stewart was a member of that class of pioneer exploiters of the public domain who considered their great fortunes as legitimate rewards of aggressive industry and opportunism. Powell, on the other hand, was a conservationist and believed sincerely that he was sworn to protect the public domain.

While the Major was facing his greatest uncertainty in the toils of Congress he was embarrassed by affairs in his own house. Just as the events attending the irrigation survey had conspired to discredit his administration, so did the conduct of a second division of the Geological Survey.

Back in the days of the rival surveys of the western territories Cope and Marsh, the paleontologists, were enjoying a field day in the great unexplored regions of the West. Cope had been making the best of his opportunities by association with Dr. Hayden. All of the fossil skeletons collected by Hayden's men were sent to Cope for examination and description. In addition, Cope was spending from his ample patrimony large amounts to further his own paleontological researches, buying books, purchasing collections, and employing assistants in his laboratory. At the same time Marsh was financing elaborate fossil collecting expeditions, engaging private collectors and assistants who in some cases were scientists in their own rights. Marsh, with a professorship at Yale and a fortune by inheritance, was able to do pretty well as he pleased.

When the combined Geological Survey was established in 1879 paleontological work was temporarily discontinued because the appropriation which accompanied the founding act did not carry sufficient funds to allow King to hire a paleontologist. Thus, he did not have to choose between these bitter professional rivals. When Powell succeeded King paleontology was immediately organized as a regular division of the survey's program. The Major invited Marsh to accept the chief position in this division and promised generous funds to allow for elaborate publication of Marsh's results. Even with this inducement Marsh was reluctant to accept an appointment, but was persuaded finally to join the survey on condition that he could remain at New Haven and carry on all of his work there.[1] Whatever salary Marsh received he put into the work. In fact he spent far more on paleontology than he ever received as remuneration.

Cope was thus frustrated in his ambition for an opportunity which offered some security. His own fortune was being dissipated and he found himself in increasingly desperate financial straits. Cope grew increasingly bitter while he watched Marsh gain in prestige and influence.

There was another bone of contention. Cope had in various stages of completion several voluminous manuscripts on materials gathered by the Hayden survey. Major Powell refused to authorize their publication because of the excessive cost involved, especially when he had commitments for regular survey manuscripts.[2] Cope quite naturally refused to accept the Major's explanation at face value, especially when the Major estimated that the cost of publication was six times the amount that Cope and Hayden had figured upon. Cope preferred to believe that a much more sinister motive was involved; specifically, that Powell intended to delay publication of these works so that Marsh could steal his material and publish them himself.

[1] There is evidence that by gentlemen's agreement Marsh was given favorable conditions for research and publication. Nothing very definite has been found but C. Schuchert and C. M. LeVene, *O. C. Marsh: Pioneer in Paleontology*, pp. 269–70, believe it was the deciding factor in Marsh's acceptance.

[2] The regular publications of the survey so taxed the budget that the Major tried to avoid allocating funds for any other manuscripts. Hayden had to exert pressure on Sec. of the Int. Teller to force Powell to publish the reports of the old Hayden survey.

That Powell could have found some means of publishing the reports if he wished cannot easily be denied, but as to a more sinister motive there simply was none. Cope had no one but himself to blame for these petty troubles and the hostility he encountered practically everywhere he went. He had buttonholed Congressmen to whisper against Powell and Marsh. He had fought Marsh's election to the National Academy and campaigned by personal attacks against Marsh's nomination and election to offices in the academy. He topped off all these activities with anonymous charges before the congressional investigation committee in 1885. It is little wonder that Cope did not fare well in Washington. In other words, the Marsh-Cope feud had waxed and waned during almost twenty years of intense rivalry. What had been a purely personal and jealous antagonism had gradually developed into a complicated issue with supporters on each side.

The combatants had four things in common: consuming interest in vertebrate paleontology, wealth, possessive pride, and eccentricity. Cope, a Quaker by ancestry though not by inclination, was belligerent, scheming, and anything but humble. Yet his outward appearance was that of an optimistic, amiable gentleman. Marsh was selfish, proud, and ambitious. Moreover he was a shrewd politician and had many friends in high places in education and government. Despite the vastness of America and the vast unexplored fields of paleontology, there simply was not room enough in the same decade for these individualists. Their differences were widely known and ridiculous charges and counter-charges were whispered over tea cups or sherry wherever geologists gathered to gossip. Probably all this feuding would have been confined to the halls of academic institutions and backstage campaigning in Congress had it not been for a keen news reporter and for a decision in which Powell had allowed himself to become involved. As for William Hosea Ballou, the reporter, he had picked up the scent of a good story and was intent on making the most of it. Thus a silly squabble among a few scientists was to become a noisy political dog fight of national significance.

During the latter part of 1889 the Honorable John W. Noble sent an order to Cope requesting him to deposit his Cretaceous and Tertiary fossils in the National Museum as required by law. This order was based on the assumption that some, if not all, of his collections were the property of the federal government, because they had been gathered by the Hayden survey at federal expense. Major Powell had initiated the request and a copy of Powell's letter to Noble was sent to Cope. Cope's pride was cut to the quick. His misfortunes had reached a crisis. The order ignored many facts: Cope had served with Hayden without salary; many of the specimens had been collected out of Cope's personal funds; and many others had been legitimately presented to him. On the other hand, some—only Cope knew which—belonged to the government. Cope jumped to the immediate conclusion that Marsh was the instigator in the whole affair and that Powell was a willing conspirator.

Early in January 1890 Mr. Ballou of the New York *Herald* called upon Major Powell and showed him the manuscript of an article in which Cope bitterly assailed Powell as a conspirator with Marsh in controlling all government scientific work as a great political machine. Ballou had prepared the article very carefully, incorporating the account which Cope had given him and augmenting it with an impressive series of communications by some of Cope's assistants and by Marsh's former assistants.

The article accused Marsh of dishonesty, plagiarism, and numerous other malpractices and Powell of crude politics, scientific patronage, general ignorance, and unfair treatment of Cope. Ballou for his own protection invited Major Powell to prepare a statement which would be printed in the same issue of the *Herald* with Cope's attack. Powell dictated to his secretary, Miss May Clark, an indignant reply, discussed it with Gilbert and McGee, mailed it on January 3rd to New York, and waited for something to happen.

The Major did not see his copy of the Sunday *Herald* of January 12th until late in the afternoon. In the middle of the section spread before him was a full page and a half of the sensational story, "Scientists wage bitter warfare," enlivened with pen sketches of Cope, Marsh, and himself. In a series of headlines Ballou outlined the argument. "Cope brings serious charges against Powell and Marsh with important collateral issues, the misuse of the National Academy of Sciences and the political control of the Geological Survey. Will Congress investigate?" [3] Apparently the only section in this long account written by Ballou was the preamble, which described how Cope had poured forth his woes to Ballou and how he had investigated the charges. The public was treated to as crude an attack on men of any profession as had appeared in the public press. Nothing like it had ever insulted reputable men in American science.

[3] New York *Herald,* Jan. 12, 1890, pp. 11–12; see also Jan. 19, 1890, p. 11. Minor notices appeared on other dates from Jan. 12th to 26th, but the heat of battle is contained in the two features cited.

All of the old charges against Marsh and Powell that had been raised in 1885 were aired again. Powell, the political boss, using much the same methods as Tammany Hall, had built a scientific monopoly which controlled all geology in America. The survey was staffed with the sons of Congressmen who would be influenced when the appropriations bill had to be passed through the Congress. Cope claimed that the National Academy of Sciences, of which Marsh was president, was being filled with men who could be relied upon to support the Geological Survey. The first article included a series of letters from Hatcher, Osborne, Williston, and Bauer, who denied that they had ever authorized Cope to quote them, and much of the thunder in Cope's charges was thus open to question.[4]

Marsh had an opportunity to reply a week later and his rejoinder obviously had been in preparation for a long time. In a full page he ridiculed every one of Cope's charges, using a tone of injured dignity. For two weeks this game of charge and countercharge embroiled scores of scientists and appeared in successive numbers of the paper until public interest subsided. Behind it all was a political motive to discredit the Geological Survey. To be sure Cope and his followers had a hand in the business. Although the Major did not fare badly during the controversy, being relegated to a minor part in the affair, many innuendoes concerning irrigation, patronage, and politics pointed in the Major's direction. The attack upon the survey, though vicious and heartless, was not primarily a personal assault upon the Major or his integrity. It was part of a general campaign to reduce expenses of the first billion-dollar Congress and to get the Geological Survey out of irrigation and off the public domain. Many of the members of Congress, particularly newcomers, could not help but be impressed by the shameful behavior of the principals in the Marsh-Cope-Powell feud and many of them, although unwilling to believe the truth of the charges, felt that irreparable damage had been done to the dignity of government supported scientific bureaus.

The whole affair resulted in a loss of confidence and ultimately cost the Major dearly when the fortunes of the survey came before the appropriations committee in the next few years. Several of the practices which the Major had used to strengthen the work of the survey were

---

[4] *ibid.*, p. 12. When the denials secured by Marsh appeared, Cope was left high and dry. H. F. Osborn, *Cope: Master Naturalist,* and Schuchert and LeVene, *op. cit.,* pp. 265–68; on pp. 290–312 the background of these disclaimers is given.

undoubtedly open to severe criticism. Marsh's original selection in pref-
erence to Cope was certainly a deliberate political move. Marsh had a
wide influence in New Haven, New York, and Washington. His prestige
could be counted upon to aid the survey in many ways. Then, Powell
admittedly indulged in nepotism both in his immediate family and the
more political nepotism of appointing relatives of Congressmen to minor
and temporary positions on the survey. College students were frequently
employed for the summer field work and these men were drawn from
families which might do the survey some good. Powell's system of hiring on a part-time or per diem basis a large number of permanent geologists and other scientists from practically every state in the Union was
questionable. These men were college professors, consulting engineers,
state geologists, and editors. Mere listing of the more prominent men
who served on the survey by this arrangement would show what powerful allies the Major had been able to organize over the years. Indeed,
Powell had been criticized on several occasions for this practice but in
each case he was able to convince his critics that the quality of work
accomplished by the survey was enormously enhanced by the employment of specialized talent. So long as the part-time employees were hired
with nonpolitical motives, admittedly the system was ideal. Without
exaggeration the Geological Survey virtually controlled the science of
geology in the United States, not officially of course, but through its
remarkably capable staff. There were many independent geologists and
some of them of great reputation, but they were lone workers, usually in
restricted fields of activity. There were many who believed that Powell
had grown in power to such a point that he wielded a potentially dangerous control over government science. While other departments in the
federal government struggled to obtain funds for their work, by sheer
endurance and organized activity Powell had seen his annual budget increase progressively until it approached, including funds for irrigation,
$900,000.

Equally unsatisfactory to Congress was the fact that Powell, ever
since 1882, had been the disbursing officer of the survey, which gave
him the unquestioned right to spend the survey funds as he saw fit without any control of Congress and subject only to the audit of the Department of the Treasury. Every other department in the federal service
had money allocated to it for specific purposes. Powell on the other hand
had a carte blanche. There was feeling that Congress would have to re-
capture its prerogative and reestablish control over the survey funds.

The Major saw the storm ahead. He had previously announced to his friends that he planned to resign [5] but now this would be impossible. Until the future of the Geological Survey was more certain and a suitable successor could be groomed Powell had to stand firm and fight for what he could save.

The Marsh-Cope affair turned out to be no serious obstacle in securing ample funds for the work of the Geological Survey. When the sundry appropriation bill was finally passed it carried $719,000, the greatest sum yet voted for the survey; in fact it was the largest endowment for a single year's work received by any scientific organization in the entire world. Little wonder that the Geological Survey became the envy and admiration of not only every other federal agency but of scientific institutions everywhere. The Major regarded this success as a vindication of the charges and insults heaped upon him. Thus he had lobbied with all his ability to acquaint every friend in Congress of his plans for continuation of his many projects; but then, he believed that he was in the right.

All of this was telling upon the Major's health. Though less than sixty, he was worn by the struggle and turmoil of national politics and especially the personal antagonisms that had dogged his administration. Moreover, the stump of his arm gave him constant annoyance. The stump was so sensitive that the slightest jarring when he was walking or riding in the saddle sent sharp pains to his shoulder. Unconsciously, he held the maimed arm with his left hand when speaking or moving about. The doctors diagnosed the trouble as regeneration of the nerves and concluded that a third operation would be necessary. The Major reaffirmed his intention to resign as soon as a capable successor could be groomed to take over the responsibilities; this time he meant it.

A new director would find his tasks easier than Powell or King had. The spading was done. Even the attitude of the great mining companies toward the Geological Survey was changing gradually. S. F. Emmons' monograph on the Leadville district had proven how economies in ore recovery could be achieved through scientific investigation of mineral deposits. The monograph had met with immediate approval. In June

[5] Powell's desire to resign from the Geological Survey has been mentioned several times because this fact has been generally overlooked. The Major declared it in testimony before congressional committees in 1885; the *Cong. Rec.* contains other allusions to his intention between 1885 and 1890. Powell wanted to devote his time to his "new science of Demononomy"—the science of humanities—and to create a bureau for the "Science of Man" on the same proportions as the Geological Survey. I believe however, without sufficient substantiation, that the unexpected opportunity to engage in an irrigation survey upset Powell's master plan.

1891 Powell received a petition signed by fifty-one mine owners inviting the Geological Survey to the Aspen, Colorado region to undertake a similar investigation. "This district," the petition read, "offers an opportunity for similarly valuable scientific work." [6] Here were private business interests seeking government assistance in solving technological problems. The Geological Survey had come a long way since 1879. Professionally the survey was becoming stronger; politically it was growing weaker with each passing year. The old champions—Garfield, Hewitt, and Schurz [7]—were gone. Too often political support was secured only for a price. The price was usually small, paid by petty patronage, such as finding jobs for relatives or friends of Congressmen. Through thick and thin Powell held his grip. His personal integrity was never doubted.

Somehow it never occurred to the Major that his position was really vulnerable. Strong, independent, and aggressive, always confident of his own power, he expected to beat down all unreasonable opposition. If Powell thought his administrative troubles were over, he was rudely shaken when, to the surprise of even the oldest political observers in Washington, the opposition succeeded the next year in reducing the appropriation. Although the cut amounted to only $90,000 the sums voted for the survey were assigned for specific salaries and for designated branches of the work. At long last, twelve years after the founding of the United States Geological Survey, Congress recaptured control of the expenditures of the bureau. To Powell it was a grave misfortune because any phase of the survey's activities could be discontinued by political whim without warning. Heretofore the opponents had to agree to all or nothing.

This misfortune was a mere foretaste of the gathering storm which broke in 1892. The appropriation bill was usually acted upon in March and passed by mid-April at the latest. But this time April slid by and the bickering and dickering showed no signs of abating. In both the House and Senate the survey—the Major in particular—was in real trouble.

Even before the appropriation for the Geological Survey was called up for debate an assault on the Geological Survey was made by Wilson of Washington:

---

[6] U.S.G.S., *letters received*, National Archives.

[7] This distinguished trio constituted the core of political support which ultimately made the Geological Survey possible. Powell met Garfield in 1868 and was on intimate terms by 1874; he met Hewitt at Cooper Union in 1871 but I do not know how early friendship matured. Hewitt delivered a remarkable speech (*Cong. Rec.*, Feb. 11, 1879) on behalf of consolidation which deserves attention in retrospect.

We make appropriations everywhere to give the Geological Bureau an opportunity to ascertain the variety and number of butterflies and to stow away
in dusty volumes the result of their examinations into prehistoric times and report whether the birds that existed in that era lived with or without teeth, but
the home builder, the settler, who is developing new country, building towns
and villages, turning vast plains into a huge granary, building an empire on the
other side of the Rocky Mountains is almost totally neglected.[8]

Wilson's garbled nonsense was greeted with applause. "Birds with teeth"
was going to be a battle cry. This was a direct thrust at Marsh, who
had published a monograph on certain fossil toothed-birds.

Hilary Herbert dragged out every charge against Major Powell repeated during the preceding ten years, from incompetence to dishonesty,
and warned of the danger of extension of the survey's activities into
every phase of the economic life of the country. The Marsh-Cope epi-
sode was aired all over again. During the debate Powell's failure to produce a geological map of the United States after thirteen years of field
mapping at a cost of six million dollars was questioned repeatedly. At
the rate he was progressing it would take fifty years and a hundred million dollars. The six million dollars was an exaggeration because that
was the total of the appropriations of the survey, topographic work
amounting to barely forty per cent of this amount.

Mr. Herbert sneered, "How is it that so much money had been expended upon a simple commission to make a geological map? Why,
simply for the reason that the Director of the Survey mapped out and
has been pursuing the most ambitious scheme of geology ever conceived
by the human mind."

"Of course," he continued, "gentlemen may say, and they will say, in
reply: 'Is not all science valuable'? No doubt about that, but why not
go into biology, physiology, or into the whole range of physics?"[9]

The Major's policy of engaging collaborators on a part-time basis
came in for more criticism. In addition to the regular staff of one hundred and fifty employees "no doubt loyal to their chief," there were
sixty-nine professional associates from nineteen states and two territories. But was this patronage—seven state geologists, twenty-four professors, four editors, four metallurgists, three mining engineers, and
several others? "Is there any room in the field for private enterprise?"[10]

Paleontology was denounced as a useless subject and Alexander Agassiz' letters, written to Herbert seven years before when on another issue

[8] *Cong. Rec.*, 1892, Vol. 23, pt. 2, p. 4144.
[9] *ibid.*, p. 4390.
[10] *ibid.*

he was attacking Major Powell, were introduced into the record. Plaintively Mr. Herbert pleaded:

There is no end to paleontology, there is no end to geology; and when the morning of resurrection shall come, some paleontologist will be searching for some previously undiscovered species of extinct beings, and some geologist will be pecking away at the rocks to find some characteristics which have never before been ascertained. There is no end to it.

Then in summation, "No other government in the world appropriates as much money as we do for science." [11]

Every one of the scientific bureaus found its appropriation in jeopardy. The Coast and Geodetic Survey was reduced by more than $200,000. The Lighthouse Commission was badly crippled. The Smithsonian, the Naval Observatory, and the Bureau of Ethnology all came in for curtailment. In this sense the battle over the Geological Survey was not, strictly speaking, an assault on Powell, but a general move for economizing at the expense of the scientific agencies. Nevertheless it gave Powell's enemies the opportunity for which they had long been awaiting. On May 18th the debate on the survey shifted again to increasing appropriations for surveying public lands by restricting the funds for pure geology. Johnson of North Dakota ridiculed expenses for holding an inquest on the mound builders or cliff dwellers or on fossils of remote geological epochs. He pointed out that $340,000 could be struck out from the survey appropriation and the money used for surveying of the public land. The desire to economize was genuine, but as is always the case the unpopular bureaus bore the brunt of the economies.

Most of the opposition which joined the chorus had other motives than economy. There was in it an attempt to starve the bureau to oust its chief. Dickerson, an old enemy of the survey, said this:

In looking over the report of the Survey for 1889 I find that a large portion of that work is given up to a discussion of irrigation . . . it can have but one result and that is to lay the basis for inaugurating a system of irrigation at the expense of the Government of the United States. . . .

We have continued in this line until the Congress of the United States is about to seize the last power that was reserved to the states and the people. We are centralizing until we are now looking after the health of the people by taking charge of their food. . . .

If this Democratic House, with such a majority as we have here, is not willing to call a halt upon this continual absorption of power and tendency toward centralization, I do not know where the people can turn for help.[12]

[11] *ibid.*, p. 4626.
[12] *ibid.*, p. 4433.

John Bingham of Pennsylvania, speaking to the Democratic majority, taunted the House:

You have already crippled not only one, but every one of these bureaus: the Light-House Board, the Light House Service, The Coast and Geodetic Survey, the Fish Commission, Smithsonian Institution—what of the paragraph under consideration? The gentleman from Kentucky is correct when he states that it is the basis of the geological survey, and when you strike out the topographical survey that wipes out the Geological Survey.

Mr. Dickerson thundered an interruption, "That is my purpose." Bingham continued:

I know that is your purpose and so that, in every line of this bill relating to any scientific proposition, of your party since 1875, with the exception of two congresses, the 47th and 51st.[13]

The year 1875 marked the turning point toward consolidation of the government surveys, the beginnings of federal support of scientific agencies, concerted agitation for federal support of irrigation and development of the arid regions. In a period of unbelievable political corruption a few honest individuals, conspicuous by their rarity, began the long battle for reform. Major Powell was an outspoken advocate of each of these movements, which shaped the course of development of the arid regions of the West. A. S. Hewitt did not overestimate the importance of consolidation of the geographical and geological surveys when, shortly before his death and after his public career had ended, he called it his most important accomplishment.[14] The early history of the Geological Survey is the history of the beginning of the conservation movement in America; it is also the history of the federal government's cautious role as a welfare state (that is, the public service as opposed to the police state, which merely maintains law and order).[15]

Over in the Senate things were no better. In other years, if the House voted reductions in appropriations for the survey, the Senate could be depended upon to restore the amounts. The appropriation for the survey carried by the Sundry Civil Bill had been practically impregnable, and the annual attack upon Major Powell and his work failed conspicuously.

Heartened by the rebellion in the House Senator Stewart renewed his efforts to reduce the sums granted for the various agencies of the survey, but he made no headway. Then, on July 14th, after two vigorous

[13] *ibid.*, p. 4437.

[14] The Geological Survey was cognizant of his role, for Hewitt's portrait hangs with those of King and Powell in its headquarters.

[15] R. H. Gabriel, *The Course of American Democratic Thought*, p. 174.

denunciations by Sen. Edward O. Wolcott of Colorado, who proposed a reduction from $562,000 to $400,000, and Sen. Joseph M. Carey of Wyoming, who went even further offering a scheme to cut the total to $336,000, nearly all the western Senators, with additional votes picked up among southern states' righters and others with personal grudges, passed the bill, twenty-eight to twenty-five, just before adjournment. The reversal was so utterly unexpected that surprise was even noted in the New York *Herald*—hostile to Powell since 1888.[16]

The Major's many friends tried to stave off severe defeat, but they were able to retrieve only a few items, so that the bill finally passed on August 5, 1892, carried the sum of $430,000 for the survey. Again, definite sums were assigned for stated salaries. This time fourteen salaries were discontinued altogether, and the amount of money allocated for topographic work was such a large part of the total that it left virtually nothing for any other division of the organization. Hilary Herbert had succeeded in amending the bill by striking out the salaries for paleontology as of July 1, 1892, and that after that date "The Geological Survey shall not expend any money for paleontologic work or researches."

The news of the reduced appropriation came so late in the season that various divisions of the geological branch of the survey were already in the field. After hasty conferences Powell directed Gilbert to telegraph to the field chiefs directing them to return at once to Washington and prepare whatever data were on hand for publication and for future use. The various men reached their desks and found their positions abolished or their salaries sadly diminished. Despite disappointments they continued to serve, some voluntarily without any pay whatsoever, to bring all of their material into systematic shape. Of these men the Major proudly wrote in his last annual report as director of the survey:

> . . . the corps of scientific assistants consists chiefly of students who labor con amore, devoting their time to research and looking upon the salaries which they receive as a means to carry out the purpose of their lives.[17]

The Major was the real target of the blow at the survey. Looking around at his men, he chose not Gilbert but Walcott as his successor. Gilbert, a brilliant scientist, did not have the disposition necessary to obtain the funds nor the desire to haggle and testify, which was the perennial obligation of the director. Walcott had done splendid work in the canyon region and had shown during the preceding fifteen years talent

[16] New York *Herald,* July 15, 1892, p. 4.
[17] U.S.G.S., *15th Ann. Rep.,* p. 7.

in research and in administrative work.[18] Without divulging immediately the extent of his plan Powell laid the groundwork for his resignation. For the year ending 1894 the appropriation was increased to
approximately half a million dollars and it was some gratification to the
staff. The economic condition of the country was still unstable and this
reassurance was a boon to the survey members. On May 4, 1894, the
Major dictated a letter of resignation:

To the President of the United States

I have the honor to tender my resignation as Director of the U.S. Geological
Survey, to take effect on the 30th day of June proximo.
I am impelled to this course by reason of wounds that require surgical opera-
tion.
With deep gratitude for the confidence you have imposed in me,
I am, with respect,

Your obedient servant,
J. W. POWELL
Director

and of his men he wrote sentimentally:

In this severance of our relations, made necessary by painful disability, I
cannot refrain from an expression of profound gratitude for the loyal and loving aid which they have given me, ever working together with zeal and wisdom
to add to the sum of human knowledge. The roster of these honored men is
found in ten-score volumes of contributions to knowledge and fifty-score maps
familiar to the scholars of the world, and their names need no repetition here.
. . . With feelings of deep endearment I say goodbye.[19]

The Major's resignation was clouded by a disappointment over the
lack of confidence which was shown to him, and his withdrawal from
office was a sad ending to the great work of creation and organization
with which he had guided the Geological Survey almost from its beginning. Whatever the Major's outward feelings, he carried this feeling of
injury to his pride for a number of years. Despite the contentment afforded by his directorship of the Bureau of Ethnology, which continued
until the time of his death, he knew that he was actually out of harness.
He had drawn no salary as director of the Bureau of Ethnology while
he was at the head of the survey.

The Major's resignation was received with mixed emotions. There
was gloating among some of the western Congressmen and their con-

[18] For an excellent characterization of Walcott's qualifications as an administrator see
Bailey Willis, *A Yanqui in Patagonia*, p. 32. There was another political consideration in
Walcott's selection; he was opposed to irrigation work as such by the Geological Survey.
[19] U.S.G.S., *15th Ann. Rep.*, p. 7.

stituents who had objected to Powell's possessive protection of the public domain. Even some of the men of the survey believed that in tying the survey to irrigation and land classification the Major had endangered the very existence of the Geological Survey; limiting the work of the survey to economic geology and mining would have been safer. Of course, they were sorry to see the chief go, but sober reflection would show that he had passed beyond his maximum usefulness.

22

1894-1895 · A Philosophy of Science

ALTHOUGH Major Powell's resignation was not to take effect until the first of July 1894 he had no desire to remain in the old surroundings any longer than necessary. In a few days he would enter Johns Hopkins Hospital to obtain relief from the incessant pain and hypersensitivity of the stump of his arm, and after that settle down to the administration of the Bureau of Ethnology. Powell had, however, committed himself to two fairly ambitious projects. The editor of the Chautauqua Century Press had persuaded him to revise the account of the exploration of the canyons of the Colorado River, and the National Geographic Society, which was planning to bring before the public a series of semi-popular monographs on various aspects of geography, had invited the Major to prepare the first in the series and thus set a standard for subsequent volumes. Powell had outlined three essays, "Physiographic Processes," "Physiographic Features," and "Physiographic Regions of the United States." He hoped to work over his notes during his stay in the hospital.

On May 13, 1894, a week after Major Powell had submitted his resignation as director of the Geological Survey, he was admitted to Johns Hopkins Hospital for the third operation on the stump of his right arm. It had been amputated two inches below the elbow. Although the stump was well covered and there was good movement of the joint, Powell could raise the arm only ninety degrees from his body. The upper arm and shoulder had atrophied moderately due in part to disuse in late years. He had tried to wear an artificial arm repeatedly but, because of the lack of mechanical strength and the extreme sensitivity of the stump, he found it impossible. It had been feared that a third amputation would be necessary but Dr. William S. Halstead, the renowned chief surgeon of Johns Hopkins, decided to remove several large nerves for a distance of six inches from the end of the stump. This comparatively simple operation succeeded in giving the Major the relief he had sought for many years.

There is a cherished tradition that Major Powell refused anesthesia for this operation, preferring to chew on a black cigar while the surgery was performed. The yarn is without foundation no matter how picturesque it may be. Chloroform was administered in accordance with approved practice. As for the cigar, Dr. Halstead would have tolerated no such eccentricity; he was a pioneer proponent of complete asepsis in surgery.[1]

The morning after the operation the Major's temperature was normal, his pulse rate, seventy-eight to eighty-four, and his respiration, twenty. During the week of convalescence in the hospital McGee and Pilling supervised the transfer of Powell's books and papers from the survey office in the Hooey building to the Adams building across the street, where the Bureau of Ethnology had been quartered for some years. Marcus Baker called daily to read John Ruskin's *Sesame,* while the Major listened; it was one of Powell's favorite essays and he could quote long passages from it.

"When men are rightly occupied, their amusement grows out of their work," Baker read.

"That's enough," the Major interrupted. "You know, Mark, I have had more than my share of amusement."

"And trouble," Baker added.

Powell raised his bandaged stump, "You mean this?" and laughed at his own evasive joke.

Baker passed a copy of the New York *Tribune* for May 11th to the Major and pointed to a dispatch which said, "For several years Major Powell has been an intense sufferer from his old army wounds and this alone induces him at this time to retire." It would be just as well that the public considered his resignation in this light. Nevertheless, behind it all was the disaster to the survey, which meant nothing less than diminished confidence on the part of Congress in his directorship.

A nurse came in with Mrs. Powell and after an exchange of pleasant greetings, Baker left. The Major called as he was going out the door, "tomorrow bring Milton." [2]

The Major did indeed have more than his fair share of enjoyment.

---

[1] Johns Hopkins Hospital provided a synopsis of the diagnosis, surgery, and recovery of the Major. It is surprising how often this anecdote of the black cigar is encountered. It is without foundation.

[2] I have two versions of this incident; the one used here is attributed to McGee who was intimate with both Powell and Baker.

He could look back over sixty years and recall no real disappointments, no serious disillusion, no overwhelming personal tragedy. The misfortune to his arm had but accentuated a fortitude and stoicism which were his since early youth. An infection in his eyes, which had kept him in darkness for several weeks in 1884 at the time of the congressional investigation, had left his sight impaired. Since that time his vision had been gradually deteriorating, but instead of curtailing his reading, it caused Powell to enlist others to read aloud to him. The resignation from the survey brought with it a tinge of regret, but he had seen it approaching.

As soon as the Major was able to go about his tasks friends raised a subscription and had a bronze bust of him made for the survey library. Ulysses Dunbar, a prominent sculptor who had made figures of many of the important personages in Washington, made an excellent likeness. During the sittings Baker, ever ready to amuse and oblige, read from Burns and Ruskin.[3]

At home Powell revised the 1875 official report of his exploration of the Colorado River, replacing with photographs many of the inadequate, ofttimes inaccurate, woodcuts and adding information on the customs of the Indians of the region. Every page of the old journals and of the printed report must have reminded him of little incidents of the exciting and anxious days afloat on the Colorado. Andy Hall was now gone; so was Bradley, who died at the home of his sister in Newburyport, Massachusetts, on November 13, 1885, shortly after returning from California.[4] Jack Sumner was having hard times prospecting for silver and for gold and doing a little ranching. Bill Hawkins was getting on well; he had a good ranch in Arizona. As a tribute to his old comrades Powell wrote:

> I was a maimed man, my right arm was gone; and these brave men, these good men, never forgot it. In every danger my safety was their first care, and in every waking hour some kind service was rendered me, and they transfigured my misfortune into a boon.[5]

Powell had been called upon many times to lecture on that grand adventure as he had one evening on the occasion of the second international irrigation congress in 1893. Popular interest in the explorations

---

[3] M. Baker, "Personal Reminiscences," *Open Court*, 1903.

[4] Jack Sumner in late life mishandled facts flagrantly. Among his many misstatements is that Bradley died in San Diego from injuries sustained in an accident.

[5] Not even in 1869 did Powell speak unkindly or critically of the Howlands and Dunn. However, the tribute given in 1895 is more paternal than he could have written in 1875. Unquestionably the Major had mellowed with the years. *Canyons of the Colorado*, p. v.

of the canyons had never lagged and the book, issued by the Chautauqua Press in attractive form, was received favorably. The volume contained nothing new and it was little more than a publisher's venture.[6] The remuneration, considering the nature of the project, was handsome and the Major planned to save the money toward the purchase of a summer cottage at some rocky shore of the ocean.

The writing of the three essays, or chapters, for the National Geographic Society monograph took considerably more time than the *Canyons of the Colorado,* and Powell labored over his manuscripts.[7] These monographs were intended to be technically accurate but simple enough to permit popular use, especially among teachers and students. For some unexplainable reason the Major wrote his essays in a most florid style. As guides for teachers of geography, the two on physiographic processes and physiographic features were almost worthless. In the original report on the Colorado explorations the Major had described the canyons with unadorned simplicity but with striking accuracy. In the essays there is an extravagant verbosity which must have mystified readers. The Major's manner of expression had changed with the years. For example: "The purple cloud is painted with dust and the sapphire sky is adamant on wings"; again, "With the revolving moon the tides sweep back and forth across the surface of the sea and alternately lash the shores with their crested waves." The essay on physiographic regions of the United States is more satisfactory and the subdivision of the country into provinces as presented by Powell has been followed by many later writers.

Honest appraisal indicates that the Major's heart was not in either of these projects. They were, with the exception of a very short article on possible causes for movement in the crust of the earth, Powell's last contributions to geology.[8] This is not saying that geology no longer held an interest for him; rather, other interests occupied his energy.

---

[6] This was *Canyons of the Colorado,* an enlarged and revised edition of the official report of 1875. The additions concern chiefly topography and the Indians of the plateau region. The illustrations are notably superior to those of the original edition.

[7] *Nat. Geog. Monogrs.,* Vol. 1, 1895. The essays were: "Physiographic Processes," pp. 1–32; "Physiographic Features," pp. 33–64; and "Physiographic Regions of the United States," pp. 75–100.

[8] *Jour. Geol.,* Vol. 6, pp. 1–9. This is the theory of isostacy, developed by Gilbert. Elsewhere, "Truth and Error," p. 53, Powell says, "This doctrine was proposed several years ago by myself, but has received little attention except among a few geologists engaged in this branch of research." Today it is recognized as one of the great theories of geology, but Powell's name is not usually associated with it. Gilbert deserves fullest credit. See "Interpretation of anomalies of gravity," U.S.G.S., *Professional Paper 85,* 1913, pp. 29–37; also W. M. Davis, *Mem. Nat. Acad. Sci.,* Vol. 21, pp. 147–48.

Released from the accumulated anxieties of the past six years—the irrigation issue, the Marsh-Cope affair, the disaster to the survey, his increasing infirmity—Powell took refuge in his own thoughts.

Schooled as a naturalist—intimate with the earth, its form, structure, and ever-changing face; equally familiar with savages and scholars, with the endless variety of plants and animals—Powell thought in terms of nature. He was a scientist seized with the optimism of discovery, with faith in the ultimate attainment of absolute truth by the methods of science. With a passion for order and organization, Powell was beguiled into making a synopsis of the sum of human knowledge.

For many years the Major had tried to harmonize his own observations on mankind with the opinions of the great "modern" philosophers —Aquinas, Bacon, Hegel, Descartes, and Kant, but he found them lacking; in the works of Comte, Mill, Darwin, and Spencer he recognized a groping for a central idea of consciousness. But the age of philosophy was past; speculation is sterile; science holds the answer. Observe and reason—the truth will out.

The error in metaphysic philosophy was the assumption that the great truths were already known by mankind, and that by the proper use of the logical, all minor truths could be discovered, and all errors eliminated from philosophy. As metaphysic methods of reasoning were wrong, metaphysic philosophies were false.[9]

Powell had disparaged "metaphysic philosophy" in the first annual report of the Bureau of Ethnology. Twenty years had passed but the essence of his belief remained unaltered. Since 1878, perhaps earlier, Major Powell had nurtured an ambition to survey man's knowledge and philosophy through the span of time from the primitive savage, the barbarian to the modern age of science and technology. He had recorded random ideas, read prodigiously, thought independently, and pieced together an outline of his project. The work was to be a trilogy: the first volume on nature, the external environment, the universe; the second on man and his philosophy, the highest attainment of nature; and the third on the human activities and mind, the ultimate union or power of man and nature. The tentative titles did not bear a close correlation with the subjects: "Truth and Error," "Good and Evil," "Pleasure and Pain."

It would be a mistake to underestimate the Major's philosophical

---

[9] Biol. Soc. Wash., *Proc.*, Vol. 1, pp. 60–70. This address, given on the occasion of the Darwin memorial meeting, May 12, 1882, is probably the most revealing expression of Powell's credo.

peregrinations, nor can they be dismissed as idle ruminations of an elderly scientist. The peculiar blend of science and philosophy is as characteristic of the man as his physical features. Powell's personalized philosophy influenced every facet of his career. They permeated his work in geology, ethnology, and economics—least, of course, in geology.

The earliest clear statement of Powell's approach to philosophy was presented in 1876. On December 29th of that year the Major read a paper, "The Philosophy of the North American Indians," before the American Geographical Society meeting in Chickering Hall, New York City. In his lecture Powell explained that "savagery is ethnic childhood." This notion of the development of philosophy was much more fully given in August 1879 at the meetings of the American Association for the Advancement of Science at Saratoga Springs. Powell as retiring vice-president of the section of anthropology was expected to give a formal address, and he prepared a paper, "Mythologic Philosophy," in which he discussed the genesis of philosophy.[10]

Year after year, Powell found ample opportunities to expand and develop his ideas. It was customary for the president of the Anthropological Society of Washington to give an annual address. Inasmuch as the Major held the office for a number of years, this was a favorite means of presenting his ever-expanding philosophy. On June 15, 1880, he read a paper on "Wyandot Government" to try out his views on tribal organization and social institutions. With only minor alterations, the lecture was redelivered in Boston in August at the meetings of the American Association.

In 1882 Powell was ready to give his "Outline of Sociology." The paper was read first before the Anthropological Society of Washington on February 7th and a few weeks later at a public lecture in the National Museum. In May the Major lectured twice on Charles Darwin's contributions to philosophy.

Two essays read publicly a month apart in 1883 shows the next important step in this development. "Human Evolution" was presented on November 6th before the Anthropological Society and "The Three Methods of Evolution" read on December 8th before the Philosophical Society of Washington. In the first paper the Major discussed the sources of human history, the origin of activities, the evolution of arts, institutions, languages, and of the mind. Already Powell had taken a stand very much apart from that of Darwin.

Without enumerating in detail the further extension of Powell's views

[10] Anthrop. Soc. Wash., *Trans.*, Vol. 1, pp. 106–29.

on man, two more papers must be considered because with them the framework of his philosophy was complete: "From Savagery to Barbarism" in February 1885 and "From Barbarism to Civilization" in March 1886. Both of these papers, read first before the Anthropological Society of Washington, were given on several occasions.[11]

Thus, at the very time Major Powell was engrossed in the administration of the Geological Survey in its period of most vigorous growth and the Bureau of Ethnology, and defending both organizations against political assault and investigations, he was devoting no little attention to philosophy. In fact, he did not distinguish between philosophy and science:

> The philosophy of biology satisfies the reason. In the universe of life, system is discovered, and biologists see visions of the origin of living beings and dream dreams of the destiny of living beings.
> Had philosophers discovered that generations of living beings were degenerating they would have discovered despair. Had they discovered that life moves by steps of generations in endless generations—that what has been is, and what is shall be, and there is no progress—the gift of science to man would have been worthless.
> The revelation of science is this: Every generation in life is a step in progress to a higher and fuller life; science has discovered *hope*.[12]

Briefly then, Powell accepted without serious question four stages of human progress: *savagery,* in which the unit is the clan and the organization is based on kinship through the maternal line; *barbarism,* in which the units are the gens and tribe, the organization based on kinship through the paternal line; *civilization,* in which the unit is in its earlier phase the city and in later phases the nation, and in which the organization is territorial; and finally, *enlightenment,* in which the units are the individual and the state, while law rests on the equality of individuals. The direction of progress is in increasing cooperation among men.

Powell accepted also four great doctrines of modern science: The *atomic theory,* that the constitution of matter is explained as the mathematical combination of ultimate particles; the *doctrine of morphology,* which holds that different kinds of bodies exhibit homologies that express degrees of relationship; the *dynamic theory,* or concept of persistence of motion, as the method for the correlation of forces; and the *doctrine of evolution,* which holds that "higher bodies are derived from

[11] *ibid.,* Vol. 3, pp. 173–96; *Am. Anthrop.,* Vol. 1, pp. 97–123.
[12] Biol. Soc. Wash., *Proc.,* Vol. 1, p. 66.

lower bodies." "The chaos of scientific phenomena collected in vast catalogues of facts are . . . explained by these laws."

Nor was the essence of these ideas of recent vintage. In 1867 the Major had given a lecture, "Motion," which was a discussion of the prevailing notions of atomic theory. This lecture, which was in all probability suggested by an address by J. B. Turner, was the direct antecedent of a paper Powell published thirty years later.

Another basis for Powell's system was "the three methods of evolution."

First, physical evolution is the result of direct adaptation to environment, under the law that motion is in the direction of least resistance.

Second, biotic evolution is the result of indirect adaptation to the environment by the survival of the fittest in the struggle for existence.

Third, anthropic evolution is the result of the exercise of human faculties in activities designed to increase happiness and through which the environment is adapted to man.

These may be briefly denominated: evolution by adaptation, evolution by survival of the fittest, and evolution by endeavor.

Civilized men have always recognized to some extent the laws of human evolution, that activities are teleologically developed and that happiness is increased thereby. In the early history of mankind the nature of teleologic endeavor was so strongly impressed on the mind that the theory was carried far beyond the truth so that all biotic function and physical motion were interpreted as teleologic activity. . . .

Thus this reaction from the ancient false philosophy of teleology has carried men beyond the truth, until they have lost faith in all human endeavor; and they teach the doctrine that man can do nothing for himself, that he owes what he is to physic and biotic agencies and that his interests are committed to powers over which he has no control.

Such a philosophy is gradually gaining growth among thinkers and writers, and should it prevail to such an extent as to control the actions of mankind, modern civilization would lapse into a condition no whit superior to that of the millions of India, who for many centuries have been buried in the metaphysical speculations of the philosophy of entology. When a man loses faith in himself and worships nature, and subjects himself to the government of and laws of physical nature, he lapses into stagnation, where mental and moral miasma is bred. All that makes man superior to the beast is the result of his own endeavor to secure happiness.

Man, so far as he is superior to the beast, is the master of his own destiny and not the creature of the environment. He adapts the natural environment to his wants and thus creates an environment for himself.[13]

Powell places himself squarely against those philosophers and biologists who interpret the evolution of man by the standards of the theories

[13] Phil. Soc. Wash., *Bull.*, Vol. 6, pp. 27–52.

of Darwin and his followers. Man is above biological evolution. Of war, a favorite argument by those who preach survival of the fittest, the Major has this to say:

That struggle for existence between man and man which we have considered and call crime is a struggle of one individual with another. But there is an organized struggle of bodies of men with bodies of men, which is not characterized as murder, but is designated as warfare. Here, then, we have man struggling with man on a large scale and here it is where some of our modern writers on evolution discover the natural law of selection—"the survival of the fittest." The strongest army survives in the grand average of the wars of the world.

When armies are organized in modern civilization, the very strongest and best are selected and the soldiers of the war are gathered from their homes in the prime of manhood and in lusty health. If there is one deformed, if there is one maimed, if there is one weaker of intellect, he is left at home to continue the stock, while the strong and the courageous are selected to be destroyed. In organized warfare the processes of natural selection are reversed: the fittest to live are killed, the 'fittest to die are preserved; and in the grand average the weak, physically, mentally, and morally, are selected to become the propagators of the race.[14]

Viewing modern industrialized society as a complex of interdependent individuals with a high degree of division of labor, Powell with unbounded optimism sees civilized man as the keeper of his own destiny, the determinator of his even greater evolution.

If all the men who have worked for me, directly or indirectly, for the past ten years, and who are now scattered through the four corners of the earth, were marshalled on the plain outside of the city, organized and equipped for war, I could march to the capitol of the world and the armies of Europe could not withstand me. I am the master of all the world. But during all my life I have worked for other men, and thus I am every man's servant; so are we all—servants to many masters and master of many servants. It is thus that men are gradually becoming organized into one vast body-politic, everyone is striving to serve his fellow man and all working for the common welfare. Thus the enmity of man to man is appeased, and men live and labor for one another; individualism is transmitted into socialism, egoism into altruism, and man is lifted above the brute to an immeasurable height. Man inherited the body, instincts, and patience of the brute; the nature thus inherited has survived in his constitution and is exhibited along all the course of history. Injustice, fraud, and cruelty strain the pathway of culture from the earliest to the latest days. But man has not risen in culture by reason of his brutal nature. His method of evolution is of those things which distinguish him from the brute. The doctrines of evolution which biologists have clearly shown to apply to animals *do not apply to man.* Man has evolved because he has been emancipated from the cruel laws of brutality.[15]

[14] *Am. Anthrop.*, Vol. 1, pp. 297–323. A condensed version may be found in *Science* (N.S.), Vol. 11, pp. 112–16; quotation from p. 113.

[15] Anthrop. Soc. Wash., *Trans.*, Vol. 3, pp. 173–96; quotation from pp. 195–96.

Of course, the Major was not alone in this philosophy; many of his contemporaries held essentially similar views.

It is not difficult to trace the genealogy of Powell's ideas. At the very foundation was his strict Methodist conscience inculcated by the exemplary lives of his parents. Then came the early guidance of Crookham, Mather, and Turner, each a naturalist and humanist and a liberal Christian. However, it was to books as much as nature that Powell owed his intimacy with the world and man. Susceptible to suggestion and ideas, Powell's early reading in Hume, Buckle, Adam Smith, Bailey, and especially Milton gave him a deeper insight into his sympathies with Whigism, Free-soilism, and Republicanism, which would otherwise have been but political opinion. After the war Powell read even more widely, at no time limiting himself to the sciences. Comte, Mill, Bagehot, Hegel, Darwin, and Spencer made deep impressions—especially Bagehot's *Physics and Politics* and Hegel's *Phenomenology*.[16]

No other book had a more immediate and obvious influence on Powell's philosophy and ethnology than L. H. Morgan's *Ancient Society*, a book which had a very wide reading in Germany, Russia, and Japan (with an emphasis Morgan would in all probability not have shared).

Interwoven with all of this complex philosophic attitude was Major Powell's personal scientific experience, which really began, in his early impressionable years, with Crookham and Mather. His whole scientific approach was that of the naturalist or the anthropologist—man in nature, the world known to man. It is a logical step to consider society as an organism responding to its environment and undergoing evolution.

Some anthropologists have said that Powell had neither the attitude nor the temperament of a scientist. He was too quick, too sure, too philosophical.[17] Presumably these criticisms should be interpreted as implying that Powell was impressionistic and dogmatic. His method of work even in purely scientific problems was as much inspiration as deduction. He never worried about substantiating his own theories or explanations, assuming with complete intellectual honesty that, if the theories were true, they would find ultimate acceptance. If false, they

16 One of the Major's intimate friends was William Torrey Harris, who came to Washington in 1889 as U.S. commissioner of education. Powell was influenced by Hegel long before he became acquainted with Harris but with the publication of W. T. Harris, *Hegel's Logic: A Book on the Genesis of the Categories of the Mind,* the influence became more pronounced. Harris, on the occasion of the Powell memorial meeting, said, "Whatever was human interested John Wesley Powell. He took the problems of his contemporaries seriously. . . . One of the first things I came upon in my acquaintance with him was his altruistic view of the world. He had made for himself a very noble concept of the relation of nature to man." *Science* (N.S.), Vol. 16, pp. 782–90.

17 Among those who have expressed this opinion are F. Boas, A. L. Kroeber, and C. Wissler.

would soon be superseded and forgotten. Powell carried this notion to an extreme which irritated even his closest colleagues. He was on occasion content to state a theory and then confuse his own statement with the proof. Though having complete faith in his own work, he had withal a modesty which seems contradictory. He took no particular pride in his work; it was his obligation.

Walcott, an intimate friend and associate of Powell for more than thirty years, said of him, "In all our talks from 1879 to our last meeting [in May 1902] I never heard him say a word of what he had done or what he himself thought of his work." [18]

Everything Major Powell accomplished, everything he worked to accomplish, can be measured in terms of his philosophy of science, his idea of the function of science.

There are many people who confuse energy and enthusiasm for ambition and avarice. Sometimes it is envy that fogs the vision. Less frequently, perhaps, the confusion is malicious or deliberate. Major Powell coveted nothing and was envious of no one, yet he acquired bitter enemies whose most persistent charges were that he was greedy and ambitious for power. His burning ambition to serve mankind was to him as much a vocation as a divine calling to religious life. The Major cared little for money, little about fame and, least of all, what others thought about him.

Powell's philosophy was science and science was to him a religion:

There be good folk in the world who love mythologic and metaphysic philosophy—one or both. . . . In my soul I find no cause for angry contention. . . . Every man's opinions are honest opinions—his opinions are the children of his own reasoning, and he loves his offspring. . . .

When I stand before the sacred fire in an Indian village and listen to the red man's philosophy, no anger stirs my blood. I love him as one of my kind. He has a philosophy not unlike that of my forefathers, though widely separated from my own. . . .

Among civilized men I find no one who has not a philosophy in part common with my own; and of those smaller portions of our philosophies which are not alike, I see no cause why anger should be kindled between us thereby. They and I are bound together by the same cord of honesty in opinion.[19]

Major Powell had unbounded faith in mankind and in the future of man.

[18] *Science* (N.S.), Vol. 16, p. 784.
[19] Biol. Soc. Wash., *Proc.*, Vol. 1, pp. 69–70.

23

1896-1898 · Haven

EARLY in 1896 Mr. Noah V. Tibbetts of the pension bureau handed to Major Powell a brochure [1] describing a little summer colony at "Haven," in Hancock County, Maine, in the town of Brooklin. Here for seven years, in the summer months, the Major was to forget department affairs, the bustle of Pennsylvania Avenue, and the cares of housekeeping in Washington—far from the more commercialized resort centers.

Mr. Tibbetts had, a few years earlier, recognized the possibilities of establishing a summer colony along the road from the Eastern Steamship Wharf to Brooklin. The name first given to the planting was "Castle View." There are two versions of the origin of this romantic title. One has it that Tibbetts named the colony for Castle Rock, marked by a prominent tripod sixty feet high, which was plainly visible from the front porch of the "Old Homestead," the trim eighteenth-century Tibbetts farmhouse. The second explanation says dryly that Noah Tibbetts named it Castle View, " 'Cause there ben't no castle and there ben't no view." Perhaps this Maine witticism so maligned the proprietor's intention that he was forced to select the more seductive name of Haven.[2]

Whatever the origin of the name, the Major and Mrs. Powell were captivated with the advertisement and rented one of the cottages for the 1896 season.

In mid-May the Powell official family, the Major, Mrs. Powell, Mary Powell, and May Clark entrained for Jersey City by way of the Penn-

---

* This chapter has been based largely upon materials provided by Mr. Eric Parson of Santa Barbara, California, who at one time contemplated writing a biography of Major Powell. Mr. Parson has read the chapter, made several corrections, and suggested certain changes (all but one of which I have accepted). Additional information has been obtained from Miss Emma Tibbetts, Mr. Winsor K. Bridges, Fred S. Herrick, M.D., and Mr. W. J. Freethey.

[1] "Where to Spend the Summer—Castle View—Brooklin, Maine" (Noah V. Tibbetts).
[2] The quotation is from Eric Parson. For a map of the vicinity showing the landmarks mentioned in this chapter see U.S.C. & G.S. coast chart, "Frenchman and Blue Hill Bays and Approaches."

sylvania Railroad. At Jersey City they crossed the river to Manhattan by the ferry from Debrossus Street and took the Fall River Line boat, *The Priscilla,* spending the night aboard ship. The ladies had never been in Boston before and, after stopping at Young's Hotel, the Major took them sightseeing—not because of any particular reverence for historical landmarks on his part. At five o'clock in the afternoon, they boarded the *City of Bangor* at Foster's Wharf on Atlantic Avenue for Rockland and the Penobscot River ports. The Major stood at the rail at the prow as the boat cut its way past Boston Light out into the open sea.

Leaving the *Boston Boat* at Rockland, Powell met for the first time Capt. Oscar A. Crockett, who, with his two sons Ralph and Lew, operated a small line of steamers which touched all of the landings in East Penobscot Bay and Eggemoggin Reach. Captain Crockett, of a sturdy seafaring family and known in all of the outermost islands, became a great friend of the Major from their first meeting on the *Juliette.*

As was his custom when traveling, the Major held in his hand a sketch map of the area and watched with excited interest the everchanging Maine shoreline up Penobscot Bay, past Ilesboro, into Eggemoggin Reach with the mainland on the left and Deer Island to the right. Brooklin, which extends from Bluehill Bay on the east to Eggemoggin Reach on the west, is a peninsula jutting southward far out into Jericho Bay toward the Isle au Haut, which rises nearly six hundred feet above the sea. To the north and eastward toward Frenchman Bay the prominent elevations of Mount Desert stood against the cloudless sky.

The irregular rocky shore was studded with boulders large and small. The land along the road was growing up with black spruce, hemlock, white pine, and tamarack—nature taking back fields which only a century before had been cleared for tillage. Farmers raised crops and families on this thin lean soil! No wonder their sons had followed the westward course of empire.

Haven consisted of four modest and comfortable cottages, "The Pioneer," "The Log Cabin," "The Morris," and "The Milton." There were also a dining hall, over the lintel of which was painted "Castle View Dining Hall," and the "Old Homestead." The Major had asked for the Milton but it had already been rented, so he took the Morris.

The Morris faced south and from the porch one had a commanding view over the entrance to Center Harbor and the southeast entrance to Eggemoggin. The Powells arrived at the cottage on May 15th before any of their neighbors, but by July 1st all of the summer rusticators had moved in, and the population swelled to twenty-five souls.

The cottages, snuggled among the half-grown trees, had considerable seclusion. The Morris, being directly south of the dining hall, had probably the least, but the colony was small enough to make the matter of seclusion unimportant.

In addition to the occupants of the cottages there were other rusticators who roomed at the Old Homestead or in other farmhouses, but who "mealed" at the common dining hall. Mr. Tibbetts charged four dollars a week per person for meals, and the fare, which was planned without the benefit of new-fangled notions on dietetics, was a bone of contention—not for lack of quantity, but for its monotony and the utter lack of imagination on the part of the cook. When confronted with deputations of the guests, sometimes polite, sometimes irate—such as when supper consisted of a few knickknacks and three kinds of cake or breakfast of eggs, doughnuts, and cookies—Mr. Tibbetts merely replied with imperturbable calm, "What do you expect, hummingbirds on toast?" There must have been some basis for Tibbetts' aplomb. His mealers returned season after season and joked all winter about the fare of the past summer. As for the Major he enjoyed the whole eating issue as a great amusement. He could live on cheese and hardtack provided there was enough coffee to wash them down.

Meal times, when all of the families were gathered together, were the occasions for meeting neighbors, passing gossip, and planning outings. There was a lively set of boys, six of them, belonging to the Parson family. The Major knew he would have a good time with them.

During the Powells' first summer at Haven the residents included, besides the family of Rev. William Parson, Prof. F. W. True of the Smithsonian and Dr. Prentiss, a medical practitioner, and their families, Col. W. B. Thompson and his attorney-partner, Mr. I. C. Slater, all of them from Washington. Some of the people did not remain for the entire season, so the complexion of the colony changed somewhat from time to time.

The Major became a familiar figure attired in sport clothes, Norfolk jacket, knickerbockers, and woolen stockings.[3] He wore a soft black fedora and carried a rough-carved spruce cane. His bearing was at first glance austere, perhaps even stern, but there was a twinkle in his eyes.

[3] Recollections by Miss Emma Tibbetts and Eric Parson, also several photographs, 1896, 1898, 1900.

He was short, thick set, and erect. The hair of his head had grayed almost completely but the beard, turning gray, was streaked with rust and stained by tobacco. The Major had been an inveterate smoker but now limited himself to six cigars a day. He was a man of established habits, relaxed somewhat by an elastic schedule.

Shortly after the rusticators had taken possession of Haven, Powell surrounded himself with the children, enjoying their frolic without entering in their fun. In the evening the older children would gather on the porch of the Morris cottage and listen while he sang songs, told stories, and recited poetry. When warmed to his audience the Major would stand up and give "Captain Irenson's Ride," rolling every "r" in the "hard hard heart."

Ordinarily he would not tell about his own experiences in the canyons or with the Indians but, if in the mood, he might allow someone to trick him into describing the Sockdologer or Marble canyon or his visits to the Utes. Then it would be a capital evening for eager listeners.

The natives, habitually rather aloof and independent but needing the income from summer guests to tide them over the long winter months, appreciated the rusticators in a peculiar and pecuniary way. With tact and friendliness, but especially with his quiet manner, the Major was able to win their esteem, and the natives were soon willing to accept him on intimate terms. He cultivated the friendship of Capt. Jud Freethey, an old salt and master spinner of yarns who had sailed the seven seas, run the blockade of Confederate ports during the war, and had lived through enough experiences for half a dozen men. Captain Freethey made his own boats, and one of them, the *Effie,* was an excellently built sloop.

Major Powell enjoyed greater freedom from cares than he had ever known before—he had unburdened all administrative responsibilities to the faithful McGee—and was now able to fill his day with work and play. Always an early riser, up before six, he would walk down to the shore in any weather, wade waist deep into the ocean, and fill a large can with water for the washstand pitchers. Before breakfast he would arrange his ideas for dictation to Miss Clark. If there had been mail from the bureau the day before, he would prepare in his mind suitable replies. By midmorning he usually finished dictation and would correct the typed copy, which accumulated like the sands of time. Most of the work pertained to his philosophical essays. Powell had sought this unhurried situation to think out and complete his trilogy.

The quiet, the leisure, and the ocean brought the buoyancy of the

Major's spirit back again. His love of the water and of boats never tired. A few weeks after he had arrived at Haven he struck a hard bargain, undoubtedly much less of a bargain than he reckoned, with Captain Freethey to sail the *Effie* around the islands at twenty-five cents a head. The Yankee captain probably looked smugly upon this, an unexpected extra dividend. Nearly the entire population of the colony turned out for the excursion as Powell's guests.

The Major had begun at once to explore the topography and observe the inhabitants of the countryside. It would be difficult to decide which of the two held the greater interest for him. Even on the *Boston Boat* bound for Rockland the down-east speech sounded like the echoes of the voices of his own childhood home. He heard English names mixed with French, Indian, and local history. The fanciful place names fascinated him: Jordan's Delight, Mahoney, Burnt Coat Harbor, Smutty Nose, the Cuckolds; Monhegan, Opechee, Maskeag; and countless others.

Before the first summer closed the Major purchased a bicycle with which to visit the more remote points of the peninsula. After one bad spill, he did not venture forth without "Ownie" MacDonald, who ran behind him with one hand on the seat to give him better balance. For longer land excursions, Powell hired Rodney Smith's carriage, sometimes taking along young Eric Parson to do the driving.

This companionship recalls Major Powell's boyhood with Crookham.

I remember in those early days the patient kindliness of his attitude toward a boy of eleven, and his establishing with young and old a common ground of interest in natural phenomena—the sea, the tides, the trees, and the orchids in the swamps along the Woods Road to Sedgwick. On expeditions into the woods between North Brooklin and Sedgwick to gather specimens of pines he showed me the difference between the pitch pine and the white pine and told me the name of the five-leaved *Pinus strobus*. He told me how cyclonic storms in the northern hemisphere revolve in a counter-clockwise direction, and how I could stand with my back to the wind and holding my left arm out at my side point to the storm center. He explained how and why the waters of the Bay of Maine are piled up in formidable tidal waves of the Bay of Fundy, and why fog creeps in after the sun goes down.[4]

But the Major never wandered very far from ethnology. He recognized an Indian shell heap along the shore barely fifty yards below the cottages and another heap directly across the bay. A little effort was usually rewarded by turning up a few arrowheads, sometimes perfect points, on the beach. For many years Powell had been interested in the earthworks of the moundbuilders of the Midwest and he had encouraged

---

[4] Eric Parson, MS; quoted with permission.

Cyrus Thomas to investigate the works of those Indians. If there was enough in the local shell heaps, he planned to bring Frank Cushing from the Smithsonian to undertake a thorough study of the Indian middens of the neighborhood.

Indian shell heaps, or middens, dot nearly the entire New England coast but are most numerous from Bar Harbor to Portland. The refuse is predominantly clamshell, though remains of oyster and other shellfish as well as bones of deer, Indian dog, and the now-extinct great auk are not infrequent. Quantities of ashes, charred acorns and nuts, and fragments of pottery and flint implements are usual. Human burials in the heaps are rare.

The shell heaps are generally stratified and the larger ones have been accumulated over many centuries, some even in pre-Algonquian times. When excavated with skill and care successive cultures can be recognized in such refuse.

The Indians did not live the year round on such sites but came to them only during the summer seasons when they were not engaged in agriculture and hunting or gathering acorns, nuts, and berries. These prolonged visits to the shell heaps were food-gathering expeditions. Great quantities of oysters were gathered and broken open. The edible portions were removed and dried over long-burning fires. The dried clams and oysters and such other dried foods as fish, lobster, and clams were packed in birch-bark containers and taken inland to the Indian villages, where they were used in the wintertime in a variety of stews, which were an important part of the Indian diet.

The Penobscot Indians still remembered their former visits down to the shores, during which they dried clams and brought them home in birch-bark boxes. The old voyagers like John Josselyn, and Pilgrims like William Wood, have left descriptions of the Indians busy at these tasks.

Jeffries Wyman, the eminent biologist of Harvard, was apparently the first to recognize, in 1867, the scientific importance of investigating the shell heaps, which were gradually being destroyed. One enterprising company had installed itself at the great heap at Damariscotta to grind the shell for lime. Professor Putnam, an old friend of the Major, had engaged amateurs to collect specimens of implements as the commercial digging progressed.

It was with some knowledge of these middens, then, that the Major during his first year at Haven engaged "Cap" Stewart to sail the *Arrival* for ten one-day trips to reconnoiter the waters to the south and east of

Brooklin to locate Indian shell heaps, which were always on the south shores of the mainland and the innumerable islands, and usually came near to the water's edge, two to eight feet above high tide. The Powells, Parsons, and from time to time a few others made up the searching party. Landings were made on many islands and inviting heaps were discovered on Torrey and Campbell islands. Before the summer had passed the Major had mapped out a program for Cushing.

Beginning with the 1897 season, and continuing for several summers, Frank Cushing dug in the shell heaps on the shores and estuaries close to East Penobscot Bay. Cushing hired several local men to assist with the work and the Major paid frequent visits to look in on the excavations. There was great excitement at the dining hall when Cushing returned from the work one day and announced that he had found, in the midden on Upper Torrey Island, a well-preserved Indian skeleton.

In all of this scientific activity the Major took, of course, an avid interest, but his greatest pleasures in those years at Haven were on the water. The pitch and roll of boats, the splash of waves, the shower of spray delighted him.

When a wind came up and a moderate storm churned the waters of the harbor, the Major would don old clothes, put on the blue hat of a sea captain, and go down to the landing and watch, with heightening excitement, the waves slap against the piling and break over the sea wall. Then turning away from the pier he would call on Jud Freethey or his son Will to hire either to row him out into the choppy water. There was always an exchange, beginning with "What do ye want t'do that fer?" The captain would yield, unwillingly, put on a sea jacket, and take him out in the *Fanny*. Neither Will Freethey nor the captain fancied these outings, but because of the remuneration, they would indulge his whim. The Major, seated in the stern, would take command and with mock severity issue orders to the captain. The Major from his position controlled the rudder with his left hand while the Freetheys frowned and looked at the bottom of the boat. The Major enjoyed the feel of rain beating on his face, and although he never went out when a severe wind was up or the rain in a deluge, he was on several occasions caught in unanticipated fury.[5]

Some of the finest hours were spent with Captain Freethey on one of his boats, usually the *Effie*, which was the largest. An excursion might be just for the sail, a reconnaissance for shell heaps, or fishing. Whatever the occasion it was a happy one for Jud Freethey was a master seaman

[5] Recollections by Will Freethey and Eric Parson.

who knew every foot of the shores of the mainland, the islands of the region, and all the soundings, and who was a master carpenter and teller of tales factual and fanciful.

At least twice a week, often more frequently, the Major went fishing, usually for cunners when the contest was for the largest catch, but occasionally, when the tides were favorable, deep-sea fishing for "big ones." He was not much of a sportsman but a sight to behold when he pulled in an eighteen- or twenty-pound cod, using his stump arm as a reel, winding the line with carefully timed motion while Jud Freethey waited at the rail to gaff the catch.

These trips were Major Powell's parties. At breakfast he would gather the boys together, plan a trip to Marshall Island, where Colonel Thompson had just built a fishing lodge, and send Eric Parson up to Uncle John Bridges' store in the village to put in an order for provisions. The lads would scatter to obtain parental consent, hurry back to the dining hall, and go down to the landing together. After weighing anchor the party sailed to their favorite fishing grounds at Marshall Ledge and Halibut Rocks.

At the approach of mealtime the Major would peek in at the clock in the cabin, then walk over to Captain Freethey, look at the sky, and remark that the sun was well up over the yardarm (even if there was no sun that day), which meant that it was high time that water should be boiling for the haddock, the captain's tea, and the Major's coffee. The fare usually consisted of native doughnuts, invariably called "sinkers," New York State cheese, and of course pilot crackers, haddock, and coffee. After lunch the Major would smoke unbranded cigars, which were known simply as "Uncle John's," and watch the boys fish during the flood tide. Such trips were often overnight affairs, in which case the *Effie* would be anchored just inside Ringtown Island and the party landed to spend the night in comparative comfort at Colonel Thompson's lodge.

When the Major's sense of humor had full play he would toy with a situation with a persistence bordering on the ridiculous—but always with mock erudition. An incident which occurred on one of the fishing trips when Reverend Parson, his boys, and Doctor Prentiss were along is a rare example. They had spent a long day fishing, first on Hat Island Bar and later out beyond Heron Island, and the hungry crowd were waiting for Captain Freethey to prepare the supper in the lodge. He had cleaned the haddock and sliced the potatoes, and called to one of the lads to fetch a couple of onions.

"The potatoes, as all reasonable men agree, should be fried with-out benefit of bermuda," announced Reverend Parson.

The Major half closed his eyes and with emphasis interjected, "With onions, of course."

"No potato is worth eating if it consorts with an onion," replied the Reverend.

"Not worth eating unless smothered with onions," said the Major with asperity.

Captain Freethey, never seeing the Major so put out before, halted his cooking until the matter could be settled.

The argument, mostly one of expressions of dislikes, continued for some minutes when Doctor Prentiss, aside, remarked, "De gustibus non est disputandum." This lifted the discussion to a more rhetorical and philosophical level. The Major remarked that Hieronymus Cardan had domesticated Solanum Tuberosum and had himself recommended its use with Allium Cepa—at least no word which contradicts this as-sumption has come down to us. The Reverend could not let this go un-challenged and retorted that the Latin *unio*, the onion, really means "oneness" and thus the onion obviously should be eaten alone. The Major now entered into a sonorous philosophical discourse, while Reverend Parson tiptoed to the kitchen and whispered instructions to put in with the potatoes all the onions in the house.

Long before the Major had finished calling upon classical authori-ties, including Hesiod and modern writers like Hegel and Kant, and quoting from his own unpublished manuscripts, the aroma of onions wafted in from the kitchen. The Major stopped, half closed his eyes again, and in a broken key sang softly to himself by the fireplace. A few minutes later the fried potatoes, crisp and brown, were placed on the table in front of the Reverend. With exaggerated politeness he passed them to the Major saying, "Eat your fill, sir; your persistence, not your reasoning, subdued me."

"Thank you, my dear Doctor," the Major acknowledged meekly, "but I never eat fried potatoes." [6]

Sometimes these verbose encounters, all in fun, held a deeper mean-ing than the younger members of the parties realized. On another fishing trip, while the *Effie* was riding at anchor, Doctor Prentiss had in the course of conversation startled the elders with a Latin sentence

[6] Recollection by Eric Parson. This anecdote is typical of Powell's humor, which played with erudition and rhetorical quips. Consider his definition of a paraphrase: "A paraphrase is a circumlocutory cycle of verbal sonorosity, circumscribing an atom of ideality, lost in verbal profundity."

to the effect that "facti maschii, parole femine"—deeds masculine, words feminine. The thought seemed appropriate, for the Major smiled, perhaps thinking he could find ample proof of half of that proverb within his own household. Reverend Parson, a good Latinist, picked up the idea and quoted the lines from Tennyson's "The Brook,"

> For men may come and men may go,
> But I go on forever,

and suggested that they must have been inspired by a garrulous woman whom the poet had known. Subdued laughter followed and the Major, taking a cigar from his mouth and dropping the ashes over the rail, recalled a chattering old dame who had been an early acquaintance of his father in upstate New York. "Can you believe it," he went on, "she had the temerity to write a poem about her love of her own protusile, lingual appendage," and quoted the verses:

> I love to wind my mouth up,
> I love to hear it go,
> I love its giddy gurgle,
> I love its fluent flow.[7]

There was much inconsequential speech in the Powell household. To be sure, these verses were never spoken there, even under duress. The Major remained unruffled when a shrill voice was dinning in his ears.[8] Like Socrates he had his Xantippe in those later years and like Socrates his philosophy never failed him. By curious coincidence, of no significance but of passing interest, Powell had a striking physical resemblance to the traditional representation of the lovable broad-nosed Socrates, a resemblance observed by a number of the Major's acquaintances.

Major Powell found in Haven the enjoyable companionship and the small pleasures which allowed him to work on *Truth and Error* unhindered. In 1897 he purchased a small lot from Noah Tibbetts and made arrangements with Captain Jud to build a cottage on the property. Jud Freethey, taking his son Will and Peal Curtis as a crew, sailed the *Effie* many times to Bangor to bring back all of the lumber for the "Bungalow."

[7] Eric Parson, MS.

[8] I have many recollections and reminiscences of Emma Powell; some of these concern intimate family affairs, others less so, but no worthy purpose would be served by perpetuating them. Langley charitably said, "the veil of which I speak should rest on the subject of his family affections, for even here, as elsewhere, he [Powell] was self-contained, and he needed not to speak of those things even as near as I was privileged to be." Wash. Acad. Sci., *Proc.*, Vol. 5, p. 129.

Another of the local men in whom the Major became interested was Will Eaton, a dependable fellow who was hired to help dig in the shell heaps. He had accompanied the Major on the preliminary excursions in 1896, and when Frank Cushing came to Haven to excavate systematically, Will Eaton became his chief assistant. Will Eaton may have been a capable assistant, but his crowning masterpiece was a stone wall constructed in front of the Bungalow down by the shore, where the boulders were built up as a seawall. Eaton would maneuver his oxen in position before a two-ton boulder, then adroitly tie a rolling hitch or a double back wall hitch to the stone and with supreme confidence begin the weight pulling contest, dragging the rock from the open field to the shore. Eaton's movements were "down-east," slow and deliberate, sometimes to the distress of an impatient onlooker, and yet with his alert eyes and ingenuity he was able to accomplish the assignment to the admiration of everyone. The Major would stand by the oxen and watch every movement, talking as any rural philosopher might of the weather, the storms, the canting-in of the wind, or the Indians that once inhabited the land, but never offering unsought advice on the boulder business.

The summer colony increased slowly in size and several new cabins were constructed among the pines and spruce. The rusticators had become an integral part of Brooklin. Spontaneously someone suggested that a public library be established not only for the summer people but also for the benefit of the permanent residents. To achieve the goal a series of lectures, at which an admission charge was made, were presented in the Brooklin town hall. The Major opened the series with a lecture on the canyon voyage. He was still able to hold an audience spellbound though he no longer looked the part of an intrepid explorer.

Professor Cushing followed with an account of his experiences with the Zuni Indians, closing the lecture with a reconstruction of the builders of the shell heaps. In the semidarkness of the room Frank Cushing nearly frightened the audience out of their seats with a Zuni war whoop. Reverend Parson came third with a travelogue on Japan and his experiences in the Orient.

The speakers succeeded in drawing a crowded house for each performance and the proceeds established the fund for the "Memorial Library," which before many months became a reality.

One evening the Major took a stroll to Uncle John's store to buy his daily allowance of cigars. His eyes caught sight of a poster announcing a camp meeting near Mountainville on Deer Isle. "Methodist?" he inquired. "Mormon," Uncle John replied. Surprised at this apparent outcropping of Mormonism, the Major at once organized a party—Mrs. Parson, three of her boys, May Clark, and her sister Fidele—and engaged Captain Jud and Will to take them to the island in the *Fanny*. This he had to see; long years had passed since he had been among the saints.

It was a disappointing excursion. The "Mormons" were actually Seventh Day Adventists and the "revival" was a mild gathering encamped for a manifestation of religious joy. On the return home the party was becalmed. The Major thereupon called upon the Freetheys to "whip up an ash breeze," which meant they would have to row the rest of the way home while he sang sea chanties and hymns remembered from revival meetings in his childhood days.

Once in a while the Major could be drawn out in conversation to reminisce about his early adventures on the Colorado River or among the Indians, but he was never a great storyteller and did not linger on his own experiences. Retrospect seemed to play almost no part in his thinking nor did he apparently have any desire to relive the variety of experiences that he had enjoyed in the past. Rather, he wished to enrich the last years of his life with such new adventures as his aging body and mind could enjoy.

At first glance there seemed to be not the slightest romantic retrospect in his makeup, yet this was not true. The Major had a penchant for composing poetry—not very good poetry perhaps, but sentimental, philosophical, and sincere. The poem most appreciated at the time, though now not a single copy is known, was "The Island." The verses alluded to the Isle au Haut, which stretched a long green arm across the limits of Jericho Bay.

Only three of the Major's unnumbered poems have been published. Most of them, written on the spur of the moment for passing fancy or to brighten a homely occasion, have been lost or forgotten. One of the hitherto unpublished poems which suggests a side of Powell known only to most intimate friends is given here:

> A picture now hangs on the library wall
> Its colors are faded, its gilding is small;
>   I know it was only a girl's little hand
>   That painted the scene in far Albion land.
> Then tell me the charm that enraptures my thought?
>   'Tis the gleam
>   Of a beam
> That no artist has caught.

A cottage with thatch and a tree standing near,
A mother and child in the foreground appear,
    The lassie uplifting her hand to enclose
    The finger of mother who stands in repose.
But the scene has a charm that no art can portray;
    'Tis a light
    Ever bright
From my earlier day.

The sky is blue silk, and the house is gray floss;
The gowns are of needlework, soft as the moss;
    The faces are painted in delicate tint;
    The rosy lips tempt a sweet kiss to imprint;
But a mystical charm and a vision sublime
    Ever lure
    And assure
Of a happier clime.

A grandmother taught a sweet girl at her side—
A daughter's delight and the child of her pride—
    To pencil, to stitch, and to deftly combine
    The paint and the floss and the azure silk fine.
As with rapture I look on the beautiful work,
    Magic sights
    And delights
In the scene ever lurk.

The picture was wrought by my mother so dear,
I gaze on it now through a crystalline tear,
    And think of the time as I silently weep
    When, kneeling beside me, she kissed me to sleep.
Oh its charm for me now is not found in its art;
    I rejoice
    In the voice
That appeals to my heart.

A voice from a temple not builded with hands,
A holy of holies where loving commands
    Are shrined and embalmed with the smiles and the tears,
    Caresses and kisses of happier years.
Oh that voice is my guide through the difficult way
    With the kiss
    And the bliss
Of the earlier day.[9]

[9] Transcripts of this poem were given to me by Miss Margaret Whittemore, a grandniece, and Mr. Francis D. Schnacke, a grandnephew of the Major.

Each summer the Major brought his family—Emma, Mary, and May Clark [10]—to Haven and found delight in the miniature world about him. He accomplished some work, but he no longer came primarily for that purpose.

The first complete draft of *Truth and Error* was completed at Haven during the summer of 1897. Since then Miss Clark retyped the manuscript many times. The Major revised each page as quickly as she handed the sheets to him. Discussions with fellow rusticators helped to clarify the arguments but Powell won no converts to his cause. Doctor Prentiss and Reverend Parson— M.D. and D.D. but metaphysicians both—challenged his conclusions, questioned his facts, disputed his definitions.

Ah, the Reverend! Disputing words. When would the religionist and the scientist meet on common ground with a common vocabulary? He scribbled the sentiment on a slip of paper, "Words are blank checks drawn on the bank of thought, to be filled with meaning by the past and future earnings of the intellect." That would go into *Truth and Error* in the first chapter.

[10] Miss May S. Clark was the daughter of Gen. W. T. Clark, adjutant general of the Army of the Tennessee. She became secretary to Powell in 1886 and in 1894 was transferred to the Bureau of Ethnology to continue in that position.

24

1898-1901 · Truth and Error

POWELL during the Nineties was without question one of the best-known scientists in America. Moreover he was the most influential. The impact of science had not been felt in the United States until the close of the Civil War; then it struck organized religion, government, industry, and education with staggering blows. The stream of western thought had been diverted and from his eminence Powell witnessed the cataclysm.

The age of religion, the age of philosophy had passed; the age of science had displaced them. When the discoveries of geology had compromised the cosmology of Genesis, and paleontology had exploded the notion of the uniqueness of man, and biology had thrown a healthy skepticism around the concept of consciousness, the age of superstition passed—at least so Powell believed.

The maze of conflicting testimony of science required an interpreter. It would be an audacious scientist who would attempt the task. The time had come when someone must find a common language or philosophy of science, a science of science; science must dispel superstition. The Major accepted the challenge to survey the universe and drew his base line.

Powell accepted, as he freely admits, the notion of natural law—absolute truth merely awaiting discovery and interpretation. This seems strange because his iconoclasm with respect to religion is so complete. Bob Ingersoll was scarcely more an atheist. Stranger still, the Major had never slipped from the grace of institutionalized respectability—even Oberlin and Illinois Wesleyan proudly claimed him as their own. Apparently his admirers overlooked his papers or failed to understand them.

It was not accidental that Powell numbered among his friends many whose views were unsympathetic, even hostile, to his own: William Torrey Harris, whose star of genius had burned out too soon; Daniel

Coit Gilman, the vigorous president of Johns Hopkins; Edward Everett Hale, the aged reformer and man of letters; Hamlin Garland, the teller of tales of the middle border; and Henry Adams, his unfathomable neighbor. In addition to these there was a veritable battery of Protestant clergymen including the Episcopal Sterrett, the Lutheran Parson, and the Unitarian Farquhar. One cleric, after a battle of wits with the Major, uttered in despair, "You cut the heart as well as the logic from my best sermon," to which Powell replied, "No, my dear Reverend, if you wish to be anatomical, I have merely cut off the legs you stand on." [1]

In an age when organized religions, particularly Evangelical Protestantism, were warding off the assaults of science upon the citadel of Biblical authority, Powell chose to be counted among the heretics. The authority of every religion is fortified by the myth of divine revelation. Destroy that myth and what remains? The clergy combined could not advance a single argument which Powell's father had not voiced years before—though they might pose their arguments in more learned words.

Science was not a destroyer; it was a method, a message, and a promise. Major Powell was a follower of the cult of science. His trilogy must be appraised in that light.

It was an ambitious plan to write an outline of modern science which would embrace every aspect of human endeavor from technology to ethics, from the earth to immortality. On his sixty-fourth birthday the Major completed the manuscript of the first volume, *Truth and Error*.

Those who knew the Major had a fairly good notion of what was coming. Some years before he had set the stage with two poems, partly in blank verse, "Immortality" published in *Open Court* in December 1894 and "The Soul" in the *Monist* in April 1895.

Immortality, Powell thought, is evidenced by heredity, labor, pleasure, justice, language, adaptation, effort, and design; the soul is evidenced by awareness, memory, sensation, perception, reflection, acception, introspection, conception, the mind, and the will. The distinctions are subtle but the definitions are quite clear. Immortality is the sum total of man's works, those things physical and ideological which each generation passes on to the next. The soul is the individual mind in its most comprehensive sense.

Lester Ward, Otis Mason, Reverend Sterrett, and Reverend Parson had contested every inch of the ground as the arguments passed through

[1] A. C. Lane to William Culp Darrah.

discussion into rough draft and manuscript. Powell, with the instruments of science, dissected the philosophies of Kant, Hegel, Spencer, and Hume and cast them away. He pushed aside those of Berkeley, Fichte, and Schelling and ridiculed Emerson's "thaumaturgy of transcendentalism." [2]

Truth and Error was written as an introduction to the philosophy of science—perhaps more precisely, the evolution of science. Seldom has a person of prominence revealed with more complete honesty his personal credo. "On the threshold," he says, "it is necessary to state certain scientific conclusions which I accept. These are the four great doctrines taught by modern science": the atomic theory, persistence of motion, morphology, and evolution. Consciousness, that is, the science of psychology, is harmonized with all these principles.

The orientation of Powell's philosophy is revealed in the opening chapter. He relates an experience on the Kaibab Plateau with Chuar in 1880. The Indian chief, replying to Powell's questions, had tried to explain the forces of nature.

Now, in the language of Chuar's people, a wise man is said to be a traveler, for such is the metaphor by which they express great wisdom, as they suppose that a man must learn by journeying much. So in the moonlight of the last evening's sojourn in the camp on the brink of the canyon, I told Chuar that he was a great traveler, and that I knew of two other great travelers among the seers of the East, one by the name of Hegel, and another by the name of Spencer, and that I should ever remember these three wise men, who spoke like words of wisdom, for it passed through my mind that all three of these philosophers had reified void and founded a philosophy thereon.

Concepts of number, space, motion, time and judgment are developed by all minds, from that of the lowest animal to that of the highest human genius. . . . [It is] impossible to expunge from human mind these five concepts. They can never be canceled while sanity remains. Things having something more than number, space, motion, time and judgment cannot even be invented; it is not possible for the human mind to conceive anything else, but semblances of such ideas may be produced by the mummification of language.[3]

Truth and Error begins conventionally though many new terms had been coined to replace established terms of perfectly good repute. The Major classified the sciences into ethnomy, astronomy, geonomy, phytonomy, zoonomy, and demonomy. When it is realized that these refer to the sciences of the "ether," the stars, the earth, plants, animals, and institutions of man, it is obvious that all but the first and

2 J. W. Powell, *Truth and Error*, p. 410.
3 *ibid.*, p. 2.

last terms are not in the least way necessary—the names, geology, botany, and zoology are generally acceptable.

The absence of mathematics, physics, and chemistry from this classification disturbed the devotees of these subjects but the Major had a ready answer; these were only tools with which man determined the properties of bodies—properties like number, space, motion, and time and with which judgments about the various categories of bodies are formulated.

Proceeding with an elaboration of his argument Powell discussed the properties of each of these groups of bodies—earth, plants, and animals—in terms of number, space, motion, time, and judgments (with generous delectable servings of physics and chemistry). "Properties" are the real attributes of bodies; "qualities" what we judge them to be. Qualities are relative. A "hill" in the Rocky Mountains would be a "mountain" in the Adirondacks, but a "mountain" in the Rockies would be but a "hill" in the Himalayas.

The Major drew a distinction between sensation and perception and explained how by "apprehension," the faculty of the mind to form judgments about sensations, "we become expert at making judgments." The method of deduction is a form of apprehension, of forming a logical sequence of judgments. When higher categories of judgments are compounded this becomes "ideation." All science, all investigation and the like, are ideation. To this whole process of thinking, from sense perception to the propounding of theory, the Major gave the name "intellection."

In this process of intellection man's faculties are such that he has but fragmentary knowledge of things and phenomena and thus, in his judgments, there may be illusions and fallacies. When experience or science provides newer knowledge, erroneous judgments are corrected or discarded. Sometimes in the great human institutions, as in tribes, governments, or religions, whole systems of thought may be constructed upon fallacies. Nevertheless, other fallacies of ideation may prevent the overthrow of false concepts, impede progress, and confuse the thinking and working of mankind.

Ideas are expressed in words which are symbols, and the word may be divested of all meaning in terms of number, space, motion, time and judgment and still remain, and it may be claimed that it still means something unknown and unknowable; this is the origin of reification. . . .

Things little known are named and man speculates about these little-known things, and erroneously imputes properties or attributes to them until he comes to think of them as possessing such unknown and mistaken attributes. At last he discovers the facts; then all that he discovers is expressed in the terms of number, space, motion, time and judgment. Still the word for the little-known thing may remain to express something unknown and mystical, and by simple and easily understood processes he reifies what is not, and reasons in terms which have no meaning as used by him. . . .

Such terms and such methods of reasoning become very dear to those . . . who love the wonderful and cling to the mysterious, and, in the revelry developed by the hashish of mystery, the pure water of truth is insipid. The dream of intellectual intoxication seems more real and more worthy of the human mind than the simple truths discovered by science. There is a fascination in mystery and . . . a school of intellects delighting to revel therein. . . .

Often the eloquence of the dreamer has even subverted the sanity of science, and clear-headed, simple-minded scientific men have been willing to affirm that science deals with trivialities, and that only metaphysics deals with the profound and significant things of the universe.

. . . All the processes of reasoning . . . proceed by inference; the inference may be correct or erroneous, and certitudes are reached by verifying opinions. . . . Incorrect conclusions are fallacies about realities.

Known realities are those about which mankind has knowledge; unknown things are those things about which man has not yet attained knowledge. Scientific research is the endeavor to increase knowledge. . . .

The history of science is the history of the discovery of the simple and the true; in its progress fallacies are dispelled and certitudes remain.[4]

In a delightfully incisive discussion Powell considers mythology "the history of ghosts," which history, he says, is "strange to say . . . well recorded, for ghosts have had more complete recognition than men in all ancient history."

. . . Ghosts, as a race, have passed through interesting stages of history. All changes are in time and require time to become discrete quantities of change that may be recognized. Hence, it is that in the evolution of ghosts we have to consider their transmutation from one to another as it appears when we consider them separated by many centuries of time. . . .

In savagery the ghosts are zoomorphic. All lower animals, stones, bodies of water, the sun, the moon, and all the stars are supposed to be animals. The universe is a universe of animals living in the seven regions. All of these animals have ghosts which can leave their bodies and journey through the world. . . . What these ghosts can do in their proper bodies is easily seen, though it is very wonderful; but what they do when they leave their proper bodies is mysterious or occult.

To the savage, lower animals seem to have attributes and to perform deeds that are more wonderful than those of human beings. The serpent is swift without legs, the bird can revel where man cannot go. . . . The spider can spin a thread and travel on it. . . . The stars can fly like birds and shine like

[4] *ibid*. Extracted from pp. 3–8.

fire. So the savage man considers the molar bodies of the world, which are all animals like himself, to have many magical or occult attributes which are very wonderful. But the wonderful things which they do are not attributed to their bodies, but to their ghosts. . . . If you strike one rock with another you can see its ghost as a spark of fire. When the clouds gather they are the ghosts of water; when angry they shine with lightning light, and when pleased the clouds shine as rainbows. . . .

In the second stage of culture, called barbarism, animals have been domesticated and thus by more intimate acquaintance with animals the lower animals are dethroned and human animals are exalted . . . . the great phenomena of nature are personified as human beings; the sun, moon, stars and the rivers and the mountains. . . . If . . . my reader will consult the Odyssey he will there find the most vivid portrayal of barbaric philosophy that has been preserved to us from antiquity.

In despotism, or the third stage of social organization, ghosts are still more exalted, in that the psychic characteristics of men are personified . . . there is a god of War, a god of Love, a god of Hate, a god of Commerce. . . . It is in this stage that we observe the transmutation of words into gods. . . . "In the beginning was the Word, and the Word was God."

. . . [Cosmology becomes more complex, the earth becomes the midworld having] a world above or a heaven, and a world below or a hell. The midworld becomes the sole theater for the development of ghosts by birth. . . . The ghosts born on earth depart to the upper or lower regions, where they are forever separated by an impassable barrier, and . . . the chief purpose of life in the body is attained by securing a happy life in ghostland.

I shall refrain from discussing the fourth stage of ghost-lore. In very modern times it has assumed a special phase which is called spiritism, and . . . on that phase which is specially represented in religion I purposely remain silent, lest I should antagonize, with my own opinions, the views of others about religion, and thus enter a field of theological disputation. Yet without expressing personal opinions about the evolution of religion, which I have elsewhere done, I shall content myself with only one paragraph upon the subject.

From the doctrine of signatures there has grown the science of modern surgery and medicine. I do not despise the early efforts of mankind to relieve their sufferings, even though they entertained many fallacies; but I rejoice in the outcome of this effort as it is exhibited in modern medicine. Astrology was necromancy at one time, but has become astronomy in modern times, and I look upon the efforts which were made in former times by astrologists as the planting of the germs of the celestial science. So I look upon mythology with no feelings of hatred, for it seems to me to have made great strides in the science of religion or ethics, out of which shall come a purified science of God, Immortality, and Freedom.[5]

[5] *ibid.* Extracted from pp. 382–90. In speaking of his "personal opinions about the evolution of religion," Powell is referring to an article published in the *Monist,* Vol. 8, pp. 183–204. The Major appears in this paper as a supreme humanist. Warman overlooked this important paper in his bibliography of Powell's works.

There is no pap nor pabulum in this philosophical diet nor meat to chew on. The stomach is not used to such indigestible stuff unless the lining is good and the juices are strong. Weak partakers the morning after had either a throbbing headache or a revolted stomach. They could pick out and name the offending ingredients but had to admit that some of it was palatable.

The cold reception which his previous philosophical essays had received probably forewarned Powell that the first volume of his trilogy would fare badly in the hands of reviewers, especially the scientists, who would naturally make up the majority of his readers.

In the magazine *Science,* Lester Ward, to whom the book was dedicated, commented sarcastically,

The author is omniscient and discovers the universe. The golden rule is never to introduce a new word when an old one will serve the purpose. Major Powell's method reverses this, and he seems never to use a word that has a popular acceptance if he can find a synonym "however rare" or can coin a new term. We know what his answer to all this would be, as he never tires of repeating it, viz., that the bane of all thinking is the use of the same word in different senses, whereby the ideas are confused by the sounds of the words.

To the glorious company of Chuar, Spencer, and Hegel, Powell must surely be added.[6]

Lester Ward's criticisms were mild compared with those of W. K. Brooks, who in the same number of *Science* ridiculed the entire book and summed up:

If I seem to some to have devoted more space to this new book on "Philosophy" than it deserves; if I sit patiently among the audience, listening attentively as the philosophers play out their little plays; it is because of my hopes that they may destroy each other like Kilkenny cats before the curtain drops, and that, in the last accounting, they, who are not philosophers but simple honest folks, may come by their own and live at ease.[7]

Undaunted, the Major made his reply. Identifying Brooks as an idealist and Ward as the champion of materialism, he concluded,

[6] L. F. Ward, *Science* (N.S.), Vol. 9, pp. 127–39. Ward also opined that Powell has "five nothings [instead of Berkeley's one] and constructed a phantom world out of nothing." Many critics seized upon the Major's pentalogic classification as evidence of some mystical interpretation of the universe. Close examination will show that the Major meant no such thing, but his emphasis was unfortunate.

Powell wrote in *Truth and Error,* p. 267, "The ultimate particles of inanimate bodies have self-activity in so far as they manifest choice or affinity." Of this Ward says, "Now this is imputation which belongs to the first or fetishistic phase of the theological stage, which as Major Powell has elsewhere so ably shown characterizes the thinking of the savage. To the glorious company of Chuar. . . ." etc. In the light of nuclear physics of the mid-twentieth century, scientists would be less dogmatic than Ward.

[7] *ibid.,* p. 123.

I find scientific men martialled into three camps, one as champions of idealism, another as champions of dynamism, and a third rejecting all philosophy as vain. I have begun on the attempt to propound a philosophy of science.[8]

Although the reviewers were hardly just in their criticism, carping about trivialities, and Ward in particular using the occasion to sound his own music, they did point out that Powell had solved nothing; he was but another monist. He was a consummate example of the scientific philosopher so typical of the nineteenth century.

The foundations for Powell's philosophy as it is recorded in *Truth and Error* are based upon Comte, Kant, Hegel, and Spencer, despite the fact that he denounces them. The old naturalism is there with a new cloak. Comte's three states—theological, metaphysical, and positive—are evident, as also the hierarchy of the sciences. Hegel held the deepest contempt for nature and its study, yet his philosophy of history profoundly influenced Powell. Spencer was so carried away with enthusiasm for Darwinian evolution that he argued against the State, contending that it interfered with freedom of the individual and thus natural law. Powell rejected Spencer's sociology emphatically, but there is more than a little Spencerian nomenclature scattered throughout *Truth and Error*. Spencer held that some things were unknowable; the Major denied this, arguing that the mind cannot conceive an unknowable thing.

To Powell all mind is matter in motion and all matter in motion is, at least potentially, "mind," perhaps better called in biological terms "irritability." This was nothing new; it was the prevailing mechanistic view of the age, a healthy skeptical view of "consciousness."

In a few words the Powellian system was nothing more than a personal brand of positivism (man must deal only with knowable things) and monism (all phenomena of the universe are interrelated in one cause).

Powell lived in the security of absolutism. He accepted (he had no basis for not accepting) the Newtonian universe. Blind faith in the perfection of science, in absolute truth, and in natural law imprisoned him just as much as doctrine imprisoned the religionists. For all his independence and iconoclasm the Major was swept

[8] *ibid.,* pp. 259–63. Powell's reply is disappointing. Ward places himself without reservation: "The direct study of nature reveals everywhere irregularity, heterogeneity, amorphism, chaos; and however laudable the effort to reduce this anarchy to law and this chaos to cosmos any attempt in this direction which goes beyond the limit set by concrete facts is, by minds trained to the scientific habit dismissed at once as not science, whatever else it may be." *ibid.,* p. 136.

along in the current of American thought. He had accepted the notion of the evolution of society through successive stages of savagery, barbarism, and civilization, envisioning like Morgan democracy as the highest attainment of human evolution. He believed with the fervor of a patriot in the mission of the United States to bring democracy to all peoples and envisioned

the ultimate spread of Anglo-Saxon civilization over the globe; the English language the language of the world; of the science, the institutions and the arts of the world; and the nations integrated as a congeries of republican states.[9]

The fundamental "truths" which were the foundations of Powell's system have weathered badly in the climate of modern science. The Newtonian universe is not a perfect edifice. "Natural law" has failed to stand the test of time. The Major was undaunted by criticism. Few of his critics comprehended his objective. It was natural that thoughts so diffuse and so sketchily developed would meet with little recognition. It took more than courage to continue. Powell's ever-expanding plan was unpremeditated, but the diversification of ideas was hardly indiscriminate. He would follow a line of argument, develop a synopsis, and publish a brief essay in one of the annual reports of the Bureau of Ethnology. Later each section was expanded and published as an essay in the *American Anthropologist*. How much time Powell actually devoted to this writing is not known. He dictated regularly to Miss Clark, ofttimes repeating the same thought in different ways. Although these sessions became less frequent and the thoughts more disconnected, there is no evidence that Powell lost interest in his ambitious project.

While *Truth and Error* was in press Powell completed a short sketch on "The Five Categories"—esthetology, the science of activities designed to give pleasure; technology, the science of industries; sociology, the science of institutions; philosophy, the science of activities designed to give expression; and sophiology, the science of activities designed to give instruction. These "categories" covered the whole gamut of human endeavor from food-gathering, homebuilding, and commerce to the fine arts, justice, and education.

Enlarged essays on esthetology, technology, and sociology appeared in 1899, on philology in 1900, and on sophiology in 1901, with the expectation that these chapters could be brought together, amplified further, and published under the title *Good and Evil,* which was to be

[9] *Am. Anthrop.* (N.S.), Vol. 1, pp. 695–745, especially pp. 724–28.

the second part of the trilogy. Certain sections extracted from each essay were then to form the framework for *Pleasure and Pain*.[10]

It is a pity that these essays were tossed off so hurriedly; a greater pity that they were written for a small professional audience. The central idea throughout the series is the need for a science of society that would ultimately provide men with the knowledge to teach them how to live together in peace and mutual cooperation. There was no panacea, no great intellectual movement: merely the urge for organizing a new science of man. It was a real disappointment, more bitter than is evident, that these views were unheeded. Powell's dream was a Bureau of Ethnology which would develop the new comprehensive science of man.[11]

[10] Powell left an unfinished manuscript of *Good and Evil*. It is composed chiefly of quotations from the earlier essays.

[11] Powell creates "a new science . . . which I call Demononomy or the science of the Humanities" which has five subdivisions: art, developed to promote pleasure; industry (or technology) developed to promote welfare; government, developed to establish justice; language, developed to express thought; and education, developed to acquire knowledge. The *Monist*, Vol. 8, p. 184.

25

1902 · The Last Days

THE Bureau of Ethnology functioned smoothly under the able administration of McGee, the Major giving less and less time to its affairs as the years slipped by. He was director in name only. Powell's office could be entered only by an elevator in the adjoining building, and to invade his sanctum a visitor had to pass the scrutiny of Tolly Spriggs, a colored messenger who stood guard at the main entrance to the bureau. McGee occupied an office on a light well leading into a large front room, which accommodated the secretarial force. The laboratories were in the rear of the building and the library, the most used room, was located on the third floor. This arrangement served a double function; visitors would by-pass the offices and no one in the bureau would ordinarily know whether or not the Major was in. When occupied with his thoughts he preferred privacy and maintained a study at home, even carrying on considerable official business from there. Spriggs would bring the mail, already twice sorted by McGee and Miss Clark, so that relatively few pieces of the voluminous official correspondence reached Powell's hand. After 1899 he rarely went down to the Smithsonian, and those few occasions when he did were visits with Samuel P. Langley. His calls to the bureau soon became as infrequent.[1]

For all practical purposes Powell had abandoned scientific pursuits. He wrote short articles on the welfare of the Indians, on education, simplified spelling, and occasionally upon current topics, but most of these were ephemeral and have lost their meaning. Some are not even included in the published compilation of his bibliography of two hundred and fifty-one titles.[2]

[1] Recollections of Dr. F. W. Hodge, Dr. J. R. Swanton, and Mr. Harry Dorsey.
[2] P. C. Warman, "Catalogue of the Published Writings of John Wesley Powell," Wash. Acad. Sci., *Proc.*, Vol. 5, pp. 131–87. Warman lists 251 numbers but there is some duplication. However, these are balanced by items omitted altogether. See, for example, Chapter 24, note 5.

However profound or distinguished the Major may have appeared in professional circles, he remained modest and unaffected to his family and friends. To some it seemed as if his sternness had softened with the years.

The Major attended regularly the famous "Wednesday evenings" of Alexander Graham Bell, which were among the most unusual social events in Washington. Twenty-five or thirty guests, distinguished men, and a small circle of younger men, gathered in Bell's handsome library for open forums on travel, invention, history, indeed on almost anything in the range of human fancy. Alexander Bell's aged father, Mr. Melville Bell, occupied the place of honor with the Major at his side.

Powell had first met the Bells in 1881 when they came to Washington to do their pioneer work with the deaf. Alexander Melville Bell had been interested in a sign language with which to instruct the deaf and had called on the Major to compare some of his problems with Powell's researches on Indian sign languages. Alexander Graham Bell was at that time also studying phonetics and training teachers of the deaf. The elder Bell, now more than eighty, was immersed in the preparation of two books, one on the science of speech, the other on elocution.

Major Powell held in his home informal "literary evenings" which vied with those of Mr. Bell. Hamlin Garland described them as "a feature of life in the capital." [3] The forums in the Major's library attracted a more cosmopolitan crowd than Bell's Wednesday nights. They were attended by celebrated visitors from out of town, by literary people, and by the Major's philosophical friends. When Edward Everett Hale was serving as chaplain of the Senate he came often to the literary evenings. Hale, perhaps best known for his *Man Without a Country,* had labored for nearly half a century to raise the standard of living of the great laboring peoples of America. He had been an advocate of abolition, justice for the Indians, liberal theology, and popular education. Lester Ward and W J McGee were the only members of the survey and the bureau who found much of interest in these gatherings. Mrs. M. D. Lincoln, who wrote under the pen name "Bessie Beech," John Hay, Henry Adams, and Gen. A. W. Greely were among the more occasional guests at these gatherings.

Simon Newcomb, Alexander Bell, and Samuel P. Langley were, during these last years, the Major's most intimate friends. In size Bell and Powell were a David and Goliath. Bell, a giant of a man with his full beard, heavy eyebrows, striking dark eyes, and thick gray hair

[3] Hamlin Garland, *Roadside Meetings,* pp. 361–63.

curled back from his forehead, towered over Powell, smallish, rather round, with small hand and small feet. On their regular rides into the country on horseback, the contrast was ludicrous.[4]

Langley was a newer friend. He had come to Washington in 1887 as secretary of the Smithsonian to succeed the lamented Spencer Baird and within a year had begun his studies of the "internal work of the wind." The Major took great interest in Langley's work on the solar spectrum and in aeronautics because they offered new approaches to the mysteries of space and time. Powell had witnessed the launchings of Langley's first two "aerodromes," those modest flying machines which weighed but twenty-six pounds and had a wingspread of only sixteen feet. The two inauspicious trials in May and November 1896 with steam-driven models proved them to be capable of sustained flight and demonstrated the practicability of mechanical flight. The first model traveled nearly half a mile, sustaining itself for barely a minute and a half when the engines stopped. The second model attained a speed of thirty miles an hour and traversed a distance of three-quarters of a mile. The scientific principle had been proved; the mechanical instrumentation would follow quickly.

Powell was as much intrigued by Langley's explorations into the infrared portion of the solar spectrum as in aeronautics. Langley proved that, with new instruments possessing greater precision than had been devised previously, unsuspected extensions of the invisible infrared band could be identified and measured. Man had made but a beginning in his exploration of the universe.

The Powells cherished family ties; the bond of affection was never broken. Wes, Bram, and Nell lived nearby in Washington. Each Sunday two of them called upon the other. Harry Thompson, inseparable from Nell when he was not at the office, came along for the weekly gossip. It was not so with Emma. She had ruled herself out of the circle. Martha, while John Davis served Congress, started the "Merry Go Round," an intimate chain newsletter sent from one member of the family to the next until it had made a complete circuit. Each person wrote a letter but before adding it to the pack, removed his old sheets. When Martha returned to Kansas she continued the custom, which survives today in the fourth generation. Thus the Merry Go Round provided the spirit of each weekly gathering of the Powells in Washington. Martha and John worried about modern theories of feeding babies on artificial diets—"What is this world coming to?" Populism, free

[4] Recollections of Mrs. Marian Bell Fairchild and Mrs. Elsie May Bell Grosvenor.

silver, and the Knights of Labor were not even mentioned. Mary and William Wheeler had retired to their farm in Minnesota. Juliet, widowed and living with Mary, taught music. Soon Juliet and Nell would make a home for Walter, whose deepening insanity grieved them all. The mental twilight had almost completely engulfed him.

In Washington Bram had his hands full. With virtually the same temperament as Wes, brooking no opposition if he was convinced of right and wrong, he had been heading for years in the direction of trouble. Bram had wrought a revolution in the public schools of Washington, lifting them out of disgrace and mediocrity; but he didn't know when to stop. He had theories of education, some progressive and ahead of the times but others of dubious value. Bram dispensed with marks and report cards, established intangible methods for grading and promotion, and rid himself of teachers and supervisors who criticized the changes too severely. So long as the dismissals hit persons without strong political friends, this was not too dangerous. When, however, he refused to reappoint a number of admittedly incompetent teachers with political influence, his own fate was sealed. All the opposition needed was a pretext and that Bram gave by requiring the teachers to answer a questionnaire which included several questions of a semi-personal nature.

Senator William Stewart of Neveda, who had a strong dislike for Powells, went after Bram with the same tactics with which he had battled the Major. It took Stewart two years, from 1898 to 1900, with a full-dress congressional investigation, to oust William Bramwell Powell as superintendent of the public schools of the District of Columbia, but he did it nevertheless.[5]

While Bram was being hounded by Stewart and difficulties piled up, there was a joy to mitigate his trouble. Bram and Minnie had the supreme pleasure of seeing Maud, a childhood prodigy, rise to the greatest heights of musical fame. Their long years of sacrifice to give her the best training available had been justified. Maud Powell achieved world-wide celebrity for her virtuosity with the violin. The Powell clan were proud of her. During her concert tours in America (she now had her headquarters in London) when Maud visited her parents in Washington, the

---

[5] *56th Cong. 1st Sess. Sen. Rep. 711.* Stewart was chairman of the investigating committee. The chief opinions of the committee were that the public schools were improperly organized and that teaching of nature study and science interfered with drilling in spelling, reading, writing, and arithmetic. There was undeniable friction within the school system. See also Washington *Star,* June 27, 1900.

Major arranged private recitals given in his own home for the family and their most intimate friends. Maud, born with an unassuming simplicity which endeared her to her relatives, entered into the spirit of these gatherings wholeheartedly. A little incident recorded by another of the Major's nieces may not comment upon Maud Powell's skill but it tells something of the personality of both Maud and the Major. "Uncle Wes teased the ladies until Maud said unless he behaved himself and stopped acting like a bad boy, she would put away her fiddle." [6] Her fiddle was a priceless Joseph Guarnerius del Jesu.

Aside from occasional visits from former colleagues and appearances at anniversary meetings, Powell had become estranged from public life.

In 1897 Sir Archibald Giekie, the great Scottish geologist, came to America to deliver a series of lectures on the "Founders of Geology" at Johns Hopkins. Major Powell and Sir Archibald had lively discussions about erosion in the Colorado country and of volcanic processes in the Henry Mountains. One of the highlights of Giekie's visit was a field trip to the falls of the Potomac. Nearly fifty geologists from Washington and Baltimore participated in the excursion. This was almost the last appearance of Major Powell at a geological gathering. After the lecture series Giekie traveled extensively in Utah, Wyoming, and Arizona to see the canyon country and found ample confirmation of his and Powell's postulates on erosion. The fourth edition of his *Textbook of Geology*, published in 1903, gives generous testimony to the Major's important contributions to the science of physiography.

During the last week in February 1899 Marsh came to Washington, primarily to make final arrangements with Walcott for the return of the survey collections which had long been in his possession at Yale. Marsh called at the Powells and remained with them for several days. The occasion was hardly a cheerful one, bringing back as it did unpleasant memories to dim more happy recollections. Marsh was sixty-eight, worn by bitter professional and financial disappointments, and remained unreconciled to adversity. He was still obsessed with paleontology, still battling Edward Cope in memory. Cope had died two years before at the age of fifty-six, untroubled by his misfortunes and enthusiastic until the very last three days of insufferable pain.

Marsh left Washington, seemingly in fair health, stopping over in New York to visit Carl Schurz. Scarcely two weeks later he was gone, stricken with a severe cold which developed into pneumonia. O. C. Marsh died on

[6] Mrs. L. T. Schnacke, daughter of Martha Ann Powell Davis. Quoted with her permission.

March 18, 1899. Thus did Cope and Marsh, the two principles of the comico-tragic feud which had rocked the scientific world, pass from the scene.

Other old associates had passed away. Pilling died in 1895, Baird in 1888, Dana in 1896. Some were not so old. Frank Cushing, whose life had for years hung by a slender thread, died of tuberculosis in 1900. Frank was but forty-two, and a promising career ended before its fruition.[7]

The Powell family had not yet been marked by death, when Martha passed away on November 6, 1900. Wes, Bram, Nell, and Mary attended the funeral services in Topeka and, realizing this would be their last time together, posed for a group photograph, joined by Harry Thompson. John Davis followed Martha a year later.

The Major never dwelled long on such thoughts. He was at peace with the world, even though some of his old associates had refused to smoke the pipe of peace with him.

Just the same he turned his mind to the days when he would be gone. His organon would be far from complete no matter how long he should live. He had been concerned a number of times and had often discussed the probability with McGee and Langley, even arranging tentatively for McGee to edit the scattered essays and manuscripts under the auspices of the Smithsonian. Langley was outwardly sympathetic but unconvinced and noncommittal. He suggested that no one else could continue such a work, an opinion no doubt influenced by his estimation of W J McGee. Whereas the Major held McGee in the highest regard, Langley believed that his was but reflected brilliance.

During one of the frequent discussions between the Major and McGee when, as usual, the talk had digressed far from the problem they had met to consider, a remark was passed about brain size and intelligence. Was abnormal intelligence correlated with abnormal brain size? The Major studied McGee's large head. W J was a large man and of uncommon ability. Powell, disregarding his own small size, observed, "McGee, I'll bet I have a bigger brain than you have."

"Nonsense," McGee replied. "That's an easy bet."

"Not so easy. This is a very serious matter," the Major bantered, nudging his forehead as he spoke.

In this vein the conversation continued until they agreed upon an ingenious plan for settling the question (some will, no doubt, view it with aversion). Each would bequeath his brain to the other. Immediately

[7] Powell published eulogies of Baird, Dana, and Cushing.

upon the death of one of them a surgeon would remove the brain and prepare the specimen for medical study.[8] The brain in preserving fluid would then be delivered to the survivor. The survivor was to bequeath both brains, his own and the preserved specimen, to Dr. Edward Spitzka, a renowned brain surgeon whom Powell had admired since their first meeting when Spitzka had testified that the assassin of Garfield was insane. Spitzka's investigations of the brains of unusual people—genius, criminal, and insane—had aroused the interests of many anthropologists.

The Major, however, did not intend to die in the near future. There was too much to do. In the winter of 1900–1901, with Holmes as a companion, he made a short expedition to Cuba and Jamaica to study the Arawak and Carib Indians. The Bureau of Ethnology had but fragmentary collections of these tribes and reports of prehistoric human remains in Cuba tantalized his curiosity.

The exertion of the trip proved to be more than Powell had bargained for. Instead of returning home tanned and rested, he was exhausted. For the first time in his life he had to be assisted even on his way to the bureau. Spriggs would call for him, and if the weather was good, help him walk down to the office. It was a warning. The Major was a keen observer. He had talked and written a good deal about sensations, apprehensions, and ideation. Time for work was growing short.

The sojourn in Haven during the summer of 1901 did not restore the vitality which the Major had lost during the Cuban expedition. Fellow rusticators noticed how feeble he looked; how much his physical powers had declined. Major Powell felt old.

A week passed after the Powells returned to Washington before the Major bothered to go down to the Bureau of Ethnology. Several times McGee and Miss Clark had been up to see him on business and assured their chief that the affairs of the bureau were running smoothly except for the publication of reports. Publication dates were running two and a half years behind appropriations, and there were a score of long manuscripts on hand.

On his first trip to the office the Major took more interest in his boys than in the publication jam. In the library he met John Swanton, who had completed a few months of service as an assistant ethnologist. Swanton was of the newer college-bred anthropologists and Powell was

---

[8] Recollections of Gifford Pinchot, to whom McGee entrusted the responsibility for properly disposing of his brain. See E. A. Spitzka, *Am. Anthrop.* (N.S.), Vol. 5, p. 38; see also pp. 585–643; McGee's brain was described by Spitzka in Vol. 15.

curious. The Major, inviting him into the office, said, "John, I want you to understand what we are trying to do." Then he tried to induce the young man to talk about his interests and his opinion of the bureau.[9]

DeLancey Gill, the staff artist, came in with a minor problem, which he said could wait, but the Major hailed him in and told him to proceed. Gill began and talked on because Powell gave no indication of replying. He was gazing at DeLancey's face and, apparently listening intently, stroking his nose slowly with his index finger. Finally Gill, unable to attenuate the question, finished and waited expectantly for a reply. There was a long pause and the Major answered, "DeLancey, when you are as old as I am you're going to have a nose just like mine." [10]

Early in November, while sitting quietly in his library, the Major gave a slight start and slumped into the chair. Emma, who had been reading, cried out and rushed to his side. He was cold, pallid, and unconscious. Dr. Prentiss came promptly and after examining him, warned that general paralysis might result. He had suffered a stroke and would be confined for many weeks. Walcott, Ward, Gilbert, and the others called quietly to inquire of their old chief. McGee made a daily visit to the Major's bedside. After several anxious days Powell showed improvement and by Thanksgiving Day he was propped up in bed.

Arthur Davis brought the tidings that President Theodore Roosevelt, in his message to Congress, urged federal participation in irrigation:

It is as right for the National Government to make the streams and rivers of the arid region useful by engineering works for water storage as to make useful the rivers and harbors of the humid region by engineering works of another kind.

Visibly moved, the Major observed, "These things take time, Arthur. You must learn to control impatience, but always be impatient." [11]

By Christmas he had made a substantial recovery and was able to sit in his library, accepting friends for brief social calls. The New Year, 1902, found Major Powell in his usual good spirits, convinced his time had not yet come. He decided to visit Charleston but Dr. Prentiss refused flatly. The Major would not give in. Dr. Prentiss, provoked but indulgent, said he would call Dr. W. W. Johnston for consultation if the Major would agree to accept their joint advice without further argument. Reluctantly the Major accepted the condition. Dr. Johnston confirmed Dr. Prentiss's "diagnosis of arteriosclerosis—degeneration of

[9] Recollection of Dr. John R. Swanton.
[10] Related by Dr. Frank H. H. Roberts, jr. of the Bureau of American Ethnology.
[11] Arthur Powell Davis to F. H. Newell, April 1904.

the walls of the arterial system. He advised moderate work, freedom of emotions, sedentary habits, drives, diet, and small doses of nitroglycerine. . . . Apoplexy may come at any time or never appear." [12]

With a good January thaw and the temperature unseasonably warm, the Major finally was allowed to walk to the office. He sent for Tolly Spriggs to assist him. He had been around the block a number of times to try his legs but the gait was labored and uneasy. The Major shuffled along on Spriggs' arm joking, "I used to climb mountains." While pausing for a rest Hamlin Garland stepped up and greeted him. Powell looked at him searchingly. Then cheerfully but "with pathetic vagueness" said, "I know you, and I ought to recall your name, but I can't. I've lost my memory." Garland was so moved by this sad meeting that he was inspired to write "The Stricken Pioneer," as a tribute to those men who "our velvet way . . . prepared." [13]

The boys from the bureau were considerate of their old chief, remembering him in many little ways. Hodge came up several afternoons to rearrange the books in the library for more convenient reference. The Major wanted the volumes he used most or was likely to want placed so that he could reach them without stooping or stretching. This request was capricious because the Major was no longer able to read for himself. Arthur Davis came every other evening, as he had done willingly for many months, to read to his Uncle Wes. Miss Clark, Marcus Baker, and McGee came to read too, sometimes technical books, more often pure literature.

Emma scanned the newspapers for him but her idea of news did not always coincide with his. Despite all his constitutional annoyances, Powell's day was filled with quiet activity. In his better moments he dabbled with the unfinished organon, knowing full well it would never be finished. He had but begun.

The Major had been ailing all winter and the dragging unpredictable spring was tortuous. He looked forward to another summer by the sea. There perhaps he could shake the cold which plagued him since the first week in March. Dr. Prentiss suggested that an early start for the "Bungalow" could do no harm and might do considerable good. On May 27th Mrs. Powell, Mary, the Major, and Miss Clark left Washington for Haven. He knew it was for the last time.

They went by the Pennsylvania Railroad to Jersey City, across the

---

[12] D. W. Prentiss to S. P. Langley, Jan. 27, 1902. Declassified from confidential files of the Smithsonian Institution, March 1948.

[13] Hamlin Garland, *Roadside Meetings,* pp. 361–63.

river to Manhattan, to the pier of the Fall River Line. Miss Clark obtained the tickets and the Major walked, Mary holding his arm, to see whether it would be the *Puritan* or the *Priscilla*. It was the *Priscilla* with accommodations for fifteen hundred persons: 440 feet long, sleek for a coastwise steamer, she weighed more than 4,800 tons. The little sailing ship which had brought Father, Mother, Martha, and Mary from England to New York Harbor seventy-two years before was but a few hundred tons. What changes time had wrought within the life span of one man!

A short distance out in the harbor the Statue of Liberty, with torch held high, beckoned a welcome to the land of freedom and opportunity. The Major had stopped to examine casually the forearm of that statue in Philadelphia at the exposition in 1876. It had meant nothing then. The Statue of Liberty was not there when the Powell family came to the land of opportunity. Father and Mother had raised eight children, every one of them worthy of their pride. Four of them had achieved distinction: Wes, Bram, Nell, and Mary.[14] If Martha's name was not to be remembered, it was because she sought a lesser place behind her distinguished husband. The third generation held promise too. Already Maud Powell and Arthur Davis had made marks for themselves.

America had been good to the Powells, but all of them had worked to make the American ideal a reality.

In Boston the Major spent the day lounging at Young's Hotel, taking a leisurely luncheon, watching the people. At five o'clock the *City of Bangor* moved from Foster's Wharf as the great paddles pushed her into the harbor. At Rockland he was greeted at the gangplank by Captain Crockett, who handed him the usual complimentary pass, good on the *Juliette* or the *Catherine* of the "Rockland-Blue Hill-Ellsworth Line." Powell may have smiled to himself; that Yankee captain gave passes to all the Haven families—even the big ones like the Parsons.

The May nights were still cold, and although June was almost upon them, summer appeared to be a long way off. The Major had brought with him a considerable quantity of work, but a full week passed before he opened his portfolio, and then only to fuss with the papers and put his notes away again. Neither the mind nor the flesh was willing.

On June 24th the Major was seized with severe chest pains, and his

[14] Ellen Powell Thompson and Mary Powell Wheeler were nationally known suffragettes. Juliet Powell Rice, a pioneer in the teaching of folk music, transcribed many Indian songs into standard notation.

neighbor, Dr. Fred Herrick, was summoned.[15] It was their first meeting of the season and how the Major had changed in less than a year! The fine physique, though deteriorated somewhat in the past few years, was worn and the old man was broken down. His movements were slow and his memory faulty. Nitroglycerine was administered and the seizure passed in a few minutes, but Dr. Herrick remained awhile. They talked together; the Major had diagnosed his own symptoms as angina, and made it clear that he understood the gravity of his illness. Dr. Herrick reassured him that the disease was not necessarily fatal, but the Major repeated his opinion that it was serious and he was a feeble man.

There were days and even weeks when he felt quite hale but the periods of distress always returned. Powell bore his condition with courage and fortitude and with merciless honesty.

The various families who made Haven their summer home took their places in the community and called on the Major frequently. Some of them he remembered; others he had forgotten. The older boys in the summer colony missed the Major's companionship, the exciting excursions, and the fishing trips. Eric Parson called one day and Mrs. Powell, taking him to the porch, said to the Major, "Eric is here to see you." He didn't even turn his head.[16]

Perhaps the most cheering news of that whole summer was the establishment of the Reclamation Bureau, which at last had been created by Congress and signed into law by Theodore Roosevelt on June 17th. For twenty-five years he had tried to convince Congress that the people needed a federal bureau of irrigation. Frank Newell was appointed its first chief, and Arthur Davis assistant chief engineer.

The bright hot days of midsummer yielded to the softer fragrant days of September. The green, gold, scarlet, and purple of the fields and woods, the departing birds, which each year the Major had observed enthusiastically, passed nature's calendar unnoticed. The Major was bundled snuggly and carried to the porch, where in the sunshine he could gaze in solitude over the blue waters of Eggemoggin Reach to the island beyond. The tide of life was ebbing fast.

[15] Fred S. Herrick, M.D., to W. C. Darrah, Aug. 11, 1946.
[16] Eric Parson, MS.

Epilogue

THERE is no better gauge of a man's character, no better testament of his spirit, than how he faces death. John Wesley Powell had strayed far from the faith of his fathers but he had grown in wisdom. His was a noble faith in man. John Wesley Powell met the inevitable with the same fearless calmness with which he met every uncertainty and decision in his full life.

On September 17, 1902, Sunday, Major Powell slipped into a coma and Dr. Herrick hurried to the bungalow as fast as he could. There was no hope. For six days the Major lingered; then, without regaining consciousness, passed away at six o'clock in the evening, September 23, 1902. Messages were telegraphed to Bram and McGee, who notified the press.[1]

Next morning Alexander Graham Bell arrived at Haven. Somehow he had learned of Major Powell's condition, but arrived too late from his retreat in Nova Scotia to have a last meeting with his friend. Emma Powell, expecting for many months the fatal outcome of Wes's illness, had been prepared for her grief. The townspeople paid their simple respects and Reverend Parson accompanied the family to Washington. Bram and McGee joined the sad party in New York.

The body of Major Powell arrived in Washington early in the morning of September 26th. It was a miserable night with a cutting cold drizzle; nevertheless, Jack Hillers, Charles Walcott, Dr. David T. Day, and Mrs. Alexander Bentley—a friend of Mrs. Powell's—had waited for hours at the Sixth Street depot. Shortly after six A.M., Dr. D. S. Lamb and Dr. Frank Baker came to the house to perform a task they had promised the Major years before: to excise the brain, preserve it, and convey it to McGee. The necropsy was finished and the body prepared to lie in state.

---

[1] Obituaries were published in metropolitan newspapers throughout the country; Washington, Bloomington, Chicago, Denver, New York, and Boston papers compiled data from their files. The Washington *Evening Star* of September 24, 1902, is typical.

The friends and associates of Major Powell gathered at one o'clock in the afternoon to hold a brief memorial service at the National Museum. It was customary to hold a private meeting to mark the passing of one of the staff. Owing however to the Major's wide friendships and reputation, the services were open to the public. Despite the inclement weather the main auditorium of the National Museum was filled to overflowing.

In the absence of Samuel Langley, who had arrived in Boston the day before but left before he could be notified, Mr. Richard Rathbun, assistant secretary of the Smithsonian, presided. W J McGee, William Dall, Otis Mason, F. W. Hodge, Marcus Baker, W. T. Harris, and Charles Walcott gave simple eulogies of a man they had come to love. Those deluded by the belief that empirical scientists are devoid of the deepest human sympathies would find inspiration in the recorded minutes of this memorial service.

The services for the family and friends were held at the Powell home on "M" street. The parlor and library were banked with floral pieces, which did not quite obliterate the rows of books which the Major had known so intimately.

At three o'clock Rev. James MacBride Sterrett gave a brief prayer and a few simple words of comfort to the grieved. He eulogized the Major for his unselfish service, his warm sympathy, his faith in mankind, and his courage in all things.

Many distinguished men crowded into the rooms to pay their last respects: from the canyon days, Harry Thompson, Jack Hillers and Fred Dellenbaugh; from the early survey days, McGee, Walcott, Gilbert, and Holmes; from the bureau, Hodge, Cyrus Thomas, and Swanton; from every walk of life, from every government department. The many organizations—scientific, literary, and patriotic—sent official representatives, in every instance a close friend to represent them.

The active pallbearers, J. K. Hillers, W. H. Holmes, H. C. Rizer, J. D. McChesney, G. K. Gilbert, and Cyrus Thomas, were drawn from the bureau and the survey. The honorary pallbearers included S. P. Langley, Charles D. Walcott, Charles J. Bell, Dr. E. M. Gallaudet, W J McGee, W. T. Harris, Gen. G. M. Sternberg, Herbert Ogden, W. F. Hillebrand, Judge M. F. Morris, Dr. C. W. Hayes, Richard Rathbun, Dr. D. C. Gilman, Marcus Baker, Dr. Frank Baker, W. B. Clark, Rev. J. MacBride Sterrett, Gen. A. W. Greely, and Rep. W. P. Hepburn. The Loyal Legion sent a delegation of friends. Powell had lived out his public career as "the Major," and the Grand Army of the Republic, in recognition of his military services though he was not a member, sent a committee from the Burnside post to take charge of the body and to accompany it with full military honors to the cemetery.

A distinguished cortege bore the remains of Major John Wesley Powell across the Potomac and laid them to rest in the western division of the officers' section of Arlington National Cemetery.

The Major was gone, missed only by the diminishing circle of intimate friends. Geology, ethnology, and irrigation had long before passed to other able hands. For thirty years he had worked for all the people.

His will read, "All my right, title, interest, and estate in and to all my property . . . of every description . . . I bequeath to my beloved wife, Emma Dean Powell." The legacy included the house on "M" street, the cottage at Haven, a collection of books, a small life insurance policy, and an insignificant bank account.

John Wesley Powell had not enriched himself. With reasonable thrift he had managed to accumulate a very modest estate, that was all. So meagerly had Major Powell provided for his family that Congress granted to Mrs. Powell a pension of twenty, increased later to fifty, dollars a month until her death. Emma survived Wes by twenty-two years, passing away March 13, 1924, at the age of eighty-nine. G. K. Gilbert in his will directed that one thousand dollars be given to Mrs. Powell in affectionate remembrance of her kindness in his hour of grief. Gilbert's estate was even smaller than the Major's. Those men of science labored *con amore*.

John Wesley Powell bequeathed a greater legacy to the nation he served—the United States Geological Survey, the Bureau of American Ethnology, and the Bureau of Reclamation. More than these, he directed the course of development of the vast semiarid region, determined the pattern of the relation of government to science, and broadened the policy of many scientific institutions. He was the most outspoken promoter of a broad program of government research in American history.

In 1930 a university professor, Walter Prescott Webb, rediscovered the significance of Major Powell's role, and in his book, *The Great Plains*, pointed out the fundamental part that Powell took in bringing about reforms in federal land policies. Then followed disastrous droughts in the region which fifty years before Powell had warned was held in perpetual mortgage by nature. In 1890 the grandparents and parents of the sufferers endured a similar drought, and with the return of rains had disregarded the catastrophe. "Droughts will come and there will be years of abundance and there will be years of disaster," was the Major's unheeded warning.

Powell's proposals for laws protecting the arid region published in 1878 are recognized as masterpieces of government. Many of the evils which Powell exposed have been corrected. Some of the measures he proposed have been enacted into law, but the fundamental problem, that there is insufficient water to irrigate all the lands that could be irrigated, remains as he left it.

The vision of harnessing the Colorado River is becoming reality. Hoover Dam in the Boulder project was erected a few miles north of a site which the Major had long ago considered feasible. The Department of Forestry and the Bureau of Mines are the two others of the long series of agencies which owe their existence to early efforts within the Geological Survey by Major Powell to create a permanent federal land policy.

In 1908 Theodore Roosevelt withdrew from public entry 1,200,000 acres of land pending an examination by the Geological Survey and the Bureau of Reclamation. The phosphate lands of the West were withdrawn and reserved until the value could be determined by the survey —barely two decades after Major Powell had been cut down for advocating this procedure. Since that time the withdrawal of lands in Alaska has been accomplished with little more than a ripple of political waters and the people have been taught to expect their government to watch over the national wealth.

The conservation movement owes not its inception but its breadth to Powell—directly in irrigation, classification of land, nationalization of irrigation projects, and indirectly through his "boys," notably F. H. Newell, A. P. Davis, and W J McGee. Newell was first director of the Reclamation Bureau and Davis one of the greatest pioneer irrigation engineers. Pinchot called McGee "the scientific brains of the Conservation Movement." Compare McGee's work in hydrology, soils, and irrigation with those of his old chief, Major Powell: contour plowing, silting of storage dams, leaching of salts—small things, perhaps, but the delicate balance in nature is upset by small things. It was McGee who carried the broader vision of conservation into the twentieth century.

The Major proposed and promoted yet another cause, a national Department of Science, a centralized administration for all of the scientific work done at government expense. Legislation for a National Science

Foundation, not very unlike that proposed sixty years ago, passed both houses of Congress in 1950. Powell's gift was perhaps vision; perhaps rare insight.

W J McGee died without worldly goods on September 4, 1912. In accordance with an old wager, McGee's and Powell's preserved brains were conveyed to Dr. Edward Spitzka. The Major had won the bet; his was the bigger. The doctor concluded the report, "Major Powell was endowed with a superior brain. What is more he used it well."

Bibliography

PRINCIPAL SOURCES

IT WOULD be impractical to enumerate more than a careful selection of the principal sources used in this biography—the more so because this study has been based primarily upon original and unpublished sources. Specific references to quoted literature are given in the footnotes.

To facilitate search by others interested in Major Powell, the important collections of manuscripts and photographs are listed below:

Public Institutions

U.S. National Archives:
    War Department
    Geological Survey
    Surveys of the Western Territories
    Smithsonian Institution
    Bureau of Indian Affairs
    Census Records
Smithsonian Institution: Bureau of American Ethnology
Library of Congress
New York Public Library, Manuscript Division:
    F. S. Dellenbaugh Collection
    R. B. Stanton Collection
    S. V. Jones Collection
Utah State Historical Society
Illinois State Normal University
New York State Museum
University of Rochester: Rush Rhees Library
Detroit Public Library: Burton Historical Collection
Denver Public Library
Harvard University Archives

Private Collections

Mr. Pearson H. Corbett
Mr. William Culp Darrah
Miss Ethel Jones

Mrs. Klotho McGee Lattin
Mr. Eric Parson
Mr. Francis Dean Schnacke
Dr. Margaret Stanley-Brown
Mrs. Laurens D. Whittemore and Miss Margaret Whittemore

MANUSCRIPTS

Adams, Samuel. 1869 Journal of the exploration of the Colorado River, July 12 to Aug. 13. (Huntington)

Allen, Rhodes. 1868 Diary, June 29—Nov. 16. (Darrah)

Baker, William Pinckney. 1912, "Early Recollections." (Mary E. Baker)

Bradley, George Young. 1869 Diary, Mar. 24—Aug. 30 (only complete journal of the 1869 expedition). (Lib. Cong.)

Darton, Nelson Horatio. 1945–1947 Letters to William Culp Darrah. (Darrah)

Dellenbaugh, Frederick Samuel. 1871–1873 Diary of the second Powell expedition of exploration down the Green and Colorado Rivers and through adjacent country, Apr. 21, 1871—Apr. 14, 1873. (N.Y. Pub. Lib.)

———. 1885 (ca.) The Colorado River expedition under the direction of Major Powell, 1871–1872. (N.Y. Pub. Lib.)

Durley, Lyle H. 1868 Diary, July 1—Nov. 20, 1868 (illegible following entry of Sept. 2). (Durley)

Garman, Samuel. 1868–1869 Letters to Gertrude Lewis. (Milner Lib., Ill. State Normal Univ.)

Griffiths, John Herbert. 1861 Marriages performed by John Herbert Griffiths, D.D. during pastorates held in Detroit, Mich. and Milwaukee, Wisc. Nov. 14, 1861—Mar. 3, 1878. (New Eng. Hist. Geneal. Soc.)

Hall, Andrew. 1869 Letters to Mrs. Mary Hall and William Hall. (Mrs. M. S. Stetson and Mrs. M. H. Laughlin)

Hamblin, Jacob. 1870 Treaty with Navajoes at Fort Defiance Nov. 5. (Corbett)

———. 1870 Letter to Erastus Snow Nov. 21 (concerning treaty at Fort Defiance). (Corbett)

Herrick, Frederick S. 1946 Letters to William Culp Darrah. (Darrah)

Illinois Institute: (1) Archives; (2) Alumni Records.

Illinois State Normal University Museum. 1867–1873 Catalogue of Accessions (includes records of birds, mammals, shells, minerals, fossils, and ethnological collections made by Major Powell).

Illinois, University of (Illinois Industrial University). 1867–1869 Proc. Bd. Trust.

Illinois Wesleyan University. 1865–1868 Faculty Minutes.

Jones, Romaine Aten (Mrs. Benner). 1949 Letters to William Culp Darrah (pertain to Jackson, Ohio). (Darrah)

Jones, Stephen Vandiver. 1871 Daily measurements and technical notes, Sept.—Oct. (N.Y. Pub. Lib.)

———. 1871 Green River, Wyoming to Lees Ferry, Apr. 21 to July 25, 1871–1872. Topographic work vicinity of Pipe Springs, Kanab, House Rock Spring, and Lees Ferry, Aug. 1 to Dec. 14, 1872. 2 vols. (N.Y. Pub. Lib.)

——— 1871–1885 Miscellaneous papers. (Jones) 1871–1872 Miscellaneous papers. (N.Y. Pub. Lib.)

Lane, Alfred Church. 1944–1946 Letters to William Culp Darrah. (Darrah)

———. 1945 "Reminiscences" dated May 6. (Darrah)

Lattin, Klotho McGee. 1945–1948 Letters to William Culp Darrah. (Darrah)

Mace, Blanche H. 1948–1949 Letters to William Culp Darrah (include interviews and reminiscences of more than thirty old-timers of the Kanab region of Utah). (Darrah)

McGee, Anita Newcomb (Mrs. W J McGee) 1891–1912 Miscellaneous papers. (Lattin)

McGee, W[illiam] J[ohn]. 1882–1910 Miscellaneous papers. (Lattin)

Medcalfe, William H. 1865 "Certification of wound of Capt. (now Major) J. W. Powell," Springfield, Ill., Jan. 3, 1865. (Nat. Arch.)

Mitchell, Joseph W. 1865 "Confirmation of wound [of J. W. Powell] at Shiloh," Springfield, Ill., Jan. 3, 1865. (Nat. Arch.)

Parson, Eric. 1946–1949 Letters to William Culp Darrah. (Darrah)

———. 1947 "Reminiscences," 4 parts. (Darrah)

Pinchot, Gifford. 1945–1946 Letters to William Culp Darrah. (Darrah)

Powell, John Wesley. 1861–1865 War Service Record. (War Dept.; Nat. Arch.)

———. 1865 "Claim for Invalid Pension," Detroit, Michigan, Jan. 31, 1865. (Nat. Arch.)

———. 1869 Journal "No. 2. Geological Notes and Sections." (Bu. Am. Ethnol.)

———. 1869 "Journal No. 1. Cañon Trip of 1869," July 2 to Aug. 28. (Bu. Am. Ethnol.)

———. 1870 "No. 8 Geological Notes of 1870 (Land trip)." (Bu. Am. Ethnol.)

———. 1871 Journal "No. 3 Steward's Notes and Sections." (Bu. Am. Ethnol.)

———. 1871 "No. 5. Journal from Green River to Brown's Park. Journal commencing Sept. 27 at Henry's Butte, with compass bearings." (Bu. Am. Ethnol.)

———. 1872 "No. 9. Geological Notes of 1872 of Marble Cañon, Grand Cañon and Paria Cañon. Also section of the Kanab in 1871" (includes vocabularies). (Bu. Am. Ethnol.)

———. 1872 "No. 10. Journal of the trip of 1872 through the Grand Cañon." (Note: Journals Nos. 4, 6, and 7 are missing. No record of their contents is known.) (Bu. Am. Ethnol.)

[———.] 1872 (1) Indenture for property—910 M Street; (2) Instrument of mortgage; (3) Deed and trust. (Recorder of Deeds, Wash., D.C.)

———. 1876–1881 Letters to Lewis Henry Morgan. (Rush Rhees Lib., Univ. of Roch.)

———. 1881–1892 Letters to James Hall. (N.Y. State Mus.)

———. 1882–1885 Letters to Alexander Agassiz. (Museum of Comparative Zoology, Harvard Univ.)

———. 1882–1901 Miscellaneous papers. (Whittemore); 1859–1902 Miscellaneous papers. (Darrah)

———. 1893 "The Last Will and Testament of John Wesley Powell," dated July 14, 1893. (Probate Ct., Wash., D.C.)

[———.] 1894 Medical history. Record—Surgery 11089. (Johns Hopkins Hosp.)

Powell, Walter Clement. 1871–1872 Diary of journey from Naperville, Illinois, to Green River Station; thence exploring the Green and Colorado Rivers and adjacent country. (Grand Canyon Mus.)

Stanley-Brown, Joseph. 1902 "John Wesley Powell. Memorial Address delivered before Washington Literary Society, December 13, 1902." (Stanley-Brown)

———. 1929 "An Eventful Career." (Stanley-Brown)

Stanton, Robert Brewster. 1889–1923 Miscellaneous Papers: (1) Personal papers; (2) Notebooks of Colorado River exploration; (3) Letters from John C. Sumner; (4) Letters from William Rhodes Hawkins; (5) Letters from John Wesley Powell. (N.Y. Pub. Lib.)

Sterrett, H. D. 1946–1947 Letters to William Culp Darrah. (Darrah)

Steward, John Fletcher. 1871 Diary of the second Powell expedition and survey down the Green and Colorado Rivers to the Paria River, thence to Kanab, Utah, May 22—Nov. 3, 1871 (originally written in shorthand; transcribed by Steward about 1900). (N.Y. Pub. Lib.)

Sumner, John C. 1869 Journal (July 6—Aug. 31) (a transcript; only a few loose pages of the original are preserved [Smith. Inst.]). (N.Y. Pub. Lib.)

Swanton, John R. 1946 Letter to William Culp Darrah dated Mar. 2. (Darrah)

Thompson, Almon Harris. 1871–1875 Journals 5 vols. (N.Y. Pub. Lib.)

United States Geological and Geographical Survey of the Western Territories. Letterbooks. (Nat. Arch.)

United States Decennial Census: 1840; 1850; 1860; 1870. (Nat. Arch.)

United States Geological Survey. Letterbooks. (Nat. Arch.)

United States War Department Records: 1861–1865 (1) Company Descriptive Book Company H 20th Regiment, Illinois Volunteer Infantry; (2) Muster rolls Company H; (3) "Captain Powell's Independent Battery" Muster-in Roll, dated December 11, 1861, Cairo, Illinois; (4) Muster rolls Battery F, 2nd Regiment Illinois Light Artillery; (5) Service Record of John Wesley Powell; (6) "Officers Casualty Sheet," State of Illinois; (7) Field and Staff Muster Out Roll, July 27, 1865; (8) "Claim and Affidavits for Invalid Pension." (Nat. Arch.)

Wheaton College. 1856–1866 Archives.
Whittemore, Margaret. 1946–1949 Letters to William Culp Darrah. (Darrah)
Willis, Bailey. 1947–1948 Letters to William Culp Darrah. (Darrah)

BOOKS

Adams, Henry. *The Education of Henry Adams*. Boston, 1918.

Adams, Samuel. *Colorado River Explorations of Samuel Adams*. 42nd Cong. 1st Sess. H.R. Misc. Doc. 37, Washington, 1871.

Agassiz, G. R. (ed.) *Letters and Recollections of Alexander Agassiz, with a Sketch of his Life and Work*. Boston, 1913.

Anderson, Robert. *Evolutions of Field Artillery*. New York, 1860.

Bailey, Paul. *Jacob Hamblin: Buckskin Apostle*. Los Angeles, 1948.

Bailey, P. J. *Festus*. Boston, 1847.

Bangs, Nathan. *A History of the Methodist Episcopal Church from Its Origin in 1776 to the General Conference of 1840*. 4 vols., New York, 1839–1842.

Bass, W. W. *Adventures in the Canyons of the Colorado*. Grand Canyon, 1919.

Bateman, Newton. *Historical Encyclopedia of Illinois and History of DuPage County*. Chicago, 1913.

Becker, G. F. *Geology of the Comstock Lode and the Washoe District*. U.S.G.S., Mon. 3, Washington, 1882.

Bell, W. A. *New Tracks in North America*. 2nd ed., London, 1870.

Bleak, J. G. *Annals of Southern Utah Mission*. 1870–1872.

Blodgett, Lorin. *Climatology of the United States*. Philadelphia, 1857.

Bowles, Samuel. *Across the Continent: A Summer's Journey to the Rocky Mountains, the Mormons, and the Pacific States, with Speaker Colfax*. Springfield, Mass., 1866.

——. *The Switzerland of America: A Summer's Vacation in the Parks and Mountains of Colorado*. Springfield, Mass., 1869.

Burnam, J. H. *History of Bloomington and Normal, McLean County, Illinois*. Bloomington, Ill., 1879.

Burt, J. S. *Past and Present of Marshall and Putnam Counties, Illinois*. Chicago, 1907.

Carter, Kate B. (ed.) *The Story of an Old Album*. Salt Lake City, 1947.

Chidlaw, B. W. *The Story of My Life*. Cleveland, 1890.

Chugarman, Samuel. *Lester Ward, the American Aristotle*. Durham, N.C., 1939.

Clarke, J. M. *James Hall of Albany, Geologist and Paleontologist*. Albany, 1921.

Colby, Charles. *Handbook of Illinois*. New York, 1855.

Cook, J. W. *Educational History of Illinois*. Chicago, 1912.

——. and McHugh, James. *A History of Illinois State Normal University*. Normal, Ill., 1882.

Cosmos Club of Washington, D.C. *Anniversary Meeting* (25th). Washington, 1904.

Cox, J. D. *The Battle of Franklin*. New York, 1897.

Curtis, J. S. *The Silver-Lead Deposits of Eureka, Nevada*. U.S.G.S. Mon. 7, Washington, 1884.

Curtiss, D. S. *Western Portraiture, and Emigrant's Guide: A Description of Wisconsin, Illinois, and Iowa; etc.* New York, 1852.

Cushing, F. H. *Zuni Folk Tales*. New York, 1901.

Dale, H. C. *The Ashley-Smith Explorations and the Discovery of a Central Route to the Pacific, 1822–1829*. Cleveland, 1918.

Dana, E. S. (ed.) *A Century of Science in America*. New Haven, 1918.

Darton, N. H. *Story of the Grand Canyon of the Colorado*. Kansas City, Mo., 1917.

Davis, A. P. *Irrigation Works Constructed by the United States Government*. New York, 1917.

Davis, W. M. *Biographical Memoir of Grove Karl Gilbert*. Nat. Acad. Sci. Memoirs, Vol. 21, 1926.

Dellenbaugh, F. S. *The Romance of the Colorado River*. New York, 1902.

——. *Breaking the Wilderness*. New York, 1905.

——. *The North Americans of Yesterday*. New York, 1906.

——. *A Canyon Voyage*. New York, 1908. 2nd ed., New Haven, 1926.

Duane, J. C. *Manual for Engineer Troops*. New York, 1862.

Dunham, H. H. *Government Handout: A Study in the Administration of the Public Lands 1875–1891*. New York, 1941.

Dutton, C. E. *Geology of the High Plateaus of Utah*. Washington, 1880.

———. *Tertiary History of the Grand Canyon District*. U.S.G.S. Mon. 2, Washington, 1882.

Dutton, E. C. *Yale University—Class of Sixty*, pp. 95–100. Boston, 1906.

Eddy, Clyde. *Down the World's Most Dangerous River*. New York, 1929.

Edwards, R. *Chicago City Guide 1869–1870*. Chicago, 1869.

Ellison, R. S. *Fort Bridger, Wyoming. A Brief History*. Casper, Wyo., 1931.

Emmons, S. F. *Geology and Mining Industry of Leadville, Colorado*. U.S.G.S. Mon. 12, Washington, 1886.

Fairchild, H. L. *The Geological Society of America 1888–1930. A Chapter in Earth Science History*. New York, 1932.

Fenton, C. L. and Fenton, M. A. *The Story of the Great Geologists*, Garden City, N.Y., 1945.

Finney, C. G. *Memoirs of Rev. Charles G. Finney*. New York, 1876.

Fletcher, R. S. *A History of Oberlin College*. 2 vols., Oberlin, Ohio, 1943.

Force, M. F. *From Fort Henry to Corinth*. New York, 1881.

Ford, W. C. *Letters of Henry Adams 1858–1891*. Boston, 1930.

Freeman, L. R. *The Colorado River Yesterday, To-Day and To-Morrow*. New York, 1923.

Fuller, M. L. *Bibliographic Review and Index of Papers Relating to Underground Waters Published by the United States Geological Survey, 1879–1904*. U.S.G.S. Water Supply Paper 120, Washington, 1905.

Gabriel, R. H. *The Course of American Democratic Thought*. New York, 1940.

Garland, Hamlin. *Ulysses S. Grant—His Life and Character*. New York, 1898.

———. *Roadside Meetings*. New York, 1930.

Geiser, S. W. *Naturalists of the Frontier*. 2nd ed., Dallas, 1948.

Geological Society of America. *Fiftieth Anniversary Volume, Geology 1888–1938*. New York, 1941.

Gerhard, Frederick. *Illinois As It Is, its history, geography, statistics, etc*. Chicago, 1857.

Gilbert, G. K. *Report on the Geology of the Henry Mountains*. Washington, 1878.

———. *Lake Bonneville*. U.S.G.S. Mon. 1, Washington, 1890.

———. (ed.) *John Wesley Powell: A Memorial to an American Explorer and Scholar*. (Reprinted, with slight changes, from *The Open Court*, Vols. 16, 17.) Chicago, 1903.

Gilpin, William. *Mission of the North American People—Geographical, Social, and Political*. Philadelphia, 1873.

Gorlinski, Joseph. (del.) *Map of the United States and Territories*. U.S. Land Office, Washington, 1868.

Hall's *Northern Counties (Illinois) Gazetteer and Directory 1855–1856*. Chicago, 1855.

Harvard University. *Historical Register of Harvard University 1636–1936*. Cambridge, Mass., 1937.

———. *Quinquennial Catalogue of the Officers and Graduates 1636–1930*. Cambridge, Mass., 1930.

Hendrickson, W. B. *David Dale Owen: Pioneer Geologist of the Middle West*. Ind. Hist. Coll., V. 24, Indianapolis, 1943.

[Henry, Joseph]. *A Memorial to Joseph Henry*. Washington, 1880.

Hibbard, B. H. *A History of the Public Land Policies*. New York, 1924.

Hinton, R. J. *Irrigation in the United States*. Washington, 1890.

Hodge, F. W. *Handbook of American Indians North of Mexico*. 2 vols., Bu. Am. Ethnol. Bull. 30, Washington, 1910.

Hofstadter, Richard. *Social Darwinism in American Thought 1860–1915*. Philadelphia, 1945.

Hopkins, Sarah Winnemucca. *Life Among the Paiutes*. Boston, 1883.

Humphreys, H. H. *Andrew Atkins Humphreys*. Philadelphia, 1924.

Illinois Adjutant General's Report 1861–66. Vols. 2 and 8, Springfield, Ill., 1888.

Illinois-Vicksburg Military Park Commission. Illinois at Vicksburg. Chicago, 1907.

Illinois Board of Education. *Proceedings*. Springfield, 1858–1875.

Illinois Institute. *Catalogues*. Jacksonville, 1855–1856, 1856–1857.

Illinois State Agricultural Society. *Transactions, with notices and proceedings of county societies, and kindred associations.* Vols. 3, 4, 1857–1860, Springfield, 1859–1861.

Ives, J. C. *Report on the Colorado River of the West.* Washington, 1861.

James, G. W. *Reclaiming the Arid West.* New York, 1917.

Jenkins, Warren. *The Ohio Gazetteer.* 1st rev. ed., Columbus, O., 1837.

Johnson, R. U. and Buel, C. C. (eds.) *Battles and Leaders of the Civil War.* 4 vols., New York, 1884–1887.

Jones, R. A. *Early Jackson.* Columbus, O., 1942.

King, Clarence. *First Annual Report of the United States Geological Survey.* Washington, 1880.

[————]. *Clarence King Memoirs: The Helmet of Mambrino.* New York, 1904.

Kolb, Emery and Kolb, Ellsworth. *Through the Grand Canyon from Wyoming to Mexico.* New York, 1920.

Lapham, I. A. *Wisconsin: Its Geography and Topography, History, Geology, and Mineralogy. . . .* 2nd ed., Milwaukee, 1846.

Lexington Historical Society. *The Battle of Lexington* (Missouri) *Sept. 18–19–20, 1861.* Lexington, Mo., 1903.

Lindsey, B. M. *Long Creek Township in Macon County, Illinois.* Decatur, Ill., 1929–1932.

Little, J. A. *Jacob Hamblin.* Faith Promoting Series, Salt Lake City, 1881.

Lyell, Charles. *Travels in America in the Years 1841–2.* 2 vols., New York, 1845.

McElroy, Robert. *Grover Cleveland, The Man and The Statesman.* 2 vols., New York, 1923.

McGee, E. R. *Life of W J McGee.* Farley, Iowa, 1915.

McLeister, I. F. *History of the Wesleyan Methodist Church of America.* Syracuse, N.Y., 1934.

Mason, George. *Illinois at Shiloh.* Chicago, 1905.

Marshall, A. O. *Army Life; From a Soldier's Journal.* 2nd ed., Joliet, Ill., 1884.

Mather, W. W. *First Annual Report on the Geological Survey of Ohio.* Columbus, Ohio, 1838.

Mather, W. W. *Second Annual Report on the Geological Survey of Ohio.* Columbus, Ohio, 1838.

Matlack, L. C. *Anti-Slavery Struggle and Triumph in the Methodist Episcopal Church.* New York, 1881.

Mayes, Edward. *Lucius Q. C. Lamar: His Life, Times, and Speeches.* Nashville, Tenn., 1896.

Merrill, G. P. *Contributions to a History of American State Geological and Natural History Surveys.* U.S. Nat. Mus. Bull. 109, Washington, 1920.

Merrill, G. P. *The First One Hundred Years of American Geology.* New Haven, 1924.

Mills, Anson. *My Story.* New York, 1918.

Mode, P. G. *The Frontier Spirit in American Christianity.* New York, 1923.

Morgan, L. H. *Ancient Society.* New York, 1877.

National Cyclopedia of American Biography

Nelson, Bruce. *Land of the Dacotahs.* Minneapolis, 1946.

Nevins, Allan. *Abram S. Hewitt: With Some Account of Peter Cooper.* New York, 1935.

Newcomb, Simon. *The Reminiscences of an Astronomer.* Boston, 1903.

Newell, F. H. *Irrigation in the United States.* New York, 1902.

Oberlin College. *General Catalogue, 1833–1908.* Oberlin, Ohio, 1909.

Osborn, H. F. *Cope: Master Naturalist.* Princeton, 1931.

Owen, D. D. *Report of a Geological Reconnaissance of the Chippewa Land District of Wisconsin.* 30th Cong. 1st Sess. Sen. Exec. Doc. 57, Washington, 1848.

Owen, Hugh. *Some Account of the Ancient and Present State of Shrewsbury.* Shrewsbury, England, 1808.

Piatt, Donn (posth., ed. H. V. Boynton). *General George H. Thomas. A Critical Biography.* Cincinnati, 1893.

Pinchot, Gifford. *Breaking New Ground.* New York, 1947.

Powell, C. S. *History and Genealogies of the Powells in America.* St. Petersburg, Fla., 1935.

Powell, J. W. *Survey of the Colorado of the West.* 42nd Cong. 2d Sess. H.R. Misc. Doc. 173, Washington, 1872.

————. *Geographical and Geological Surveys West of the Mississippi.* 43rd Cong. 1st. Sess. H.R. Rept. 612, Washington, 1874.

———. *Expedition of the Colorado River of the West and Its Tributaries.* Washington, 1875.

———. *Report on the Geology of the Eastern Portion of the Uinta Mountains and a Region of the Country Thereto.* U.S.G.S. Territories, Washington, 1876.

———. *Introduction to the Study of Indian Languages.* 1st ed., Washington, 1877. 2nd (rev.) ed., Washington, 1880.

———. *Report on the Lands of the Arid Region of the United States, with a More Detailed Account of the Lands of Utah.* 45th Cong. 2nd Sess. H.R. Exec. Doc. 73, Washington, 1878.

———. *Report on the Methods of Surveying the Public Domain to the Secretary of the Interior at the Request of the National Academy of Sciences.* Washington, 1878.

———. *Second Annual Report of the United States Geological Survey (1880–1881).* Washington, 1882.

———. *Canyons of the Colorado.* Meadville, Pa., 1895.

———. *Truth and Error or the Science of Intellection.* Chicago, 1898.

———. and Ingalls, G. W. *Report of Special Commissioners on the condition of the Ute Indians of Utah; the Paiutes of Utah, northern Arizona, southern Nevada, and southeastern California; the Go-si-utes of Utah and Nevada; the northwestern Shoshones of Idaho and Utah; and the western Shoshones of Nevada; and report concerning claims of settlers in the Mo-a-pa Valley, southeastern Nevada.* Washington, 1874.

Rammelkamp, C. H. *Illinois College: A Centennial History.* New Haven, 1928.

Reagan, J. H. (ed. W. F. McCaleb) *Memoirs, with special reference to secession and the civil war.* New York, 1906.

Reed, D. W. *The Battle of Shiloh.* Washington, 1909.

Rich, J. W. *The Battle of Shiloh.* Iowa City, 1911.

Richardson, Harriet Fyffe. *Quaker Pioneers.* Milwaukee, 1940.

Robbins, R. M. *Our Landed Heritage: The Public Domain 1776–1936.* Princeton, 1942.

Rodgers, A. D. *American Botany 1873–1892.* Princeton, 1944.

Rogers, E. S. *William Barton Rogers—Life and Letters.* 2 vols., Boston, 1896.

Schmeckebier, L. F. *Catalogue and Index of the Publications of the Hayden, King, Powell and Wheeler Surveys.* U.S.G.S. Bull. 222, Washington, 1904.

Schuchert, Charles. *Stratigraphy of the Eastern and Central United States.* New York, 1943.

———. and LeVene, C. M. *O. C. Marsh: Pioneer in Paleontology.* New Haven, 1940.

Schurz, Carl. *The Reminiscences of Carl Schurz.* 3 vols., New York, 1908.

Scott, W. B. *Some Memoirs of a Paleontologist.* Princeton, 1939.

Shaler, N. S. *Autobiography.* Boston, 1909.

Siebert, W. H. *The Underground Railroad.* New York, 1898.

Smith, T. C. *The Life and Letters of James Abram Garfield.* 2 vols., New Haven, 1925.

Smithsonian Institution. *Essays in Historical Anthropology in North America Published in Honor of John R. Swanton.* Smith. Misc. Coll. V. 100, Washington, 1940.

Smythe, W. E. *The Conquest of Arid America.* New York, 1900.

Stanton, R. B. (Chalfant, J. M., ed.) *Colorado River Controversies.* New York, 1932.

Statesman's Yearbook (Macmillan's). New York.

Stern, B. J. *Lewis Henry Morgan: Social Evolutionist.* Chicago, 1931.

Steward, J. F. *Last Maramech and Earliest Chicago.* Chicago, 1903.

Steward, J. H. *Basin-Plateau aboriginal socio-political groups.* Bu. Am. Ethnol. Bull. 120, Washington, 1938.

Stewart, W. M. (Brown, G. R. ed.) *Reminiscences of Wm. S. Stewart of Nevada.* New York, 1908.

Stone, J. F. *Canyon Country.* New York, 1932.

Summers, R. A. *Conquerors of the River.* New York, 1939.

Taft, Robert. *Photography and the American Scene.* New York, 1942.

Taylor, Bayard. *Colorado: A Summer Trip (1866).* New York, 1867.

Tewksbury, D. G. *The Founding of American Colleges and Universities Before the Civil War.* New York, 1932.

Thoron, Ward (ed.) *The Letters of Mrs. Henry Adams.* Boston, 1936.

Tibbetts, N. V. *Where to Spend the Summer—Castle View—Brooklin, Maine.* Washington.

United States Congress. *Report of the Special Committee of the United States Senate on the Irrigation and Reclamation of Arid Lands.* Washington, 1890.

United States Congressional Record (including its predecessor, the *Congressional Globe*).

United States Engineers (War) Department. *Map of the Siege of Vicksburg 1863.* Washington, 1869.

United States Bureau of Ethnology (Smithsonian Institution). *Annual Reports.*

United States Geological Survey. *Annual Reports.*

United States Statutes at Large. Washington.

U.S. Surgeon General. *Medical and Surgical History of the War of the Rebellion.* 4 vols., Washington, 1888.

Utah Historical Quarterly. Records of the Powell Colorado expeditions. Vols. 15–17, Salt Lake City, 1947–1949.

War of the Rebellion. Official Records. Washington.

Ward, L. F. *Dynamic Sociology, or applied social science.* . . . 2 vols., New York, 1883.

Ward, Lester. *Glimpses of the Cosmos.* 6 vols., New York, 1913–1918.

Warden, R. B. *Account of the Private Life and Public Services of Salmon Portland Chase.* Cincinnati, 1874.

Warman, P. C. *Catalogue and Index of the Publications of the United States Geological Survey, 1880–1901.* U.S.G.S. Bull. 177, Washington, 1901.

Warren, H. V. *The History of Putnam County, From Its Earliest Settlement to the Year 1876.* Hennepin, Ill., 1877.

Webb, W. P. *The Great Plains.* Boston, 1931.

Wheeler, G. M. *Chronological Account of Explorations of the Colorado River of the West.* Washington, 1880.

————. *United States Geographical Surveys West of the 100th Meridian. Vol. 1 Geographical Report.* Washington, 1889.

White, A. D. *History of the Warfare of Science with Theology in Christendom.* 2 vols., New York, 1898.

White, L. A. (ed.) *Pioneers in American Anthropology.* Albuquerque, N.M., 1940.

Willard, E. B. (ed.) *The Hanging Rock Iron Region of Ohio.* 2 vols., Chicago, 1916.

Williams, Daniel Webster. *History of Jackson County.* Columbus, 1915.

Willis, Bailey. *A Yanqui in Patagonia.* Stanford, 1947.

Wilmarth, M. Grace. *Lexicon of the Geologic Names of the United States.* U.S.G.S. Bull. 892, 2 vols., Washington, 1938.

Worthington, Thomas. *A Correct History of the Battle of Shiloh.* Washington, 1880.

ARTICLES

Beaman, E. O. "The Cañon of the Colorado and the Moqui Pueblos." *Appleton's Journal,* 11: (Apr.–May), 1874.

Beecher, C. E. "Othniel Charles Marsh." *Bull. Geol. Soc. Am.,* 11:521–37, 1899.

Bishop, F. M. "Journal—August 15, 1870—June 3, 1872." (Charles Kelly ed.) *Utah Hist. Quart.,* 15:159–238, 1947.

————. "Personal Reminiscences of John W. Powell." *Trans. Utah Acad. Sci.,* 2:16–27 (1918), 1922.

Brewer, W. H. "John Wesley Powell." *Amer. Jour. Sci.,* 14:377–82, 1902.

Bryant, H. C. "John Wesley Powell." *Cosmos Club Bull.,* 1(8):2–5, 1948.

Byers, W. N. "First Ascent of Long's Peak." (Reprint of account published in *Rocky Mountain News,* Denver, 1868.) *The Trail,* 7(5):21–23, 1914.

Canby, W. M. and Rose, J. N. "George Vasey: a biographical sketch." *Bot. Gaz.* 18:170–83, 1893.

Cope, E. D. "Unification of the Geological Survey—an editorial review." *American Naturalist,* 13:35–37, 1879.

Dall, W. H. "Charles Abiather White (1862–1910)." *Nat. Acad. Sci. Biog. Mem.,* 7:225–43, 1911.

Darrah, W. C. "Biographical sketches and original documents of the first Powell Expedition of 1869." *Utah Hist. Quart.* 15:9–148, 1947.

———. "Three Letters by Andrew Hall." *Utah Hist. Quart.*, 16–17:505–8, 1949.

Darton, N. H. "Memoir of W J McGee." *Ann. Assn. Am. Geog.*, 3:103–10, 1914.

Davis, C. W. "The Exhaustion of Arable Lands." *Forum*, 9:461–74, 1890.

Dawson, T. F. "Lost Alone on Bear River Forty Years Ago." (Story of W. H. Bishop, with Powell in 1868.) *The Trail*, 11(2):13–20, 1918.

———. "More Light on James White's Trip Through the Grand Canyon." *The Trail*, 11(9):5–14, 1919.

DeMotte, H. C. "Six Days on the Kaibab." *Ill. Wesl. Alumni Jour.*, 1:233–39, 1872.

Dickason, D. H. "Henry Adams and Clarence King, The Record of a Friendship." *New Eng. Quart.*, 17:229–54, 1944.

Emmons, S. F. "Clarence King (1842–1901)." *Nat. Acad. Sci. Biog. Mem.*, 6:27–55, 1906.

Ganoe, J. T. "The Desert Land Act in Operation 1877–1891." *Agr. Hist.*, 11:146–49, 153–54, 1937.

Gary, O. J. "Wheaton Seventy Years Ago." *Jour. Ill. State Hist. Soc.*, 20:128–37, 1926.

Gilbert, G. K. "John Wesley Powell." *Science* (n.s.), 16:561–67, 1902.

Hack, J. T. "The Changing Physical Environment of the Hopi Indians of Arizona." *Peabody Mus. Am. Arch. and Ethnol. Harv. Univ.*, 35(1):1942.

Hague, Arnold. "Samuel Franklin Emmons (1841–1911)." *Nat. Acad. Sci. Biog. Mem.*, 7:309–34, 1912.

Hobbs, W. H. "John Wesley Powell 1834–1902." *Sci. Monthly*, 39:519–29, 1934.

Iddings, J. P. "Arnold Hague (1840–1917)." *Nat. Acad. Sci. Biog. Mem.*, 9:21–38, 1919.

Jones, S. V. "Journal, 1871–1872." (ed. Herbert E. Gregory). *Utah Hist. Quart.*, 16–17:11–174, 1949.

Keplinger, L. W. "The First Ascent of Long's Peak." *Kans. Hist. Coll.*, 14:340–53, 1915.

———. "First Ascent of Long's Peak." *The Trail*, 7(8):13–15, 1915.

Manning, T. G. "The Influence of Clarence King and John Wesley Powell on the Early History of the United States Geological Survey." *Interim Proc. Geol. Soc. Am.*, part 2, 23–29, May 1947.

Merrill, G. P. "John Wesley Powell." *Am. Geol.*, 31:327–33, 1903.

Moulton, F. R. "The American Association for the Advancement of Science: A Brief Historical Sketch." *Science*, 108:217–18, 1948.

National Academy of Sciences. "Report for 1878–1879." Washington, 1879.

Osborn, H. F. "Edward Drinker Cope (1840–1897)." *Nat. Acad. Sci. Biog. Mem.*, 13:126–317, 1930.

Powell, J. W. "Scientific expedition to the Rocky Mountains. Preliminary report of Prof. J. W. Powell." *Proc. Ill. State Bd. Ed.*, 9–13, 1867.

———. "Report of the Survey of the Colorado River of the West, March 25, 1872." *42nd Cong. 2nd Sess. H.R. Misc. Doc. 173*, 1872.

———. "Report of the Survey of the Colorado River of the West. Jan. 17, 1873." *42nd Cong. 3d Sess. H.R. Misc. Doc. 76*, 1873.

———. "Some remarks on the geological structure of a district of country lying to the north of the Grand Cañon of the Colorado." *Am. Jour. Sci. and Arts (3d ser.)*, 5:456–65, 1873.

———. "Report on the Survey of the Colorado River of the West. April 30, 1874." *43rd Cong. 1st Sess. H.R. Misc. Doc. 265*, 1874.

———. "Remarks on the structural geology of the Colorado of the West." *Bull. Phil. Soc. Wash.*, 1:48–51, 1874.

———. "The Cañons of the Colorado." *Scribner's Monthly*, 9:293–310, 394–409, 523–37, 1875.

———. "Physical Features of the Colorado Valley." *Pop. Sci. Monthly*, 7:385–99, 531–42, 670–80, 1875.

———. "An overland trip to the Grand Cañon." *Scribner's Monthly*, 10:659–78, 1875.

———. "The ancient province of Tusayan." *Scribner's Monthly*, 11:193–213, 1876.

———. "Types of orographic structure." *Am. Jour. Sci. and Arts (3d ser.)*, 12:414–28, 1877.

———. "A discourse on the philosophy of the North American Indians." *Jour. Am. Geog. Soc. N.Y.*, 8:251–68, 1878.

———. "Mythologic Philosophy." *Pop. Sci. Monthly*, 15:795–808; 16:56–66, 1879–1880.

———. "On the evolution of language, as exhibited in the specialization of the grammatic processes, the differentiation of the parts of speech and the integration of the sentence; from a study of Indian languages." *Bu. Ethnol. (1st Ann. Rep.)*, 1–16, 1881.

Powell, J. W. "Sketch of the Mythology of the North American Indians." *Bu. Ethnol. (1st Ann. Rep.)*, 17–56, 1881.

————. "Sketch of Lewis H. Morgan, president of the American Association for the Advancement of Science." *Pop. Sci. Monthly*, 18:114–21, 1881.

————. "Outlines of Sociology." *Trans. Anthrop. Soc. Wash.*, 1:106–29, 1882. (Smith. Misc. Coll. Vol. 25.)

————. "Darwin's Contributions to Philosophy." *Proc. Biol. Soc. Wash.*, 1:60–70, 1882. (In Smith. Misc. Coll. Vol. 25.)

————. "Human evolution." *Trans. Anthrop. Soc. Wash.*, 2:176–208, 1883.

————. "Review of Ward's *Dynamic Sociology.*" *Science*, 2:45–49, 105–8, 171–74, 223–26, 1883.

————. "The three methods of evolution." *Bull. Phil. Soc. Wash.*, 6:27–52, 1884. (Smith. Misc. Coll. Vol. 33.)

————. "On the state of the interior of the earth." *Science*, 3:480–82, 1884.

————. "On the fundamental theory of dynamic geology." *Science*, 3:511–13, 1884.

————. "Address delivered at the inauguration of the Corcoran School of Science and Arts, in the Columbian University, Washington, D.C., October 1, 1884" (pamphlet). Washington, 1884.

————. "From savagery to barbarism." *Trans. Anthrop. Soc. Wash.*, 3:173–96, 1885.

————. "The organization and plan of the United States Geological Survey." *Am. Jour. Sci. (3rd ser.)*, 29:93–102, 1885.

————. "The administration of the scientific work of the general government." *Science*, 5:51–55, 1885.

————. "The larger import of scientific education." *Pop. Sci. Monthly*, 26:452–56, 1885.

————. in "Testimony before a joint commission to consider the present organization of the Signal Service, Geological Survey, Coast and Geodetic Survey, and the Hydrographic Office of the Navy Department, with a view to secure greater efficiency and economy of operation." *49th Cong. 1st Sess. Sen. Misc. Doc. 82*, Washington, 1886.

————. "The cause of earthquakes." *Forum*, 2:370–91, 1887.

————. "From barbarism to civilization." *Am. Anthrop.*, 1:97–123, 1888.

————. "Competition as a factor in human evolution." *Am. Anthrop.*, 1:297–323, 1888.

————. "The laws of hydraulic degradation." *Science*, 12:229–233, 1888.

————. "Methods of geologic cartography in use by the United States Geological Survey." *Cong. geol. internat., C.R. 3 Sess. (Berlin)*, 221–40, 1888 (read by W J McGee).

————. "The personal characteristics of Professor Baird." *Bull. Phil. Soc. Wash.*, 10:71–77, 1888.

————. "The Lesson of Conemaugh." *North Am. Rev.*, 149:150–56, 1889.

————. "The Non-Irrigable Lands of the Arid Regions." *Century Illus. Monthly Mag.*, 39:915–22, 1890.

————. "The Irrigable Lands of the Arid Region." *Century Illus. Monthly Mag.*, 39:766–76, 1890.

————. "Institutions for the arid lands." *Century Illus. Monthly Mag.*, 40:111–16, 1890.

————. in "Irrigation and reclamation of public lands." *51st Cong. 1st Sess. Sen. Rep. 1466*, 1890.

————. "Evolution of music from dance to symphony." *Am. Assn. Adv. Sci. Proc. 38th Meet.*, 1–21, 1890 (read by G. K. Gilbert).

————. "The new lake in the desert." *Scribner's Magazine*, 10:463–68, 1891.

————. "Indian linguistic families of America North of Mexico." *Bu. Ethnol. 7th Ann. Rep.*, 1–142, 1891.

————. "National Agencies for scientific research." *Chautauquan*, 14:37–42, 160–65, 291–97, 422–25, 545–49, 668–73, 1891–1892.

————. "Our recent floods." *North Am. Rev.*, 155:149–59, 1892.

————. "The geologic map of the United States." *Trans. Am. Inst. Min. Eng.*, 21:877–87, 1893.

————. "The mineral exhibits at Chicago" (unsigned). *Brit. Trade Jour.*, 31:520–22, 1893.

————. "Are our Indians becoming extinct?" *Forum*, 15:343–54, 1893.

————. (Address). *Proc. Internat. Irr. Cong.* (Los Angeles), Oct. 1893. 106–20, 1893.

————. "Simplified spelling." *Am. Anthrop.*, 6:193–95, 1893.

————. "The water supplies of the arid region." *Irrigation Age*, 6:54–65, 1894.

————. "Ownership of lands in the arid region." *Irrigation Age*, 6:143–49, 1894.

————. "The North American Indians." in Shaler, N.S., *The United States of America, A Study of the American Commonwealth.* 1:190–272, New York, 1894.

————. "On the nature of motion." *The Monist*, 5:55–64, 1894.

————. "Immortality" (verse). *Open Court*, 8:4335–37, 1894.

————. "Physiographic Processes." *Nat. Geog. Mono.*, 1:1–32, 1895.

————. "Physiographic features." *Nat. Geog. Mono.*, 1:33–64, 1895.

————. "Physiographic regions of the United States." *Nat. Geog. Mono.*, 1:65–100, 1895.

————. "Proper Training and the Future of the Indians." *Forum*, 18:622–29, 1895.

————. "The Soul" (verse). *The Monist*, 5(3):app. 1–16, 1895.

————. "Relation of Primitive Peoples to Environment Illustrated by American Examples." *Ann. Rep. Smith. Inst. 1895*, 625–37, 1896.

————. "On primitive institutions." *Am. Bar Assn., Rep. 19th Ann. Meet.*, 573–93, 1896.

————. "Seven Venerable Ghosts." *Am. Anthrop.* 9:67–91, 1896.

————. "James Dwight Dana." *Science* (N.S.), 3:181–85, 1896.

————. "On Regimentation." *Bu. Ethnol. 15th Ann. Rep.*, civ–cxxi, 1897.

————. "An hypothesis to account for the movement in the crust of the earth." *Jour. Geol.*, 6:1–9, 1898.

————. "The five categories of human activities—esthetology, technology, sociology, philology, and sophiology." *Bu. Am. Ethnol. 17th Ann. Rep.*, xxvii–xxxviii, 1898.

————. "The Evolution of Religion." *The Monist*, 8:183–204, 1898.

————. "Esthetology, or the science of activities designed to give pleasure." *Am. Anthrop.* (N.S.), 1:1–40, 1899.

————. "Technology, or the science of industries." *Am. Anthrop.* (N.S.), 1:319–49, 1899.

————. "Sociology, or the science of institutions." *Am. Anthrop.* (N.S.), 1:475–509, 695–745, 1899.

————. "The Lessons of folklore." *Am. Anthrop.* (N.S.), 2:1–36, 1900.

————. "Philology, or the science of activities designed for expression." *Am. Anthrop.* (N.S.), 2:603–37, 1900.

————. "Sophiology, or the science designed to give instruction." *Am. Anthrop.* (N.S.), 3:51–79, 1901.

[————]. "In Memory of John Wesley Powell." Minutes of a meeting held at the U.S. National Museum (ed. S. P. Langley). *Science* (N.S.), 16:782–90, 1902.

[————]. "Proceedings of a Meeting Commemorative of His Distinguished Services." February 16, 1903. *Proc. Wash. Acad. Sci.*, 5:99–187, 1903.

Ruffner, E. H. "Report of a Reconnaissance in the Ute Country made in 1873." Washington, 1874.

Schuchert, C. "Othniel Charles Marsh." *Nat. Acad. Sci. Biog. Mem.*, 20:1–78, 1939.

Shoup, F. A. "The Art of War in '62—Shiloh." *United Service* (ser. 3), 8:67–80, 1905.

Smith, H. N. "Rain Follows the Plow: The Notion of Increased Rainfall for the Great Plains, 1844–1880." *Huntington Lib. Quart.*, 10:169–93, 1947.

————. "Clarence King, John Wesley Powell, and the Establishment of the United States Geological Survey." *Miss. Vall. Hist. Rev.*, 34:37–58, 1947.

Spitzka, E. A. "A Study of the Brain of the Late Major J. W. Powell." *Am. Anthrop.* (N.S.), 5:585–643, 1903.

Stegner, Wallace. "Jack Sumner and John Wesley Powell." *Colorado Magazine*, 26:61–69, 1949.

Sterling, E. W. "The Powell Irrigation Survey 1888–1893." *Miss. Vall. Hist. Rev.*, 27:421–34, 1940.

Steward, J. H. "Notes on Hillers' Photographs of the Paiute and Ute Indians Taken on the Powell Expedition of 1873." *Smith. Misc. Coll. 98*, No. 18, 1939.

Thompson, A. H. "Diary of Almon Harris Thompson, Geographer, Explorations of the Colorado River of the West and Its Tributaries. 1871–1875" (ed. Herbert E. Gregory). *Utah Hist. Quart.*, 7:1939.

Walcott, C. D. "John Wesley Powell." *U.S.G.S. 24th Ann. Rep.*, 271–87, 1903.

Ward, Lester. "Professor John Wesley Powell." *Pop. Sci. Monthly*, 20:390–97, 1882.

Warman, P. C. "Catalogue of the Published Writings of John Wesley Powell" (lists 251 titles, with some duplication. It is an incomplete catalogue). *Proc. Wash. Acad. Sci.*, 5:131–87, 1903.

White, C. A. "Ferdinand Vandiveer Hayden, 1839–1887." *Nat. Acad. Sci. Biog. Mem.*, 3:395–413, 1893.

White, C. A. "John Strong Newberry, 1822–1892." *Nat. Acad. Sci. Biog. Mem.*, 6:1–25, 1906.

Zwemer, R. L. "The National Academy of Sciences and the National Research Council." *Science*, 108:234–35, 1948.

Zuidema, H. P. "Discovery of Letters by Lyell and Darwin." *Jour. Geol.*, 55:439–45, 1947.

NEWSPAPERS

Bloomington (Illinois) *Pantograph*
Boston *Transcript*
Cheyenne *Leader*
Chicago *Daily Republication*
Chicago *Interocean*
Chicago *Tribune*
Denver *Rocky Mountain Daily News*
Denver *Post*
Detroit *Free Press*
Hennepin (Illinois) *Putnam County Record*
Jackson (Ohio) *Standard*
Lacon (Illinois) *Home Journal*
Naperville (Illinois) *Clarion*
New York *Herald Tribune*
New York *Times*
Salt Lake City—*Deseret Evening News*
Salt Lake City *Tribune*
Washington *Chronicle*
Washington *Evening Star*

Index

Abbott, Henry L., 298
absolutism, 382
Adams, Capt. Samuel, 116, 145, 146, 183, 220
Adams, Henry, 247, 251, 376, 386
Adrian, Michigan, 213n
Agassiz, Alexander, 244, 293, 294, 344
Agassiz, Ida (Mrs. Henry Lee Higginson), 294
Agassiz, Louis, 76, 293, 332
Agriculture, U.S. Department of, 309, 287, 333
Ah Chug, 117, 162
Aiken, John, 94
Alabama, geological survey of, 317
Alatoona, Georgia, 69
Albany, New York, 3
Alberger, Col., 180
Allegheny observatory, 292
Allegheny River, 6, 43
Allen, Rhodes C., 94, 95n, 96, 103, 104, 106
American Anthropologist, 383
American Antiquarian Society, 266
American Association for the Advancement of Science, 219, 263, 355; memorializes Congress on forest reserves, 227; Powell's speech as retiring president, 327
American Express Company, 81
American Geographical Society, 262, 355
American Journal of Science, 150, 215
Ames, Oliver, 333
Ancient Society, 262, 359
Andrews, Elisha B., 112
Anthropological Society of Washington, 264, 265, 355
arid regions, 222, 223, 234, 399; land classification of, 236; problems of, 312
Arizona, 153, 154, 157, 183, 194, 195, 200, 211, 212, 230, 304, 316, 324, 352
Arkansas River, 237
Arlington National Cemetery, 398
Army Medical Library, 219
Arrival, the, 366

artesian wells, use in irrigation, 309, 310
Asey, Joseph, 144
Ashley Falls, 123, 166
Ashley, Wm. H., 123
Aspen, Colorado, 343
Aspen Mountain, 104
Atkins, John D. C., 246, 249, 251
Atlanta, battle of, 69
Aurora, Illinois, 162, 213, 326

Bacon, Mr., 167
badlands, 81, 82, 194
Bagehot, Walter, 359
Bagley, boat builder, 113, 161
Bailey, P. J., 40, 359
Baird, Spencer, 112, 152, 205, 214, 218, 259, 261, 265, 268, 271, 298, 390
Baker, Frank, 396, 397
Baker, Morris, 328, 351, 352, 397
Baker, Wm. Pinckney, 32n
Ballou, Wm. Hosea, 338, 339
Bandelier, A. F., 263
Bangor, Maine, 370
Barbenceta, Chief, 159
barometers, 119, 126
Battery F, Second Illinois Artillery, 52-57, 59, 60, 62, 63, 65, 69
Bauer, George, 340
Beaman, E. O., 161, 164-166, 168, 169, 173, 175, 176, 178, 182, 187
Bear Creek Canyon, 97
Bear Lake, Utah, 301, 305
Bear River, see Yampa River
Beaver Canyon, Utah, 252
Bell, Alexander Graham, 386, 396
Bell, Alexander Melville, 386
Bell, Charles J., 397
Bell, Wm. A., 120n, 148, 150
Belleville mission, 176
Beloit, Wisconsin, 18
Benn, Charlie, 154
Bennett, F. F., 158, 159
Bentley, Mrs. Alexander, 396

Moapa Valley, 201
Monist, the, 376
Monongahela River, 43
monopoly of land, 234, 235
monopoly of water, 234, 235
Montana, 307, 316
Montgomery, Samuel, 9
Moore, Ira, 45, 75
Morgan, J. T., 227
Morgan, Lewis H., 227, 258, 262, 267, 359, 383; *Ancient Society,* 262, 359
Mormons, 4, 109, 135, 140, 143, 144, 153, 154, 156, 158, 159, 171-175, 194, 195, 198, 231
Morris, M. F., 397
Morrison, Wm. R., 71n
Mount Desert, Maine, 362
Mount Lincoln, 89, 91, 99
Mount Morris, New York, 5
Mount Trumbull, 154, 155, 192
Munsell, O. S., 74

Naperville, Illinois, 31, 162
Narrow Canyon, 172
Nashville, Tennessee, 65, 69, 73; battle of, 70
Natchez, Mississippi, 68
National Academy of Sciences, 226, 279, 286, 288, 289, 291, 292, 339, 340; Powell becomes member, 283; recommends consolidation of surveys, 243-247, 249
National Geographic Society, 328, 350
National Science Foundation, 399, 400
natural law, 383
Nautical Almanac, 287
Naval Observatory, 287, 345
Navy Department, U.S., 287, 292
Nebeker, A., 154
Nebraska, 309
Nellie Powell, the, 164, 189
Nettleton, E. S., 302, 308
Nevada, 157, 194-197, 200, 201, 301, 304, 307, 316
Newberry, John S., 109, 239-241, 244, 328
Newbury, Massachusetts, 111
Newburyport, Massachusetts, 352
Newcomb, Simon, 218, 244, 279, 283, 287, 292
Newell, Frank, 311, 395, 399
New Haven, Connecticut, 337
New Jersey, geological survey of, 317
New Mexico, 157, 195, 301, 302, 307, 311, 316
New Orleans, Louisiana, 38, 42, 67
Newtonian universe, 382, 383
New York, 3, 249, 267; geological survey of, 317
New York Herald, 339, 347

New York, New York, 262, 278
New York Tribune, 226, 330, 351
Noble, John W., 338
Noettling, C. F., 185n, 186n
No-Name, the, 118, 120, 124, 126; loss of, 125; wreckage sighted by 1871 party, 168, 170
Normal, Illinois, 46, 75, 78, 81, 91, 94, 102, 112, 128, 180, 187
North Carolina, geological survey of, 317
North Dakota, 223, 235, 304, 345
North Park, 97
Northwest Territory, 9
Noyes, Alex. G., 71

Oberlin College, 10, 25, 37-40, 71, 261, 328, 375
Ogden, Herbert, 397
Ogden, Utah, 252
Ohio, 6ff, 17, 19, 249, 261
Ohio Canal, 6
Oklahoma, 223, 235
Olean, New York, 6
Omaha Bee, 308, 309
Omaha, Nebraska, 95
Omaha Republican, 145
Open Court, 376
Oraibi, Arizona, 157
Oregon, 261, 304, 316
osage orange, 37, 40
Osborne, A. C., 180
Osborne, H. F., 340
Ottawa, Illinois, 44

Packard, A. S., 246, 247
paleobotany, 280
paleontology, 278
Palmer, J. M., 148
Palmyra, New York, 4
Panamit Mountain, 195
Paria River, 136, 153, 164, 173, 188, 189
Parke, C. R., 77
Parson, Eric, 361n, 365, 368-370, 395
Parson, Mrs. Wm., 372
Parson, William, 363, 368-371, 374, 376, 396
pasturage lands, 232, 233, 234
Patterson, T. M., 249
Paul, Caroline, 327
Paul, William, 327
Peale, A. C., 214, 291
Pearson, F. W., 247
Pemberton, John C., 63, 66
Pennsylvania, geological survey of, 317
Pennsylvania State College, 332
Penobscot Bay, Maine, 362, 367
Perkins Landing, Louisiana, 60
petroleum, 289, 290
phenomenology, 359

U. S. Geological Survey (*Continued*) 348; regional offices, 274, 278; Walcott's administration, 347

U.S. Military Academy, 13, 244

U.S. National Museum, 186, 246, 250, 338, 355, 397

U.S. Thirty-sixth Infantry, 111

Urbana, Illinois, 82

Utah, 108, 127, 153, 154, 157, 179, 194, 195, 197, 200, 201, 212, 214, 215, 223-225, 230, 231, 280, 281, 311, 316, 330

Utica, Mississippi, 61

Utica, New York, 3, 4

Vasey, George, 45, 82, 94, 183, 185

Vasey's Paradise, 190

Vegas Wash, 109

Vermilion River, 110, 212

Vermont, 114

Vicksburg, Mississippi, 60, 62, 73; battle of, 62-66, 319

Vilas, Wm. F., 300, 305

Virgin River (Río Virgen), 109, 141, 143, 155, 173, 178

Walcott, Charles D, 279, 347, 360, 392, 396, 397

Walker, F. A., 197, 268, 279

Wallace, W. H. L., 54-57, 59

Walworth, Wisconsin, 16, 17, 19, 21, 25

Wampum, 296

War Department, U.S., 81, 92, 114, 152, 181, 207-210, 215, 237, 242, 244, 246, 287, 292

Ward, J. D., 98

Ward, Lester, 3n, 264, 278-283, 320, 322, 328, 376, 381, 382n, 386, 392; *Dynamic Sociology*, 280

Warman, P. C., 380n, 385n

Washington, 304, 316, 343

Washington, District of Columbia, 81, 92, 112, 152, 180-184, 205ff, 264, 363; center of science, 218, 264

Washington Gazette, 219

Washington, Utah, 188

water companies, 234; monopoly of, 234, 235; natural economy of, 223, 224, 232; ownership, 234; California doctrine, 303; Colorado doctrine, 303

Weather Bureau, U.S., 333

Webb, Walter P., 398

welfare state, 272, 346

Welling, J. C., 248

Wells, Fargo and Company, 81

Welsh communities in Ohio, 6

Wesley, Charles, 4

Wesley, John, 10

Wesley, Susanna, 5

Wesleyan Church (Connection), 10, 17, 39

western territorial surveys, see surveys

Wheaton College, 38n, 39, 148; see also Illinois Institute

Wheaton, Illinois, 28-31, 38, 41, 51, 65, 71-73, 81, 113, 147, 148, 175, 213

Wheeler, George, 152, 181, 182, 195, 207-212, 214, 220, 237, 243, 246, 248-250, 296

Wheeler, John, 94

Wheeler, Mary Powell (Mrs. Wm. Wheeler), 3, 11, 15, 19, 24, 334, 388, 390, 394

Wheeler, William, 23, 24, 388, 390

Whirlpool Canyon, 127

White, Charles A., 214, 310

White, I. C., 290

White, James, 109, 137, 138, 182, 183

White River, 103, 112, 128, 177; junction with Green River, 128, 131; Powell's winter camp, 104, 105, 106, 107

White River Agency, 118, 128, 129; Powell visits, 129, 130, 169; Thompson visits, 169, 170

Whittlesey, Charles, 13

Wigginton, Peter D., 249

Wilberforce, Wm., 4

Wilbur, C. D., 45, 78, 79

Williams, Professor, 14

Williamson, J. A., 227, 228, 252

Williamsport, Pennsylvania, 331

Willis, Bailey, 279, 324, 328

Williston, F. H., 340

Willson, Annie, 5

Willson, George, 5

Wilson, John L., 343, 344

Wing, Henry, 94

Wisconsin, 17ff, 27, 213, 223, 227, 261

Wolcott, E. O., 336, 347

Wood, Henry, 94

Woodward, Wm., 94

Worcester, Massachusetts, 266

Worthen, A. H., 46

Wyman, Jeffries, 366

Wyoming, 127, 154, 162, 347

Yale University, 149, 209, 239, 251, 278, 286, 292

Yampa Canyon, 168

Yampa Plateau, 212

Yampa (Bear) River, 104, 105, 110, 212; junction with Green River, 128, 168

yankee kitchen choir, 148

Yarrow, H. C., 211, 266, 267

Yates, Richard, 52

Yocona River, Mississippi, 60

Yosemite Canyon, 149

Young, Brigham, 143, 153, 174

Young, C. A., 292